Prince Henry Revived

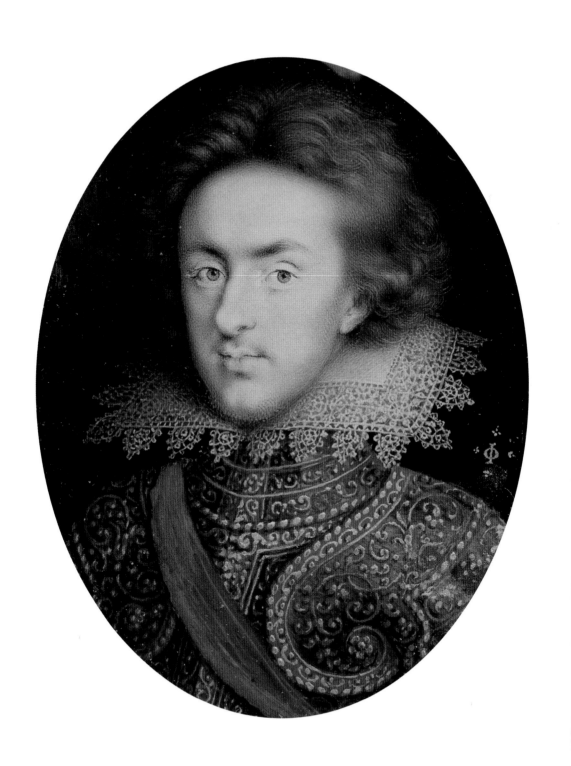

Prince Henry Revived

Image and Exemplarity in Early Modern England

Edited by Timothy Wilks

Southampton Solent University
in association with
Paul Holberton publishing

Contents

ISBN 978 1 903470 57 2

British Library Cataloguing in Publication Data
A catalogue record for this book is available from the British Library

Produced by Paul Holberton publishing,
89 Borough High Street, London SE1 1NL
www.paul-holberton.net

Template designed by Roger Davies
Pre-press at Paul Holberton publishing by Laura Parker

Printed by Graphic Studio, Bussolengo, Verona, Italy

Jacket Image: artist unknown, *Henry, Prince of Wales, in Armour,* oil on panel, Cambridge University Library

Frontispiece: Isaac Oliver, *Henry, Prince of Wales,* miniature, watercolour on vellum, National Museum and Gallery of Wales, Cardiff

Foreword

The idea for this volume emerged at the annual conference of the Renaissance Society of America, held at Cambridge in April 2005, at which papers were given by four of the following contributors. We are indebted to Michael Ullyot for assembling the panel on that occasion, and for bringing into contact various scholars who had been working independently on aspects of the court of Henry, Prince of Wales. Prior to the conference, Michael extended invitations to the pioneering Henrician scholars of the 1970s and 1980s, Sir Roy Strong and J.W. Williamson, who, in declining, both replied to the effect that they had long since made their statements on Prince Henry, and had left the field to others. It is testament to the influence of their publications that these are cited frequently in the endnotes to the following chapters.

It was always intended that any resultant publication should comprise much more than a collection of conference papers, and should reflect the new directions which research on Prince Henry has taken. This volume, accordingly, includes the work of art historians, cultural historians and literary historians, whose disciplines have separately negotiated cultural turns over the last two decades. A generous sharing of ideas and information between authors has increased the interdisciplinary strengths of these following essays, and it is hoped the small 'Republic of Letters' established over recent months will encourage further collaboration.

Grateful acknowledgement is made to Southampton Solent University for its generous support, and to the publishers for their enthusiasm, expertise and patience.

TW

Notes on the Contributors

Gilles Bertheau (PhD University of Paris III – Sorbonne Nouvelle) is a Senior Lecturer at the Centre d'Etudes Supérieures de la Renaissance (University of Tours). He wrote his doctoral dissertation (2002) on the tragedies of Chapman, and has published several articles, mainly on the drama of Chapman. He has recently edited 'Sir Thomas More by Munday, Shakespeare *et al.*' in the Pléiade edition of *Shakespeare's Complete Works*.

John Buchtel (PhD Virginia) is Head of the Special Collections Research Center in the Georgetown University Library. Since 2004, he served as Curator of Rare Books in The Johns Hopkins University's Sheridan Libraries, prior to which he was Curator of Collections at Rare Book School, an independent institute for the history of books and printing at the University of Virginia. He earned his doctorate in English literature at the University of Virginia, writing on 'Book Dedications in Early Modern England and the Literary Patronage of Henry, Prince of Wales (1594–1612)'. His article 'Book Dedications and the Death of a Patron: The Memorial Engraving in Chapman's Homer' appeared in *Book History*, vol. 7.

Dr Elizabeth Goldring (PhD Yale) is an Associate Fellow at the Centre for the Study of the Renaissance, University of Warwick. She has co-edited *Court Festivals of the European Renaissance: Art, Politics and Performance* (Aldershot, 2002), and *The Progresses, Pageants, and Entertainments of Queen Elizabeth I* (Oxford, 2007), and is General Editor of the forthcoming, five-volume new edition of *John Nichols's The Progresses and Public Processions of Queen Elizabeth I*. Her next monograph will be a study of the culture of collecting in Renaissance England.

Alexander Marr is a Lecturer in Art History at the University of St Andrews. He has published widely on topics such as automata, collecting, mathematics, architecture, instrumentation, book history, and landscape aesthetics from the fifteenth to the nineteenth century. Recent publications include (with R.J.W Evans), *Curiosity and Wonder from the Renaissance to the Enlightenment* (Ashgate, 2006). He is currently completing a monograph entitled *Mathematics and Material Culture in Late Renaissance Italy*.

Gregory McNamara (PhD West Virginia) is an Assistant Professor at Clayton State University. He gained his doctorate for a thesis, '"A perfect diamond set in lead": Henry, Prince of Wales, and the Construction of Early Stuart Majesty' (2000), and among his published articles are several on the emergent majesty of Henry, and on the material aspects of English Renaissance fashioning.

Michelle O'Callaghan is a Reader in Early Modern Literature at the University of Reading. Her publications include *The 'Shepheards Nation': Jacobean Spenserians and Early Stuart Political Culture* (Oxford, 2000) and *The English Wits: Literature and Sociability in Early Modern England* (Cambridge, 2007).

Aysha Pollnitz (PhD Cambridge) is a Research Fellow at Trinity College, Cambridge. She is completing a monograph based on her doctoral thesis, 'Princely education in sixteenth-century Britain' (2006), and has written on humanism and Tudor court culture, Shakespeare's political thought and Mary I.

D.J.B. Trim is Lecturer in History in the Department of Humanities, Newbold College, and a Visiting Research Fellow in the Department of History, University of Reading. He has published a number of articles and chapters on England's relationship with Europe in the sixteenth and seventeenth century, and has edited *The Chivalric Ethos and the Development of Military Professionalism* (Leiden, 2003), and co-edited *Cross, Crown and Community: Religion, Government and Culture in Early Modern England* (Oxford, 2004), and *Persecution and Pluralism: Calvinists and Religious Minorities in Early Modern Europe 1550-1700* (Oxford, 2006).

Michael Ullyot (PhD Toronto) is an Assistant Professor of English at the University of Calgary. His doctoral thesis on Prince Henry and the 'genres of exemplarity' (2005) has led to a wider study, now nearing completion, *Exemplarity, Biography, and Interpretation in Early Modern England*. He has published on elegies, anecdotes, and Senecan drama, and his continuing work on Prince Henry includes the annotation of an old-spelling edition of William Fowler's *True Report of the … Baptisme of … Prince Henry* (1594).

Gail Capitol Weigl, (PhD Michigan) is an independent scholar researching Elizabethan and Jacobean painting, since retiring from teaching East and South Asian art history, specializing in Japan, at the University of Maryland, Georgetown University and the Corcoran College of Art and Design, Washington, D.C.

Timothy Wilks (DPhil Oxford) is a Senior Lecturer in the Visual Arts at Southampton Solent University. Since completing his doctoral thesis on the court culture of Prince Henry (1988), he has maintained an interest in the early Stuart court, and has written several articles illuminating more clearly the development of art collecting in England prior to the reign of Charles I. His published work on Prince Henry includes studies of projects at Richmond Palace and the picture gallery in St James's Palace. He is currently completing, with Edward Chaney, *The Jacobean Reconnaissance*, a study of England's cultural re-engagement with continental Europe through travel.

Introduction | Image and Exemplarity

Timothy Wilks

Though the attachment of a pair of abstract nouns to the title of a scholarly work is an over-used practice, 'image' and 'exemplarity' have emerged as two unsolicited, yet recurring pre-occupations of this collection of essays, which deserve notice. While 'image', despite bearing multiple and subtle meanings, is still a heavily and shrewdly used word, it is to be doubted whether 'exemplarity', with its roots in classical rhetoric, is nowadays encountered at all beyond academia.[1] Present-day society seems obsessed with the one, yet wholly unconcerned with the other, whereas the Early Modern world in which Prince Henry lived remained deeply concerned with both, and, moreover, saw a connection between them.

Exemplarity, especially where it addresses virtuous or heroic action, would seem to re-quire the following: a culture of rhetoric, suitable models, and also a desire to emulate them. While these criteria would all have been very evident in England four centuries ago, their sur-vival in the twenty-first century is somewhat harder to detect. In our Post-Modern age, char-acterized by scepticism, pluralism, and emphasis on the uniqueness of the individual, exemplarity has little place. It may even be argued that disenchantment with exemplarity set in long ago, and that even the Early-Modern episteme was already uncomfortable with it. Montaigne, we are informed, in declaring the pursuit of exemplars to be silly, was merely re-flecting the scholarly mood of late sixteenth-century France.[2] England, as it straggled along the path of the Renaissance behind continental Europe, held faith with exemplarity for some-what longer.

To map oneself as nearly as possible on to a previous life, and to attempt to release one's innate virtue by repeating the actions of an earlier virtuous life, might have been an ancient practice, but, none the less, it lent itself well to medieval Christianity. Thomas à Kempis's *De imitatione Christi*, a text of enduring influence, though never one of much assistance to those willing to engage with a harsh and corrupt world, and never much favoured by Protestants, stands as a reminder that the life of Jesus of Nazareth offered a perfect model for Christians. Exemplarity was also of central importance to Dante, as revealed in his encounter with his an-cestor, Cacciaguida, crusader-knight and imitator of Christ, in the *Paradiso*. In view of what will be said later concerning the connection between exemplarity and image, it is worth noting that an iconic source, the Byzantine mosaic in the apse of S. Apollinare in Classe, has been suggested for Dante's vision of jewels upon the Cross appearing to him as Cacciaguida and his companions.[3]

More immediate historical examples offered themselves to a would-be English Renaissance prince. The late Tudor crisis brought about by Elizabeth I's lack of a uterine heir and the desire for a Protestant hero figure is familiar enough to us. Sir Philip Sidney, Robert Dudley, Earl of Leicester, and Robert Devereux, Earl of Essex, were all projected in this role. None of them, however, could be wholly satisfactory or convincing, as it was plain they would never reign; though Leicester played suitor, then regent (in the Netherlands), Essex exercised vicariously the powers of the Crown in France and Ireland, even knighting several of his closest followers, and Sidney, it was said, was offered the throne of Poland. After the execution of the Duke of Norfolk in 1572, Elizabeth even distanced the throne from the aristocracy by having no dukes at all. Of these three, it was Sidney whose exemplary life was immediately seized on by writers – Molyneux's account appearing in the 1587 edition of Holinshed's *Chronicles*, in the year following Sidney's death at Zutphen. Fulke Greville's influential 'Life of Sidney', though not published until 1652, was written by 1612, and though Greville was probably increasingly unhappy with the earlier literary treatments of his friend, one can only conclude that after desisting for a quarter of a century he was stirred to write partly by witnessing the rise of the court of Prince Henry.[4] Samuel Daniel, who would later write for Henry the masque *Tethys' Festival*, took a greater risk with his *The Tragedie of Philotas* (1605), even though the old Essexians were being re-embraced by the new king, as it was interpreted as an allegory of the fall of Essex.[5] The drawing of parallels between the lives of Philotas and Essex was exemplarity at one remove; similarly, the account of the mortally wounded Sidney like Alexander the Great redirecting water to one more needy. As Gilles Bertheau reveals, exemplarity crossed the Channel, and re-crossed; a form of hero-'laundering'. Thereby, a life such as Essex's might be safely paralleled by Chapman with that of Marshal Byron.

These three fallible Elizabethan heroes (arguably, there were more) at least served to sop up some of the national yearning and frustration until the Queen's death and the arrival of the Stuarts in 1603.[6] James VI of Scotland, now James I of England, had long since fashioned a highly idiosyncratic form of kingship that accentuated his personal abilities and dispensed with those regal qualities he lacked, which included all heroic inclination. Here was a king who would never wear, or even be depicted wearing, a single piece of armour. *Rex Pacificus*, his preferred persona, was itself founded on an Old Testament *exemplum*, and he was only the latest of several European kings keen to be seen as another King Solomon.[7] It offered no solution, though, to England's deepening crisis of heroic leadership. Fortunately, the new king brought with him his son and heir apparent, Henry.

Whenever Henry's tutors and mentors urged him to have regard to exemplary figures he readily complied. Henry was hardly supine, and saw that in acquiescing he would gain the attributes of leadership quickly. To become the embodiment of an exemplary hero-figure was to gain the approbation of one's instructors and the adoration of one's audience. After all, the non-compliant, wayward, rebellious heir to the throne was, and is, a more familiar figure in history and literature than its opposite. If one extreme of Renaissance princely behaviour were to be witnessed in the abstemious and diligent Henry, the other extreme had earlier been witnessed in the psychopathic Don Carlos, roaster of live hares, slasher of stabled horses and, until his removal, heir to the Spanish Empire. For both princes there are, curiously, anecdotes involving their shoemakers that, when compared, testify to the differences in their characters. Henry's shoemaker once brought him new boots that did not fit well, but Henry silenced his protesting gentlemen, reassured his servant, and waited patiently while his boots were altered. On a similar occasion, Don Carlos forced his shoemaker to cut up the offending boots and eat the pieces. England's general joy, after such a long wait, at the seemingly perfect match of their prince to the princely ideal was given the fullest expression. Ben Jonson observed two tall men and a short companion merrily arrange themselves as an 'H' to toast their prince.[8] Pewter beakers engraved with the Prince of Wales's feathers and motto were raised by drinkers not only within proximity of the court but also in remote villages.[9] The 'HP' (Henricus Princeps) cypher was branded on the backs of the pictures once in Henry's collection;[10] is found in the plasterwork decoration of a room above the Inner Temple Lane archway,[11] and also beneath the figure of 'Hope' in a wall painting in a merchant's house in far-off King's Lynn.[12] In Sherborne Abbey hangs a hatchment bearing the 'HP' cypher and feathers. It was made in 1611 at the time Henry took possession of nearby Sherborne Castle, intending to return it to its imprisoned former owner, Raleigh, who for Henry was a hero and patriot.[13] Henry's arms are seen in the stained glass of the 'King's House' in Salisbury,[14] and his badge is on the great oak bed in Montacute House.[15] All manner of artefacts created in England between 1603 and 1612 offered surfaces upon which the presence of Henry and the great hopes attached to him could be proclaimed.

At the beginning of the seventeenth century a millenarian atmosphere hung heavy over Europe. Doctrinal differences sharpened antagonisms, and general warfare of the bitterest kind was widely expected. Continental warfare lasting a generation, to be known as the Thirty Years' War, did break out, though after Henry had died. Many of his followers had believed the Prince would play a heroic part in the coming conflict, and one aspect of the court culture constructed around him gave expression to this belief. Increasingly, Henry's image was only intelligible as part of this narrative. As Michael Ullyot elucidates, the book of Henry was already written, though it would never be played out. Underlying such *exemplum*-based, prophecy-fulfilling fashioning was an assumption that individual lives, as well as the broader lives of societies and states, had a limited number of possible enactments. Those concerned with the unfolding of worldly affairs could find confirmation of this in many historical parallels, and in the repetition of the actions of men, either for good or for ill.

Henry's image, therefore, was only fully comprehensible in a narrative context, that is, as illustrative of the book of his life. In art, where a portrayed figure is a participant in a familiar history, it may be reduced to an iconic assemblage of signs, provided they are sufficient to direct the thoughts of the viewer to the narrative. Henry's image is iconic in this sense. It could still offer much detail, as in precisely rendered apparel, jewels and weapons, all there to be appreciated as indicators of station, wealth, authority and – importantly – intention. Such incidental details caught and delighted the Jacobean eye just as they had the Elizabethan eye before. Within a few short years, however, visiting and immigrant Dutch artists, such as Blyenberch, Mytens (who painted a posthumous portrait of Henry for Charles) and Van Dyck, would banish much of the detail with a broad brush, would set their sitters against inchoate, brown backgrounds, and leave English viewers no alternative but to look afresh, and perceive form-in-time:[16] the truth of the moment captured with mere gesture. Henry's image, therefore, remains essentially Pre-Modern, though if he had lived longer it might not have remained so. His younger brother Charles (for whom, inevitably, Henry's own life became exemplary) succeeded in attaining this fundamentally new way of seeing, and it is notable that above all other painters he admired Titian, whose art was essentially concerned with transience (in this regard Titian has more affinity with Degas than Mantegna or, indeed, any of his Renaissance predecessors). Charles even admitted into his collection a painting by the upcoming Rembrandt van Rijn, an artist wholly concerned with capturing the moment. It was presented to him by Robert Kerr, Earl of Ancram, formerly one of the sophisticated young courtiers of Prince Henry's privy chamber, who had since made his personal leap into a modern way of seeing.

Henry's vigour and his natural inclination to action were obvious to all. Perhaps this was the single-minded and supremely confident *virtù* prescribed by Machiavelli, although, as Gilles Bertheau reminds us, Henry's first biographer, Hawkins, rejected any such suggestion. No doubt, Nietzsche would have attributed to Henry the 'will to power', but we must ask whether the notion of the hero really finds a place within the Modern paradigm. Now, it seems that heroes, such as they are, are raised, hailed, and depicted without expectation of detecting any virtue in them (indeed, we recognize such as being as the 'anti-hero'). They are raised without reference to *exempla*, and simply for that thrill to be gained from the act of adoration. As this is being written, a new statue of our living Prince Harry is being displayed in London.[17] It owes much to the funerary monument. A recumbent Harry, hands clasping a locket bearing the miniature images of his parents, lies dead, a vulture perched at his foot. With this, the sculptor Daniel Edwards commemorates another un-acted narrative, as if history had followed an alternative course. In some respects it is comparable to the funeral effigy of Prince Henry – here discussed in the essays of Elizabeth Goldring and Greg McNamara – as the earlier effigy formed the centrepiece of a funeral for a hero denied only the time to enact his heroism. All too easily dismissed, this sham memorial demonstrates most effectively that this is not an age for heroes. Were it so, Harry would have been allowed to join his troops in the theatre of war, and, alive or dead, return as hero. He is, instead, retained; deprived of a life-narrative; precious yet purposeless.

Although the placing of value on both exemplarity and iconic imagery of the kind that defined Prince Henry persisted into the Early Modern period, these practices became increasingly outmoded until they disappeared altogether. The outlook in which a life was fitted to an external purpose and framed within a coherent world, and for which the metaphor of a book was entirely appropriate, gave way to a sense of the moment, of perpetual change, and of unpredictability. Individuals finding themselves within this unsettling, 'Modern' episteme required a new strategy for living, much of which came to consist of improvisation. Henry lived at the turn of an age, a turn discernible in every facet of early seventeenth-century culture, including literature.[18] In 1605, the year in which Prince Henry matriculated at Oxford and was appointed an honorary tutor, in Spain Cervantes' *Don Quixote* was published, which, in its various modern characteristics, was unlike any book previously written. One of those characteristics was its depiction of an improvisational approach to life. Though Quixote has a quest, he has no real plan of action in a world of unpredictable events. He is sometimes improvisational and sometimes reactive, and at these times he is capable of being perceptive and wise – only when he attempts to be chivalrous is he delusional. Cervantes, of course, was satirizing that major literary genre of his own age, the chivalrous romance that invariably featured the heroic knight. He was also deriding a European court culture that took chivalry seriously.[19] As a young man Cervantes had attempted to be the heroic knight, but if he ever saw his own life complacently as a pre-written chivalric romance, his capture by Algerian corsairs and his subsequent sufferings led to utter disillusionment. *Don Quixote* – more than a subversive text, an indicator of the existence of a new world-view – soon became widely read throughout Europe. Within Prince Henry's lifetime the first part of the work was translated into English by Thomas Shelton, and published as *The delightfull historie of the wittie knight, Don Quiskote* (1612).

Running parallel with the publishing history of *Don Quixote* is its iconography. Cervantes's word-image of Quixote wearing his great-grandfather's tarnished armour topped by a helmet fitted with a cardboard visor, and astride a bravely renamed hack, has been interpreted by a succession of artists including Fragonard, Daumier, Dalí and Picasso, who in turn have influenced the cinematic Quixotes of Welles and Wasserman.[20] The first of these illustrators is now thought to be Andreas Bretschneider, whose engraving of 1613 appears in Tobias Hübner's *Cantel-Auffzüge* (Leipzig, 1614), an account of a German court celebration in which a 'Don Quixote' takes part in the procession.[21] This same Hübner was responsible for *Beschreibung der Reiss* (1613), the publication that described the journey to and festive entry into Heidelberg of the newly married Frederick, Elector Palatine, and Henry's sister, Princess Elizabeth, at which Henry should have been present (considered in this volume by Elizabeth Goldring).[22] The first illustration of Quixote to be published in England, the title-page of the first part of the second edition of Shelton (1620), was a partial copy of the title-page engraving of a 1618 French edition. Very soon, therefore, after the collapse of Prince Henry's court, not only the book but also the image of Don Quixote began to proliferate in Europe. The great equestrian portrait of Prince Henry, an icon of chivalry, derives much of its authority from its very derivativeness (re-examined here by Gail Weigl), and this tradition would endure somewhat longer. It would from this point, however, have to contend with the subversive image of the mounted knight of La Mancha. This was not merely an exercise in debunking chivalry, for the iconic, classical image and the preposterous, self-fashioned knight-errant represent fundamentally different attitudes to time.

Is there perhaps something pertaining to the nature of the heroic that requires the hero to be placed out of time? Is, therefore, the depiction of the heroic necessarily iconic? Certainly, the philosophical challenge to the heroic portrait coincided with the beginnings of a visual revolution in art. It is harder to identify the moment at which the heroic portrait disappeared in Britain than to note the presence of an alternative view that could not accommodate it. Edgar Wind considers that divergence in his perceptive essay, 'Hume and the Heroic Portrait', in which he draws a convincing parallel between the opposing artistic principles of Thomas Gainsborough and Sir Joshua Reynolds and the opposing philosophical positions of David Hume and James Beattie.[23] Hume, as a Sceptic, discountenanced immoderate pride, while Beattie, supported by no less a trenchant advocate than Samuel Johnson, defended heroism and enthusiasm. Wind leaves us in no doubt that these late eighteenth-century rivalries among artists and philosophers were parts of the same large conflict. In it, we may see the emergence of a new, post-Enlightenment episteme in which there is far less room for the celebration of heroism in the classical sense, and, consequently, less room for the heroic portrait. If we compare Wind's summary of Hume's contention, 'The enthusiast must learn from the sceptic that to believe he can aspire to supernatural heights with impunity is to ignore the limits and weakness of human understanding',[24] with Prince Henry's easy declaration that '… I have pleasure in overcoming difficult things',[25] we see that Henry and all his supporters are grouped far away from the camp of the Sceptics.

If one may overlook the six or seven generations separating their lives, Gainsborough, with his 'simple style', would surely have wished neither to paint Henry nor to have been called upon to do so; whereas Reynolds, one feels, would have been entirely at ease with such a commission. It was Reynolds who still attempted to communicate the Platonist 'idea', while Gainsborough aspired merely to paint what he saw. It was not so much that Georgian Britain no longer cared for heroes; on the contrary, in an age of colonial and imperial expansion, and repeated military intervention on the continent, it not only had a need for heroes, but it consistently found them. Benjamin West, Reynolds's successor as president of the Royal Academy, persisted in painting death scenes of heroes, enjoying great popularity, and in referring to his royal commission of 1771, felt that his *Death of Epaminondas* 'would, as a classic subject, and with Grecian circumstances, make a suitable contrast with the *Death of General Wolfe*'. West may have succeeded in providing an interesting contrast of periods for the room in Buckingham House in which the paintings were displayed (there was, in fact, a third painting in the series, the *Death of the Chevalier Bayard*), but they were also unmistakably connected by exemplarity, as Wolfe had already been compared to the Theban Epaminondas in at least two publications.[26] West, however, did take one bold step away from the timeless, classicized heroes insisted upon by Reynolds towards contemporary and, therefore, more realistic depiction, by including the figures of an American ranger and an American Indian attending the dying Wolfe. West's 'Epic Compositions' would culminate in the *Death of Lord Nelson* (1806).[27] The heroic portrait seems, therefore, to have perished slowly as part of the general demise of *invenzione*: the resolving of the problem of communicating the 'idea' through *disegno* and *colorito*. Neither Gainsborough nor Turner nor, certainly, any of the Impressionists, were especially concerned with it.

Just as many people had feared the onset of a new age at the beginning of the seventeenth century, so many entered the twentieth century with a sense of foreboding. While the validity, still less the utility, of comparing such sentiments across centuries is debatable, previous millennial apprehensions hold an undeniable fascination for us. It was generally agreed that the Modern Age would be delivered by machines, though the nature of the delivery remained in debate until the outbreak of the First World War. Among those who returned disillusioned from the Western Front some became introspective while others were drawn to radical, even revolutionary, politics. This seemed not to be a time for recognizing heroes, except in Lloyd-George's inclusive 'homes fit for heroes' sense. An artist such as Wyndham Lewis, in rejecting realism, rediscovered in Vorticism something of the icon's potential as a carrier of meaning. More of his contemporaries than he cared to admit, such as C.R.W. Nevinson, shared his disdain for the fleeting nature of retinal impressions. It might even be proposed, if only in this respect, that the idiosyncratic Stanley Spencer (another war veteran), saw things similarly. Spencer, it is often claimed, was influenced by Gauguin, a perception possibly based on Gauguin's essential interest in formal representation rather than in attempting to capture transient appearances. Beyond Britain, a proliferation of art movements reflected this cultural turn, at which the 300-year Western consensus on the time aspect of imagery, and the aesthetic consensus based on it, ended.

It might be possible to continue in this vein, separating all figurative artists into two camps; a sort of dinner-party game in which even Prince Henry's household painter, Robert Peake, who had only a very raw technique, but strove always to capture the 'idea' of his master, might be sent to join a stylistically disparate group including not only Gauguin and Lewis, but also the likes of Picasso, Klee, and (returning to the equestrian theme) Marino Marini, rather than to the group of Gainsborough, Delacroix, Sisley and John Singer Sargent. We would discover that those artists fitting the first are hardly to be found after Peake's time (he died in 1619), but begin to reappear in significant numbers after Gauguin and Cézanne, while the second, headed by Giorgione and Titian – these are artists concerned with happening – proliferate in the intervening years.

Those able to contemplate iconic images tend to find some affinity with the Modernists of the early twentieth-century, who uniformly recoiled from the Impressionist perception of the world. If it may be held that the truly heroic image has something of the icon about it, then we might expect to find a place again for heroism within Modernism. Indeed, that godfather of Modernism, Hegel, not only allowed the existence of heroes (his 'world-historical men'), but also deemed them essential, for they alone were able to perceive what their age lacked. Yet, for Hegel, each age fashioned its own heroes, and the very notion of the *Zeitgeist* seems to preclude new heroes from appearing in the guise of old ones. This ran counter to the view that pertained to the end of the Renaissance which saw the heroes of the classical age displaying virtues through their actions, and allowed that new heroes faced by similar challenges might, by acting similarly, also find within themselves the same virtues. In the 'New Epoch', without exemplarity, and with virtue replaced by economic value, who could tell what kind of person might become a hero? Those great espousers of Modernism, Walter Gropius and his Bauhaus colleagues, though practitioners of the arts, proposed themselves, in all seriousness, as heroes of their age. Imbued with such a sense of self-importance, artists in the twentieth century lost the necessary reverence to create icons. They also lost the humility to represent others as heroes, except as pastiche.

If there are exceptions, they are to be found where one might least expect to find them: in the hyper-real medium of photography. A hero is found in Karsch's painstaking portrait of Winston Churchill, and another in Korda's accidental snapshot of Che Guevara. If it is not too preposterous to compare Korda's *Guevara* and Isaac Oliver's three-quarter face portrait of a tousle-haired Prince Henry in armour (see frontispiece), both may be seen to represent a narrative of ideological struggle, and to impart, through the serene detachment of the subject, absolute confidence in the outcome. Western art has, in fact, long familiarity with the disengagement of the subject from circumstances, acquired through innumerable depictions of the sufferings of saints.[28] Isaac Oliver, with the assistance of other miniaturists, made several versions of his two studies of Henry (the profile and the fuller face) to satisfy a courtly demand for portraits that could be kept on the person. Often, these miniatures were set within valuable jewels, befitting the reliquary nature they acquired after Henry's death. The reverential treatment accorded Henry's image is in marked contrast to the ultimate fate of Korda's *Guevara*. Whereas Oliver's preparatory life drawings (now lost) were used as guides for engravings by means of which Henry's image was widely spread, Warhol's dissemination of the Guevara image was by means of silk-screen processing that reduced photo-realist qualities to monochrome patterns that barely allow recognition and signification. Warhol went on to replicate the image in blocks, as a further challenge to the notion of art as sacred object. Despite all this, Warhol's *Guevara* remains an icon no less than the venerated *Christ Pantocrator* of St Catherine's Monastery, Mt Sinai, all of whose original Byzantine encaustic is long gone; only the idea endures.

It was earlier suggested that Jacobeans would have perceived a natural connection between image and exemplarity. It might further be suggested that this connection depended on a particular understanding of time. The Jacobean mind still conceived of time as a narrative, and, moreover, a narrative that was already written. This, incidentally, did not disallow free will – Man still could make choices, though the actions and events stemming from those choices had always existed as part of the future, were known to God, and therefore open to prophecy. All time was laid out; not just the present, or even the present and the past, but future, present, and past. If God could survey the whole span of history, being, as St Augustine had taught, outside time, then Man might also switch his attention back and forth between past and future. Exemplarity was perfectly suited to such an approach. As for experiencing the present, it was sensed more as the brink of what was to come than as the ever-happening moment of what for us is reality.[29] As Gail Weigl elucidates in her essay on the Parham portrait, Henry, astride his great horse, is, essentially, poised on the brink of his future; all is anticipation.

Stepping out of time seemed very possible to the pre-Modern mind. It, moreover, enabled a prudent person, especially a ruler, to equivocate. Frank Kermode discusses Shakespeare's repeated use of the word in *Macbeth*, and finds a compatible notion of 'a kind of interim between thought or intention and act' also in *Julius Caesar* and *Hamlet*.[30] Equivocation recognized the possibility of taking different courses of action, and by allowing those courses equal voice a considered decision could then be made, and found acceptable. 'Now you have my distinctions, wherein I hope you will not tax me for aequivocation', wrote Henry's mentor in statecraft, Robert Cecil, to Henry's secretary, Adam Newton, concerning a suit brought by two gentleman with the Prince's backing.[31] In this, Cecil contrived to use the word itself equivocally, that is, jokingly in the Jesuitical sense, and also in Shakespeare's sense; for he had paused on the brink of a policy decision, in order to assess the foreseeable consequences of various courses of action. More broadly, there was a sense that all of youth, at least male, aristocratic youth, was a pre-narrative, waiting period.[32] There was, of course, very much to be done within the seclusion of the 'courtly college', and Aysha Pollnitz, Michael Ullyot and Michelle O'Callaghan reveal the rich diet of instruction and vicariously experienced travel upon which Henry was fed.

Galileo had finally shattered the Ptolemaic fixed spheres with the publication of *Siderius Nuncius (The Starry Messenger)* in 1610, and Henry had, like several other princes of Europe, obtained a copy of the book and one of the new telescopes to see for himself that the universe was space, and (no less disconcertingly) that all was in flux.[33] "Tis all in pieces, all coherence gone': this oft-cited line from John Donne's *The First Anniversary* was written only a year before Donne, the son-in-law of Henry's Receiver-General, would compose his elegy on the Prince. Still – but only just – the present moment was of more interest for what it would be as part of the past, and for what it pointed to in the future, and it was of least interest for itself. In contrast, our own age gives primacy to the present, and at the extreme there is a measure of agreement in current Western thought with Zen Buddhist teaching that there is no past or future, only the present. Our subconscious presentism (even historians, paradoxically, might possess it) obstructs our understanding – even our ability to recognize – many of the common assumptions held by those who lived on the threshold of the Early Modern period. That a philosophical struggle, reflected in art and literature, was already underway in the court culture of Prince Henry, where patronage had gathered many of the best minds, is apparent. A struggle over much the same issues has taken place over the last century, and continues. Wyndham Lewis, mentioned earlier, declared, 'I loathe anything that goes too quickly. If it goes too quickly it is not there.'[34] More than merely declaring a dislike of the sleek contraptions that so inspired the Continental Futurists, it reveals his refusal to accept that he is in a bubble of the present as it shoots along a track, past behind, and future ahead.[35] Louise Bourgeois, an artist who has lived in awareness of this disagreement through almost the whole of the previous century and into this one, has created her own dialectic, and found synthesis through recourse to memory: 'You cannot arrest the present. You just have to abandon every day your past. And accept it. And if you can't accept it then you have to do sculpture. If your need is to refuse to abandon the past, then you have to re-create it.'[36] Anti-narrativists, however, remain in the ascendant, pre-occupied with the fetishization of the continual, yet ever-changing, moment, and absorbed by media output.[37] For them, there is no history, and *ergo* no exemplars, for to search would be to grasp into emptiness; but there are images; in fact, little else for them but images – flickering and fleeting – hinting at nothing beyond. For those of us for whom there is history, we might do well to recall T.S. Eliot's lines:

> Time present and time past
> Are both perhaps present in time future
> And time future contained in time past.[38]

If so, perhaps Prince Henry might, indeed, be 'Revived'.[39]

NOTES

1 Scholarly interest in the place of exemplarity within Renaissance society is relatively recent; see John D. Lyons, *Exemplum: The Rhetoric of Example in Early Modern France and Italy* (Princeton, 1989); Timothy Hampton, *Writing from History. The Rhetoric of Exemplarity in Renaissance Literature* (Ithaca, 1990); Alexander Gelley (ed.), *On the Rhetoric of Exemplarity* (Stanford, 1995).

2 See François Rigolot, 'The Renaissance Crisis of Exemplarity', *Journal of the History of Ideas*, LIX, 4 (October, 1998), pp. 557–68. 'I often say it is pure silliness which sets us chasing after foreign and textbook exemplars. They are produced no less abundantly nowadays than in the times of Homer and Plato', Michel de Montaigne, *The Complete Essays*, trans. M.A. Screech (London, 1991), p. 1227.

3 See Jeffrey T. Schnapp, *The Transformation of History at the Center of Dante's 'Paradise'*, (Ithaca, 1986), pp. 170–238.

4 Alan Stewart, *Philip Sidney: A Double Life* (London, 2000), gives more attention to the mythic Sidney than Katherine Duncan-Jones, *Sir Philip Sidney, Courtier Poet* (New Haven and London, 1991); see also Jan van Dorsten, Dominic Baker-Smith and Arthur Kinney (eds.), *Sir Philip Sidney: 1586 and the Creation of a Legend* (Leiden, 1986); Kevin Pask, '"The mannes state" of Philip Sidney: Pre-scripting the life of the poet in England', *Criticism*, 36, 2 (Spring, 1994), pp. 163–88.

5 See H. Gazzard, ' "Those Graue presentments of antiquitie", Samuel Daniel's *Philotas* and the Earl of Essex', *Review of English Studies*, li, no. 203 (2000), pp. 423–50. For the re-embracing of the Essexians, see T. Wilks, 'The Peer, the Plantsman, and the Picture-Maker: The English Embassy to the Court of Christian IV of Denmark, 1603', *The Court Historian*, 12:2 (December 2007), pp. 155–71.

6 It should be acknowledged that alongside the quest for the Elizabethan hero there was another major diversionary, cultural response to the problem of a virgin queen, encapsulated in the title of Roy Strong's seminal work, *The Cult of Elizabeth. Elizabethan Portraiture and Pageantry* (London, 1977).

7 See R. Malcolm Smuts, 'The Making of Rex Pacificus: James VI and I and the Problem of Peace in an Age of Religious War', in D. Fischlin and M. Fortier (eds.), *Royal Subjects: Essays on the Writings of James VI and I* (Detroit, 2002), pp. 371–88; also Paul J.E. Kershaw, 'Rex Pacificus: studies in royal peacemaking and the image of the peace-making king in the early medieval West' (unpublished Ph.D. diss., London, 1999).

8 C.H. Hertford and P. and E. Simpson (eds.), *Ben Jonson*, 11 vols (Oxford, 1925–52), I, p. 146.

9 Such a beaker, found in a well in Hurstbourne Tarrant, Hampshire, was recently sold at auction; see Christie's, London, King Street sale, 1 May 2007, lot 98. Other similar examples are known.

10 See Timothy Wilks, '"Paying special attention to the adorning of a most beautiful gallery": the Pictures in St James's Palace, 1609–49', *The Court Historian*, x, 2 (December 2005), pp. 152, 170–71.

11 The so-called 'Prince Henry's Room', 17 Fleet Street.

12 M. Bardwell, 'Greenland Fisheries Building, King's Lynn. Paintings discovered in two rooms after the house was bombed in the War', *Norfolk Archaeology*, xxi (1957), pp. 198–99.

13 See A.R. Wagner, 'A Note on Hatchments', *Antiquaries Journal*, xxxvi (1956), pp. 71–73; *Inventory of the Historical Monuments in Dorset* (RCHM, 1952), plate 25.

14 Formerly the home of Sir Thomas Saddler, registrar to the bishop of Salisbury, who twice played host to the royal family, in 1610 and 1612.

15 See Anthony Wells-Cole, 'An oak bed at Montacute; a study in Mannerist decoration', *Furniture History*, xvii (1981), pp. 1–19.

16 'Form-in-time' is a term more usually found in the discussion of music, though its application to imagery seems appropriate, not least as it qualifies 'form', and therefore bears an inherent challenge to 'formalism'.

17 Daniel Edwards, *Iraq War Memorial Featuring the Death of Prince Harry, Martyr of Maysan Province*, Bridge Art Fair, London, 11–14 October 2007.

18 The extent to which certain Medieval traits of mind were still discernible at a date when the Renaissance is supposed to have largely completed its task strikes the Early Modern specialist on reading J. Huizinga, *The Waning of the Middle Ages* (London, 1924). Huizinga observes: 'People feel an imperious need of always and

especially seeing the general sense, the connexion with the absolute, the moral ideality, the ultimate significance of a thing. What is important is the impersonal. The mind is not in search of individual realities, but of models, examples, norms' (1979 reprinting, p. 207).

19 Pulci's *Morgante* had earlier ridiculed the aspiring hero, but without lasting effect.

20 See Johannes Hartau, *Don Quijote in der Kunst: Wandlungen einer Symbolfigur* (Berlin, 1987); Ronald Paulson, *Don Quixote in England: the Aesthetics of Laughter* (Baltimore, 1998); Rachel Schmidt, *Critical Images: The Canonisation of Don Quixote through Illustrated Editions of the Eighteenth Century* (Montreal, 1999). See also the online digital archive that forms part of 'El Proyecto Cervantes', hosted by Texas A&M University: http://cervantes/tamu/edu.

21 See A.G. Lo Ré, 'A New First: an Illustration of Don Quixote as "Le Capitaine de Carnaval", Leipsig, 1614', *Cervantes*, 10, 2 (1990), pp. 95–100.

22 See Helen Watanabe-O'Kelly, 'The Iconography of German Protestant Tournaments in the Years before the Thirty Years War', *Image et spectacle: Actes du XXXIIe Colloque international d'études humanistes du Centre d'études supérieures de la Renaissance (Tours, 29 juin–8 juillet 1989), CHLOE: Beihefte zum Daphnis*, 15 (Amsterdam, 1993), pp. 47–64.

23 See Edgar Wind, *Hume and the Heroic Portrait*, ed. Jaynie Anderson, (Oxford, 1986), pp. 1–52.

24 *Ibid.*, pp. 4–5.

25 *Nugae Antiquae*, ed. Thomas Park, 2 vols. (London, 1804), I, pp. 389–90.

26 'J.P.', *The Life of General James Wolfe* (London, 1760); John Knox, *An Historical Account of the Campaigns in North America* (1769); see Helmut von Erffa and Allen Stanley, *The Paintings of Benjamin West* (New Haven and London, 1986), p. 214.

27 *The Paintings of Benjamin West*, cat. no. 108; *nota bene*, also the smaller *Death of Lord Nelson in the Cockpit of the Victory* (1808), cat. no. 109. West also painted two versions of *The Death of Sir Philip Sidney*, cat. nos 79 and 80, both depicting his Alexander-like refusal of water.

28 As the subject becomes removed from the immediate, the viewer is necessarily distanced. This elicits respect and awe, but it also permits the unreturned observation: the gaze. Oliver's miniature and Korda's photograph both show an unconscious, youthful, male beauty that encourages a romanticized view of the hero-figure.

29 Students of the theory of time will recognize that I am suggesting that eternalism maintained the upper hand over presentism.

30 Frank Kermode, *The Age of Shakespeare* (London, 2004), pp. 145–47.

31 Thomas Birch, *The Life of Henry, Prince of Wales* (London, 1760), p. 135.

32 See Pask, "The mannes state".

33 National Archives, Kew, E.351/433/15: payment to the widow of one Francesco Petrozani. See also *HMC Downshire III*, p. 238.

34 Paul O'Keeffe, *Some Sort of Genius A Life of Wyndham Lewis* (London, 2000), p. 153.

35 Lewis sets out his position, as best he can, in *Time and Western Man* (London, 1927); a critique of the philosophical positions of Alexander, Whitehead, Bergson, and Croce.

36 Lecture, 'Partial Recall', MOMA, New York, 1982, quoted in Frances Morris (ed.), *Louise Bourgeois* (London, 2007), p. 256.

37 See, for example, Leo Charney, *Empty Moments, Cinema, Modernity, and Drift* (Durham, N.C., 1998).

38 T.S. Eliot, *Burnt Norton* (1935), later published as the first of 'The Four Quartets'.

39 Henry Peacham, *Prince Henrie revived Or A poeme vpon the birth, and in honor of the hopefull yong Prince Henrie Frederick, first sonne and heire apparant to the most excellent princes, Frederick Count Palatine of the Rhine, and the mirrour of ladies, Princesse Elizabeth, his wife, only daughter to our Soueraigne Iames King of Great Brittaine, &c.* (London: W. Stansby for Iohn Helme, 1615).

1| Humanism and the Education of Henry, Prince of Wales

Aysha Pollnitz

During Prince Henry's lifetime and in the thirty years after his death, he was described in letters, dedications, biographies and other treatises as an ideal student prince. In 1609 William Cecil, Viscount Cranborne, reported from Bordeaux that 'the rare perfections both of [Henry's] mind and body, daily increased by [his] studies and exercises, do most gloriously shine abroad'.[1] Daniel Price lauded Henry as 'a young *Ptolomey* for studies and Libraries; such a young *Alexander* for affecting martialisme and chiualrie, such a young *Iosiah* for religion and piety'.[2] Henry's great princely potential and the glories of his future reign were anticipated and then mourned on the basis of his upbringing.

Henry was undoubtedly a young man of great energy but the nature of the praise he attracted owed a great deal to the preoccupations of sixteenth-century northern humanism. In Price's and Cranborne's commendations, for instance, one might see an echo of Thomas Elyot's description of Philip of Macedon in his *Boke Named the Gouernour* (1531), as having 'such lernyng as well in actes martiall as in other liberal sciences that he excelled other kings'.[3] The idea that the upbringing of royal children was critical for the fame of kings and the health of the common weal gained considerable momentum in England and Scotland following Erasmus's presentation of the *Institutio principis Christiani* to Henry VIII in 1517.[4] Erasmus had argued that the *bonae litterae* fashioned princes towards personifying virtue, governing with moderation and ruling for the common good. Subsequently, pedagogical works including Elyot's were dedicated to British princes, and humanists such as John Cheke, Roger Ascham and George Buchanan were engaged to provide Tudor and Stuart royal children with liberal educations.[5] Adult princes were praised (or blamed) on the basis of their learning. In many respects the argument for careful princely instruction reached its self-conscious apogee in James VI and I's *Basilicon Doron* (1599 and 1603). The monarch himself propounded aspects of the humanists' case in a work dedicated to his eldest son and heir, Prince Henry.

Subsequently, Henry developed a reputation on both sides of the border for being an ideal prince-in-training. The Prince's great potential for government was mythologized by his seventeenth-century biographers and later by scholars of the Stuart court. In the last twenty years, the most influential restatement of Henry's respect for learning, his 'capacity for sustained application' and his 'unremitting curiosity' has been Roy Strong's biography *Henry Prince of Wales and England's Lost Renaissance*.[6] Often neglected manuscript evidence of Henry's schooling, held in the British Library and the Wren Library of Trinity College, Cambridge, however, invites a reassessment of two aspects of Strong's magisterial study: his suggestion that father and son were invariably rivals; and the extent and nature of Henry's commitment to the idea of princely education.

Historical depictions of Henry

Seventeenth-century commendations of Henry reflect humanist concerns but the volume of praise heaped upon the prince by his contemporaries had a great deal to do with political circumstances. As the first male heir to the throne that England had had since 1537–47, Henry was immensely popular on both sides of the border. According to Isaac Wake, secretary to Sir Dudley Carleton, the Prince's premature death on 6 November 1612 'cawsed a fearefull outcrie among the people as if they felt at the present their owne ruine in that losse'.[7] Following Henry's demise, over forty works were published celebrating his life in the most exalted terms and mourning his loss as the guardian of England's and Scotland's futures.[8] These cries have echoed down the centuries, leading Strong, among others, to declare Henry's demise a 'lost Renaissance' of cultural achievement for Britain.

Strong's highly persuasive account characterized Henry's popularity and independence as causing rivalry between James and his son. Strong acknowledged that Henry did not inherit his father's scholarly mind but claimed that the Prince was intellectually astute and possessed wider sporting and cultural interests than the pedantic James. James's court was condemned as a hotbed of financial excess, debauchery and corruption but his son was accredited with frugally managing a centre of artistic and scientific innovation, piety and chivalry. James was called a pacifist by nature while Henry was pronounced a European Calvinist, who favoured military intervention and colonizing schemes. Many of these dichotomies are based firmly on contemporary evidence and Strong's analysis has proved invaluable for scholars of Stuart court culture.[9] Nevertheless, the divisions he asserts do not tell the whole story.

Firstly, the seventeenth-century accounts on which these polarities have been anchored need to be read with an eye to their authors' circumstances. Those within Henry's household and those who sought his patronage praised him wildly and self-interestedly during his lifetime. After his early death, many turned their attention to Charles, only to be disappointed for a second time when his household was established without them. Henry's comptroller Sir John Holles lamented that Henry's clients had been left like Tantalus 'to see the fruit and not to taste of it'.[10] The early accounts of Henry's life were often penned by characters like Sir Charles Cornwallis, who had fared badly, or at least failed to rise, after Henry's death.[11]

Secondly, Henry was naturally attractive to those who had political or religious reasons to be dissatisfied with his father and brother. The Prince was the hope of militant Calvinists, for instance, who were frustrated by James's and Charles's readiness to consort with Spain and with Catholics. Certainly, few English or Scotsmen used Henry to criticize James directly before 1620, but the Venetian ambassadors showed no such restraint. They praised the 'brave' and 'forward' young prince and sniped at his 'jealous' father.[12] Their favour seems to have sprung from a letter that Sir Henry Wotton, who was trying to convert the Venetians to Protestantism during the dispute between the Signoria and Pope Paul V, claimed Henry had sent him in 1607. Apparently, the Prince had protested that 'if he were of age, he would come in person to serve the Republic' in its battle. By 1609, the story was legendary. Paolo Sarpi criticized James for offering nothing but words against Rome, while his son desired action.[13] Calvinists and Venetians looked to Henry and designated him a champion of their cause.

In the 1620s, Henry became a vehicle for local criticism of his father and brother. The posthumous image of Henry as a Protestant knight was used against James on the subject of Charles's Spanish marriage and was revived to inspire Parliamentary generals in the Civil War. In this context, Sir Simonds D'Ewes lamented Henry's death in much the same way as the Marian exiles mourned Edward VI's premature demise: this 'shipwreck' of Protestantism had been caused by the sins of the British. D'Ewes added that many suspected that Henry had been poisoned, like Germanicus, the popular military hero and heir to the corrupt, idle and homosexual emperor Tiberius.[14] As Jason Scott-Warren has pointed out, Henry, like Elizabeth I, was 'a beneficiary of the blackening of James' in the 1650s. Anthony Weldon and Francis Osborne both lamented the 'hopeful Prince Henry' with Weldon even hinting that James was responsible for his early death. Thomas Birch's foundational *Life of Henry* (1760) followed D'Ewes in comparing the loss of his princely promise to the death of Germanicus. Subsequently, the suggestion that the reign of Henry may have produced an alternative to the political 'shipwreck' of the Civil War has become entrenched in the historiography of early Stuart Britain.[15]

As Timothy Wilks, Kevin Sharpe and Grant Tapsell have emphasized, however, one can only maintain this depiction of Henry by neglecting other pieces of contemporary evidence. With respect to the glittering court, Strong associated innovative figures like Inigo Jones with Henry, but Jones was originally promoted by the Earls of Rutland and Salisbury, and by Anne of Denmark, and came to full prominence under Charles. Indeed, as Wilks and Sharpe have argued, James was the founder of Henry's court in the first place and continued to shape it until 1610. Henry's image as a chivalrous warrior was won entirely in the tiltyard. And the great hope of militant European Calvinism actually had a number of Catholics in his household.[16] The extent of the disparity between the dominant representations of Henry and the reality of his life suggest that we cannot assume that he and his father were invariably at loggerheads, either.

This chapter is concerned with the first dichotomy I mentioned: the representation of James as a myopic, pedantic scholar and his son as intellectually curious but with wider artistic, scientific and sporting interests. Certainly evidence for such a depiction does exist. The Earl of Northampton wrote to Henry in 1605, for instance, praising him for achieving a perfect balance between learning and chivalric training, 'in all degrees matching Mercury with Diana, and study with exercise'. John Hawkins reported that once his household had been established in Oatlands, Henry had 'begun to ply his Booke hard for two or three yeares, continuing in all his Princely Sports' which included hawking, hunting, running at ring, leaping and riding. Henry's court did include a number of innovative mathematicians and natural philosophers including Edward Wright and Thomas Lydiat. William Haydon, a member of Henry's household, reported that James unleashed 'sharpe speeches, and other demonstrations of fatherlie severitie' on his son, for failing to reach the high academic standards the king himself had maintained as a boy.[17] Yet what is sometimes missing from accounts of James and Henry, indeed what is frequently absent from discussions of larger-than-life royal characters, are arguments based upon their own words and deeds.

The Basilicon Doron (1599 and 1603)

When all the evidence is taken into account one of the most important aspects of Henry's education is the extent to which his image as an exemplary student prince was actually cultivated by his father. The key document in shaping Henry's reputation was the *Basilicon Doron*, James's treatise of princely pedagogy, which he dedicated 'to Henry my dearest sonne, and natural sucessor'.[18]

The *Basilicon Doron* was first published in 1599 with a print-run of just seven copies. At this stage, James's intention seems to have been to address the issue of Henry's education for its own sake. The printing coincided with the beginning of Henry's formal lessons. James presented him, his tutor Adam Newton and his governor, the Earl of Mar, with copies of the work and, later, the King referred Henry to precepts contained in the book on at least two occasions.[19] James's own schoolmaster, George Buchanan, had addressed three nominally pedagogical works to James, however, and the King was well aware of the capacity of such texts to shape subjects' expectations of monarchical rule.[20] Subsequently, the *Basilicon Doron* became a text which was meant to fashion both Henry's education and the public perception of it.

On the eve of his succession to the English throne in 1603, James arranged for large printruns of the *Basilicon Doron* in both British capitals. Jason Scott-Warren has pointed out that James made a great number of changes to his 1599 text before it was printed in large numbers in 1603. Yet the 'rhetorical force' of the 1603 preface falsely implied that the second edition was identical to the first. The point of this subterfuge, Scott-Warren has argued, was to convince readers that they were eavesdropping on an intimate conversation between father and son, king and heir.[21] James was, of course, playing to one of his great virtues in the eyes of his subjects: his paternity. Readers of the *Basilicon Doron* would 'overhear' James instructing his son to 'acknowledgeth himselfe ordained for his people' and countless other pious sentiments (p. 20). They would observe the great care that James was taking for their welfare and his efforts to groom his son for their benefit. The *Basilicon Doron* portrayed James as a careful king and father. It put Henry's education at the heart of James's representation of his own sovereignty.

James was a member of a line of English and Scottish princes who were conscious that they were being evaluated by their contemporaries on the basis of their education. Reformers had emphasized Edward VI's learning in order to refute Stephen Gardiner's claim that, as a minor, he could not authorize changes to the structure or practices of the English Church. Elizabeth I made repeated references to her education in public speeches and James, of course, published (thinly veiled) testimony to his princely erudition from 1584 onwards.[22] By the turn of the sixteenth and seventeenth centuries, then, British subjects expected their monarchs to be well-educated. What 'well-educated' meant was frequently debated by pedagogues. The King warned Henry, however, that, as with most things, one's subjects would typically 'iudge of the substance' of one's upbringing 'according to the outward appearance' (p. 49). With the 1603 edition of the *Basilicon Doron*, then, James was attempting to influence how Henry's education and his own rule were viewed 'upon a publike stage' (p. 4): he portrayed himself as the philosopher-king begetting a student prince.

According to the *Basilicon Doron*, Henry's education would teach him to rule both church and state. James explained that he was cultivating his son to possess 'knowledge in all the points of [his] calling' and to 'study to know well [his] owne craft … which is to rule [his] people' (p. 47). Particularly, the king emphasized the importance of mathematics, which Henry was to apply to 'the arte militarie, in situations of Campes, ordering of battels, making fortifications, and the placing of batteries' (p. 47). In peacetime, Henry needed sufficient knowledge of scripture to 'containe [his] Church in their calling, as *Custos utriusque Tabulae* ['the Guardian of both Tables']' of their laws (p. 45). With respect to secular jurisdiction, James similarly instructed his son to 'studie well [his] owne Lawes' so that he could discern existing statutes and institute new legislation (p. 45). With respect to ruling more generally, the king recommended reading historians like Xenophon and Caesar. By describing practical action, they allowed princes to gain 'experience by Theoricke' which they could apply 'to the present estate' (p. 46). These subjects, James argued, would enable Henry to discharge his duty toward God and his royal office.

The King claimed to be sceptical about the value of many of the 'liberal arts and sciences', which had been praised by sixteenth-century humanists including Erasmus, Elyot, Roger Ascham and Buchanan. It was entirely appropriate for princes to show an interest in liberal disciplines and be 'reasonably versed' in them (p. 46). Attempts at Greek and Latin composition, however, and extensive knowledge of rhetoric and poetry, were more appropriate for scholars than future rulers. Henry should not be 'preassing to bee a passe-master' of the liberal arts since it might distract him from his princely duties (p. 46). Indeed, a number of courtly exercises and recreations – including hunting, naturally – were equally useful in enabling a prince to 'goe before all his subiects' (p. 55). Outward shows of physical dexterity, like riding, served 'greatly for allurements to the people', encouraging subjects to 'embrace and follow [the King's] vertue' in more substantial things (p. 59). The point of many of James's instructions was to differentiate the training of a prince from the education of scholars or subjects more generally.

It may sound surprising that James, who fought his own princely battles with a liberally educated pen, had not trumpeted the value of the *bonae litterae*. In part, James was undoubtedly trying to distinguish his prescriptions for Henry from the 'laws' of kingship that his own tutor, the humanist Buchanan, had set out for him. Buchanan had championed a liberal curriculum for kings in his poem 'Genethliacon' (1567) and then argued in the *De iure regni apud Scotos* (1579) that the point of princely education was to teach a monarch to personify the virtues for his subjects' imitation.[23] Buchanan might well emphasize the need to cultivate rulers' moral authority: he denied them most other powers. In contrast, James insisted that Henry needed to understand Church ordinances and municipal law because he had invested his heir with sovereign legislative responsibility. He focussed on knowledge which was important for the maintenance (and possibly extension) of monarchical authority and skills which would enhance a prince's pre-eminence.

Additionally, James's emphasis on vocational skills, shows of physical virtuosity and his seemingly sceptical attitude towards rhetoric were not out of step with the prescriptions of some contemporary pedagogues. Humphrey Gilbert, Sir Francis Bacon and Sir George More also questioned whether the study of rhetoric and extensive explications of the 'discourse of the Cardinall virtues' ('so troden a path', wrote James, p. 43) were, on their own, adequate to prepare men for government.[24] These humanists still meant to cultivate virtuous behaviour in civic life but they were searching for more practical and effective means to encourage it.[25] Bacon praised the *Basilicon Doron* as 'a woorke ritchlye compounded of *Divinity, Morality and Policy* with great aspersion of all other artes' and consequently he found it 'apt for action'.[26] In 1603 James introduced Henry to Scottish and English subjects as a prince who might be a 'lampe' of virtue (p. 42) but he insisted that this status was commensurate with training in the 'crafte' of kingship.

The philosopher-king and the student prince

James's depiction of Henry's education was widely disseminated. As Jenny Wormald has argued, the *Basilicon Doron* 'was undoubtedly a best-seller' in Britain and was published widely on the Continent.[27] Its influence is evident in the large number of treatises which were dedicated to Henry after 1603 and which reference James's work. In the imagination of would-be clients, Henry was a prince-in-training, and the obvious recipient of pedagogical texts.

Joshua Sylvester, for instance, made most successful use of the *Basilicon Doron* in his bid for royal patronage. He presented his English verse renderings of Guy du Faur's *Quadrains* to

Henry in 1605. Sylvester's dedicatory verses claimed that he was reinforcing the 'golden Rules of State, Religious Lessons, Moral Precepts graue' which had been contained in Henry's 'Father's Royal-Gift'.[28] In the same year, he dedicated his English translation of *Bartas his Devine Weekes & Workes* (1605) to James. Du Bartas was one of James's favourite authors and he had recommended the poet to Henry in the *Basilicon Doron* (p. 58). King and heir were linked once more in the dedication of Sylvester's 1607 *Posthumus Bartas* in which the translator thanked Henry for his gracious receptions of the earlier *Quadrains*.[29] Sylvester's 'Royal-Gifts' were heeded and he became the first poet of Henry's court when his pension was awarded in 1608. On 17 February 1610, James became the poet's patron too, presenting Sylvester £300 for his efforts.[30] By mirroring James's self-depiction and his presentation of Henry in the *Basilicon Doron* Sylvester pleased both 'Great Britain's Solomon' and its 'great hope'.

As the dedications piled up, so Henry's reputation for learning increased. When Sir Clement Edmondes, Remembrancer for the City of London, dedicated his 1604 edition of *Observations upon Caesars Commentaries* to the prince, he did so on the grounds that Caesar confirmed 'those manie principles of warre which his Maiestie hath set downe by way of precept' in the *Basilicon Doron*. By the 1609 edition, Edmondes was one of Henry's clients and his debt to the *Basilicon Doron* had grown: 'in the deepe Iudgement of his most excellent Maiesty', Caesar had been offered as 'as a cheefe paterne and Maister-peece of the Art of Warre'.[31] The publishing value of representing Henry as an eager prince-in-training evidently increased over time. His enthusiasm for learning was becoming an article of faith.

In addition to rewarding authors who praised him in the terms of James's *Basilicon Doron*, Henry began to cultivate this image himself, commissioning works which demonstrated his love of learning. When Queen Anne and her ladies performed Ben Jonson's *Masque of Queens* for the court on 2 February 1609, Henry asked Jonson to provide him with a bibliography of the classical authorities he had used. Jonson offered Henry a copy of the masque with annotations and explanations in his own hand, commending the Prince's 'favor to letters, and these gentler studies'.[32] Henry's next commissions would be for the wider reading public: George Chapman's English translations of Homer, published in 1609, 1611 and 1616.[33] As Henry aged, he made a graceful transition from student prince to literary patron.

Individuals patronized by Henry were frequently deemed his 'tutors', though it is impossible to determine that their attendance in the schoolroom was formal or frequent. Thomas Lydiat was appointed as Henry's chronographer and cosmographer for the sum of forty marks a year. In return, he dedicated *Emendatio temporum compendio facta ab initio mundi ad praesens usque* (1609) to the Prince. Alfonso Ferrabosco, who received a pension of fifty marks per annum for instructing the Prince in music, dedicated his *Ayres* to Henry in 1609. Salomon de Caus gave the Prince some lessons in perspective and mathematics and dedicated his *La Perspective avec la raison des ombres et mirroirs* (1612) to his royal student.[34] John Protheroe, a Welsh patron of mathematics and executor of Thomas Harriot, was also described as amongst his 'tutors'.[35] Henry used patronage to parlay his father's depiction of him as a prince-in-training into an image of himself as the 'Maecenas of the learned'.[36] He was publicly fashioning himself into the ideal cultivated by the *Basilicon Doron*.

Henry's reputation for learning was further assisted by events which showed him engaging in study. Between 27 and 30 August 1605, he entered Magdalen College, Oxford as part of a royal visit and became the first British prince to matriculate at university. Oxford set out to entertain, and James had a wonderful time. Apart from a few dramatic performances which bored him to sleep, the King was in his element, interjecting cheerfully in disputations regarding the use of tobacco, pottering around Sir Thomas Bodley's newly opened library, and making Latin orations. James's auditors 'pronounced our Countrie to be that Commonwealth, which *Plato* affirmed, to be happie and blessed, under the gouernment and protection of a King so learned, wise, and vertuous'.[37] Isaac Wake, the University Orator, similarly entitled his account of the visit *Rex Platonicus* and described Henry as an Alexander to James's Philip and Aristotle.[38] James went to Oxford as a king and philosopher and Henry attended him as a son and pupil destined for great things.

It is clear that the Prince was not actually expected to study in Oxford. His 'matriculation' consisted of a round of learned entertainments and a feast. Anthony Wood registers that he was appointed a tutor, John Wilkinson, Bachelor of Divinity and later President of Magdalen, but there is no record of further contact between the two.[39] While the University addressed James in Latin, Henry was saluted in the vernacular; Oxford dons had few illusions about the Prince's linguistic competence.[40] Henry's 'matriculation' was actually a variation of the standard royal progress and a novel way of showing royal favour to Magdalen and Oxford. Nevertheless, prior to his departure to the university, Henry received a letter from Henry Howard, Earl of Northampton, the Jacobean controversialist. Northampton expressed his sorrow that Oxford was to have 'the first fruits of your resort to the temple of the muses' and hoped in time to see him in Cambridge.[41] Henry's 'matriculation' had evidently been discussed in courtly and university circles in a way that amplified his image as a student prince.

There had been 'a great labour' to admit Henry to the degree of MA on the final day of his visit to Oxford. On the morning of the ceremony, however, the Prince had been carefully tucked out of the concourse's way, watching a play by Samuel Daniel with his mother.[42] Strong has attributed James's refusal to allow his son to take the degree to his jealousy of Henry's growing popularity, but the King could have been admitted to an even higher degree himself had he wished it.[43] Actually, James's refusal was entirely consistent with his discussion of princely education in the *Basilicon Doron*. As we have seen, the King had specified that his son should become only 'reasonably versed' in the liberal arts 'but not preassing to be a passe-master in any of them' (p. 46). Matriculation demonstrated that Henry was a patron of the university but the conferral of a degree suggested the wrong kind of learning for a future ruler. Despite the attendance of increasing numbers of aristocrats the university was still closely associated with the seminary. Henry was to become a king not a cleric.

Rather than install Henry in a university, James preferred that his son be educated in a 'collegiate court'. In a 1607 letter to the Chancellor of the Exchequer, Sir Julius Caesar, Henry's governor Sir Thomas Chaloner begged for more funds for what was 'intended by the King for a *Courtly College* or a *Collegiate Court*'.[44] In his *Hero-paideia or The Institution of a young nobleman* (1607) James Cleland, who as tutor to Sir John Harington of Exton (1592–1614) was part of Henry's Nonsuch household, recommended 'the *Academie* of our Noble Prince' as the best place for 'a young Noble man [to] learne to fashion himselfe'. By encouraging the study of civil matters, the liberal arts and sciences and the 'exercise of the body' Henry's collegiate court prepared one to become a '*Privie Counseller*, a *Generall* of an Armie, to rule in peace, & commande in warre'. [45] Cleland obviously offered an idealized picture: Henry's householders were not always propelled towards learning and civic virtue. One young collegiate courtier, William Sidney, was even expelled for stabbing his tutor, Mr Bird.[46] In its ideals, however, the court mimicked the prescriptions of the *Basilicon Doron* in stressing practical training towards political leadership. Moreover, Wilks has discovered evidence to suggest that, at the time of his death, Henry was planning to expand the collegiate court into a permanent, national academy for wards of the court.[47] As with his literary patronage, James had created the initial venture and Henry had begun to amplify it.

Father and son also worked together on what Strong has rightly termed the 'refoundation' of the Royal Library. Following the death of Lord Lumley on 11 April 1609, Henry acquired his library of some 3,000 titles in around 2,800 volumes. Most of the books were relocated to St James's, where Henry was to take his court after his investiture as Prince of Wales.[48] James built a new library in the palace for his son, paying for the construction work, fittings, ornamentation and furniture himself. Henry, in turn, employed at least one librarian, Edward Wright, purchased additional volumes and paid for the binding of works in his collection.[49]

As T.A. Birrell has shown, Wright and others set about assembling a vast and scholarly library of books. Its catalogue of titles in mathematics, natural philosophy and geography was especially impressive; the collection was probably intended to be a resource for explorers and colonizers in Henry's service.[50] The library also held works donated by the Prince's clients, who were frequently friends and collaborators of Wright. In 1600, for instance, Wright had assisted in the publication of William Gilbert's *De magnete*. After Gilbert's death his brother (also confusingly called William) presented Henry with a manuscript edition of the natural philosopher's final work, *De mundo nostro sublunari philosophia nova* (completed in its present form in 1603) 'either for publishing for public use or for preserving in your truly princely library'.[51] His adjectives are telling. For men of mathematics and natural philosophy, Henry's collection – under Wright's intellectual aegis – was a welcome indicator of the prince's present and future support of their endeavours. They praised the library and its owner accordingly. Once again, James's and Henry's shared scientific patronage furthered Henry's reputation as a promising prince.

Far from the antagonism which Strong argued had invariably characterized James's and Henry's relationship, father and son actually worked together to cultivate their complimentary images as philosopher-king and student prince. Authors who mirrored the terms of the *Basilicon Doron* were well rewarded for their services. Henry's affiliation with Oxford and his collegiate court sent specific messages about the pattern of his education which were consistent with James's text. And the refoundation of the royal library, sponsored jointly by king and heir, promised subjects that Henry had been fashioned for a 'truly princely' reign.

Sources for Henry's schooling

In order to determine how this widely disseminated 'patterne' of Henry's education related to the reality of the Prince's schooling it is necessary to go beyond the printed, biographical accounts of his life. The most frequently cited of these allegedly eye-witness testimonies is Sir Charles Cornwallis's *Discourse of the most illustrious Prince Henry* (written 1626; published 1641). Cornwallis, Henry's treasurer, claimed that the Prince divided his time between 'the service of God' and 'apting himselfe to the office hee was borne unto',[52] just as the first two sections of the *Basilicon Doron* had intimated he ought (pp. 12, 19). Cornwallis claimed that the Prince also followed his father's instructions by reading history 'to enable his knowledge in government civill'. Then 'in the military', Henry also respected James's prescriptions by studying mathematics, cosmography and the construction of fortifications. Cornwallis reported that Henry rode daily, ran at ring and tilted 'with so great a comelinesse … he became second to no Prince in Christendom'. In fact, far from being an eye-witness to Henry's upbringing, Cornwallis was stationed in Spain until 1609 and only appointed to Henry's household after his investiture in 1610.[53] His description matches the prescriptions of the *Basilicon Doron* because it was probably the main source for the *Discourse*.

More reliable testimony is to be found in the neglected exercise books and papers collected by Prince Henry's schoolmaster Adam Newton. Newton was born the son of an Edinburgh baker but managed to graduate from the University of Glasgow in 1582. Thereafter he worked as an advocate in Edinburgh, contributing a small amount to the pension of James Melville, the nephew of Andrew, who had been exiled to England for his support of ecclesiastical parity.[54] At some point, Newton travelled to France to teach at St Maixent in Poitou, where he tutored the young André Rivet in Greek. By 1594 he had returned and was recommended, albeit unsuccessfully, for a post at the College in Edinburgh.[55] At the time of his appointment to Henry's household, Newton was evidently a promising young scholar. He did not have an international reputation of his father's preceptor, Buchanan, but this may have enabled him to obscure his early Presbyterian sympathies for James's benefit. Once in royal service, Newton followed his sovereign assiduously in matters of religion and ecclesiastical government.[56] He was handsomely rewarded for his efforts on Henry's behalf and on James's.

Despite being a layman, he was made Dean of Durham in 1606 and Henry's principal secretary in 1610. After the Prince's death he served as secretary of Charles's council and retired from his office at Durham to accept a baronetcy on 2 April 1620. Eight years later, Newton received the reversion to the Marches of Wales, a post worth £2000 per annum.[57]

Newton followed previous royal tutors in his commitment to the *bonae litterae*. His commonplace books were well-developed compendiums of Plautus, Cicero, Sallust, Horace, Demosthenes, Seneca, Virgil and Tacitus.[58] His pedagogical sympathies are evident from a copy of the Hans Holbein portrait of *Erasmus writing*, which Strong has shown he presented to one of the Stuart princes.[59] Somewhat more unusually for a royal tutor, Newton continued to read law while in Henry's service.[60] Perhaps James hoped that he would assist Henry with the knowledge of municipal statutes that the King had recommended in the *Basilicon Doron*.

While in Henry's household Newton kept a number of the Prince's letters, school exercises and books. Around 1610 a selection of Henry's schoolbooks were bound in white vellum and tooled with gold. It was the same binding that the librarian Patrick Young had arranged to preserve some of the schoolbooks of Edward VI and James VI.[61] After the death of both Newton and his heir in the early 1630s, these books and papers were inherited by his second son, Henry. Henry Newton was a staunch royalist during the Civil War, and changed his last name to 'Puckering' in 1652 to inherit his uncle's estate and title. After the death of his wife in 1689 he retired from political life to Trinity College, Cambridge, and two years later he gave most of his books – including the set bound in white vellum – to the Wren Library of that college, where they remain. He died in 1701. On 9 July 1713, George Paul of Jesus College, Cambridge, wrote to Robert Harley, Earl of Oxford and Lord Treasurer, to say that his landlady had come into possession of a collection of letters by and to Prince Henry previously owned by Puckering.[62] Perhaps the baronet had offered them to his landlady in the same manner as he had presented other books and papers to Trinity: as payment or in gratitude for board and care during his declining years. They are now held as part of the Harleian manuscripts in the British Library and, alongside the Wren documents, provide a source for reconstructing Henry's upbringing prior to 1610.

Henry's early schooling, 1599–1607

In the *Basilicon Doron*, James had warned his son against becoming distracted by philosophy (p. 46). From what can be pieced together from manuscript evidence, Henry's princely potential was not unduly blighted in this respect. Between 1599 and 1607, the Prince's curriculum followed a relatively conventional route in an unhurried fashion. Like his father, grandmother and Tudor royal children, he commenced by studying Latin grammar and elementary rhetoric, learning French and acquiring an italic hand.

With respect to Latin grammar, Newton's teaching followed the well-established methods of Erasmus. Between 1599–1601/02, Henry almost certainly studied the parts of speech. In this endeavour Newton probably used the *Brevissima institutio* also known as Lily's Grammar. At some point, Henry consulted a manuscript treatise by Henry Wright which argued that there were a number of errors and (more importantly, Wright thought) omissions in that text.[63] Wright sought Henry's patronage for developing and publishing his corrections and additions but the Prince does not seem to have been persuaded that schoolboys needed longer Latin textbooks. Disheartened, Wright dedicated his subsequent work, *The Disquisition of Truth, concerning Political Affairs* (1616), to the mayor and aldermen of London. There he described 'all credit, countenance, honors, and authority' gained in court as 'slippery'.[64] Many 'uncorrected' editions of the *Brevissima institutio* also came with a series of pious excerpts for young scholars, including the Creed, the Ten Commandments, the Lord's Prayer, William Lily's 'Carmen de moribus' and sometimes Erasmus's *Christiani hominis institutum*, which Henry may have read too.[65] The point of these short texts was to develop a pupils' vocabulary and understanding of syntax. They paved the way to the reading of Latin authors.

Two letters that Henry wrote to his father in 1603 confirm that he had indeed progressed to those Latin authors which were studied in the junior years of grammar schools. The first was dated 19 February, Henry's ninth birthday. The Prince explained that he was writing to demonstrate his progress in Latin. He had read 'Terence's *Hecyra*, the third book of Phaedrus' *Fables* and two books of the Selected Epistles of Cicero'.[66] In the middle years of the sixteenth century, Ascham and John Cheke had expressed concern as to the immodesty of Terence's subject-matter, but Newton was not so squeamish. Neither was Henry, who in a subsequent letter to James, dated 15 July 1603, claimed that Terence, Caesar and Phaedrus were among the noblest authors of the Latin language. The only one of these that James had not studied himself was Phaedrus but his fables were largely Latin verse renderings of Aesop's. Newton gave Henry a verse regarding Tiberius's report to an officious and self-seeking slave, entitled 'Tiberius Caesar ad Atriensen'.[67] Henry's introduction to Latin authors, then, reflected standard practice in Early Modern Britain.[68]

As Henry's letters to James and his early study of Cicero's letters suggest, from at least 1601 the Prince had been learning to imitate the vocabulary, grammar and compositions of Roman authors by writing Latin epistles. He may have relied on a copy of Erasmus's *De conscribendis epistolis* (1523) in the Lumley Library to develop his understanding of epistolary genres and techniques.[69] When the time came to practise letter-writing, Newton would compose the epistle – often drafts exist in his hand – and then the Prince would take it down.[70] Henry's first drafts usually contained a number of errors, evidence that Newton had dictated the text to him or perhaps had instructed him to commit it to memory and then reproduce it later. There is no suggestion that his early study of letter-writing followed Ascham's and Cheke's method of double translation.[71] After making corrections to his text, the Prince was expected to practise a few words or letters in the margins of his page to improve his italic script or spelling.[72] The only difference between Henry's epistles and the letter-writing training of his contemporaries

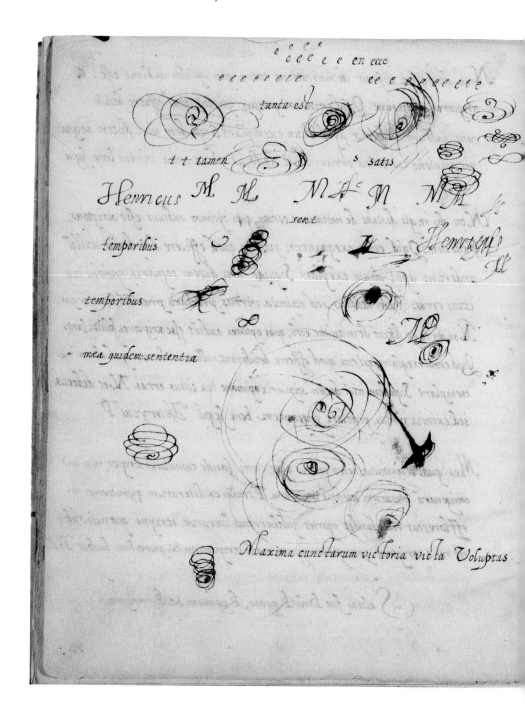

6

Mea quidem sententia, nemo poterit esse omni laude cumulatus scriptor, nisi erit omni-

genarum literarum scientiam consecutus: Etenim ex literarum cognitione efflorescat

& redundet oportet pulcherrima literarum scriptio: quæ nisi subest res a scriptore

percepta & cognita, inanem scriptionem et puerilem habet   Henricus Princeps

Mea quidem sententia, nemo poterit esse omni luade cumulatus scriptor

nisi erit omnigenaru literaru scientiam consecutus: Etenim ex literaru cogni-

tione efflorescat & redundet oportet pulcherrima literaru scriptio: quæ

nisi subest res a scriptore percepta & cognita, inanem scriptione & puerile habet

Mea quide sententia nemo poterit esse omni laude cumulatus scriptor, nisi erit

omnigenaru literaru scientia cosecutus: Eteni ex literaru cognitione efflores-

cat et redudet oportet pulcherrima literaru scriptio: quæ nisi subest res a scrip

tore percepta go cognita, manem scriptione & puerilem habet. H.P.M.

+a

Mea quide sentetia, nemo poterit esse omni laude cumulatus scriptor, nisi erit omnigena-

vu literarum scientia consecutus: Eteni ex literaru cognitione effloreat & redudet oportet

pulcherima literaru scriptio: quæ nisi subest res a scriptore percepta & cognita, ina-

nem scriptionem et puerilem habet. H P.   Henricus Bing

Mea quidem sententia Princeps Henricus vix est mediocri laude

dignus scriptor, adeo puerilem scriptionem habet.

Wren Library, Trinity College, Cambridge
MS R.7.23, I, fols. 5v–6r

35

Eruditio litterarum naturam laudabilem eximie reddit ornatam ibi prudens inuenit vnde sapientior fiat; ibi bellator reperit vnde animi virtute roboretur, inde Princeps accipit, quemadmodum populos sub æqualitate componat. Nec aliqua in mundo potest esse fortuna quam literarum non augeat gloriosa notitia. HP W   Cassiodorus

Eruditio literarum naturam laudabilem eximie reddit ornatam: ibi prudens inuenit vnde sapientior fiat; ibi bellator reperit vnde animi virtute roboretur, inde Princeps accipit; quemadmodum populos sub æqualitate componat. Nec aliqua in mundo potest esse fortuna, quã literarũ non augeat gloriosa notitia

Eruditio literarum naturã laudabilem eximie reddit ornatam: ibi prudens inuenit vnde sapintior fiat; ibi bellator reperit, vnde animi virtute roboretur, inde Priceps accipit quemadmodum populos sub æqua litate componat.

Eruditio literarũ naturam laudabile eximie reddit ornatũ . s

Eruditio literarũn naturam laudabilem eximie reddit ornatam: ibi prudens inuenit vnde sapientior fiat ibi bellator reperit vnde animi virtute roboretur inde Princeps accipit quemadmo dũm populos sub æqualitate componat. Nec aliqua in mundo potest esse fortuna quam literarum non augeat gloriosa notitia. Henricus Prrinceps W

Eruditio literarum naturam laudabilem eximie reddit ornatam ibi prudens inuenit vnde sapientior fiat, ibi bellator reper

Wren Library, Trinity College, Cambridge, MS R7.23, I, fol. 8r

favour given to one onlie, causeth the prince to be deemed
a weake and unwise man, it fretteth much, & alienateth
particulerlie the mindes of the greatest and worthiest
subiecte, and so disordereth the whole goverment, that
that State seemeth naked of counsell and deprived of
Justice. But as a Prince is but a man, and man being
naturallie sociable cannott in what estate soever
live chearfullie w.th out some inward friend w.th whom
hee may communicate the passion of his mind, and
this friend of the prince beinge the favorite, hee ought
to have so much prudence that hee can temper in
such sort the affections of friendshipp, that hee corrupt
not the effecte of soveraigntye.

It hath bene said before, that distributive Justice propor-
tioneth greevances, by reason that if the distribuçon
of them be not ballanced w.th the condiçons & quallities
of the subiecte, Uniustice wilbe alwayes powerfull
to rayse the state, whose dutie is to give so many forces
to their prince that hee may maintayne them w.th
iustice, and defend them from open violence.

The greevances ymposed vppon the people are pecu-
niarye contribuçons, psonall service reservinges of
ryalties and comodities of lodginge ~~Pecuniarie~~.

Pecuniarie contribuçon is of two sortes; ordinarie &
extraordinarye; ordinarie consisteth in the auntient
right of customes, Tenthes, and other tribute; extra-
ordinarie in the increase of ordinarie paymentes &
taxaçons ymposed for a tyme accordinge to the
Prince his necessitie.

Parsonall service is likewise of two sortes, eyther
by the

Wren Library, Trinity College, Cambridge, Trinity MS R7.23, II, fol. 16v

knights will plaie, w:th you two knights: that are noe
gentlemen. this was somewhat wittie; but to sharpe
w:th all. All thes taunts, and descants are no less
scornefull to the dignitie: then reproachfull to the
abuse thereof. But wee maye finde, and reade in our
anncyent recordes, and cronacles: that our famous, and
victorious kinges in reward of virtue, and valour
haue confered that title vppon theire worthiest subiects:
and oftentymes on theire owne brothers, and soms: as
a high grace, and therevnto gaue sundrie prerogatiues,
though nowe growne out of date; whereby few or none
striue att this daie, to make themselues worthie of that
callinge for other virtue, or seruice: then for attiringe
them selues in sumptious apparell, toowell knowinge,
that y honorable tytle is nowe to be attayned by farr
easier meanes: then by virtuous endeuours, or martiall
toyles. But in this sorte doe our gallants carrie all
theire reputations, and wealth on theire backes: and
runn so deepelie indebted to the marchaunts, and Ar=
tifycers: as that they make them banckrouts, and
afterwardes to keepe them companie, like true vnthrifts,
they conclude theire brauerie in prisons, & goales.
What a number are there, both of English, and Scotts,
on whome the kinge yo:r father hath bestowed greate,
and bountifull giufts: thatt cann shewe no other
testimonie thereof, nor are thereby enabled to doe

hym

Wren Library, Trinity College, Cambridge, MS R7.23, III, fol. 7r

hym better seruice: then to seeke protections to saue them
from arests, or els are readie dailie to begg newe suites?
Thes men perswade themselues that in this foolish,
and lauish pride, they make the worlde admire theire
woorth: but they are onelie admired for theire inconsiderate vanitie, and prodigalitie: that cann couerte
to no better vse, the bountie of theire Soueraigne,
then to turne it into clouts: and to wast more on theire
backes, then manie of theire parents haue wherew:all
to feed theire families. And if his Ma:tie did rightly
value many of his seruaunts by theire loue to hyme,
and theire care of his estate; hee shoulde verie soone
finde iust cause to hold his bountifull hande, from
opening his purse vnto them, soe often, and plentifully:
as hee doth. For if I maye (vnder pardon) presume
to reason by example: (wch is the plainest waye of
instruction of all others) I shoulde iudge yt seruaunte
of myne to nourishe little affection in his harte towards
mee: that wthout all respect of my estate, my occasions,
and necessities, did daylie studie to drawe from mee,
what he coulde: and hauinge obtayned more, then
standes wth his merit, or my fortunes to afoorde hym:
is not onlie not satisfied therewth, but doth contynewe
in spendinge moste vainelie. not onelie that, wch hee

hath

Cum principio rerum homines ad fastigium regiæ
dignitatis moderatione potius quam ambitione prove-
herentur, atq̧ intra suam cuiq̧ patriam regna fini-
rentur; Ninus omnium primus auitum hunc morem
mutauit, & inferens bella finitimis non contentus
gloria victoriæ gentium deuictarum possessionem
occupauit.　　Henricus Princeps scripsi Maio 1605

Sæpe licet videre fœminas assumere sibi viriles
animos, & vicissim homines muliebres & molles
gerere animos. Nam Semiramis mentita sexum
res gessit magnas, q quibus non solum auxit maiesta-
tem
regni, sed etiam existimationem suam: quod fœmina
vel homines anteiret virtute. Sed filius Nini
ia contra contentus regnis acquisitis aparentibus, omnia studia bellica deposuit, & maluit in cœtu mu-
lierū consenescere, quam amplitudine actionum inter
homines conclarescere. Hen L

1

6.

Licet in Sardanapalo aliud videre exemplum
muliebris in viro animi: qui vna cum habitu virilem
exuens animum, ~~cum~~ vestem foemineam induit, nebat
colo inter scortorum greges, deuidebat pensa inter ea,
& armorum loco filum & lanam tractabat, prebens se
virum nulla re, nisi vltima actione. Nam cum impul-
su Arbacti quidam optimatum in eum coniurassent,
cum fugam & tenebras non posse iuuare perspiceret
post prelij stragem se & diuitias in incendium
misit.

Cyrus ille, per quem Imperiũ a Medis ad Persas
erat translatũ, est nobis insigni documento, et quã
mira vis fatorum sit, et quãta sit benignitas Dei, in ijs conseruandis, quos rebus gerendis magnis destinauit. Nam quid aperti-
us potestatem Numinis declarat, quã quod ab eodẽ seruatus sit
cui tradebatur necandus. Et itorum pastorem videre et coniu-
gem et ipsam canem foeminam misericordia moueri, cum parens
necare decreuit, argumentum est eius inscrutabilis bonita-
tis eius qui omnes actiones hominum in suas fines dirigit

Rex Sere.^{me} & amantissime Pater,

2

Offero Ma.^{ti} Tuæ strenæ loco, manum simul et mentem
meam. Manum quæ in pauculis Bibracii tetrastichis
describendis facile in oculos incurrit. Mentem etiam,
quæ eisdem e Gallico in Latinum transferendis, et ipsis
Gallicis memoriæ commendandis, non leuiter desudauit: ac
iam nunc experimentum sui dare non recusat. Et
profecto non indigna mihi res videbatur, in qua et manus
operam, & mentis ingenii, aciem intenderem: quòd cum
præcepta hîc contineantur ad mores informandos apprime
vtilia, tum bona eorum pars principibus ipsis instituendis
potissimum videtur conscripta. Quodsi Deus aliquando
mihi dederit, vt Ma.^{ti} T.^e vestigiis insistens, vita
factisq; eadem exprimere valeam: tum non mediocre
operæ nauatæ pretium consequutum me Ma.^{tas} Tua
existimabit. Quam, vt ille ipse Deus quàm diu-
tissimè viam mihi ad virtutem præire, ac (vt cœpit,)
ab immanibus perditissimorum hominum ausis intactam
conseruare perpetuo velit, toto pectore rogo. Kal.
Jan.   Ma. T. filius obsequentissimus,

Henricus

Wren Library, Trinity College, Cambridge, MS R7.23, VII, fol. 2r in the grammar schools was that Henry's letters were addressed and sometimes sent to Continental heads of state, establishing his presence on the European political landscape.[73]

After Cicero's letters and Terence, Henry probably moved on to Virgil. In 1604 John Harington of Kelston presented James with a translation of the sixth book of the *Aeneid* for Henry, using marginal notes to draw the Prince's attention to James's use of Virgil in the *Basilicon Doron*.[74] Simon Sturtevaunt prepared an autographed and illuminated collection of sentences from the poet for Henry, entitled *Virgills Gnomologie*. Sturtevaunt described excerpts of Virgil, 'namelie his Weightier Verses, his Wittier sayings', as 'being next unto Divinitie better appliable for [Henry's] high estate yeares & Condic[i]on' than any other author.[75] Despite Sturtevant's claims, his gnomology was no key to political philosophy. Sturtevaunt instructed schoolmasters to explain the literal sense of each excerpt, discuss its context and argument, and propose additional occasions upon which the quotation might be employed, before requiring the pupil to rehearse these three steps by himself. This method was not significantly different from the practice set out by Cardinal Wolsey in his 1529 statutes for Ipswich school or indeed from Erasmus's prescriptions in *De ratione studii* (1511).[76]

Henry did not escape philosophy or rhetoric entirely. Like his princely predecessors and grammar school counterparts, he read *De officiis* and annotated his copy throughout. He underlined unusual words and phrases to transfer them into a copybook like those made by Edward VI. Henry numbered the stages in many of Cicero's arguments, such as his discussion of the role of the advocate in court. He made marginal indications of *sententiae*, often marking passages which advocated participation in public life, then reused them in his compositions.[77]

Unlike Edward, James VI and Elizabeth I, however, Henry appears not to have studied Cicero alongside Greek authors like Isocrates or Demosthenes. It is always dangerous to make an argument from silence, but, given that Newton preserved so much of Henry's schoolwork, it seems odd that so little evidence of Greek remains. Some does exist: Henry transliterated the Greek terms in his copy of *De officiis*; one of his lost exercises was a Latin thesis composed out of a sentence of Menander; and in an oration from 1609, Henry included a single Greek phrase and cited Plutarch, Xenophon and Plato.[78] All of these authors, however, were available in parallel text editions or Latin translation at the time he was studying them. In all probability, Henry had a 'name-dropping' acquaintance with Greek. His capacity to produce and transliterate the alphabet and to quote some of the major authors in Latin was a sufficient badge of culture for the heir to the throne. The rhetorical and religious impetus to teach princes Greek – emphasized in the sixteenth century by Elyot and reformers like Cheke – seems to have subsided.[79]

Henry may have embarked on Italian instead. In an undated letter to his mother he thanked her for the gift 'of some Italian and French books, [as he] is able to become more wise and virtuous by the reading of them'.[80] In 1603, he and the Princess Elizabeth told the Venetian ambassador that they intended to learn Italian. Perhaps on account of this, Henry received letters in Italian from the Venetian Doge Leonardo Donato.[81] Henry certainly had

Hominis probi Deus est præsidium, etiam
tum cum ab omnibus derelinquitur: quin hoc
ipso minus animo consternatur suo, quòd Deum
sui curam gerere exploratum habet.

Bona corporis ac fortunæ si propriè loquamur bona
nuncupanda non sunt, cùm minimis quibusq mutati =
onibus sint obnoxia. virtus autem eadem semper
permanet.

24

De l'homme droict Dieu est la sauuegarde,
Lors que de tous il est abandonné,
C'est lors que moins il se trouue estonné,
Car il scait bien que Dieu lors plus le garde.

God is the iust-man's Anchor and his Ayde,
His sure Defence, when all the World forsakes-him;
And therefore, then is he the least dismayde,
Knowing that God then most to safe-gard takes-him.

25

Les biens du corps, & ceux de la Fortune,
Ne sont pas biens, à parler proprement,
Ils sont subiects au moindre changement,
Mais la vertu demeure tousiours vne.

The Goods of Fortune and the Body (call'd)
They are not Goods, if we them rightly name;
For, to least changes they are euer thrall'd :
" But Onely Vertue still persists the same,

26

Vertu qui gist entre les deux extrèmes,
Entre le plus & le moins qu'il ne fault;
N'excede en rien, & rien ne luy default :
D'autruy n'emprunte, & suffit à soy-mesmes.

Vertue, betweene the Two extremes that haunts ;
Betweene too-mickle and too-little sizes ;
Exceedes in nothing, and in nothing wants :
Borrowes of none : but to it-selfe suffixes.

Qui

opportunity to learn the language. Princess Elizabeth took lessons with John Florio and Theodore Diodati, so he may have had some tuition from one of them. Adam Newton also had enough Italian to teach him: he was, of course, the Latin translator of Paolo Sarpi's *Historia del Consilio Tridento* (1619). While I have not found an instance of Henry writing the language, Benvenuto was sufficiently confident in his reading ability to dedicate a book of introductory dialogues in Italian and English, *The Passenger*, to him in 1612.[82]

The other language Henry definitely studied was French. Like James, Henry was surrounded by French speakers from a young age. His first known letter, dated 1 September 1600, was in French, suggesting that he began it at the same time as Latin, if not earlier.[83] As he grew older, Henry continued to write to the French court, his mother and his sister in French. Indeed it was necessary to address Princess Elizabeth in that language since, unlike Elizabeth and Mary Tudor, she had not been taught Latin.[84]

Henry studied French in the same way he learnt Latin: via morally improving texts. According to a New Year's Day letter to his mother Anne in 1604, his early reading centred on Guy du Faur's *Quadrains*, a series of adages written in verse in imitation of Cato's *Distiches*, which, as we have seen, were translated into English for the Prince by Sylvester.[85] In part the Prince studied them to improve his French and Latin grammar (he attempted a Latin translation of the *Quadrains* in 1605) but he persistently referred to their ethical value.[86] In a letter to his mother, Henry insisted that the verses 'deserved to be imprinted in the minds of men'.[87] To his father, he even claimed that a 'good part' of the *Quadrains* were 'most powerfully written for the education of princes themselves'.[88] Here, Henry declared, was literature which reinforced his princely authority. Certainly, they proved to be useful in advancing the fortunes of the Prince's preceptor. Henry quoted one of du Faur's quadrains (on the rewards due to schoolmasters) in his successful petition to James for Newton's appointment to the Deanery of Durham.[89] To the modern reader, the *Quadrains* are less persuasive. The classically derived commonplaces were either straw men for Christian homilies or reminders of filial duty. James's early study of French had taken in translations of Ovid and the works of Calvin.[90] The *Quadrains* suggest that less was expected of Henry.

Throughout much of the period that Henry was studying French and Latin he was also learning to write in these languages using an italic hand. His first writing master was Peter Bales, who had the most famous hand in late sixteenth-century England. Bales had fallen into disgrace after participating in the 1601 Essex rebellion, but by 1604 he was back in favour and claiming a pension from Salisbury for presenting the king with 'his *Basilicon Doron* for the Prince, in a small volume to be worn as a tablet book'. It may well have been this presentation which led to his position in Henry's schoolroom, where he served until 1606.[91] Once again, the *Basilicon Doron* had proved the vehicle for linking father and son in pedagogy and patronage.

The fruits of Bales's tuition from 1604–06 are to be plucked from the sixteen-folio bound manuscript, 'Prince Henry's Copybook'. Henry began by copying the letters of the alphabet and progressed to copying out Latin phrases in an italic hand from the top of the page to its foot. Eventually, Bales set Henry Latin *sententiae* from approved authors such as Terence, Cicero, Valerius Maximus, Virgil, Horace and Pliny.[92] Bales was particularly drawn to texts which stressed the import of education for virtuous leadership. Only through learning, Cassiodorus emphasized, could 'the Prince understand how the people may be ordered'.[93] More particularly, Henry's exercises rehearsed the value of good hand-writing as a branch of learning. Henry copied out an adapted passage from Cicero's *De Oratore* in which the role of 'the orator' was replaced by 'the scribe'. To the argument that no one is a really good 'scribe unless [he has] a knowledge of all important letters and learning' Bales had Henry add: 'indeed, in my opinion, Prince Henry has such a childish hand that he is hardly worthy of even mediocre praise as a writer'.[94] One suspects Bales of having a healthy sense of humour.

Henry developed a reputation for militant Calvinism, but there is little evidence of him studying Scripture. He must have done so, and Joseph Hall and John Harington of Kelston were among those who presented religious treatises to him.[95] The only such tract bound amongst his schoolbooks, however, was a work by Benjamin Carier, who was one of Henry's chaplains before converting to Catholicism. Carier's *Ad Christianam sapientiam breuis introductio* (which probably dates from around 1606) made the conventional argument that real wisdom lay not in the human arts or sciences, nor the good administration of government, but in 'being a servant to the faith of Christ' and showing Christian charity. Henry was reportedly a keen auditor of sermons but reading Scripture and theology does not seem to have taken the same pre-eminence in his daily study as it did in his father's.[96]

Thus far, it is possible to conclude that Henry's education from 1600–06/07 was rooted firmly in the Erasmian traditions of the English lower-grammar school, with the customary additions for nobles of French and italic handwriting. In the *Basilicon Doron* James may not have made the liberal arts and sciences pre-eminent, as they had been in the *Institutio principis Christiani*, but Erasmus's methods for studying grammar provided the foundation of Henry's schooling. There were hints of James's insistence that future rulers should study the liberal arts to ameliorate their princely authority: Henry's schoolroom epistles were actually directed to European rulers and nobles; and he justified his reading of Guy du Faur's *Quadrains* in terms of its application to princes. Overall, however, expec-tations as to the extent and depth of his study were lower than those placed on Edward VI or James VI and I himself.

It was a less demanding curriculum but Henry showed little enthusiasm for it. Like James and the Tudor princes before him, Henry was expected to make annual shows of his learning for his father and the court but his performances were almost invariably marked by failure. In 1604 Henry sent James a Latin poem which contrasted the riches that Zeus expected on feast days to the meagre literary offering he was making to his father.[97] James replied with the literary equivalent of a bolt of lightning. While he was pleased to see that Henry's handwriting had improved, he suspected that his son had simply copied the poem rather than composed it himself. James longed 'to ressave a letter from ye, that maye be … as well formid by youre mynde, as drawin by youre fingers; for ye maye remember, that, in my booke to ye, I warne ye to be waire with that kynde of *witte*, that maye flye out the ende of youre fingers'.[98] While there was no specific discussion of 'wit' in the *Basilicon Doron*, James had insisted that princes should avoid publishing in Latin or Greek and opt for prose rather than verse (p. 55).

Henry's 'litle counterfitte' had also offended James's fundamental belief that a prince should 'goe before all his subiects' in his writing (p. 55). By copying a poem, Henry had demonstrated a lack of faith in his own princely powers of invention and, by analogy, his authority. 'Trust a little more to youre owin strenth', James implored his son, '*audaces fortuna iuuat timidosque repellit* [fortune favours the brave and rejects the timid] … what ever you are about, *hoc ages* [carry it off]'.[99] Henry's show of learning had failed because James, the only spectator in a position to do so, had pointed out that the emperor had no clothes on.

In 1605/06 Henry tried again, attempting to convert Sylvester's English version of du Faur's *Quadrains* into Latin. On this occasion, the Prince did not complete his gift and the translations were never sent.[100] No Tudor prince would have dared be suspected of such idleness. While father and son continued to demonstrate their united commitment to princely education in public there were uncharacteristically critical murmurs from the Venetian ambassador, Nicolò Molin. He alleged that Henry studied 'chiefly under his father's spur, not of his own desire' and that James had threatened 'that if he did not attend more earnestly to his lessons the crown would be left to his brother, the Duke of York, who … studied more earnestly'. Molin's assessment of Charles is confirmed by the extant evidence of his schooling. Yet Henry thought that this rendered Charles suitable for a mitre, not a crown: 'I know what becomes a Prince. It is not necessary for me to be a professor, but a soldier and a man of the world. If my brother is as learned as they say, we'll make him Archbishop of Canterbury.'[101] Certainly, Henry's authoritative performances on horseback, in masques and at the chase confirm his commitment to the chivalric ideal.[102] As the praise (or panegyrics) of men like Northampton and Daniel Price indicates, however, what was generally required of a prince in the seventeenth century was the capacity to balance Mars and Minerva. A contemporary student prince was praised for possessing 'The Courtiers, Soldiers, Scholars: Eye, tongue, sword'. James had called it going 'before all' in all things. Henry's scales were weighted too heavily on one side.

The King vaunted Henry's learning in public and tried to maintain the united front he had established with the *Basilicon Doron*. In private, however, James was distressed that Henry failed to meet the less strenuous academic standards he had advocated for princes. As Sir Francis Bacon remarked, Henry was a 'favourer of letters, though rather in the honour he paid it than the time he spent upon it'.[103]

Henry's princely learning, 1607–1610

As Henry grew older, his curriculum diverged from that of the grammar school and began to reflect James's preference for disciplines which would teach the 'craft' of monarchy, particularly history and politics. This may well have been the time, too, when he took the occasional lesson from the mathematicians and geographers at his court or used the instruments they made him.[104] Henry seems to have been more committed to this second stage of his schooling.

In his 1609 oration on the value of education for monarchs, neglected in previous studies of the Prince, Henry specified which subjects were particularly useful for rulers.[105] The exercise of the oration represented the culmination of the grammar school syllabus, and it seems likely that Henry's performance was intended as a rite of passage marking the end of his formal education. Henry's 'Oratio' was as substantial as Edward's weekly declamations had been and its structure met the full requirements of the neo-Ciceronian oration: exordium; narration; arguments in favour; refutation of arguments against and conclusion. It was authorized using classical and historical *exempla*, argued using quotations from approved authors and amplified with rhetorical techniques.[106] After almost a decade of inadequate academic performances, Henry's 'Oratio' was probably meant as a final bid for James's approval and a *tour de force* for the rest of the court. It is strange then, that no record of Henry's performance was made by an admiring auditor. Perhaps, his nerve failed him, and the oration was never given – was it another botched performance?

In its textual form, however, the 'Oratio' was an act of princely self-fashioning. Henry's exordium described the oration as a response to a discussion which James, his intended audience, had initiated 'concerning the preeminence of letters'. James was the schoolmaster who had 'supplied [Henry with] the central planks of reasoning, on which [he] constructed the building' of his oration. Indeed, Henry acknowledged that the importance of education for princes had been 'explained for [his] information by Your Most Serene Majest in theose golden books'[107] of the *Basilicon Doron*. In his 'Oratio' then, Henry defended the value of princely education to a monarch, James, who had regularly presented himself as a responsible king on the basis of the careful cultivation of his heir. It was a moment of supreme self-consciousness for the theory of princely education in Britain and a direct statement from Henry that father and son were united in this pedagogical enterprise.

Like James's argument in the *Basilicon Doron*, Henry's case developed from the position that monarchy was the best form of government and that the king should not be 'bound fast by the chains of laws and decrees'.[108] Henry was clearly aware of contemporary arguments in favour of subjecting monarchs to the law. In August 1607, Robert Cecil, Earl of Salisbury, sent him a copy of *Conference about the Next Succession to the Crowne* (1595), then attributed to the exiled Jesuit Robert Parsons, to teach Henry to appreciate James's refutation of it in *The Trew Law of Free Monarchies* (1598).[109] The 'Oratio' confirms that Henry followed his father's case. For a divinely appointed monarch, education was not about moderating government. Instead Henry argued that it enabled a prince to rule more effectively, restore his energies and be remembered in posterity.[110] Yet Henry seemed to propose a more conventional list of liberal arts than James had recommended for rulers: philosophy, eloquence, politics and history. With respect to philosophy, Henry argued that its study gave one self-mastery over the passions, which was 'required more in a prince since he exercises it for the greater good of the public'.[111] James had certainly not denied the importance of self-discipline in the *Basilicon Doron* (p. 12), but Henry's emphasis on a universal standard (that rulers had an additional responsibility to personify) was more decisively Stoic.

In contrast, Henry recommended eloquence to princes on entirely vocational grounds. It helped rulers to direct judges, the council and Parliament and to 'restrain all sedition, factions and those passionate impulses … for internal dispute' in peacetime. It is unlikely, then, that parliamentary speech would have been much freer under Henry IX. In war, the Prince continued, eloquence enabled a ruler to 'impress courage and military strength on the nation'.[112] James had been cautious about the value of rhetoric in the *Basilicon Doron*. He had insisted, however, that the Prince adapt his oratory to circumstance, speaking 'grauely and with a maiestie when yee sit in iudgement, or give audience to Embassadours … and let your countenance smell of courage and magnanimitie when ye are at the warres' (p. 54). Henry followed his father in adapting Quintilian's broad prescription for rhetorical decorum for princes by emphasizing situations peculiar to their office.

With respect to the other two disciplines Henry recommended in his 'Oratio', their study and corresponding profit were more peculiarly princely. 'Does the prince wish to preserve the laws, to assign rights [*iura*] and to rule the people with supreme power [*imperium*]?' he asked. 'Politics [*politica*] will give this'.[113] James had not spoken directly of *politica* in the *Basilicon Doron*, but he had insisted that princes must learn the 'craft' of kingship (p. 44). To the extent that *politica* refers to the management of *imperium*, Henry could be referring to this 'craft'. While his father had suggested that such study began with Scripture and law, however, Henry proposed that it began with an examination of the practical operation of power or civil policy.

From at least 1607, Salisbury had been sending Newton and Henry regular updates from James's court. Salisbury invited the Prince to Whitehall to hear a dispute between the Merchant Taylors' Guild and the Mint, since it would contain 'so many things of Civill Pollicy' which were worthy of 'that Excellent Mynd, moulded (in his owne dew tyme) for the Government of Kyndoms'.[114] Salisbury insisted that understanding operational politics was a necessary supplement to, rather than a practical application of, a liberal education. The Earl argued that reading dispatches from Ireland would 'everyday prove more proper for the Prince of Britain than Aristotle or Cicero'.[115] Salisbury, like James, was looking for a prince cognisant of the arts of management and control, rather than simply *honestum*. The Earl had moved a step beyond James in proposing that the best way to acquire such knowledge was by studying the procedures of government itself, and Henry followed in his wake.

This picture is confirmed by Henry's discussion of the final discipline promoted in the *Basilicon Doron*: history. While 'any member of the public will take great delight in the solitary reading of history' a prince sees 'his affairs born by another person, he reads about the beginnings of wars between the most powerful rulers and bellicose nations, he observes arts and strategies of excellent leadership'.[116] As we have seen, James had recommended that princes read Caesar for these reasons and Henry had been introduced to this vein of history some years earlier. In May 1605 he had begun to study an author who often sat alongside Caesar in school statutes: Justin, or more specifically the first book of his *Historiarum Philippicarum T. Pompeii Trogi*. Henry composed an epitome of Justin's account of Cyrus's rise to power in a copybook which had been presented to him by an R.W.[117]

The result was one of the most promising exercises to be preserved among Henry's schoolbooks. Henry had evidently read over each section in the first book of Justin's *Historia* then summarized it briefly. He focussed on the exciting (not to say illicit) moments (such as the account of the Persian women who shamed their sons and husbands back on to the battlefield by exposing themselves), which suggests that he may have been working from memory.[118] Nevertheless the Prince made a conscientious effort to reuse some of Justin's choice phrases in his prose. Henry was also careful to preserve the literary shape of the *Historia*. The bellicose Queen Semiramis who 'feigned her sex by great deeds', was followed by her son, a peace-lover, who 'grew old in the company of women' and Sardanapalus 'another example of a womanly soul in a man'. Not only was Henry learning rhetorical skills (in this case antithesis) through imitation, but he was encouraged to structure his narratives so that they functioned as *exempla*. In the above case, the moral to be extracted was that 'often one may see women take upon themselves manly spirits, while womanly men bear effeminate souls'.[119] It was a useful adage in a country still mourning Elizabeth I. Indeed Henry's main addition to Justin's text was to present episodes in the *Historia* as fodder for humanist commonplaces. The Prince's study of history provided him with material to reuse in his orations but Henry had also grasped how an *exemplum* could reveal his political 'affairs born by another person'. In the same year that the Prince was saved from the Gunpowder Plot, he described the rescue of the infant Cyrus from exposure as 'our sign and example, of how wonderful the power of the fates is, and how great the goodness of God, in preserving those he has destined for greatness in public affairs'.[120]

In *historia* as in *politica*, however, Henry took his father's concern for learning the 'craft' of princely authority a step further. Around the time Henry was composing his oration, the type of history he was interested in shifted from the practical example of Justin to a less uniformly approved author. John Harington of Exton wrote to Henry during his European tour to ask for the Prince's assistance in making out a fairly obscure passage on corn prices in Tacitus's

Agricola. In his reply, Henry confessed his ignorance, 'I have not dared to examine Tacitus whose practical wisdom [*prudentia*] I have heard described by all but whose style, crowded by concise and pointed sentences, is too obscure for my ability'.[121] Since receiving Harington's letter, however, Henry had been spurred on. He sent his friend a translation of two sentences concerning Agricola's precocious moral rectitude and the ease and justness with which he carried out his early civic responsibilities.[122] They are much simpler to make out than Harington's passage, confirming that Henry was still no great Latinist. Like Henry's character-isation of Cyrus, however, these lines suggest the Prince's readiness to identify with examples and adages drawn from histories.

Henry's excerpts from the *Agricola* reinforced the conventional humanist emphasis on moral rectitude and responsible government.[123] Nevertheless, Tacitus's reception in late Elizabethan and Jacobean England was often associated with subversive, anti-absolutist im-pulses. Contrary to Henry's pronouncement, Tacitus's 'practical wisdom' was not 'described by all' as 'admirable'.[124] In the 1599 edition of the *Basilicon Doron*, James scorned Justus Lipsius, one of the greatest contemporary Tacitean scholars and author of *De constantia* (1584), as 'in-constant' in his religion.[125] In the 1603 version James broadened his criticism to condemn the British champions of Tacitus for 'their inconstant behauiour in their owne liues' (p. 48). By 1610, James had seen enough of Tacitus's influence on British politics to agree with Isaac Casaubon that the historian provided little more than a list of immoral deeds.[126]

Yet members of Henry's circle, including Sir Charles Cornwallis, Ben Jonson, Sir Thomas Chaloner, Robert Dallington and John Hayward, embraced aspects of the negative British vein of neo-Stoicism.[127] In writing treatises for the Prince, some of these authors drew on Tacitus's descriptions of Tiberius's corrupt court in the *Annals* in order to present Whitehall as simi-larly sunk in deceit and flattery. Charles Cornwallis's *Discourse* described him as surrounded by 'moaths & mice of court in that time … maligners of true vertue, & only friends to their own ambitions and desires'.[128] Henry also received an anonymous tract, entitled 'An Instruction to Princes', warning him to avoid favourites (as his father had failed to do) since they caused 'the prince to be deemed a weak and unwise man' and 'disordereth the whole government'.[129] Sir Arthur Gorges urged Henry to reduce the number of parasitical gallants of James's court 'on whome the kinge, your father hath bestowed great and bountifull guifts'.[130] With varying de-grees of directness, three of his clients were depicting James's court as dominated by pretty, amoral youths who were ruining the state and making a mockery of the King. Henry received these tracts and kept them alongside his own copybooks. His letter to Harington suggests that he had come to think of himself as an Agricola in his father's empire.

What did Cornwallis and others propose that the Prince of Wales should do in such a cor-rupt court? He could hardly withdraw to the country. As Markku Peltonen has argued, British authors often met the Tacitean account of court corruption with a Ciceronian call to virtuous action.[131] This hardly made their appeals less politically contentious for Henry. Gorges, for instance, argued that since princes 'have more meanes, and opportunities to expresse theire wothines, and virtue', it behoved Henry to intervene in James's government and correct the 'decaye' of the state.[132] Both Gorges and the author of 'An Instruction to Princes' used Tacitus as part of their petition to Henry to expand his princely authority and interfere with his father's rule. For a number of clients, educating Henry was now about encouraging the Prince to reject the 'patterne' James had set out for him. Strong was correct to claim that a chasm opened between Henry and James but it was not until the last two years of the Prince's life that potential clients encouraged the Prince to set himself against his father's model of kingship.

Even more dangerously, Henry began to approve of treatises which encouraged him to meet dissimulation at court with dissimulation. In Sir Charles Cornwallis's 'Short Remembrances to Prince Henry', Cornwallis insisted that in protecting their estates, 'princes may touch upon the Verge of Vice'. Henry thanked him for his 'obseruations' and asked to be further acquainted 'in that kind as occasions shall be offred'.[133] He showed similar appreciation of Robert Dallington's 'Aphorismes Civill and Militarie'. Indeed, Dallington attributed the 1609 manuscript of his work to the prince's sponsorship.[134] As J.H. Salmon pointed out, Dallington used the 'Aphorismes' to set aside the foundational argument of the second book of Cicero's *De officiis* (that nothing was profitable that was not honest) as 'too straight-laced'. Rather, he proposed 'a middle way between both [*honestum* and *utile*] which a right statesman must take'. Dallington drew on an infamous passage in Tacitus's Annales, which permitted injustice for the good of the state. 'Upon the theatre of public employment', Dallington argued, 'actors must of necessity wear vizards, and change them in every scene'. The 'good and safety of a state' was to be the end of all their actions, 'to which men cannot always arrive by plain paths and beaten ways'.[135] Phrases lifted from Tacitus's histories could be used to authorize a model of government which made dissimulation and injustice central skills for a prudent monarch.

Cornwallis's and Dallington's arguments contradict the importance that both Henry's 'Oratio' and James's *Basilicon Doron* placed on moral probity for rulers. What had drawn the Prince to condone their use of Tacitus? Like many educated Jacobeans, Henry sought his own reflection in the mirror of the past: his reading of Justin, the *Agricola* and his praise of history in the 'Oratio' are testimony to this. In the year leading up to his creation as Prince of Wales, Henry was envisaging the extension of his own powers – evident in his commission to Richard Connock to compose a tract urging the speedy grant of his title – and treatises like Gorges's encouraged and justified his desires.[136] James claimed to despise Tacitus but in one sense his argument that a prince's first care should be his 'craft' may have prepared Henry to accept the need for an occasional digression from the path of *honestum*. If the art of ruling, rather than the personification of virtue, was the real end of princely education, then, as Cornwallis had claimed, one might even walk on the 'Verge of Vice' to protect one's estate. Dallington's image of princes acting a variety of parts in a public theatre could similarly be regarded as developing James's metaphor of the monarch as an actor playing before a hostile audience. James had argued in the *Basilicon Doron* that outward shows were critical in maintaining obedience. During the first fifteen years of his life, Henry had obliged his father by performing the role of the student prince, despite the fact that he generally found the mechanics of learning tedious. In Dallington's Tacitean justification of dissimulation, Henry may have located an explanation for the necessity of presenting himself in this guise.

Conclusion

In the final two years of his life, Henry became an oppositional figure in the Stuart court, but events during and after 1610 should not obscure the long standing public partnership which had existed between the student prince and philosopher-king. James was the engineer of Henry's curriculum and of his collegiate court. He cultivated the public perception of his son as a student prince in his widely circulated *Basilicon Doron* and then supported a range of initiatives which printed its pattern on his subjects' consciousness. Henry played his part for the public with great aplomb. There were the occasional murmurings of dissent but generally the public fashioning of Henry as a student prince must be regarded as a success.

The public paeans heaped upon Henry did not necessarily equate with academic brilliance or even much enthusiasm for learning. He followed a well-trodden path through the early stages of grammar and rhetoric leaving a trail of incomplete and unsatisfactory school exercises behind him. It was only when Henry came to the study of history, or more specifically the *exempla* and aphorisms which could be extracted from it, that his mind was engaged. Henry's interest in treatises which justified the extension of monarchical authority and princely dissimulation or vice are not necessarily in keeping with his posthumous image as Britain's Germanicus. Nevertheless, they reflect a growing perception in seventeenth-century northern humanism that the key to government was not the prince but the state itself. Had Henry lived, his reign might have spawned a renaissance of British political history and philosophy, but indications are that it would have been in the tradition of Francesco Guicciardini.

NOTES

1 William, Viscount Cranborne, letter to Henry, 9 September 1609, Bordeaux, in Thomas Birch, *Life of Henry Prince of Wales, Eldest Son of King James* (London, 1760), p. 175.

2 Daniel Price, *The Creation of the Prince* (London: Printed by G. Eld for Roger Jackson, 1610), sig. D2r.

3 Thomas Elyot, *The Boke Named the Gouernour* (1531), ed. Henry Herbert Stephen Croft, 2 vols. (London, 1880), I, pp. 36–37.

4 Cecil H. Clough, 'A Presentation Volume for Henry VIII: The Charlecote Park Copy of Erasmus' *Education of a Christian Prince*', *Journal of the Warburg and Courtauld Institutes*, 44 (1981), pp. 199–202.

5 Thomas Baldwin, *William Shakespere's Small Latine and Lesse Greeke*, 2 vols. (Urbana, 1944), I, pp. 185–284, 532–56. This paragraph and much of the chapter which follows draw on the research in my 'Princely Education in Sixteenth-Century Britain', unpublished PhD dissertation (University of Cambridge, 2005).

6 Roy Strong, *Henry Prince of Wales and England's Lost Renaissance* (London, 1986), p. 13.

7 Isaac Wake, letter to Lady Carleton, 19 December 1612, National Archives, Kew, State Papers 14/71, fol. 130r.

8 Many are discussed in: Birch, *Life of Henry*, p. 367; Elkin Calhoun Wilson, *Prince Henry and English Literature* (Ithaca, 1946), pp. 128–76; Graham Parry, *The Golden Age Restor'd: The Culture of the Stuart Court, 1603–42* (Manchester, 1981), pp. 87–91, and Michael Ullyot, 'The Fall of Troynovant: Exemplarity after the Death of Henry, Prince of Wales', in *Fantasies of Troy: Classical Tales and the Social Imaginary in Medieval and Early Modern Europe*, ed. Alan Shepard and Stephen Powell, CRRS Texts and Studies, vol. 4 (Toronto, 2004), pp. 269–90.

9 Strong, *Henry, Prince of Wales*, pp. 9, 13–15, 141–42, 171–72. A similar set of polarities are propounded by Christopher Hill, *Intellectual Origins of the English Revolution Revisited* (Oxford, 1997), pp. 190–95. J.W. Williamson, *The Myth of the Conqueror, Prince Henry Stuart: a Study of Seventeenth-Century Personation* (New York, 1978) had previously emphasized the militaristic, imperial and chivalric aspect of Henry's reputation. Strong's characterization of Henry has influenced: Jonathan Goldberg, *James I and the Politics of Literature: Jonson, Shakespeare, Donne, and their Contemporaries* (Stanford, 1989), pp. 122–24, 135–36; Martin Butler, 'Courtly Negotiations', in *The Politics of the Stuart Court Masque*, ed. David Bevington and Peter Holbrook (Cambridge, 1998), pp. 20–40; Parry, *The Golden Age Restor'd*, pp. 61–94, and 'The Politics of the Jacobean Masque', in *Theatre and Government Under the Early Stuarts*, ed. by J.R. Mulryne and Margaret Shewring (Cambridge, 1993), pp. 87–117; and R. Malcolm Smuts, *Court Culture and the Origins of a Royalist Tradition in Early Stuart England* (Philadelphia, 1987), pp. 24, 29–31, and 'Court Culture and Court Politics', in *Mental World of the Jacobean Court*, ed. Linda Levy Peck (Cambridge, 1991), pp. 99–112. John Peacock also used these dichotomies in his interpretation of Robert Peake's 1610 portrait of Henry: 'Politics of Portraiture', in *Culture and Politics in Early Stuart England*, ed. Kevin Sharpe and Peter Lake (Basingstoke, 1994), pp. 199–228, (p. 215). Brian Nance draws on the divisions to explain the controversy surrounding Henry's cause of death in *Turquet de Mayerne as Baroque Physician: the Art of Medical Portraiture* (Amsterdam, 2001), pp. 172–73.

10 Sir John Holles, letter to Sir John Digby, 28 November 1612, St James, in R.F. Isaacson (ed.), *Historical Manuscripts Commission Report on the Manuscripts of His Grace the Duke of Portland, Preserved at Welbeck Abbey*, 10 vols. (London, 1923) IX, p. 37. Hereafter *HMC Portland*.

11 Chris R. Kyle, 'Cornwallis, Sir Charles (*c.* 1555–1629)', *Oxford Dictionary of National Biography* (Oxford: 2004) [http://www.oxforddnb.com/view/article/6337, accessed 31 March 2006]; hereafter ODNB. Kyle fails to attribute either *A Discourse of the Most Illustrious Prince, Henry, late Prince of Wales: Written anno 1626* (London: John Benson, 1641) or BL, Egerton MS 3876 to Cornwallis. Instead, he attributes *The Life and Death of Our Late Most Incomparable and Heroique Prince, Henry Prince of Wales* (London: John Dawson for Nathaniel Butter, 1641) to Cornwallis, despite BL, Additional MS 30075, which indicates its author was a John Hawkins. Strong, *Henry Prince of Wales*, p. 227, identified Hawkins as one of the Tower Gunners and in possession of the reversion to the office of Whiffler. Nevertheless, Kyle's account of Cornwallis's imprisonment under James and subsequent retirement from court may be relied upon.

12 Nicolò Molin, 'Report on England presented to the Government of Venice in 1607', calendared in *Calendar of*

State Papers and Manuscripts Relating to English Affairs Existing in the Archives and Collections of Venice, 37 vols. (London, 1864–1939) X, no. 739, pp. 513–14; hereafter *CSP Venetian*. See also Correr, 'Despatches to the Doge and Senate', 16 June and 23 June 1610, calendared in *CSP Venetian*, XI, no. 945, pp. 507–09 and no. 954, 515–16.

13 For Henry's letter to the Doge, see 'Report of an audience of the English Ambassador', 7 May 1607, calendared in *CPS Venetian*, X, no. 728, p. 495. Paolo Sarpi, letter to Leschassier, 22 December 1609, cited by David Wootton, *Paolo Sarpi: Between Renaissance and Enlightenment* (Cambridge, 1983), p. 92.

14 *The Autobiography and Correspondence of Sir Simond D'Ewes During the Reigns of James I and Charles I*, ed. by James Orchard Halliwell, 2 vols. (London, 1845), I, pp. 48, 49. On posthumous uses of Henry's image against his father and brother see J.S.A. Adamson, 'Chivalry and political culture in Caroline England' (pp. 161–98), in Sharpe and Lake (eds), *Culture and Politics*, pp. 167, 191–93.

15 Anthony Weldon, *The Court and Character of King James* (London: R.I., 1650), sig. A2r-v and Francis Osborne, *Historical Memoires on the Reigns of Queen Elizabeth and King James* (London: J. Grismond, 1658), sigs M1r –M6r. These texts are cited and discussed by Jason Scott-Warren, *Sir John Harington and the Book as a Gift* (Oxford, 2001), p. 204. See also Birch, *Life of Henry*, p. 1. For other accounts of Henry's death as a shipwreck for Britain's fortunes, see: Joseph Morgan's 'Preface' to his edition of Charles Cornwallis's *Discourse*, entitled *The Life and Character of Henry Frederic, Prince of Wales*, ed. Joseph Morgan (London, 1738), sig. A3r; George M. Trevelyan, *England Under the Stuarts*, ed. Charles Oman, 4th edn, *A History of England* (London, 1910), V, p. 112; Hill, *Intellectual Origins*, pp. 13, 195.

16 Timothy Wilks, 'The Court Culture of Prince Henry and his Circle 1603–1613', unpublished DPhil. Dissertation (University of Oxford, 1987), pp. 22, 37, 52, 60–62, 67–69; Kevin Sharpe, *Politics and Ideas in Early Stuart England: Essays and Studies* (London, 1989), pp. 290–91; Grant Tapsell, 'The Prince and the Papists: Henry Frederick, Prince of Wales and his relations with Catholics', unpublished undergraduate dissertation (University of Cambridge, 1998), pp. 8–19. For Inigo Jones's patrons, see John Summerson, *Inigo Jones* (New Haven, 2000), pp. 9–13, 21–22, 33–61, 67–132. For Henry's exploits in the tilt-yard, see Antonio Foscarini, 'Despatch to the Doge and Senate', 6 January 1612, calendared in *CSP Venetian*, XII, no. 409, 270 and Correr, 'Despatch to the Doge and Senate', 26 December 1608, calendared in *CSP Venetian*, XI, no. 393, 206.

17 Henry Howard, Earl of Northampton, letter to Henry, *c.* September 1605, though no date or place cited, BL, Harleian MS 7007, fol. 69r. Hawkins, *The Life and Death*, p. 10. Wright's and Gilbert's book dedications to Henry refer to his patronage: Edward Wright, *Certaine Errors in Navigation* (London: Felix Kingston, 1610), sig.*10v and William Gilbert's treatise BL, Royal MS 12 F. XI, later published (although not from this MS) as William Gilbert, *De mundo nostro sublunari philosophia nova*, ed. William Gilbert [half-brother of the author] and Isaac Gruter (Amsterdam, 1651), sig. *2r. For James's sharp speeches, see W.H., *The True Picture and Relation of Prince Henry* (Leiden: William Christian, 1634), p.3, see also pp. 5, 8, 10, 11, 26–27. The *True Picture and Relation* seems to be drawn from BL, Harleian MS 6391. With respect to W.H.'s identity, Birch, *Life of Henry*, p.451 records that a 'William Haydon' was a senior groom of thePrince's bedchamber. Strong, *Henry, Prince of Wales*, p. 227 identifies 'William Haydon' as a possible author for the *True Picture*.

18 James VI and I, *Basilicon Doron* in *James VI and I: Political Writings*, ed. Johann P. Somerville (Cambridge, 1994) pp. 1–61 (p. 2). Henceforth, reference to this edition will be made in brackets in the text.

19 There has been some controversy as to James's motivation for his political writing. Jenny Wormald, 'James VI and I, *Basilicon Doron* and *The Trew Law of Free Monarchies*: the Scottish Context and the English Translation', in *The Mental World of the Jacobean Court*, ed. Peck, pp. 36–54 (p. 49) described it as a philosophical exercise. Alternatively, see: Johann P. Sommerville, 'Introduction' in *James VI and I: Political Writings*, pp. xviii–xix; J.H. Burns, *True Law of Kingship: Concepts of Monarchy in Early-Modern Scotland* (Oxford, 1996), pp. 249–64; and Peter Lake, 'The King (the Queen) and the Jesuit: James Stuart's *True Law of Free Monarchies* in context/s', *Transactions of the Royal Historical Society*, 14 (2004) pp. 243–60. In support of my claim regarding James's pedagogical intentions in 1599, see his letter to Henry dated 7 April 1603, BL, Harleian MS 6986, fol. 39r and an undated letter to Henry, printed in Birch, *Life of Henry*, pp. 36–37. That Henry began his schooling shortly after

receiving his father's treatise is confirmed by his first extant letter, addressed to the States General, 1 September 1600, Stirling, in BL, Harleian MS 6986, fol. 61r.

20 George Buchanan, *Baptistes, sive calumnia, tradgoedia* (London: Thomas Vautrollier, 1577), sigs Aiir–Aiiir; Buchanan, *De iure regni apud Scotos* (Edinburgh: John Ross, 1579), sig. A2r–v; and *Rerum Scoticarum historia* (Edinburgh: Alexander Arbuthnet, 1582), sig. A1r.

21 Scott-Warren, *Sir John Harington*, pp. 7–8, quotation from p. 10.

22 Hugh Latimer argued for Edward's precocious wisdom in *The Seconde Sermon of Maister Hughe Latimer* (London: John Daye, 1549), sigs. C3v–C4r. Elizabeth swung between emphasizing and denying her learning. See for instance: Elizabeth's 'Latin Speech to the University, at the Conclusion of Her Entertainment in Saint Mary's Church', in *Desiderata Curiosa; or, a Collection of Divers Scarce and Curious Pieces Relating Chiefly to Matters of English History*, ed. Francis Peck, 2 vols (London, 1779), II,VII, pp. 271–72; 'Her Majesty's Speech in the Parliament House at the Prorogation of the Last Session, 29 March, 1585', BL, Additional MS 15891, fol. 148r and 'Speech to the Heads of Oxford University, 28 September 1592', in Bodleian Library, Oxford, MS Bodley 900, published in *Elizabeth I: Collected Works*, ed. by Leah S. Marcus, Janel Mueller and Mary Beth Rose (Chicago and London, 2000), pp. 182 and 327–28 respectively; and her 'Latin reply to the Polish Ambassador', Hatfield House, Salisbury MS 7, fol. 53r published with an English translation as an appendix to Janet M. Green, 'Queen Elizabeth I's Latin reply to the Polish ambassador', *Sixteenth Century Journal*, 31, no. 4 (2000), pp. 987–1008 (pp. 1005–08). James first put his name to *The Essayes of a Prentise in the Divine Art of Poesie* (Edinburgh: Thomas Vautrollier, 1584), sig. A1r.

23 George Buchanan, 'Genethliacon Jacobi sexti regis Scotorum', in *George Buchanan: the Political Poetry*, ed. and trans. Paul J. McGinnis and Arthur H. Williamson (Edinburgh, 1995) pp. 154–63, and *De iure regni*, sigs G2v–G3r.

24 See Humphrey Gilbert, 'Queene Elizabethes Achademy' (1572), in *Queene Elizabethes Achademy; a Boke of Precedence; the Ordering of a Funerall; Varying Versions of the Good Wife; the Wise Man; Maximus; Lydgate's Order of Fools; a Poem on Heraldry; Occleve on Lord's Men*, ed. Frederick James Furnivall (London, 1869), pp. 1–12 (pp. 3–4). Francis Bacon, *The Advancement of Learning*, ed. Michael Kiernan, *The Oxford Francis Bacon IV* (Oxford, 2000), pp. 22–23, 6; George More, *Principles for Yong Princes* (London: Nicholas Oakes, 1611) pp. 4, 26–28.

25 Markku Peltonen, *Classical Humanism and Republicanism in English Political Thought 1570–1640* (Cambridge, 1995), pp. 139–45.

26 Bacon, *Advancement of Learning*, p. 143.

27 Wormald, 'James VI and I, *Basilicon Doron* and *The Trew Law of Free Monarchies*', p. 51

28 *Tetrastika; or, the Quadrains of Guy de Faur, Lord of Pibrac*, trans. Joshua Sylvester (London: Humphrey Lownes, 1605), sig. Yy2r.

29 *Bartas his Devine Weekes & Workes*, trans. Joshua Sylvester (London: Humphrey Lownes, 1605), sigs A2r–B1r; *II Posthumus Bartas: The Fore-noone of the Fourth Day of his Second Week*, trans. Joshua Sylvester (London: Humphrey Lownes, 1607), sig. A3v. Sylvester inscribed the back of the title-page of his presentation copy to Henry with an anagram on the prince's name, '*Hic strenuus ratus*': Wren Library, Trinity College, Cambridge, Grylls 32.73.

30 NA, Kew, E 101/433/9 and E 351/2793. See also *Bartas his Devine Weekes & Workes*, sig. Kkk2v, and James's gift of £300 to Sylvester, 17 February 1609, reported in *Calendar of State Papers, Domestic Series, of the Reigns of Edward VI, Mary, Elizabeth and James I*, ed. Robert Lemon with addenda by Mary A.E. Green, 12 vols. (London, 1856–72), Addenda 1580–1625, no. 77, p. 515; hereafter *CSP Domestic*.

31 Clement Edmondes, *Observations upon Caesars Commentaries Setting Forth the Practise of the Art Militarie in the Time of the Romaine Empire for the Better Direction of our Moderne Wars* (London: William Ponsonby, 1604), sig. *f*3r–v and then his second edition (London: Matthew Lownes, 1609), sig. Aiiv. Joshua Sylvester's commendatory sonnet describing Edmondes as one of Henry's clients is at sig. Aiiir.

32 Ben Jonson, dedication, *Masque of Queenes, Celebration from the House of Fame*, 21 February 1609, BL, Royal MS 18A XLV, fol. 2r–v.

33 *Homer Prince of Poets. Translated According to the Greeke, in Twelve Bookes of His Iliad*, trans. George Chapman (London: Humphrey Lownes, 1609); *The Iliads of Homer Prince of Poets*, trans. by George Chapman (London: Richard Field for Nathaniel Butter, 1611); *The Whole Works of Homer; Prince of Poetts in his Iliads, and Odysses. Translated According to the Greeke*, trans. George Chapman (London: Richard Field and William Jaggard for Nathaniel Butter, 1616).

34 Thomas Lydiat, *Emendatio temporum compendio facta ab initio mundi ad praesens usque* (London: Felix Kingston, 1609), sigs. A3r–A7v and Salomon de Caus, *La Perspective avec la raison des ombres et mirroirs* (London: Richard Field and J. Mommeart, 1611), sig.π2r. Lydiat's and de Caus's pensions are recorded in NA, Kew, E 351/2793. Alfonso Ferrabosco, *Ayres* (London: T. Sodham for John Brown, 1609). His pension was awarded on 21 February 1605, calendared in *CSP Domestic*, VIII, p. 198.

35 *The Hartlib Papers*, published on CD-ROM by HROnline, 2nd edn (Sheffield: 2002) Ephemerides, 1653 Part IV, MS 28/2/80A. See: Stephen Clucas, 'Samuel Hartlib's Ephemerides and the Pursuit of Scientific and Philosophical Manuscripts: the Religious Ethos of an Intelligencer', *The Seventeenth Century*, 6:1 (1991), pp. 33–55 (pp. 44–45); Gordon R. Batho, 'Thomas Harriot's Manuscripts', Appendix B, in *Thomas Harriot: an Elizabethan Man of Science*, ed. Robert Fox (Aldershot, 2000), pp. 286–97 (pp. 287–89). I would like to thank Timothy Wilks, Stephen Clucas and Richard Serjeantson for identifying Protheroe's connection to Henry's household.

36 Henry is addressed in this manner in by William Tooker, Dean of Lichfield, in *Duellum siue singulare certamen cum Martino Becano Iesuita, futiliter refutante apologiam et monitoriam praefationem ad imperatorem, reges et principes, et quaedam orthodoxa dogmata serenissimi ac pietissimi Iacobi Regis magnae Britanniae* (London: G. Elder for Nathaniel Butter and R. Mab, 1611), sig. A3r.

37 The court's visit to Oxford is reported by: Anonymous, 'An Account of the Entertainment of King James, with the Queen and Prince at Oxford anno 1605', in the University Library, Cambridge, Additional MS 34, fols 28r–45v. John Elliot has made a hesitant identification of the author as a man named Mowtlowne, a fellow of King's College, Cambridge: John R. Elliot, 'Drama', in *The History of the University of Oxford*, ed. by Nicholas Tyacke (Oxford: 1997), IV, pp. 641–58, (p. 649). Thomas Baker of Jesus College, Cambridge, copied his report in BL, Harleian MS 7044, fols 100r–107r. Baker's transcript forms the basis of John Nichols's account in *The Progresses, Processions and Magnificent Festivities of King James the First, his Royal Consort, Family and Court*, 2nd edn, 4 vols. (London, 1828), I, pp. 543–56. James was described as a philosopher-king by: Anthony Nixon, *Oxford's Triumph: in the Royall Entertainement of his Moste Excellent Maiestie, the Queene, and the Prince* (London: Edward Allde, 1605), sig. C4v.

38 Isaac Wake, *Rex Platonicus: sive, de potentissimi principis Iacobi Britanniarum Regis, ad illustrissimam academiam Oxoniensem* (Oxford: Joseph Barnes, 1607), sig. A2v.

39 BL, Harleian MS 7044, fol. 103r; Nixon, *Oxford's Triumph*, sigs. B2v–B3r; Birch, *Life of Henry*, p.53; Nichols, *Progresses*, I, p. 552. During the Civil War, John Wilkinson 'most ungratefully sided with the rebels, and took up arms against the younger brother of the said prince, King Charles I': Anthony Wood, *Fasti Oxonienses or Annals of the University of Oxford*, ed. Philip Bliss, 4 vols. (London, 1815), I, p. 316. He had evidently had enough of philosopher-kings.

40 Nixon, *Oxford's Triumph*, sig. B1r–v.

41 Henry Howard, Earl of Northampton, letter to Henry, *c.* September 1605, though no date or place cited, BL, Harleian MS 7007, fol. 69r.

42 Nixon, *Oxford's Triumph*, sig. E3r–v. For an account of the ceremony see BL, Harleian MS 7044, fols 105r–6v.

43 Strong, *Henry Prince of Wales*, p. 14.

44 Thomas Chaloner, letter to Sir Julius Caesar, November 1607, in Birch, *Life of Henry*, p. 97.

45 James Cleland, *Hero-paideia or The Institution of a Young Nobleman* (Oxford: Joseph Barnes, 1607), sig. E2r–v. Cleland's claim to be Harington's tutor is at sig. Q2v.

46 Wilks, 'Court Culture', p. 79. Cornwallis, *Discourse*, sig. C1r, acknowledged the 'passions and appetites' of Henry's collegiate courtiers.

47 Wilks, 'Court Culture', pp. 57–59. The evidence for Henry's plans is: Bodleian Library, Oxford, Tanner MS 94, fols 6r–9v; Marc Antonio Correr, 'Despatch to the Doge and Senate, 6 February 1609, calendared in *CSP Venetian*, XI, no. 430, p. 227; and Sir John Holles, letter to Lord Grey, 27 February 1613, HMC *Portland*, IX, 8–11.

48 Strong, *Henry Prince of Wales*, p. 211. Wilks, 'Court Culture', pp. 60–71. T.A. Birrell, *English Monarchs and their Books: from Henry VII to Charles II* (London, 1986), p. 39. Wren, TC, MS O.4.38, edited in Sears Jayne and Francis R. Johnson, *The Lumley Library: the Catalogue of 1609* (London, 1956) and Sears Jayne, *Library Catalogues of the English Renaissance* (Bury St Edmunds, 1983), p. 45.

49 James's payments: NA, Kew, E 351/3244, and SP 14/57 fols 34r, 107r, and H.M. Colvin *et al.*, *The History of the King's Works: 1485–1660*, 5 vols. (London, 1982), IV, II, p.245. Henry's payments: 'A schedule of divers papers, chiefly relating to public affairs, in the beginning of the 17th century', BL, Cotton MS Titus B. VIII, fol. 334r; NA, Kew, SP 14/71, fols 19r, 127r–125r; E 351/2793 and E 351/2794; 'Docquet', 23 January 1608, and 'Accounts for 1609', calendared in *CSP Domestic*, VIII, pp. 398 and 577 respectively; Birch, *Life of Henry*, p. 452; and Wilks, 'Court Culture', pp. 64, 68.

50 Birrell, *English Monarchs and their Books*, pp. 32–39.

51 'tibi dedicare, vel in publicos usus exponendam, vel in Bibliotheca tua, vere Regia, custodiendam': British Library, Royal MS 12 F. XI, and Gilbert, *De mundo*, sig. *2r.

52 Cornwallis, *Discourse*, sigs. C4r.

53 Cornwallis, *Discourse*, sigs. C4r–D1v. Kyle, 'Cornwallis, Sir Charles (*c.* 1555–1629)', *ODNB*.

54 Stuart Handley, 'Newton, Sir Adam, first baronet (d. 1630)', *ODNB*: [www.oxforddnb.com/ view/ article/20046, accessed 7 February 2005]. Other than this notice, the best biographical information is contained in John Durkan and James Kirk, *The University of Glasgow 1451–1577* (Glasgow, 1977), p. 379 and Birch, *Life of Henry*, pp. 16–17, 371–75. Newton is treated briefly by Strong, *Henry Prince of Wales*, pp. 27–28 and at greater length by Wilks, 'Court Culture', pp. 29–30, 43.

55 Johannis Henricius Dauberius, 'Oratio funebris', in André Rivet, *Operum theologicorum* (Rotterdam: Arnold Leers, 1660), sig.**2r–v; Durkan and Kirk: University of Glasgow, p. 379.

56 Newton translated two theological treatises into Latin for James: the King's own *Declaratio serenissimi magnae Britannie Regis, qua quid cum generalibus foederatarum Belgii prouinciarum ordinibus super re Vorstii actum tractatumue sit, singillatim explicatur*, trans. Adam Newton (London: J. Norton, 1612) from the French original; and the first six books of Paolo Sarpi's, *Historiae concilii Tridentini libri octo, ex Italicis summa fide & accuratione Latini facti*, trans. Adam Newton and William Bedell (London: Bonham Norton and John Bill, 1620).

57 Handley,'Newton, Sir Adam, first baronet (d. 1630)', *ODNB*. With respect to the Deanary of Durham, see Henry, letter to James, 23 January 1605, Richmond, in BL, Harleian MS 6986, fol. 73r–v; Birch, *Life of Henry*, p. 16; and Scott-Warren, *Sir John Harington*, p. 229. For Newton's role in Charles's household and council, see his accounts NA, Kew, E 101/434/15; 101/435/5; 101/435/9; 101/435/12, and Ward 10/47; 11/411. For his baronetcy and reversion to the Marches of Wales see Newton, letter to Puckering, 7 June 1620, from St James's, in BL, Harleian MS 7004, fol. 77r; and Birch, *Life of Henry*, p. 373.

58 Wren, TC, MSS R. 9.30 and R.14.10.

59 Strong, *Henry Prince of Wales*, p. 28, and Wilks, 'Court Culture', p. 44. Henry would seem the obvious choice but Strong notes that Charles's 'brandmark' appears on the reverse.

60 Wren, TC, MS R.10.9.

61 Patrick Young presented Edward's notebooks to the Bodleian Library, Oxford, in 1639: MS Arch.F.e.26, previously catalogued as MS Autog.e.2, and MS Bodley 899. James's library is recorded in BL, Additional MS 34275. Henry's schoolbooks are in Wren, TC, MS R.7.23*.

62 Jan Broadway, 'Puckering [Newton], Sir Henry, third baronet (*bap.* 1618, *d.* 1701)', *ODNB*: [www.oxforddnb.com/view/article/20057, accessed 28 March 2006]; and Birch, *Life of Henry*, p. 328. W.A. Speck, 'Harley, Robert, first earl of Oxford and Mortimer (1661–1724)', *ODNB*:[www.oxforddnb.com/view/ article/12344, accessed 28 March 2006]. See also Harleian MS 7007 for an index and report of the manuscripts' provenance inserted before the first folio.

63 Henry Wright, 'De erroribus Lilli corrigendis', Wren, TC, MS R.7.29, I. Henry's signature appears on fol. 23r which was the final folio of the tract in its original binding.

64 Henry Wright, *The First Part of the Disquisition of Truth, Concerning Political Affairs* (London: Nicholas Oak, 1616), p. 19.

65 The model for subsequent editions of the *Brevissima institutio* was: *Institutio compendiaria totius grammaticae, quam et eruditissimus atque; idem illustrissimus Rex noster hoc nomine euulgari [sic] iussit ut non alia haec una per totam Angliam pueris praelegeretur*, ed. by John Colet, William Lily, Richard Cox et al. (London: Thomas Berthelet, 1540/3). Edward VI's copy is in BL, C.21.b4.

66 'Terentii hecyram, fabularium Phaedri librum tertium, et duos libros selectarum Epistolarum Ciceronis edidici': Henry, letter to James, 19 February 1603, in BL, Harleian MS 7007, fol. 14r. For the use of these authors in grammar schools, see Peter Mack, *Elizabethan Rhetoric: Theory and Practice* (Cambridge, 2002), pp. 13–15, 18–19, 23–24.

67 Roger Ascham, *The Scholemaster: or a Plain and Perfite Way of Teaching Children to Understand Write and Speake the Latin Tonge* (London: John Daye 1570), sig. R3r. Cheke removed Terence from the first year curriculum in Cambridge: Joan Simon, *Education and Society in Tudor England* (Cambridge: Cambridge University Press, 1966), pp. 252–53. For Henry, however, 'Studia quoque ab tempore facta sunt auctiora. Nam ad Terentium et Julium accessit optimus ut ego Lingu[ae] Latina[e] magister Phaedrus': Henry, letter to James, 15 July, BL, Lansdowne MS 1236, fol. 66r. In the margins, Henry referred to having studied Phaedrus's 'Tiberius Caesar ad Atriensen' in *Fabulae Aesopiarum*, II. v.

68 Simon Sturtevant had recently published English translations of Aesop's and Phaedrus' fables together: *The Etymologist of Aessops Fables … Also the Etymologist of Phaedrus Fables … Both Very Necessarie Helps for Young Schollers* (London: Richard Field for Robert Dexter, 1602).

69 Erasmus, *De conscribendis epistolis* (Cologne: Heronis Alopecius, 1523), BL 1083.d 1. The work had come from the Cranmer library to Lumley and contains the archbishop's autograph on the title-page.

70 See, for instance, the draft letter to Princess Elizabeth in Newton's hand: BL, Harleian MS 7007, fol. 22r.

71 For examples of Henry's correction of his own work see: Henry, letter to James, 19 February 1603, in BL, Harleian MS 7007, fol. 14r; Henry, letter to James, April 1603, Stirling, BL, Harleian MS 7007, fol. 17r. For an example of Newton's corrections, see Henry, letter to Anne, no date, BL, Harleian MS 7007, fol. 22r. For Ascham's and Cheke's use of double translation, see William Cecil, letter to John Harington, 6 June 1578, in John Harington, *Nugae antiquae*, ed. by Henry Harington and Thomas Park, 2 vols. (London, 1804), I, p. 134; and Ascham, sigs B2v, B3r, C1v–C2r.

72 In Henry, letter to James, 19 February 1603, BL, Harleian MS 7007, fol. 14r, Henry practised his Italic 'r' in the top left-hand corner, the phrase 'post discess' in the bottom left; 'ma tua obsequent' in the bottom centre of the page and multiple 's's in the bottom right corner.

73 See the index and copies in BL, Harleian MSS 7007 and 7008.

74 *The Sixth Book of Virgil's Aeneid, Translated and Commented on by Sir John Harington (1604)*, ed. by Simon Cauchi (Oxford, 1991) stanza 127, p. 59. See also Scott-Warren, *Sir John Harington*, pp. 213–18.

75 Simon Sturtevaunt, 'Virgills Gnomologie: Contayinge his principall Sentences and best applicable speeches', British Library, Additional MS 15234, fol. 2r. I am grateful to Richard Serjeantson for drawing my attention to this manuscript.

76 Mack, *Elizabethan Rhetoric*, pp. 15–16. Thomas Wolsey, *Rudimenta grammatices, & docendi methodus* (Antwerp: Martin Caesar, 1530) sigs Aiir–Aivr. Erasmus, *Ratio studii ac legendi interpretandique auctores*, in Erasmus,*Opera omnia*, ed. J.-C. Margolin (Amsterdam, 1971), I, II, pp. 148–51.

77 Henry's copy was Cicero, *De officiis libri tres, collatione optimorum ac vetustissumorum librorum, & recenti emendatione*, ed. Dionysius Lambinius and Francis Fabricius (Cologne: apud Maternum Cholinuna, 1581), BL C.28.a11. Henry has signed his name on the fly-leaf. He numbered the argument on pp. 105–06, amongst other places. His marginal markings highlighted passages on pp. 9, 17 and 18, amongst many other places. He reused a quotation from I, 13 of *De officiis* in his, 'Oratio Serenissimi Principis ad Regem', BL, Harleian MS 7007, fols. 229r–231v, at fol. 229v.

78 Henry transliterates the Greek terms in his Cicero, *De officiis*, p. 11 onwards. He refers to his thesis on Menander in his letter to James, 1 January 1608, in BL, Harleian MS 7007, fol. 171r. In his 'Oratio', BL, Harleian MS 7007, fols 229r–231v, Henry cites Plutarch, *Moralia*, 354f, 371e at fol. 229v though this particular description is contained in Erasmus, *Institutio principis Christiani* (1516) in *Opera omnia*, ed. O. Herding, IV.i, p.171; Xenophon, *Cyropaedia*, at fol. 231v and Plato, *Republic*, Book V, 472d and Book VI, 499b–c at fol. 230r, though he may have acquired this idea from Cicero's *Epistola ad Quintum fratrem*, I, X, 29. Henry includes a Greek phrase at fol. 231r.

79 Elyot, *The Boke named the Gouernour*, I, pp. 54, 75, 76. Cheke and Thomas Smith worked on a new pronunciation scheme for Greek in Cambridge and Cheke became Regius Professor of the language in 1540: Thomas Smith, *De recta et emendata linguae Graecae pronuntiatione* (1568), in *Sylloge altera scriptorum, qui de linguae Graecae vera et recta pronunciatione commentarios reliquerunt, videlicet D. Erasmi, Stephani Vintoniensis episcopi*, ed. Sigebertus Haverkamp (Leiden, 1740), (pp. 554–74), pp. 556–58; Paul S. Needham, 'Sir John Cheke at Cambridge and Court', 2 vols., unpublished PhD dissertation (Harvard University, 1971), I, pp. 138, 149n, and more generally, pp. 136–49. For Edward's study of Greek, see Needham, I, pp. 208–09; BL, Additional MS 4724, fols. 214r–222v. For James's study of Greek, see Peter Young, in Thomas Smith, 'Vita Petri Junii', in *Vitae quorundam eruditissimorum et illustrium vivorum* (London, 1707), p. 6.

80 '*Quelque livre Italien ou francois par la lecture duquel je pourray devenir ou plus sage ou plus vertueux*': Prince Henry, letter to Queen Anne, no date, BL, Harleian MS 7007, fol. 22r.

81 Giovanni Carlo Scaramelli, Despatch to the Doge and Senate, 6 August 1603, in *CSP Venetian*, X, par. 104, 74. Leonardo Donato, letters to Henry, 1 August 1608, 3 October 1609 and 11 November 1610, tucked in the cover of Adam Newton's commonplace book, Wren, TC, MS R.10.9.

82 Sarpi, *Historiae concilii Tridentini*, and Benvenuto, *The Passenger of Benvenuto* (London: Thomas Snodham for Richard Redmer, 1612). Frances Yates, *John Florio: the Life of an Italian in Shakespeare's England* (Cambridge, 1934), pp. 247–48, 297, and Wilks, 'Court Culture', p. 82.

83 Henry, letter to States General, 1 September 1600, Stirling, in BL, Harleian MS 6986, fol. 61r.

84 Henry, letters to Elizabeth, BL, Harleian MS 7007, fols 22r, 62r 64r and 66v; Elizabeth, letters to Henry, BL, Harleian MS 6986, fols 84r, 85r, 87r, 89r, 91r, 93r, 95r, 97r, 99r, 101r, 103r, 105r, 107r, 109r, 111r.

85 Henry, letter to Anne, 1 January 1604, in BL, Harleian MS 7007, fol. 27r, and Henry, letter to James in Wren, TC MS R.7.23*, VII, fol. 2r, which also contains his attempted translations.

86 Wren, TC, MS R.7.23*, VII.

87 Henry, letter to Anne, 1 January 1604, in BL, Harleian MS 7007, fol. 27r.

88 '*bona eorum pars principibus ipsis instituendis potissimum videtur conscripta*': Henry, dedicatory letter to James, Wren, TC, MS R.7.23*, VII, fol. 2r.

89 Henry, letter to James, 23 January 1605/06, Richmond, BL, Harleian MS 6986; fol. 73r, is Henry's draft and fol. 73v is Newton's.

90 James was in possession of *La Metamorphose d'Ovide figurée*, ed. B. Salomon (Lyon: Ian de Tourne, 1533). Peter Young recorded James's juvenile apophthegms on Ovid: 'The Library of James VI, 1573–1583: from a Manuscript in the Hand of Peter Young, his Tutor', in *Miscellany of the Scottish History Society (First Volume)*, ed. George F. Warner (Edinburgh, 1898), XI–LXXV (pp. LXI and LXXIII respectively). At the age of eleven, James began Jean Calvin, *L'Institution de la religion Chrestienne*, possibly in the Genevan edition of 1566 (XLIX).

91 Peter Bales, letter to the Earl of Salisbury, 1604, in *Calendar of the Manuscripts of the Most Hon. the Marquess of Salisbury*, ed. M.S. Giuseppi (London: Historical Manuscripts Commission, 1933) XVI, p. 402. Bales had signed the inside cover of Henry's copybook, Wren, TC, MS R.7.23*, I. For Bales's career see: H.R. Woudhuysen, *Sir Philip Sidney and the Circulation of Manuscripts* (Oxford, 1996), pp. 32–33. His role in Henry's household, where he was succeeded by the Catholic writing-master, John Davies of Hereford, is discussed by Wilks, 'Court Culture', p. 82.

92. In 'Prince Henry's Copybook', Wren, TC, MS R.7.23*, I: Cicero, *De oratore ad Quintum*, I.xxviii.129 is quoted fol. 9r; Cicero, *De legibus*, I, XVIII, 41 is quoted fol. 16r; Virgil, *Aeneid*, VI, 851–53, is quoted fol. 15v; Horace,

Sermones, II, 2 is quoted fol. 16r, and Pliny, *Epistolae*, 7, 9, 11 is quoted fol. 16r; Valerius Maximus, *Factorum et dictorum memorabilium libri IX*, II.10 is quoted fol. 13 r.

93 'Princeps accipit, quemadmodum populos sub aequalitate componat': 'Prince Henry's Copybook', Wren, TC, MS R. 7.23*, I, fol. 8r. The citation is drawn from Cassiodorus, *Variae Libri duo decim*, X, 3, 4.

94 'nemo poterit esse omni laude cumulatus scriptor, nisi erit omni genarum literarum scientiam consecutus' and 'mea quidem sententia Princeps Henricus vix est mediocri laude dignus scriptor, adeo puerilem scriptionem habet': Henry, 'Henry's Copybook', Wren, TC, MS R.7.23*, I, fol.6r. Bales has adapted Cicero, *De oratore* I, vi, 20.

95 In 1608 Harington, in consultation with Newton, presented the prince with an edition of Francis Godwin's *Catalogue of the Bishops of England* (London: George Bishop,1601). Harington had added marginalia and two indexes to the *Catalogue* in order to refute the suggestion that the future Henry IX would 'pull down Bishops and bells': BL, Royal MS 17 B.XXII, fol. 403v. Joseph Hall dedicated both editions of his *Epistles* to Henry (1608 and 1611) and his *The Peace of Rome Proclaimed to all the World, by her Famous Cardinall Bellarmine and the No Less Famous Casuit Navarre* (London: John Winclet for Eleazer Edgar, 1609).

96 Benjamin Carier, 'Ad Christianam sapientiam breuis introductio', Wren, TC, MS R.7.29, II, fol. 11r. Carier published *A Sermon Preached Before the Prince, at Richmond, This Present Yeere, 1606* (London: I. R. for Edmund Matts, 1606). For James's biblical and theological reading see: 'Library of James VI', pp. xli, xlvii, pp. lii–liv. James's *Paraphrase upon the Revelation of the Apostle Saint John* (pre-1586) and 'meditations' on Revelation 20 and 1 Chronicles 15 (pre-1589) suggests that his early theological reading had been extensive: *The Workes of the Most High and Mightie Prince, James … King of Great Britaine, France and Ireland*, ed. James Montague (London: Robert Barker and John Bill, 1616), pp. 7–72, 73–80 and 81–89 respectively.

97 Henry, 'A Regem carmen', part of a letter to James, 1 January 1604, BL, Harleian MS 7007, fol. 25r.

98 James, letter to Henry, 1604, BL, Harleian MS 6986, fol. 67r.

99 James, letter to Henry, 1604, BL, Harleian MS 6986, fol. 67r. On James's preference for *inventio*, see Rebecca Bushnell, 'George Buchanan, James VI and Neo-Classicism,' in *Scots and Britons: Scottish Political Thought and the Union of 1603*, ed. Roger Mason (Cambridge, 1994), pp. 91–112.

100 Henry, translations of the *Quadrains*, Wren, TC, MS R.7.23*, VII.

101 Nicolò Molin, report on England presented to the government of Venice in the year 1607, calendared in *CSP Venetian*, X, no. 739, p. 513. The anecdote grew to mythical proportions in histories of the King's reign published during the Commonwealth: see William Lily, *Life and Death of Charles I* (London: [1651] 1774), pp. 177–78; Peter Heylin, *A Short View of the Life and Reign of King Charles* (London: Richard Royston, 1658), pp. 6–7 and Richard Perrinchief, *The Royal Martyr or the Life and Death of King Charles* (London, 1667), pp. 5–6. Charles's early letters to James and Henry suggest he studied similar authors and also used letter-writing to practice compositional techniques: Charles, letter to Henry, 1609, BL, Harleian MS 6986, fol. 159r. Peter E. McCullough, *Sermons at Court: Politics and Religion in Elizabethan and Jacobean Preaching* (Cambridge, 1998), pp. 195–96, has argued that Charles's chaplains were of the same Calvinist ethos as Henry's. Charles's greater enthusiasm for learning can be seen in his 'edition' of James's juvenile poetry: 'All the kings short poesis that ar not printed', BL, Additional MS 24195, especially fols 6r–v, 44r–45v. He also made a collation of quotations from Latin poets for his father: Charles, 'Forum flores', BL, Royal MS 12 D. VIII.

102 Cornwallis [assigned to], *Life and Death*, pp. 12–15; Edmond Howe, *The Annales, or a General Chronicle of England, Begun First by Maister John Stow* (London: Thomas Dawson for Thomas Adams, 1615), p. 897; Birch, *Life of Henry*, pp. 21, 68; Nichols, *Progresses*, I, pp. 23, 34, 80; and Strong, *Henry Prince of Wales*, pp. 76–77, 141, 151.

103 'Amator … literis quoque plus honoris attribuit quam temporis': Francis Bacon, 'In Henricum principem Walliae elogium', in *The Works of Francis Bacon, Baron of Verulam Viscount St Alban, Lord High Chancellor of England*, ed. and trans. James Spedding and others, 7 vols. (London, 1857–61), VI, pp. 324 and 328. This translation has been modified.

104 Wilks, 'Court Culture', pp. 40–41, 79–81, 103, 117–124; Lesley B. Cormack, 'Twisting the Lion's Tail: Practice and Theory at the Court of Henry Prince of Wales', in *Patronage and Institutions: Science, Technology and Medicine at the European Court, 1500–1750*, ed. by Bruce T. Moran (Rochester and New York, 1991), pp. 67–84.

105 Henry, 'Oratio serenissimi princips ad regem', 1 January 1609, BL, Harleian MS 7007, fols. 229r–231v.

106 The importance and form of the oration in the school and university curricula is discussed in: Juan Luis Vives, *Vives: on Education. A Translation of the 'De tradendis disciplinis'* (1524), ed. and trans. Foster Watson (Cambridge, 1913), p. 184, and John Brinsley, *Ludus literarius* (1612), ed. E.T. Campagnac (Liverpool, 1917), pp. 178–79, 185. See also Quentin Skinner, *Reason and Rhetoric in the Philosophy of Hobbes* (Cambridge, 1996), pp. 85–86; Baldwin, *William Shakespere's Small Latine*, II, pp. 69, 97, 289, 339, and Mack, *Elizabethan Rhetoric*, pp. 28, 29–30, 65–67.

107 'de l[itte]rarum pra[e]stantia sermonem haberet', 'His quae mens ac lectio mihi suppeditat ra[tio]num firmamentis, astruendam duxi' and 'Imo ha[e]c est illa philosophia, accurata magis quam arguta, quam Ma[jes]tas Ve[stra] S[erenissima] aureis suis ad me informandum libris est complexa': Henry, 'Oratio', fols 229r, 231r.

108 'legum sanct[i]orumq[ue] vinculis constringi': Henry, 'Oratio', fol. 229v.

109 Salisbury, letter to Henry, BL, Lansdowne MS 90, fol. 61r. He was referring to Robert Parsons, *A Conference about the Next Succession to the Crowne of Ingland* (Antwerp: Arnout Conincx, 1595).

110 Henry, 'Oratio', fols. 229v–230r.

111 'hoc magis in Principe requiritur quo maiorem adfert in publicum usum': Henry, 'Oratio', fol. 229v.

112 'In consultationibus, in iudiciis, in Senatu, in Comitiis vult quae iusta, quae honesta, quae salutaria suadere, a seditionibus, a factionibus, ab intestinis dissidiis concitatos populi animos revocare? In bello rursum fortitudinem et militare robur suis imprimere, metum periculorum etiam mortis demere, generosum animum ad gloriam inflam[m]are, abiectos timidosq[ue] spiritus excitare? ~~Rursum fortitudinem et militare robur suis imprmere~~ [sic] Haec ministrabit Eloquentia': Henry 'Oratio', fols. 229v–230r.

113 'Vult Princeps leges condere, iura describere populos imperio regere? Hoc dabit Politica': Henry, 'Oratio', fol. 229v.

114 Salisbury, letter to Newton, 1611, BL, Harleian MS 7002, fol. 87r.

115 Salisbury, letter to Newton, no date or place, BL, Harleian MS 7002, fol. 95r. See also Salisbury, letters to Newton, 24 August 1607, Kensington, and 27 September 1607, Hampton Court, BL, Lansdowne MS 90, fols. 61r and 59r respectively.

116 'Ex solius Historiae lectione quiuis e vulgo incredibilem capit oblectationem … At Princeps qui suum sub aliena persona negotium geri videt, dum initi[i] bella inter potentissimuos Reges, bellicosissimas nationes legit; ducum excellentium artes et strategemata obseruat', Henry, 'Oratio', fol. 230r.

117 For Justin's popularity in grammar schools see: Baldwin, *William Shakespere's Small Latine*, I, pp. 119, 188, 219, 354, 491, 535, 542. R.W., Dedicatory Epistle, Wren, TC, MS 7. 23*, VI, fols 1r–3r. Henry's epitome is on fols. 5r–11r. On fol. 12r he begins an epitome drawn from the end of the third book of Justin's *Historiae*.

118 'Ubi cum acies Persiarum cedere primum cogeretur matres & conuiges occurrere iis obviam orantes in proelium reverterentur, & cum perspicerent eos cunctari sublatis vestibus & obscaenis corporis detectis, rogarunt num in uteros maternum et uxorum ['vellent redire' inserted]. Qua exprobratione repressi redeuntes in proelium valida impressione quos fugiebant fugere compellunt': Henry, Wren, TC, MS R.7.23*, VI, fols 8r–9r.

119 'Semiramis mentita sexum res gessit magnas'; Ninyas was content 'in coetu mulieru[m] consenescere'; 'Licet in Sardanapalo aliud videre exemplum muliebris in viro animi'; and 'Saepe licet videre foeminas assumere sibi viriles animos, & vicissim homines muliebres & molles genere animos': Henry, Wren, TC, MSR.7.23*, VI, fols. 5r, 6r.

120 'Cyrus ille… est nobis insigni [sic] documento, et qua[m] mira vis fatorum sit, et qua[n]ta sit benignitas Dei, in iis conseruandis, quos rebus gerendis magnis destinauit': Henry, Wren, TC, MS R.7.23*, VI, fol. 6r.

121 John Harington, letter to Henry, no date, in Birch, *Life of Henry*, pp. 419–21. The passage was Tacitus, *Agricola*, 19. 'Non ausus sum inquam Tacitum inspicere quem prudentia [sic] admirabilem, brevibus & acutis sententii refertum, stylo, pro meo captu, nimis obscuram, ab omnibus praedicari audiveram': Henry, letter to Harington, 1608, BL, Harleian MS 7007, fol. 226r.

122 Henry, letter to Harington, 1608, BL, Harleian MS 7007, fol. 226v. Henry cites passages from Tacitus, *Agricola*, 5 and 9.

123 Peltonen, *Classical Humanism and Republicanism*, p. 135.

124 On politically contentious uses of Tacitus in England, see: Peter Burke, 'Tacitism', in *Tacitus*, ed. T.A. Dorey (London: Routledge & Kegan Paul, 1969), pp. 149–72 (pp. 159–67); Alan T. Bradford, 'Stuart Absolutism and the Utility of Tacitus', *Huntington Library Quarterly*, 46:2 (1983), 7–34; J.H.M. Salmon, 'Stoicism and Roman example: Seneca and Tacitus in Jacobean England', *Journal of the History of Ideas*, 50, no. 2 (1989), pp. 199–225 and 'Seneca and Tacitus in Jacobean England', in Peck (ed.), *Mental World of the Jacobean Court*, pp. 169–88; Richard Tuck, *Philosophy and Government 1572–1651* (Cambridge, 1993), pp. 39–64 and 104–19; and Blair Worden, 'Ben Jonson among the Historians', in Sharpe and Lake (eds), *Culture and Politics*, pp. 67–89.

125 *James VI and I: Political Writings*, p. 278 note 341.

126 This anecdote is related by Isaac Casaubon, *Epistolae*, 704, edited by Theodore Janson (Rotterdam, 1709), referred to by Mark Pattison, *Isaac Casaubon: 1559–1614*, 2nd edn. (Oxford, 1892) pp. 280–81 and Salmon, 'Seneca and Tacitus in Jacobean England', p.186.

127 Salmon, 'Stoicism and Roman example', pp. 207–09, 215–17, and 'Seneca and Tacitus in Jacobean England', pp. 177–86. Henry commissioned John Hayward's *The Liues of the III Normans, Kings of England, William the first, William the second, Henrie the first* (London: R. Barker, 1613).

128 Cornwallis, *Discourse*, p. 3.

129 Anon, 'An Instruction to Princes. To knowe how to governe state well', Wren, TC, MS R. 7.23*, II, fol.16v.

130 Arthur Gorges, 'A Breefer discourse tendinge to the wealth and strength of this kingedome, of Greate Brittayne', 1610, Wren, TC, MS R. 7. 23*, III, fol. 7 r. See also fols 5 r ,17 v, 19 v.

131 Peltonen, *Classical Humanism and Republicanism*, pp. 124–36.

132 Gorges, 'A Breefer discourse ', fol. 3 r.

133 Charles Cornwallis, 'Short remembrances to Prince Henry', 1609?, BL, Egerton MS 3876, fols. 1r–3v (fol. 3v). Printed in Richard Connak, *An Account of the Prince of Wales, from the First Institution till Prince Henry, Eldest Son to King James I* [1609] (London, 1751), p. 72. Henry's letter of thanks is dated 24 May 1609, BL, Harleian MS 7007, fol. 266r.

134 Robert Dallington, *Aphorismes Ciuill and Militarie Amplified with Authorities, and Exemplified with Historie, out of the First Quarterne of Fr. Guicciarine [Francesco Guicciardini]* (London: M. Flesher for Robert Allot, 1613), sig. A3v.

135 Dallington, *Aphorismes Ciuill and Militarie*, sigs. Ss1 v–Ss2 r. Dallington refers to Cicero, *De officiis*, II, 9, and Tacitus, *Annales*, XIV, 44. See Salmon, 'Seneca and Tacitus in Jacobean England', p. 181.

136 Richard Connock, 'A Collection of the Names of all the Princes of this Kingdome', Wren, TC, MS R. 5.25, printed in Connak, *An Account of the Prince of Wales*.

2| James's Reception and Henry's Receptivity: Reading *Basilicon Doron* after 1603

Michael Ullyot

With mirth in funeral verses and dirge in panegyrics, poets greeted the accession of James I with a decorous balance of feeling.[1] 'Eliza's dead, and can it be, | Eliza's death brings ioy to me?' Phineas Fletcher asked on their behalf.[2] Samuel Daniel, Henry Chettle, Richard Johnson and legions more confronted two mutually awkward subjects: mourning a queen whose death was politically sensitive and praising a king whose accession was 'a mittigation of sorrow'.[3] Thomas Rogers would recollect this contest of sentiments as 'Ioy and griefe at one instant equally weighing in the ballance of the heart, striuing for victory'.[4]

Joy won, inevitably. James's accession offered England not only a new and well-experienced king, but a decisive break from Elizabethan crises of succession. The most propitious difference between the foreclosed Tudor and the fledgling Stuart dynasties was the King's son and heir, Prince Henry Frederick. Except for the aged few who remembered the closing years of her father's reign, none had ever seen a living Prince of Wales. Naturally curious onlookers met the royal family on their separate approaches to London from Edinburgh in the spring of 1603. One of the King's first proclamations that July addressed those who had travelled to London before his coronation expressly 'for [the] comfort they take in the sight of our Person, of the Queene our deare wife, and of our children'.[5]

Prince Henry was subjected to particularly intense scrutiny after his father's accession. The Oxford writing master John Davies, whose 1613 memorial volume for the Prince declared that he could be 'nere-too-mvch praised', likened Henry's English arrival to a celestial intervention: 'He, vpon whome the *Nations* Eyes were bent | As on a most auspitious blazing-*Starre.*'[6] In the same year Daniel Price, Henry's sometime chaplain-in-ordinary, rhapsodized about the Prince's approach from Scotland in terms usually reserved for his father: '*Salomon* the Prince renowned through the *Christian* world, al *beames* of expectation *reflexed* vpon him, the *lines* of the whole *circumference* met in Prince HENRY as in the *Center.*'[7] Everything the Prince would achieve, it had seemed, lay in his indeterminate yet assured future reign as Henry IX.

When Henry died in 1612, these beams of expectation collapsed into unwilling nostalgia for an optimistic, if naïve, era. These memoirs and recollections of Henry's English reception reflect what Francis Osborne would, decades later, describe with incredulity as 'so much *expectation*, as it may be doubted, whether it ever lay in the power of any Prince meerly humane, to bring so much *felicity* into a Nation, as they did all his Life propose to themselves at the Death of *King James*.[8] 'They' are the authors of more than a hundred books and manuscripts dedicated to the Prince before 1612: a heterogeneous collection of sermons, prayers, panegyrics, histories and treatises.[9] Their expectations for Henry IX range from Samson Lennard's and Richard Niccols's calls for his conquest of Rome to George Chapman's appeals for peace and temperance; from Thomas Coryate's and Thomas Palmer's enthusiasm for foreign reportage to Samuel Daniel's endorsement of domestic self-sufficiency.[10] The loudest and most influential voices were those of militant Protestants like Lennard, George More, Robert Pricket and George Marcelline. When Osborne refers to hopes of 'felicity' after James's death he means these men's plans for future military campaigns. Their encouragement of the young, athletic prince to prepare for war through chivalric exercises was well received: by most accounts, Henry was more than willing to expend his energy riding horses, tilting at barriers, camping outdoors and enduring privations as if on campaign, re-enacting battles with toy soldiers, and revelling in drums and trumpets – typical activities of aristocratic youth.[11] As Osborne suggests, however, these activities were intended to prepare Henry for the campaigns he would pursue after his father's death.

These preparations owed directly to the commissions and omissions of King James, as I will argue. James's reputation for pacifism, deserved or not, fuelled these impatient urgings toward Henry's militant future. This advice was inspired by James's promotion of his son as a symbol of the advantages of the Stuart succession, particularly its future prospects. More directly, it took inspiration from James's own book of advice to Henry, *Basilicon Doron* (1598). In this book James encouraged Henry to prepare for war and to wage it when necessary – but the King's actions gave little reassurance to militant factions that he would do so himself. The book's broader implication was that Henry was a receptive object of advice and education; as he wrote at the close of his dedicatory sonnet in the first, seven-copy edition printed in 1599: 'Your father bids you studie here and reede. [*sic*] | How to become a perfite King indeede.'[12] In this era of expanded access both to books and to their means of production, many were willing to offer such advice. The popular reception of *Basilicon Doron* in England after 1603, as I will show, fostered first derivative imitations and then ideological interpretations of James's original advice.[13]

I will compare these interpretations with James's text to determine whether they are false or merely overzealous. I will begin with the King's promotion of Henry as a tangible benefit to the Stuart accession (its promise of a dynasty), a promotion that inadvertently subjected Henry to the interests and intentions of his subjects. Henry became an object not only of his father's pedagogical influence but of his subjects' rhetoric and imaginations – of unsolicited advice that drew inspiration from his father's own counsel.

All of these expectations centred or 'reflexed' on a child aged nine years. Despite his youth, Henry's 'childhood promis'de greater hope of praise, | Then ever Prince attained in his time'. Robert Allyne also wrote these wistful words in 1613, recalling that Henry had seemed an elect ruler for his inborn royalty augmented by his acquired virtues. Notably, Allyne recalls witnessing not hope of greater praise but an enlargement of hope itself, for

> ... a Prince,
> Whome nature grace'd with such divine perfection,
> That all that e're were borne before, or since,
> Did choose him for their chiefe by rare election.
>   Famous for learning, valor, wisedome, worth:
>   Royall by vertue, beauty, bounty, birth.[14]

Nostalgia has distorted his memory, but Allyne neatly summarizes the distinction that had informed every address or entreaty to this future king: between his acquired 'worth' and natural, albeit socially determined, 'birth'. Back in 1604 Sir William Alexander acknowledged this distinction in his *Paraenesis to the Prince*, a poem advising Henry on princely conduct and virtues. Henry's ancestors are reason enough for most observers to find ways for him to deserve his social position. But Alexander is forthright about the Prince's duties both to the past and to the future:

> ... happie *Henrie*, that art highly borne,
> Yet beautifiest thy birth with signes of worth,
> And though a child, all childish toyes doest scorne,
> To show the world thy vertues budding forth.[15]

This 'yet' is a crucial reminder of the expectations of virtue accompanying high birth. Alexander acknowledges and approves of Henry's maturity, his scorn of childish toys, because it signals these budding virtues.

Both Allyne and Alexander cite Henry's virtue because it is the surest embodiment of aristocratic nobility. It entails Henry's 'divinely endowed gifts and powers' that, when cultivated by education, 'would carry the authority of example and could change the world'.[16] It reinforces the election of birth that has placed Henry in a position to rule. But virtue necessitates, in Allyne's words, 'learning, valor, wisedome, worth': in sum, a princely education to 'beautify' birth by eliding its distinction from worth.

Henry was born at the right time and of the right parents, both the culmination and the instrument of dynastic narratives. 'To haue good ancestors t'is a great gaine', Alexander succinctly concluded after a lengthy discourse on Henry's 'annointed blood'.[17] It is also a great burden. Ancestors, having set a noble youth on what James Cleland called his 'vertuous course', are imperative guides for its remainder. Cleland wrote to Henry in 1607 that 'Nobility consisteth not in the glorious images of ancestors, nor ... should it bee worne in the shooheeles, but their vertue should be a pattern for thee to imitate, and a spur to pricke thee forward in that vertuous course, wherein they haue placed thee.'[18] Henry's own virtues would only be realised if his actions resembled theirs, 'a spur to pricke thee forward', to reflect their exemplary virtues. Thus Barnabe Riche suggested in 1604 that Henry's past foretold his future: 'As you are knowne to be descended from a most royall and princely progenie, and to be the vndoubtfull heire of your worthie fathers Crowne and Scepter, so you may growe in renowne & honour equall to your auncestors, & may succeed your royall parents in their vertues'.[19]

More than anyone, perhaps, James appreciated the advantages and imperatives of ancestry. At the beginning of his reign he was determined to secure the future of his provisional Stuart dynasty by underscoring the historical precedents it both sustained and enhanced. His inaugural speech to Parliament, the rhetoric of which would be echoed by the likes of Cleland and Riche, recalled Henry VII's reconciliation of the Lancastrians and Yorkists: 'which as it was first setled and vnited in him, so is it now reunited and confirmed in me, being iustly and lineally descended' from both warring houses. James then promised a peace more fruitful than what had come before: 'the Vnion of these two princely houses is nothing comparable to the Vnion of two ancient & famous Kingdoms, which is the other inward Peace annexed to my Person'.[20] While the union of England and Scotland remained symbolic until 1707, in 1603 it was a eulogistic commonplace – a symbol of the historical precedents and future prospects of James's accession.[21]

Citing the ancestor he shared with his immediate predecessor was also a way for James to repudiate Elizabeth's legacy. If his antipathy toward her was fuelled by the memory of his mother tried and executed by her cousin, James transmuted filial pieties into paternal ones. As father both to his kingdom and to his son, James would steward both to mutual security. As Riche noted in 1604, Henry was his father's 'vndoubtfull heire'. At Henry's 1610 investiture as Prince of Wales, to formalize and reassert his right of succession, James was explicit about its tangible and intangible benefits: 'by the hopefull Succession of Princes, the State of the Church and Comon wealth is settled, the flames of Competition and Conspiracies are quenched, and the feares of future Ages, dissolued'. Addressing Parliament in his customary paternalistic tones, James cited Henry as a symbol of his own largesse.[22] Witnesses to the investiture, he said, 'may see his [Henry's] Fortunes established, in whome their owne, are so much secured; and in whome, the world obserueth so many rare and eminent gifts of nature, and choise parts of vertue and reuerence to vs his Father'.[23] These 'choise parts of vertue', the pearls gleaned from Henry's education, combine with such 'rare and eminent gifts of nature' as his patrimony, youth, strength, and intellect to 'establish' the prince's fortunes, his promised inheritance to (and in) which his subjects' hopes 'are so much *secured*' – in both senses of the word.

Thus in James's public rhetoric he assumed responsibility for Henry's natural and acquired attributes, his birth and his worth. To promote elisions between the two, James conceived of Henry's education as a means to prepare him for high public office, to legitimate his dynastic inheritance. He had not always concocted these plans in public. Some years before his accession, in 1598, James wrote *Basilicon Doron* for Henry in Middle Scots, in which he advised his son to emulate the examples and precepts of others. The story of this book's publication, its progress from a coterie manuscript to 'the runaway bestseller of 1603', is a story of the unintended dissemination, reception, interpretation, and recapitulation of ideas about princely education, specifically that of his heir.[24] I will relate this story to argue that the culture of militant expectations surrounding Prince Henry after 1603 originated in and was coloured by the publication of his father's private words.

*

James's scholarly reputation does not recommend him as the author of a highly practical manual of kingship. The King's prevailing image both in his time and today is of an aloof, bookish figure – who once reflected that had he not been born to rule, he would have become an Oxford don.[25] James's longing for the scholarly life, his considerable learning and his love of contemplation, combined with his doctrine of absolutism and his habit of addressing his subjects in didactic tones, creates the impression that he dismissed political exigencies for scholarly isolation, pursuing knowledge as an end to itself.[26]

This private life might have been James's desire, but it was tempered by the recognition of his public duty. James's reputation for learning did not preclude his humanist belief that it could be instrumental to practical purposes, particularly for princes. James claimed the authority to prescribe cures to what he calls 'the particular diseases of this kingdom'. His experience ruling Scotland reinforced this authority: 'hauing learned both the theoricke and the practicke thereof, more plainely to expresse, then any simple schoole-man, that onely knowes matters of kingdomes by contemplation'.[27] James's disdain for 'pure' contemplation was manifested in his book's concrete lessons in princely education and exemplarity.

The education of princes is a subject of recurring interest in the humanist pedagogical tradition, because of its claims of learning's practical applications in the public sphere over which the prince will rule. Xenophon's *Cyropaedia* was the narrative of princely education commonly idealized by writers of humanist educational treatises for princes and governors from Guarino to Ascham, Piccolomini to Elyot – and to James himself.[28] Cultivation was the prevailing metaphor, originating with Quintilian, for the education of young noblemen.[29] This metaphor depicted the pupils' education as a flowering of innate abilities, with the aid of conscientious teachers and a favourable environment for growth. In *The Boke named the Governour* (1531), Elyot describes the ideal method of 'forming the noble wits of noble men's children, who … shall be made propitious or apt to the governance of a public weal' as 'the policy of a wise and cunning gardener' overseeing the placement, nourishment, and protection of his seedlings in rich (noble) soil.[30] Thus in *Foure Birds of Noahs Arke* (1609), a compilation of prayers for the royal family and other public figures, Thomas Dekker prays for those 'set ouer him [Henry] as tutors or guardians': 'As yet he is but a greene plant; O drop the deaw of thy graces vpon his head, that he may flourish till the shadow of his branches be a comfort to this whole Iland.' Dekker's arboreal and fountain metaphors, common in pedagogical treatises, reinforce the public aims of Henry's education. They also underscore the importance of his educators' cultivations to realize his potential.[31]

James sought to control Henry's education at every stage, from the Prince's guardianship in Scotland to his private and public reception of *Basilicon Doron*, to his initial appearances before his future English subjects, to his household and finally his court. The early stages of Henry's education were essentially those prescribed for noble children in Elyot's *Boke named the Gouernour*: the first by a governess until the age of seven, and the second by a male tutor without female company, to avoid further risk of falling prey to their 'voluptuositie'.[32] Against the strident objections of Queen Anne, James sent Henry to be raised by the Earl and Countess of Mar almost immediately after his baptism in 1594.[33] When the family moved to England, James established Henry's household, which was designed explicitly for the Prince's education.[34] In 1607, Henry's governor Thomas Chaloner recalled that the household 'was intended by the King for a *Courtly College*, or a *Collegiate Court*'.[35] James surrounded his son with influential men to groom him for his future, creating 'an academy filled with aristocratic youths' in each of the Prince's successive households.[36]

Henry's household was distinct from those of his parents, beginning in 1606 as a primarily educational institution before its independence and self-sufficiency were increased after his 1610 creation as Prince of Wales.[37] As it emerged as a centre of humanist learning, many sought to join it despite its lesser status to the King's court.[38] Cleland, tutor to one of Henry's fellow pupils, recommended the Prince's court as 'the true *Panthæon* of Greate Britaine, where Vertue herselfe dwelleth by patterne, by practise, by encouragement, admonitions, & precepts of the most rare persons in Vertue and Learning that can be found'. Praising its 'glorious and laudable emulation among Peeres', Cleland described Henry 'sympathising' with his teachers and other exemplars to the degree that he becomes a model of virtue himself.[39] Henry's education endowed the Prince with, in the words of *Great Brittans Mourning Garment*, 'those rare vertues, which his mind adorn'd' – and 'virtue' is a word frequently invoked to describe a prince who 'from his Cradle liu'd in vertues Court'.[40] Henry appears to have responded well to these promptings, at least in his father's eyes: his New Year's gift to James in 1608/09 was a Latin prolusion whose 'main point was to shew, that learning is more necessary to Kings, Princes, and persons in the highest stations, than to others; and then to answer what might be alledged on the contrary side of the question'.[41] Having the right conditions and evidently the right attitude prepared Henry for the education that would make his virtues commensurate to his birthright.

James could not hope to control every facet of Henry's education, but he was fully invested in its outcome: the creation of a suitable heir to the new dynasty. The process of that creation lay open to uninvited influences, and soon became inadvertently collaborative.

James's writing of *Basilicon Doron* was one means of shaping the influences over his son, but one that further diffused his power as sole author of Henry's virtues.

When James composed the book in the antiquated language of Middle Scots, he wrote expressly for the eyes of his son alone – adding in the 1599 preface that it was '*for exercise of mine owne ingyne, and instruction of him, who is appointed by God (I hope) to sit on my Throne after me*'.[42] When he anglicized it for its exceptionally limited edition of seven printed copies in 1599, it was nominally to ensure that the book would be preserved for Henry, by distributing these copies among influential readers.[43] When James revised *Basilicon Doron* for its second Edinburgh edition of 1603, however, his motives are subject to debate. According to his address to the reader, James felt this wider dissemination was necessary to satisfy popular demand and to prevent either perceived or probable misreadings – mitigating, for example, his exhortation to Henry not to forgive the English their persecution of Mary, Queen of Scots.[44] Peter W.M. Blayney suggests a different motive: that James knew his book would be in demand after he succeeded Elizabeth, and that with the help of Robert Cecil, 'several hundred unsold copies [of the Edinburgh edition] were stockpiled somewhere in London'.[45] Many would have bought it out of interest in their new king, an unknown foreign quantity in 1603.[46] When Elizabeth died on 24 March 1603, at least one copy found its way to the stationer John Norton, who oversaw the production by ten different printing houses of 6,000 copies of James's book in the space of nine working days. Two months and two pirated editions later, the number of copies of *Basilicon Doron* printed and sold wholesale in London was no less than 15,000.

James thus had limited control over how and in what format English readers would encounter his book. Whether or not he ultimately intended his book to be disseminated so widely, both in England and overseas,[47] James initially intended Henry to be its primary if not its sole reader. As he wrote in its preface, *Basilicon Doron* was intended not to instruct general readers in 'the perfite institution of a King; but onely to giue some such precepts to my owne Sonne, for the gouernement of this kingdome'.[48] When this private advice to his son became public knowledge, James was either resigned or eager to use this exposure to his advantage.

Interest in Henry's education, his cultivation of virtues and capabilities suitable to a future king, was widespread long before his 1610 creation as Prince of Wales made the succession official. James acknowledged in *Basilicon Doron* that kings, 'being publike persons', stand 'vpon a publike stage, in the sight of all the people'.[49] Its English readers eagerly reinforced its message by writing and dedicating books to Henry with educational themes. Some adapted James's lessons to their own texts – in a few cases, literally translating the book into their own words. Translation was one way to praise Henry and James simultaneously, as William Willymat did in his preface to *A Princes Looking Glasse* (1603). An enthusiastic Willymat explains that after reading *Basilicon Doron*, he read it 'againe and againe' before excerpting 'the fittest and principallest precepts and instructions' and translating them into Latin and English verse.[50]

Willymat's excerpts reflect humanist pedagogy's traditional emphasis on *sententiæ* or pithy maxims. They also distort James's emphasis on practical matters of 'perfite' kingship. Willymat praises King James for urging Henry to foster honesty, justice, temperance and valiance, but places special emphasis on the latter – particularly as courage can be taught through admiration of past exemplars.

Willymat's concentration on James's text is broken by the presence, in his paraphrase, of other pedagogical texts. Foremost among them is Erasmus's *Institutio principis Christiani* (*The Education of a Christian Prince*), which outlines the ideal educational programme for the future emperor Charles V. The best way for tutors to reinforce virtues in their pupils, writes Erasmus, is to illustrate these precepts in action: 'The deeds of famous men fire the minds of noble youths, but the opinions with which they become imbued is a matter of far greater importance, for from these sources the whole scheme of life is developed'.[51] Knowledge is nothing without interpretation, Erasmus implies: the lessons pupils take from these narratives are even more important than their familiarity with them. While 'famous men' are instrumental to a prince's education, he must not read their exemplary narratives without guidance, interpreting them as he pleases. Willymat similarly recalls Plato's advice to teach courage by considering historical examples while studying theoretical principles and developing physical fortitude. Plato's teachers, he writes, exposed princes to 'many things concerning fortitude, theoricall vertues, and the worthie acts of kings, Princes, and noble men, and exhorted them diligently to imitate good examples, and to eschew, hate, and vtterly detest the badde examples, and shamefull enterprises of wicked tyrants'.[52]

James has occasional recourse to good and bad examples, but emphasizes in *Basilicon Doron* that a king must himself serve as a law-book and model to his subjects. The primary model for Henry is to be found in the worthy acts and precepts of his father, rather than in the more distant past. James briefly advises Henry to read 'authenticke histories and chronicles', to apply 'the bypast things to the present estate', but largely to appreciate the variability of human fortunes.[53] James is far more concerned with the immediate influence of verifiable knowledge, and with the king's public responsibility to exemplify virtue:

> And therefore (my Sonne) sith all people are naturally inclined to follow their Princes example (as I shewed you before),[54] let it not be said, that ye command others to keepe the contrary course to that, which in your owne person ye practice, making so your wordes and deedes to fight together: but on the contrary, let your owne life be a law-booke and a mirrour to your people; that therein they may see, by your image, what life they should leade.[55]

Words and deeds, reading and living – no facet of Henry's education is undertaken for his private benefit alone, but always with a public benefit in mind. As a public figure and exemplar of virtue, Henry's life must serve his people as a law-book, as his own reading has served him. This commonplace of humanist pedagogy, in Erasmus and other sources, informed poets' praise of the King – but also, and unintentionally, encouraged other writers to offer their own advice to the Prince.[56]

*

James's book of advice to Henry had effects beyond these explicit imitations, which sought equally to flatter the King and to influence his son. The wider phenomenon of advice-giving was predicated on Henry's apparent receptiveness, but soon devolved into implicit and even blatant ideological departures from Jacobean policy, specifically in several authors' efforts to contrast James's pacifism with Henry's enthusiasm for chivalry (as preparation for future military campaigns). As will become clear, however, this was a false opposition based on a misreading of James's advice and his practical temperament: he not only counselled Henry to wage war when necessary, but resisted his pacifist characterizations.

No author possessed James's authority over Henry, so those who addressed their entreaties to him found other ways to assume the right to offer him advice. Willymat's translation permitted him some license by trading on the King's authority, while others like Henry's chaplain Andrew Willett had recourse to the unstable hierarchy between noble students and humble teachers.[57] Willett used his position to present his 1607 *Harmonie vpon the First Booke of Samvel* to Henry as a book of prayers. Posing as a supplicant, Willett suggests that the Prince's openness to counsel and influence brings him closer to divinity. Using this topos, Willett reveals the congruent motives between prayers and dedications:

> Nothing maketh a mortall Prince more like in earth to the immortall Prince
> and great King in heauen, then to be willing to heare, as Gods eares are open
> vnto the complaints and suits of all: So your princely humilitie and humanitie
> beeing apt to receiue and regard, what is presented and exhibited, hath embold-
> ened me thus to write.[58]

Willett negotiates the paradoxical division between Henry's acquired and inherent virtues. To exercise his divinity the Prince requires the guidance and counsel of requests, submitted for his consideration only because of his earthly resemblance to that divinity. The translator W.C. described these obsequies, in 1605, as the prerogative of Henry's birth: 'there are, and shall be many zealous prayers, as incense offered daily vp vnto God, in your behalfe'.[59] One such prayer, for 'the Queene and Prince, and other the King and Queenes children', was installed in the Book of Common Prayer after the 1603–04 Hampton Court conference.[60]

W.C. is one of few voices amid the zeal attending the Stuart accession to warn Henry against this onrush as he adjusted to his new privileges and duties: 'accustome your selfe, in your yong yeares, to a diligent consideration of all those vnspeakeable blessings, that are heaped vpon you'.[61] Others responded with more specific dismay at the militant advice offered to the Prince. This advice continued a tradition established at Henry's birth, when the classical scholar Andrew Melville forecast his conquest of Catholic Europe, particularly Spain and Rome.[62] Warlike formulations of Henry's future were common enough to inflame even Ben Jonson, who – like Sir Walter Raleigh and Sir Robert Cotton – would later urge Henry toward more peaceful endeavours like trade and civil industry.[63] But in 1603, as the nine-year-old Henry approached London from Edinburgh for his father's coronation, Jonson closed his entertainment at Althorp with this eulogy:

> And when slow Time hath made you fit for warre,
> Looke ouer the strict Ocean, and thinke where
> You may but lead vs forth, that grow vp here
> Against a day, when our officious swords
> Shall speake our action better then our words.[64]

In 1610 Richard Davies used the same phrase to urge Henry to lead his people in active service: 'in thy right, our Hearts, Liues, Limmes, and Swords, | Shall stretch our Actions farre beyond our Words'.[65] Both men praise the Prince as a harbinger of military valour and expansion, who will 'speake our action' for his subjects in military campaigns.

While both Davies and Jonson rhyme 'swords' with 'words' to reinforce their predictions, they remain nothing more than words. It falls to princes to realise these predictions, 'it being more necessary for a Prince to doe well, then to speake well', as Sir George More writes in *Principles for Young Princes* (1611). More also advises Henry that 'a Prince … ought to bee a Martiall man, stoute and couragious, as well to defend his subiects, as to offend his enimies'.[66] By many accounts, the Prince was impatient to prove his valour and to enact these military adventures. George Marcelline's *Triumphs of King Iames* (1610) uses Homer's episode of single combat between Hector and Ajax in the *Iliad* to illustrate Henry's eagerness:

> This young Prince is a warrior alreadie, both in gesture and countenance, so
> that in looking on him, he seemeth vnto vs, that in him we do yet see *Aiax*
> before *Troy*, crowding among the armed Troops, calling vnto them, that he may
> ioyne body to body with *Hector*, who standes trembling with chill-cold feare, to
> see him seek to determine the difference in the inclosed Field or Lists.[67]

Thus Henry's eagerness 'seemeth vnto vs', Marcelline writes on behalf of Protestant militants like More, Davies, Andrew Melville, Robert Pricket and Samson Lennard – men whose anti-papism grew out of their frustration with James. As James's reign progressed without any significant military conflicts, those who grew displeased with his apparent pacifism turned his heir into a symbol of future action.[68] Their desire to distinguish Henry from his father was manifested in repeated and successful attempts to turn him into a military figure.[69]

Among literary and other historians, the orthodox perception of James's pacifism is often used to characterize his disagreements with Henry on the ends and the nature of kingship as fundamental conflicts. Those who argue that Henry's militarism was antagonistic toward his father's pacifism are right to suggest that the two men were at odds, but they often exaggerate both the differences between their positions, and the degree to which Henry deliberately fomented this opposition.[70] It is more accurate to say, with Curtis Perry, that Henry 'encouraged a structure of feeling that tended to chafe under Jacobean pacifism', and that his household was 'the site of an ambitious Elizabethan revival which fostered support for a number of positions opposed to James's policies', allowing these positions to be exercised (and exorcized) in this limited forum.[71]

James's practical approach to the exigencies of statecraft complicates the half-truths and idealized images of the King after 1603. From the beginning of his reign he was perceived as the *rex pacificus* who would bring religious unity to the warring factions of Europe – a position reinforced by the panegyrics welcoming James to England, such as Daniel's *Panegyrike Congratulatorie*.[72] James certainly modelled himself on biblical exemplars of peace and good government, and encouraged Prince Henry to do the same,[73] but his image as the king of peace is attributable more to the international mood and the desires of his English subjects than to his own desire to promote pacifism.[74] 'Like all statesmen, James never enjoyed the luxury of a purely theoretical approach to the major issues confronting his contemporaries', writes Malcolm Smuts.[75]

Characterizations of James's idealistic pursuit of peace, or his scholarly aversion to militarism, belie his readiness to wage war when necessary. James also instilled these values in his son to prepare him for his future reign. In *Basilicon Doron*, James advises Henry to balance contemplation with physical activity, and to learn and practise the arts of war. He counsels him to enter into war with the necessary provisions, to hazard himself in battle but not rashly, and above all to 'be slow in peace-making', for 'a honourable and iust warre is more tollerable, then a dishonourable and dis-aduantageous peace'.[76]

Before long, James effectively lost control over the interpretations of his advice when his ideas were co-opted by those with political agendas to promote. Protestant militants took up his emphasis on Henry's practical education to promote chivalric training for Henry's future wars. Few would identify their position as open opposition to James; instead, they treated James and Henry as complementary. Sir William Alexander's previously cited injunction to Henry to 'show the world thy vertues budding forth' goes on to define those virtues in militant terms:

And though a child, all childish toyes doest scorne,
To show the world thy vertues budding forth,
Which may by time this glorious yle adorne,
And bring eternall Trophees to the North:
While as thou doest thy fathers forces leade,
And art the hand, while as he is the head.[77]

Alexander foresees Henry's leading James's forces into battle as the active complement of his father's more contemplative persona (his 'hand' enacting the will of James's 'head'), his 'eternall Trophees' a sign of his worthiness to rule 'this glorious yle'. Alexander also praises Henry's military training as a son's duty to his father, because kings are well served by martial prowess ('In *Mars* his mysteries t'acquire renowne, | It giues Kings glorie, and assures their place'):

This well becomes the courage of thy Sire,
That traines thee vp according to thy kind.
He, though the world his prosp'rous raigne admire,
In which his subiects such a comfort find,
Hath (if once mou'd the bloudie art t'imbrace)
That wit for to make warre, which now keepes peace.[78]

Thus Henry's militarism is reconciled to his father's wishes: James has the 'wit' to wage war, but chooses instead to maintain peace. Even if he distorts its message, Alexander is an attentive reader of *Basilicon Doron*. In 1610, George Marcelline assures Henry with unintended irony that he need 'neuer feare that the victories of My King will leaue you nothing to conquer'.[79] Until his 'fit season', Henry's 'stronger desire' to wage war must be checked by the 'order of Nature': his youth, inexperience and obedience to his father's will. '[L]et it not be imagined', Marcelline adds, 'that the execution of great desseignes, are vtterly lost by deferrence and delay'.[80] Henry need simply await the proper time and place for his conquests, even before his father's death. Like Alexander, Marcelline posits king and prince as a conjoined figure whose study of books and use of swords are both instrumental to military success:

Yours shall bee the arme and strength, but his the head and Counsel; Yours the paine and endeauour, his the effect; Yours the Action, but he the Agent: You for him, & he for you, and you and hee ioyntly together, shall win an immortal glory; to the end, that al the world may see you in effect after the same manner, as one figured Cæsar, aloft, deposing or treading a Globe vnder him, holding a book in one hand, and a sword in the other: so that it may be saide of you, *That for the one & other you are a Cæsar*.[81]

'His pen hath made way for your sword', Samson Lennard describes James to Henry, 'and his peace, if God giue long life, may farther your warres.'[82] James's pen and book had, in their way, endorsed precisely this view; Marcelline is recalling the King's advice to Henry to read, and thus to reenact, Caesar's commentaries for their 'precepts in martiall affaires'.[83] These militant readers of *Basilicon Doron* could not be charged with misinterpreting James's book, but only with reading it too literally. By positing father and son as a conjoined figure, they carefully circumvent charges of fomenting ideological divisions.

Neither James nor Henry would lift a sword in battle, despite these heroic urgings and inclinations. Neither was capable of doing so: James because of the balance of power in Europe and because his own near insolvency prevented him from waging war (even to intervene on behalf of his daughter, Elizabeth of Bohemia, besieged in Prague by Spanish troops in late 1620); and Henry only because his youth and position delayed his confronting the same exigencies.[84]

Yet the prospects of youth made Henry the depository of ambitions from every corner: from his father, to signal the advantages of a Stuart dynasty; and from his subjects, to complement or to counterbalance his father's policies. What neither source could predict or, later, would acknowledge was the degree to which Henry would play these roles before his father's death. Had he lived to 1625, Henry IX might have succumbed to pride and tyranny, as Arthur Gorges speculated in *The Olympian Catastrophe*.[85] Or he might have been as ill-fated as his brother Charles I. 'The truth is', Osborne reflects through the lens of regicide, '*Prince Henry* never arrived at *the great test, Supremacy in power*, that leaves the will wholly to its owne guidance.'[86] Until that emancipation, Henry would remain – has remained – an object of others' interpretative ambitions.

NOTES

1 Research for this article was supported by the Social Sciences and Humanities Research Council of Canada. I am grateful to Joseph Black for comments on a previous version of its argument.

2 *Sorrovves Ioy. Or, A Lamentation for our late deceased Soveraigne Elizabeth, with a triumph for the prosperous succession of our gratious King, Iames* (Cambridge, 1603), sig. D2r. Samuel Daniel's *Panegyrike Congratvlatorie Delivered to the Kings most Excellent Maiestie at Bvrleigh Harrington in Rvtlandshire* (1603) and a multitude of other texts published in 1603 echo Fletcher's ambivalence – as do the broadsheet *Weepe with Ioy* (1603); Henry Chettle's *Englands Mourning Garment: Worne here by plaine Shepheardes, in memorie of their sacred Mistresse, Elizabeth; Queene of Vertue while she liued, and Theame of Sorrow being dead* (1603); Joseph Hall's *The Kings Prophecie: or Weeping Ioy* (1603); Richard Johnson's *Anglorum Lachrimae: In a sad passion complayning the death of our late Soueraigne Lady Queene Elizabeth: Yet comforted againe by the vertuous hopes of our most Royall and Renowned King Iames* (1603); H.S.'s *Queene El'zabeths losse, and King Iames his welcome* (1603); and Anthony Nixon's concatenated *Elizaes Memoriall. King Iames his arriual. And Romes Downefall* (1603).

3 *Weepe with Ioy*, n. p. On the mourning for Elizabeth see Dennis Kay, *Melodious Tears: The English Funeral Elegy from Spenser to Milton* (Oxford, 1990), pp. 78–90.

4 Thomas Rogers, *Gloucesters Myte, Delivered vvith the mournefull Records of Great Britaine, into the Worlds Register. For the inrolement of the euerlasting Fame and perpetuall remembrance of our late most gratious Prince Henrie. With Motiues to Repentance* (1612), sig. A4r.

5 James VI and I, 'A Proclamation signifying the Kings Majesties pleasure, touching the resort of people to his Coronation [6 July 1603]' in *Stuart Royal Proclamations*, ed. James F. Larkin and Paul L. Hughes (Oxford, 1973), I, pp. 37–38 (p. 37). James's coronation itself took place on St James's Day (25 July) 1603, but plague delayed his ceremonial entry until the following March; see Graham Parry, *The Golden Age restor'd: The culture of the Stuart Court, 1603–42* (Manchester, 1981), pp. 2–21.

6 John Davies of Hereford, *The Mvses-Teares for the losse of their hope; heroick and nere-too-mvch praised, Henry, Prince of Wales* (1613), sig. A2r. 'The light hee lent', continues Davies, 'Fore-shew'd he would haue thundred lowd, in War; | For, in his *Eares* no *musick* sweet did sound, | But *Trumpets, Drummes*, and *Phifes*' (sig. A2r).

7 Daniel Price, *David his Oath of Allegiance to Iervsalem* (Oxford, 1613), sig. B4v; p. 16. Price remained devoted to Henry throughout the Prince's life and for two years after his death, when he preached anniversary sermons. In 1610, he referred to Henry's 'Princelie goodnes, to whose service I haue consecrated my tongue, and pen, and heart, and all the offices of my life' (*The Defence of Trvth against a booke falsely called The Trivmph of Trvth sent over from Arras A. D. 1609. By Hvmfrey Leech late Minister* (Oxford, 1610), sig. *2r). On James as Solomon, embodying divine wisdom and authority, see Parry, *The Golden Age restor'd*, pp. 24–32. Imagery of expectant beams was common for the Jacobean accession; for example, Thomas Dekker's *Magnificent Entertainment: Giuen to King Iames, Queene Anne his vvife, and Henry Frederick the Prince, vppon th day of his Maiesties Tryumphant passage (from the Tower) through his Honourable Cittie (and Chamber) of London, being the 15. March. 1603. As well as by the English as by the Strangers: With the speeches and Songs, deliuered in the seuerall Pageants*, in *The Dramatic Works of Thomas Dekker*, ed. Fredson Bowers, 4 vols. Cambridge: Camridge University Press, 1953–61, 2:229–309, describes 'All mens eyes … turnd to the North … like the points of so many Geometricall needles, through a fixed and Adamantine desire to behold this fortie-fiue yeeres wonder now brought forth by *Tyme*', ll. 1–16.

8 Francis Osborne, *Traditionall Memoyres on the Raigne of King Iames* (1658), sigs. M1r–M1; pp. 113–14.

9 John Buchtel has verified 107 individual books and reprints dedicated to the Prince between 1599 and 1612 ('Book Dedications in Early Modern England and the Literary Patronage of Henry, Prince of Wales (1594–1612)' (University of Virginia, unpublished Ph.D. diss., 2004, Appendix). (See also his contribution to

this volume.) His list relies on what are presently the most comprehensive studies of (respectively) dedications in general, and dedications specifically to Henry: Elkin Calhoun Wilson, *Prince Henry and English Literature* (Ithaca, 1946); and Franklin B. Williams, Jr., *Index of Dedications and Commendatory Verses in English Books before 1641* (London, 1962). For details of Henry's bibliographic acquisitions, see Roy Strong, *Henry, Prince of Wales and England's Lost Renaissance* (London, 1986), pp. 154–57; and Timothy V. Wilks, 'The Court Culture of Prince Henry and his Circle, 1603–1613' (University of Oxford, unpublished D. Phil diss., 1987), pp. 54–70.

10 See Lennard, *The Mysterie of Iniqvitie: That is to say, The Historie of the Papacie* (1612); Niccols, *The Three Sisters Teares. Shed at the Late Solemne Funerals of the Royall deceased Henry, Prince of Wales, &c.* (1613); Chapman, *Euthymiae Raptus; or the Tears of Peace* (1609); Coryate, *Coryats crudities … dispersed to the nourishment of the trauelling members of this kingdome* (1611); Palmer, *An Essay of the Meanes howv to make our Trauailes, into forraine Countries, the more profitable and honourable* (1606); and Daniel, *The Brotherton Manuscript. A Study in Authorship*, ed. John Pitcher (Leeds, 1981).

11 Among other sources, see John Chamberlain, *The Letters of John Chamberlain*, ed. Norman Egbert McClure, 2 vols. (Philadelphia, 1939), I, p. 330; and Charles Cornwallis [assigned to], *The Life and Death of ovr Late most Incomparable and Heroique Prince, Henry Prince of Wales. A Prince (for Valour and Vertue) fit to be Imitated in Succeeding Times* (1641), sigs. B5v–B7r; pp. 20–25.

12 James, *Basilicon Doron*, in *Political Writings*, ed. Johann P. Sommerville (Cambridge, 1994), pp. 1–61; 1.

13 James Cleland explicitly imitates the King: 'I have essaied espetiallie to imitate our Soveraigne and Roiall Doctor' (*Heropaideia, or The Institvtion of a Yovng Noble Man* (Oxford, 1607), sig. ¶3r).

14 Robert Allyne, *Funerall elegies vpon the most lamentable and vntimely death of the thrice illustrious Prince Henry, Prince of VVales* (1613), sig. B2r.

15 William Alexander, *A Parænesis to the Prince* (1604), sig. B1r. In *The Triumphs of King Iames the First* (1610), Marcelline refers to 'my *Parænesis*, or accomplishment of my wish' (*Triumphs of King Iames*, sig. M4v). In 1637, Alexander rededicated the poem to Charles.

16 Blair Worden, *The Sound of Virtue: Philip Sidney's* Arcadia *and Elizabethan Politics* (New Haven and London, 1996), p. 23.

17 Alexander, *Parænesis*, sigs. B3r, B2r.

18 Cleland, *Heropaideia*, sig. B1r. Cleland's equestrian metaphor reflects Henry's lifelong interest in horsemanship, particularly in chivalric tilts and tournaments.

19 Rich, *The Frvites of long Experience. A pleasing view for Peace. A Looking-Glasse for Warre. Or, Call it what you list* (1604), sig. A3v.

20 James, *The Kings Maiesties Speech, as it was deliuered by him in the vpper house of the Parliament, to the Lords Spirituall and Temporall, and to the Knights, Citizens, and Burgesses there assembled, On Munday the 19. day of March 1603: Being the first day of this present Parliament, and the first Parliament of his Maiesties Raigne* (1604), sig. A4v. 'That peace' was the end of the Wars of the Roses, brought about by Henry's marriage to Elizabeth of York, unifying the warring parties and inspiring the Tudor rose; see Parry, *The Golden Age restor'd*, p. 64.

21 Curtis Perry, *The Making of Jacobean Culture: James I and the renegotiation of Elizabethan literary practice* (Cambridge, 1997), p. 156.

22 For a description of the investiture ceremony see Strong, *Henry, Prince of Wales*, pp. 115–16. Daniel had praised James's generosity in 1603: 'We haue, by thee, far more the[n] thine own worth | That doth encourage, strengthen, and relieue | Our hopes in the succession of thy blood' (*Panegyrike Congratulatorie*, sig. A6v).

23 *Calendar of State Papers Domestic: Edward VI, Mary, Elizabeth, and James I*, ed. R. Lemon and M.A. Everett Green (1856–72), IX, p. 597. The preamble James read was in Latin, composed by Sir Francis Bacon and Sir Henry Hobart; this anonymous translation is the more elegant of two written soon after Henry's creation.

24 I am very grateful to Peter W.M. Blayney for allowing me to make use of his unpublished research on *Basilicon Doron*'s English printings: 'Nothing Succeeds Like Succession: The Runaway Bestseller of 1603', (Washington, D.C., unpublished lecture, 2001), p. 5. See also James Doelman, '"A King of Thine Own Heart": The English Reception of King James VI and I's *Basilikon Doron*', *The Seventeenth Century*, 9 (1994), pp. 1–9.

25 Charles Carlton, *Charles I: The Personal Monarch* (1983), p. 10; no source is cited.

26 On James as the 'schoolmaster' of Britain, and his uniting of the three roles of sovereign, tutor and father, see Rebecca W. Bushnell, *A Culture of Teaching: Early Modern Humanism in Theory and Practice* (Ithaca, 1996), pp. 68–71. In January 1603, Harington recounts an audience with James in which the King, quoting Aristotle, 'and suche lyke writers', and praising Harington's 1591 translation of Ariosto, inquires 'Whether a Kynge shoulde not be the beste clerke in his owne countrie; and, if this lande did not entertayne goode opinion of his lerynge and good wisedome?', *The Letters and Epigrams of Sir John Harrington*, ed. N.E. McClure (Philadelphia, 1930), pp. 110–11.

27 James, *Basilicon Doron*, p. 10.

28 James borrowed from Xenophon so heavily that Cleland would later claim that 'his Maiesties instructions haue worne Xenophon out of credit in al other Countries' (sig. T4). (I am grateful to Jane Grogan for this reference.) Two of these treatises appear in *Humanist Educational Treatises*, ed. and trans. Craig W. Kallendorf (Cambridge, MA, 2002): Battista Guarino's *A Program of Teaching and Learning* (pp. 260–309); and Aeneas Silvius Piccolomini's *The Education of Boys* (pp. 126–259). For Elyot, see note 32 below.

29 Quintilian compares 'dry' teachers to 'a dry and arid soil for plants that are still young and tender' in *Institutio Oratoria*, ed. and tr. H.E. Butler (London and Cambridge, MA, 1920–22), p. 229. For a discussion of cultivation imagery to signal the divisions and the 'fruition' of knowledge in human affairs in Bacon's writings, see Brian Vickers, *Francis Bacon and Renaissance Prose* (Cambridge, 1968), pp. 193–98.

30 Cited in Bushnell, *A Culture of Teaching*, p. 82. Alan Stewart calls Elyot's *Boke named the Governour* (1531) 'the first major vernacular articulation of an English humanism' (*Close Readers: Humanism and Sodomy in Early Modern England* (Princeton, 1997), p. xxix). Bushnell identifies in Elyot 'an ambivalence in concert with *The Governour*'s pervasive oscillation between the teacher/adviser's self-promotion and his subservience'. Moreover, she finds in humanist pedagogy more broadly 'a persistent and productive tension between a compulsion to order and a respect for nature's claims' (pp. 83, 90). Bushnell outlines how the contest between nature and nurture or art takes in a wide array of subjects in Renaissance literature, including innate or learned virtue and character, and agency and social difference (p. 75 n. 5).

31 Thomas Dekker, *Foure Birds of Noahs Arke: Viz. 1. The Dove. 2. The Eagle. 3. The Pellican. 4. The Phoenix* (1609), sigs. E4r–E4v; pp. 12–13. (I am grateful to Elizabeth Hanson for the latter point.)

32 Thomas Elyot, *The Boke named Governour*, Ed. Donald W. Rude, New York and London: Garland, 1992, p. 31.

33 This separation of Henry from Queen Anne caused a rift between James and his wife. See J.W. Williamson, *The Myth of the Conqueror: Prince Henry Stuart, A Study of 17th Century Personation* (New York, 1978), pp. 16–21; Wilson, *Prince Henry and English Literature*, pp. 5–6; and Leeds Barroll, *Anna of Denmark, Queen of England: A Cultural Biography* (Philadelphia, 2001).

34 Henry's early household first occupied Oatlands Palace (in Surrey), then Nonsuch Palace (also in Surrey); after 1610 it moved between St James's Palace and Richmond Palace, and occasionally Woodstock. His tutor from 1600 was the Latinist Adam Newton (Strong, *Henry, Prince of Wales*, pp. 13–14). Peacham's 1612 emblem book, *Minerva Britanna or A Garden of Heroical Deuises, furnished, and adorned with Emblems and Impressa's of sundry natures, Newly devised, moralized, and published, by Henry Peacham, Mr. of Artes*, London: 1612, includes an emblem dedicated to Newton (sig. G3v); another presents an armoured knight on horseback and praises Henry's militarism (sig. D4v).

35 Cited in Parry, *The Golden Age restor'd*, p. 69. James is said to have decreed that it should 'rather imitate a

College than a Court' (National Archives LS 13/280/304). Chaloner had the charge of Henry after 1603, when he accompanied the Prince and his mother from Edinburgh to London; in 1610 he was granted the position of chamberlain (Strong, *Henry, Prince of Wales*, p. 13). Price would lament the dissolution of 'this *Collegiate societie*' in a sermon addressed to the household the day before their master's funeral (*Spiritvall Odovrs to the Memory of Prince Henry* (Oxford, 1613), sig. O2v).

36 Strong, *Henry, Prince of Wales*, p. 20. Among these youths were John Harington (cousin to the poet of that name; both are discussed below) (1592–1614); Robert Devereux, 3rd Earl of Essex (1591–1646); and William Cecil, Viscount Cranborne, later 2nd Earl of Salisbury (1591–1668) (Strong, *Henry, Prince of Wales*, pp. 20–23). Adds Wilks 'From 1603 … and for as long as he lived, Henry was the receptive object of unrelenting and painstaking instruction', ('The Court Culture', p. 55).

37 Even before Henry's creation, James mentions the three courts as distinct entities in a proclamation of 2 June 1610: 'A Proclamation for the due execution of all former Lawes against Recusants [2 June 1610]', in *Stuart Royal Proclamations*, I, pp. 245–50 (p. 247). Neil Cuddy characterizes queens' and princes' 'satellite courts' throughout the Stuart era (1603–88) as 'dwarfed by the patronage and power at the direct disposal of the monarch' – a sweeping generalization, but an important reminder of the relative status of these households: 'Reinventing a Monarchy: The Changing Structure and Political Function of the Stuart Court, 1603–1688', in *The Stuart Courts*, ed. Eveline Cruickshanks (Stroud, 2000), p. 63. For treatments of Henry's household, see Wilks, 'The Court Culture', pp. 38–70; and Parry, *The Golden Age restor'd*, pp. 64–93.

38 Figures like Sir John Holles and Sir John Harington of Kelston allied themselves with Henry only after making fruitless advances to James (Wilks, 'The Court Culture', p. 33).

39 Cleland, *Hero-paideia*, sigs. E2r–E2v. Cleland was Harington's tutor (Parry, *The Golden Age restor'd*, p. 69).

40 'To the sad houshold of Prince Henry', in Anon., *Great Brittans Mourning Garment. Given To all faithfull sorrowfull Subiects at the Funerall Of Prince Henry* (1612), sigs. C3v–C4r (C4r).

41 Thomas Birch, *The Life of Henry Prince of Wales, Eldest Son of King James I: Compiled chiefly from his own Papers, and other Manuscripts, never before published* (London, 1760), sig. K5v (p. 138). A prolusion was an educational exercise, outlining opposing positions on a given question.

42 James, *Basilicon Doron*, p. 4. Jenny Wormald, describing the manuscript as a 'lovely mess' of revisions and interpolations, argues that *Basilicon Doron* was, 'initially at least' a tentative exercise ('James VI and I, *Basilikon Doron* and *The Trew Law of Free Monarchies*: The Scottish Context and the English Translation', in *The Mental World of the Jacobean Court*, ed. Linda Levy Peck (Cambridge, 1991), pp. 36–54 (p. 49). For the significance of its language, see p. 50.

43 Namely Queen Anne, Prince Henry, his tutor, the Marquis of Hamilton, and the Earls of Huntly [*sic*], Erroll, and Angus; its printer Robert Waldegrave was sworn to secrecy (Wormald, 'James VI and I, *Basilikon Doron* and *The Trew Law of Free Monarchies*', pp. 50–51; Jason Scott-Warren, *Sir John Harington and the Book as Gift* (Oxford, 2001), p. 5).

44 Scott-Warren, *Harington*, p. 6. More broadly, James defused charges that the book was anti-English – but whether these charges were ever laid, or were motivated by his anticipation of the book's release to the English market, is uncertain. On the latter possibility, see discussion below.

45 Blayney, 'Nothing Succeeds Like Succession', p. 5.

46 Wormald memorably describes it as 'the equivalent of a coronation mug' ('James VI and I, *Basilikon Doron* and *The Trew Law of Free Monarchies*', p. 52).

47 The book's international audiences also well surpassed James's intended audience(s). Some thirty translations (in Latin, French, Italian, Welsh, and other languages) appeared during James's lifetime (*ibid.*, p. 52; Blayney, 'Nothing Succeeds Like Succession', p. 5).

48 *Basilicon Doron*, p. 9.

49 *Ibid.*, p. 4. Scott-Warren cites this passage as an illuminating example of the alterations (discussed below) that James made to *Basilicon Doron* between its Scottish printing in 1598 and its English printing in 1603 – adapting his private counsel to Henry for broader public consumption, and acknowledging that 'The king's most private sphere is a theatrical sphere' (*Harington*, p. 8).

50 William Willymat, *A Princes Looking Glasse, or a Princes Direction* (Cambridge, 1603), sig. A3r. These dual-language verses were printed on facing pages.

51 Desiderius Erasmus, *The Education of a Christian Prince [Institutio principis Christiani]*, Trans. Lester K. Bron, New York: Octagon, 1965, p. 145.

52 Willymat, *A Princes Looking Glasse*, sig. A2v.

53 *Basilicon Doron*, p. 46.

54 '[T]each your people by your example: for people are naturally inclined to counterfaite (like apes) their Princes maners' (James, *Basilicon Doron*, p. 20).

55 *Basilicon Doron*, p. 34.

56 See Erasmus, *Institutio principis Christiani*, p. 157. Daniel praised James in 1604 as a 'great exemplare prototipe of Kings' whose subjects behold him, and read his words, to 'see what we must be, and what thou art' (*Panegyrike Congratulatorie*, sig. A3v). Augustine Taylor concurs in *Encomiasticke Elogies* (1614): 'Our King's, our stay, [sic] | Whose actions we may imitate' (sigs. B1r-B1v).

57 See note 32, above.

58 Willett, *An Harmonie vpon the First Booke of Samvel … The diuers readings compared, doubtfull questions explaned, places of Scripture reconciled, Controuersies briefly touched, and morall collections applied. Wherein aboue foure hundred Theologicall questions are handled, with great breuitie and much varietie* (1607), sig. ¶2r.

59 W.C., *False Complaints*, sig. A3r.

60 The king's royal printer Robert Barker inserted this prayer after one for King James: 'Almightie God which hast promised to be a Father of thine Elect, and of their seed, wee humbly beseech thee to blesse our gratious Queene *Anne*, Prince *Henry*, and all the King and Queenes Royall progenie: indue them with thy holy Spirit, enrich then with thy heauenly grace, prosper them with all happinesse, and bring them to thine euerlasting Kingdome through Jesus Christ our Lord, Amen' (*The booke of common prayer, and administration of the sacraments by Church of England* (1603), sig. B5r; italics signify Roman proper names in this black-letter text). For a discussion of this inclusion, see David N. Griffiths, *The Bibliography of the Book of Common Prayer 1549–1999* (2002), p. 8.

61 W.C., *False Complaints. Or The Censure of an vnthankfull mind* (1605), sig. A3r. Alexander, *Parænesis*, also warns Henry to 'flatter not thy selfe with those faire showes' of love (sig. B1r).

62 See Barbara Lindsay and J.W. Williamson, 'Myth of the Conqueror: Prince Henry Stuart and Protestant militancy', *The Journal of Medieval and Renaissance Studies* 5 (1975), pp. 203–22 (pp. 204–05). They cite dedications that urged Henry to pursue a military path to glory: Dudley Digges's 'Of the Worthiness of War and Warriors' (in *Foure Paradoxes, or politique Discourses* (1604)); and Riche's *Frvites of long Experience*. Lindsay and Williamson claim that a fifth of all the books dedicated to Henry between 1603 and 1612 concerned subjects like horsemanship, archery, navigation, exploration, military history, political history, and the education and training of princes. Their estimate of the number of dedications Henry received may be inaccurate (see note 9, above), but there can be no doubt that Henry received a large number of military books.

63 The question whether Henry ought to pursue a military future was played out in a series of manuscript treatises and poems advocating opposite positions: Raleigh's included 'Observations and Notes concerning the Royal Navy and Sea Service' (1609?); 'Concerning a Match … Between the Lady Elizabeth and the Prince of Piedmont' (1611); and 'Touching a Marriage between Prince Henry and the Daughter of Savoy' (1612). See Leonard Tennenhouse, 'Sir Walter Raleigh and the Literature of Clientage', in *Patronage in the Renaissance*, ed. Guy Fitch Lytle and Stephen Orgel (Princeton, 1981), pp. 235–58 (pp. 248–49).

Cotton's treatise was more pointed: 'An answer made by command of Prince Henry, to certain proposi-tions of war and peace, delivered to his Highness by some of his military servants' (Daniel, *Brotherton Manuscript*, p. 21).

64 Ben Jonson, *The Entertainment at Althorp*, in *Ben Jonson*, ed. C.H. Herford and Evelyn Simpson (Oxford, 1925–52), VII, pp. 119–31 (p. 131). Jonson reinforces Henry's preference for action over words, a convention of military rhetoric that recurs in Christopher Brooke and William Browne's *Two Elegies, Consecrated to the Never-dying Memorie of the most worthily admyred; most hartily loued; and generally bewayled Prince; Henry Prince of Wales* (1613): 'Hee knew that Souldiers vs'd n'affected words, | Whose Tongues are speares, their Oratory swords' (sig. B4v).

65 Davies, *Chesters Trivmph in Honor of her Prince. As it was performed vpon S. Georges Day 1610. in the for said Citie* (1610), sig. A2r.

66 More, *Principles for Young Princes* (1611), sig. A9v. Riche similarly tells Henry that 'in a Prince there is nothing so glorious as to be called a great captain or a worthy soldier' (sig. A3v).

67 Marcelline, *Triumphs of King Iames*, sig. L3v.

68 The main source of dissatisfaction lay with James's religious tolerance, whether of domestic religious dis-senters, or of foreign papists antipathetic to all Protestant nations: at James's accession in March 1603, there were unfounded fears of a Scottish Presbyterian influence on Anglican ceremony. For the king's pleas for consensus, see Kenneth Fickham and Peter Lake, 'The Ecclesiastical Policy of King James I', *Journal of British Studies*, 24 (1985), pp. 169–207; and William B. Patterson, *King James VI and I and the Reunion of Christendom* (Cambridge, 1997), chapter 2.

69 After the Prince's death in 1612, the line between praise of Henry and criticism of James was blurred, parti-cularly in the elegies celebrating his expected military exploits in broader terms. On opposition to James in the 1610s among poets formerly under Henry's patronage, see David Norbrook, *Poetry and Politics in the English Renaissance* (Oxford, 2002), pp. 173–98; Michelle O'Callaghan, *The 'shepheards nation': Jacobean Spenserians and Early Stuart Political Culture, 1612–1625* (Oxford, 2000), pp. 98–113. It has become a historio-graphical commonplace that James and Henry were divided along religious lines, or at least that Henry's Protestantism – which Strong aptly describes as 'a kind of precursor of the Low Church muscular Christianity produced by the Victorian public schools' – was evident in the religious makeup of his house-hold (*Henry, Prince of Wales*, pp. 7–8). If Henry stoked Protestant hopes for a more militant foreign policy, Scott-Warren argues that his circle was as diverse as that surrounding the second Earl of Essex in the 1590s. Neither repudiated 'loyalist Catholics' like the Earl of Worcester, Lord Lumley, and John Davies of Hereford – all members of Henry's circle (*Harington*, p. 213).

70 Badenhausen, for example, claims that James was 'forced … to wage a vigorous campaign to halt the growth of a potentially dangerous myth' (p. 20) and that he sought 'to disarm his son and neutralize … his power' (p. 23): see Richard Badenhausen, 'Disarming the infant warrior: Prince Henry, King James, and the chivalric revival', *Papers on Language and Literature*, 31 (1995), pp. 20–37. Smuts describes Henry reviving Elizabethan chivalry expressly 'to encourage opposition to the pacific policies of his father' ('Political Failure', p. 185).

71 His household and (after 1610) his court 'provided a more or less containable site for dangerously opposi-tional passions, as overlapping loyalties, deferral, and the fact that no heir wants to encourage disobedience in his future subjects kept the oppositional energy surrounding the prince in check', Perry adds (*The Making of Jacobean Culture*, pp. 169, 166, 172).

72 'Peace Greatnesse best becomes: calme power doth guide | With a farre more imperious statelinesse, | Then all the force of violence can doe' (Daniel, *Panegyrike Congratulatorie*, sig. A5r). Francis Bacon praises James as a successor to Elizabeth's peaceful legacy, while emphasizing that her desire for peace did not

preclude the 'honour of war' (*In Felicem Memoriam Elizabethæ, Angliæ Reginæ*, in *The Works of Francis Bacon*, ed. and trans. James Spedding, Robert L. Ellis, and Douglas D. Heath (Boston, 1857–74), XI, pp. 411–61 (pp. 452, 447).

73 James urged Henry to read the books of Kings and Chronicles, 'wherein shall ye see yourself as in a mirror, in the catalogue either of the good or the evil' (cited in Malcolm Smuts, 'The Making of *Rex Pacificus*: James VI and I and the Problem of Peace in an Age of Religious War', in *Royal Subjects: Essays on the Writings of James VI and I*, ed. Daniel Fischlin and Mark Fortier (Detroit, 2002), pp. 371–87; 376). On James as David, Samuel and Solomon, see Linda Levy Peck, 'The mental world of the Jacobean Court: an introduction', in Peck, *The Mental World of the Jacobean Court*, pp. 1–17 (p. 8).

74 James later expressed his surprise at this attribution in *A Meditation vpon the Lords Prayer, Written by the Kings Maiestie, For the benefit of all his subiects, especially of such as follow the Court* (1619): 'I know not by what fortune the *dicton* of PACIFICVS was added to my title, at my comming in England; that of the Lion, expressing true fortitude, hauing been my *dicton* before: but I am not ashamed of this addition; for King *Salomon* was a figure of CHRIST in that, that hee was a King of peace' (sig. G8v; p.93). For the international political atmosphere contributing to James's reputation for pacifism, see Smuts, 'Making of *Rex Pacificus*', pp. 374–75.

75 *Ibid.*, pp. 384, 385.

76 *Basilicon Doron*, p. 33.

77 Alexander, *Parænesis*, sig. B1r.

78 *Ibid.*, sig. C3v.

79 Marcelline, *Triumphs of King Iames*, sig. M2v. The book is a triumphant call to arms for 'the extermination of Antichrists race, by that of *Steuart*' (sig. L2v).

80 *Ibid.*, sigs. L3v–L4r.

81 *Ibid.*, sigs. M2v–M3r. He describes James as holding both a book and a sceptre (sig. E2r). After Henry's death under what some viewed as suspicious circumstances, there was a certain urgency to reinforce James and Henry's mutual love. George Chapman's *An Epicede or Funerall Song: On the most disastrous Death, of the Highborne Prince of Men, Henry Prince of Wales* (1612) describes their bodily conjunction in terms similar to Marcelline's: 'The Humor bred | In one heart, straight was with the other fed; | The bloud of one, the others heart did fire; | The heart and humour, were the Sonne & Sire' (sig. B3r). Henry's dying words to James call him 'Soule to my life, and essence to my Soule' (*Triumphs of King Iames*, sig. D4v).

82 Lennard, *The Mysterie of Iniqvitie*, sig. ¶3r.

83 James, *Basilicon Doron*, p. 46.

84 I am grateful to Malcolm Smuts for this point.

85 Arthur Gorges, *The Olympian Catastrophe*, in *The Poems of Sir Arthur Gorges*, ed. Helen Estabrook Sandison (Oxford: Clarendon Press, 1953), pp. 135–82; 172-73.

86 Osborne, *Traditionall Memoyres* sig. M2r; p. 115. On Henry's presumed circumvention of the civil war, see Wilson, *Prince Henry and English Literature*, p. 174.

3 | *Coryats Crudities* (1611) and Travel Writing as the 'Eyes' of the Prince

Michelle O'Callaghan

'… it may perhaps yeeld some litle encouragement to many noble and generose yong Gallants that follow your Highnesse Court, and giue attendance vpon your Peerelesse person, to trauell into forraine countries, and inrich themselues partly with the obseruations, and partly with the languages of outlandish regions, the principall meanes (in my poore opinion) to grace and adorne those courtly Gentlemen, whose noble parentage, ingenuous education, and virtuous conuersation haue made worthy to be admitted into your Highnesse Court: seeing thereby they will be made fit to doe your Highnesse and their Country the better seruice when opportunity shall require.'

Thomas Coryate, 'Epistle Dedicatorie, *Coryats Crudities* (London, 1611), sig. A4v–5r

When Thomas Coryate commended his travel book, *Coryats Crudities* (1611), to Prince Henry and his court, he took it as given that while the heir to the throne may not venture abroad, the young gentlemen of his court must be encouraged to do so in order the better to serve their prince. Sir Thomas Palmer made a similar point when he dedicated his advice book on travel, *An Essay of the Meanes how to make our Trauailes, into forraine Countries, the more profitable and honourable*, to Henry in 1606. He began with the argument that, although in former ages princes 'vndertook voluntarie trauaile & aduentures into forraine parts', custom now dictated that they are 'restrained of that recreation and renowne'. Instead, they could receive information from the safety of their courts by reading tracts such as Palmer's, and surrounding themselves with gentlemen who had made 'themselues more Compleat in all things' and thus more serviceable to their prince through travel abroad.[1]

Prince Henry attracted a number of dedications of travel books that either, like Palmer, proffered advice on the method or means of travel or set out observations of foreign states. European travel was increasingly an element of elite male education; it provided the opportunity to study foreign languages, statecraft, art and architecture, and to polish manners. As has often been noted, James VI brought with him to the English throne a young family and, most importantly, a male heir to the throne who would one day take his place on the European stage. In order to equip the Prince for this role, the young noblemen of his household needed to be trained in the arts and discipline of travel in order to act as the 'eyes' of the young Prince on their travels abroad.

Prince Henry's court provided a two-fold opportunity for travel writers both to educate the elite in the arts of travel and to offer their own travel observations to the prince. Coryate, like others, justified his travel book in civic humanist terms, extending the rationale of elite travel to the travel writer, who like the courtier could profitably act as the 'eyes' of the Prince, since their 'maine scope' was 'to benefit their country and common-weale'.[2] Coryate ostentatiously presented his 1608 travels through France, Italy, Switzerland, Germany and the Low Countries to Prince Henry and 'those courtly Gentlemen' of his household. He carefully secured Henry's sponsorship of his book before its publication in 1611. The manuscript of his travel journal was personally presented to the prince, accompanied by an oration before an 'assemblie of courtiers'. Once Henry had formally accepted the dedication of the volume, Coryate was able to draw on the Prince's support to ensure his book's smooth passage through the licensing system.[3] Henry's own copy of the *Crudities*, now in the British Library (shelfmark: G 6750), is particularly handsome: bound in crimson velvet and embossed with his arms, the fine engravings by William Hole which illustrate the book, including the elaborate frontispiece, are coloured carefully by hand. Coryate presented this book to Henry at St James's Palace with one of his characteristic bombasted orations, later printed in his *Coryats Crambe* (1611).

The extensive prefatory matter to the *Crudities* goes to great lengths to give the impression that the book issues from Henry's youthful court. Alongside the usual dedicatory epistles from the author is an elaborate compilation of jesting verses and other material, most significantly the mass of parodic, mock 'Panegyricke Verses' contributed by over fifty wits. Coryate describes how he read these playful mock-encomiastic poems to the Prince, who then *'gaue me a strict and expresse commandement to print all those verses'* (sig. c1v). Members of Henry's court feature prominently among the contributors: gentlemen of his privy chamber, such as Sir Robert Phelips (son of Henry's chancellor, Sir Edward Phelips), Sir Robert Yaxley, and John Paulet; tutors and others who held office in his household, including Walter Quin, Henry's music tutor, John Davies of Hereford, the writing-master, and Inigo Jones, his surveyor of works; and those associated with the court from Sir John Harington to the literary men, John Owen, Henry Peacham, Hugh Holland and Michael Drayton. Coryate's own position at Henry's court is unclear. He was awarded a pension of £10, possibly on account of his *Crudities*. The Phelips family were long-standing patrons of Coryate – the late Sir Thomas Phelips had been his godfather, and his son, Sir Edward, had continued to support Coryate. Given that Phelips was the Prince's chancellor, he could have easily assisted Coryate to a place at Henry's court. Office-holding, however, does not appear to have been Coryate's ambition. Rather, he sought his fame through travel; his rush to print his book was fuelled, in part, by his desire to 'goe abroad againe', this time to the Holy Land and the East.[4]

Coryats Crudities can tell us much about the role of travel within elite circles not simply because of its close connections with Henry's court, but also because of the way it responds to the changing character of travel in this period. Travel, particularly in the service of princes, continued to have a political purpose. Robert Dallington, a member of Henry's household, dedicated his observations of France, first compiled in 1598, which included a commentary on the French wars of religion, to the Prince in 1605.[5] Coryate's own observations of Europe, as I will argue in the last section of this essay, similarly fed the Prince's own interests in foreign affairs by providing observations on the religious climate of countries that held Henry's attention in 1611. At the same time, the 'light' matter at the front of Coryate's book seeks to give travel a different kind of purpose at court. The educative role of travel was beginning to incorporate what would later be termed virtuoso interests – training in the observation of art, architecture and antiquities, alongside the conventional courtly skills. Albert Meier's influential travel guide *Certaine Briefe, and Speciall Instructions*, translated into English in the late sixteeenth century, advised the traveller to study closely monuments and other architectural features alongside the structures of state and church.[6] Coryate extends the scope of the humanist travelogue to encompass the careful observation of novelties, antiquities and aspects of architecture. These are the features which are presented to Henry as an aspect of his travel book that is very different to other works in this area, and they offer another mode of seeing and acting as the Prince's eyes. This was a time when Henry was establishing his own collections of art and embarking on building projects. Coryate offered the Prince a book that would serve these aesthetic interests and educate gentlemen of the court in such matters while, at the same time, entertaining them with details of foreign customs and novelties.

Travel and Prince Henry's court

Henry was eager to travel to Europe, although not so much to observe rival princes' courts as to engage in the arts of warfare. As early as 1607 (when Henry was thirteen), Sir Henry Wotton, the ambassador to Venice, informed the Doge of the young prince's desire to help defend Venice against the Pope following the rift with Rome. Again, during the Jülich-Cleves crisis of 1609–10, rumours circulated that Henry intended to head an army in defence of the Protestant states.[7] Such ambitions were prevented by his youth, at least in 1607, and more pertinently by the fears of his father and the Privy Council. Instead, Henry could receive information from the safety of his court by surrounding himself with gentlemen who had made themselves more serviceable to their prince through travel abroad. Many of the young noblemen who joined Henry's household when it was first established in England travelled on the Continent in 1608, the same year that Coryate was himself in Europe. In fact, Coryate just missed his distant kinsman, Robert Devereux, the third Earl of Essex, at an inn in Lyons. Essex had been educated with the Prince, and set off on a European tour in the summer of 1608 – his entourage included Henry's riding master, Monsieur de St Antoine. In this same year Henry's close companion, the young Sir John Harington of Exton, was also sent on a tour which included France, Italy, Germany and the Low Countries. His other young companion, William Cecil, Lord Cranborne, set off on his grand tour just a few days after his marriage in December 1608.[8]

Coryate's emphasis on the courtly aspects of travel in his dedicatory epistle to the prince was therefore timely and nicely judged. It participated in a debate at Henry's court about the value of travel in the education of the nobility.[9] The argument that foreign travel corrupted the young and impressionable was well rehearsed. Even Palmer, who advocated travel for the ruling classes, worried about the vanity of travel for the sake of personal pleasure, particularly given the seductive delights of Italy. Italy may be the 'ancient nurcerie and shop of libertie', but there were 'infinite corruptions, almost ineuitable, that inuest Trauailers after small abode there' (pp. 43–44). One danger that particularly concerned English writers was the vulnerability of the Protestant gentleman abroad to Jesuits and to Rome.[10] Dallington was a tutor in Henry's household, and presumably helped to prepare the Prince's young companions for their travels. In his *A Method for Travell*, he advocated rigorous mental and spiritual training to provide the traveller with the self-discipline necessary to combat the Catholic threat and other corrupting influences.[11] Prince Henry was said to support the foundation of an academy for the education of the nobility at home in England; these academies would prepare young gentlemen for travel so 'they should go with minds better confirmed; with less expence of tyme and mony; and be able to show themselves less ignorant at their coming hither, than now they do; whereby we yield the *French* and other nations an occasion to undervalue us; and therein cause our country to suffer more dishonour than needs'.[12] Throughout the sixteenth century, privy councillors and humanist scholars had discussed the need for a European-style academy for training royal wards and the nobility. James's arrival in England with a young heir requiring education and suitable companions among the English nobility provided the ideal opportunity to create a type of collegiate court along the lines of European academies.[13] Palmer clearly had Henry in mind when he argued that Englishmen had no need to travel to Italy to acquire 'ciuilitie and humanitie', since

> the Court of *England* at this day is the most compleat in all things and vnto all people of other nations & Courts in the world and that which can make men (if they be as studious therin as abroad, to enforme themselues) perfect in ciuility & good manners, & obseruant enough; both for that the puritie of Religion (which is the best Ciuilian) and the long continuance thereof with vs, hath framed our Nobilitie in fashion, and our Prince in State, to recommend the Court of England aboue anie that I could euer heare of.[14]

Coryate weighed into this debate on the side of travel, and turned much of the front matter of his book over to a defence of its civic and civil virtues. Hence, he incorporates a lengthy essay by Hermann Kirchner, a professor at the University of Marburg, in support of the proposition 'That young men ought to Trauell into forraine Countryes' (sig. B1r). Its argument is that travel strengthens and civilizes rather than weakens and corrupts, since those men are 'by the bent of vertue inclined to a good discipline, whose wits the heat of diuers trauels hath ripened, the performance of many iourneys hath mollified, and the knowen manners and discipline of other men haue instructed' (sig. B6v).

Travel for all its dangers was essential to princes' courts. Courts were hubs of information. They were places where men would gather to learn of the latest affairs in England and on the Continent, and to exchange information in order to cement their social position and allegiances with others. Travel was fundamental to these processes of exchange and fed an appetite for foreign news: Coryate said his book would prove 'very delectable to euery Reader that loueth to heare of forraine affairs' (sig. a8r). Those who had recently returned from foreign courts were an essential resource in that they could provide first-hand information about the political situation in Europe, particularly in the unsettled times after the assassination of Henri IV in 1610 when treaties were re-negotiated and marriage alliances between foreign powers were brokered and broken. The soldier serving on foreign soil was recognized as a particular kind of traveller, who was required to 'make diligent and true relation' of military events.[15] Henry patronized a number of military commanders, including Sir Horace Vere and Sir Edward Cecil. Both men had extensive military experience of Continental politics, and were generals in the army of the Netherlands, under the command of Maurits of Nassau. During the Jülich-Cleves crisis in 1610, a conflict which divided Europe along confessional lines and led to the outbreak of the Thirty Years' War, Vere and Cecil acted as Henry's eyes. Cecil provided detailed descriptions of the siege defences of Jülich, while Vere was in regular correspondence with Henry's secretary, Adam Newton, and supplied 'eye-witness accounts' of events in the Rhineland, as well as news of the Prince's future brother-in-law, Frederick, Elector Palatine.[16]

Travel focuses attention on this international dimension of English political and cultural life. The traffic between England and Europe was two-way. Giovanni Botero wrote of princes' courts in his *The Magnificence and Greatness of Cities* that 'all matters of importance have recourse to that place; all Princes and all persons of account, Embassadors of Princes and of common weales, and all Agents of Cities that are subiect, make their repaire thither'.[17] Henry's court attracted foreign visitors, from European princes and their ambassadors to artists and craftsmen. The diverse conversations conducted at his court – military and political, aesthetic and architectural – were predicated on a wide range of travellers and modes of travel. Princes consulted and hoped to attract men of learning to their courts. James I courted the Huguenot man of letters Isaac Casaubon, who had lived in Paris since 1600, where he was employed by his patron, Henri IV, on various projects, including overseeing the royal library. Casaubon finally accepted the invitation of the Archbishop of Canterbury, Richard Bancroft, after

Henri IV's assassination left him without a royal protector, and was received by James at Theobalds soon after his arrival from Paris in October 1610. James quickly put him to work in the pamphlet war he was waging with Jesuit scholars on the Continent.[18] These conversations between princes and men of learning are the point of intersection between the royal court and the humanist Republic of Letters.

Travel and the 'common weale of learning'

Nicolas-Claude Fabri de Peiresc, writing from his estate in Provence in the early seventeenth century, spoke of the Republic of Letters able 'to unite all Mankind, through the whole World, by the Commerce and Correspondence of Letters'.[19] Travel offered something more than this – it made actual rather than virtual dialogue possible, providing the opportunity for face-to-face conversations with men of learning. 'What a singular and incomparable comfort is it to conferre with those learned men in forraine Vniuersities and noble Cities', Coryate declared in his epistle to the reader, 'whose excellent workes we read in our priuate studies at home' (sig. b3r). Peiresc left Provence to travel to England in the summer of 1606, where he met his Huguenot friends and correspondents who were now living in London.[20] Travel guides, such as Meier's *Certain briefe, and speciall instructions*, advised the traveller to search out learned men in foreign cities, particularly 'Antiquaries, that is men excellently seene in antiquities and ancient monuments'.[21] Travel-writing is a literary form that has 'commerce and correspondence' at its centre. It sets out and participates in a range of conversations – the benefits of travel, the nature of the ideal polity – and contributes to the flow of information, providing the reader with details of the social, political, and ecclesiastical government, the art and architecture, and local customs of foreign countries. As such, travel writing dedicated to Henry presents itself as the eyes and ears of the prince and his court, providing privileged access to memorable sights, news at courts, and the conversations of learned men.

In *Coryats Crudities* we can overhear the conversations about politics, art and architecture that engaged Henry's court around the time of its publication in 1611. Andrew Hadfield has argued that the political heart of the *Crudities* lies in its section on Venice, which Coryate marks out for Henry's particular attention in his dedicatory epistle (sig. a5r). Coryate compares his own observations with Gaspar Contarini's *De magistratibus et republica Venetorum* (1543), and refers the reader to the English translation of this work (sig. a6r-v). This is Sir Lewis Lewkenor's *The Commonwealth and Government of Venice* (1599) – Lewkenor's mock-encomiastic verses on Coryate follow on from those of Sir John Harington of Kelston, another admirer of Venice, in the 'Panegyricke Verses'. Coryate's account of Venice participates in a broader political conversation about the virtues of the Venetian republic at Henry's court.[22] Yet, as he says, his book is different. If the 'iudicious Reader' wants to 'instruct himself with the forme of the Venetian gouernment', then he'd best go to either Contarini or Lewkenor's translation. What

Coryate's book offers is a detailed study of 'the antiquities and monuments of that famous Citie, together with the description of Palaces, Churches, the Piazza of S. Marke' (sig. a6r). There is an avowed admiration for Venice as an independent city-state in the *Crudities*, and it is expressed primarily through architectural description and not through a discourse on statecraft.

The manifold civic splendours of Venice that are etched into its architecture and on display in its museums and galleries arose out of the mercantile and naval supremacy of this republic. Coryate's enthusiastic observations of the great arsenal in Venice extend over five pages: he relates in admiring detail the shipyards and the armoury (even giving a summary of the pension system), describes rope-making, and finally the great Venetian ships, including the *Bucintoro* – a 'worke so exceeding glorious, that I neuer heard or read of the like in any place of the world' (p. 218). Venice has survived the onslaughts of the papal 'Imperialists' and the Turks because of the might of its arsenal (p. 221). Behind Coryate's account lies the classical humanist and republican tenet that the wealth and strength of the commonwealth resides in its ability to command the sea.[23] His observations are clearly written with Prince Henry in mind – he interrupts his description of the *Bucintoro* to give the assurance that Henry's brand-new *Prince Royal*, which had been launched in September 1610, surpasses not only the finest Venetian ships but 'any ship else (I beleeue) in Christendome' (p. 219). Roy Strong speaks of the navy as 'a major obsession' of the Prince, in 1611 was overseeing the proposed rebuilding of the fleet. Sir Walter Raleigh produced a pamphlet for Henry that went through the various aspects of naval reform, from the building of ships to where to put the kitchen. He countered arguments that such reforms were unnecessary given the treaty with Spain, pointing out that peace must not be simply passively enjoyed but actively maintained, the 'means of our defence and safety being shipping and sea-forces'.[24] Like his mentor, Henry was convinced by the argument that dominion over the sea was the primary means of ensuring peace and prosperity and combating the imperialist designs of Spain in Europe and the New World.[25]

Coryate sees the Venetian Republic, with its history of resistance to Rome, as an ally of a renewed Protestant league. He devotes a lengthy passage to the Protestant zeal of its resident English ambassador, Sir Henry Wotton, whose chaplain, William Bedel, was conducting Anglican services at his house, 'which I thinke was neuer before permitted in Venice', and would soon 'draw diuers of the famous Papists of the City to the true reformed religion' (pp. 240–41). Wotton was taking advantage of the current conflict between Venice and Pope Paul V, who had placed the city under an interdict in 1606.[26] Coryate sees other evidence of Venice's Protestant sympathies marked out on the cityscape. He recalls seeing a painting of James I 'very gallantly aduanced … at the Rialto bridge, with Queene *Anne* and Prince *Henry* on one side of him, and the King of France [Henri IV] on the other; a thing that ministred singular contentment vnto me' (p. 289). Henri IV had commanded the Huguenot armies during the French civil wars. Although he converted to Catholicism in 1593 in order to accede to the French crown, he remained hostile to Spain and sympathetic to Huguenots, securing the Edict of Nantes in 1598 which gave some protection to Protestants.[27] These political ideals inform Coryate's architectural descriptions of other cities on his travels. Observations of major cities include a great deal of detail about military architecture, accompanied by relevant and often recent memorable histories. The great citadel at Milan, for example, is described in extensive detail, including the strength of its structure, depth of foundations, materials used in its construction, the incorporation of a mill for grinding gun-powder, the size of the storehouse, the extent of the arsenal, and number of soldiers (pp. 102–05). Again the citadel stands as testimony to the tyrannical hold of Spain over a resistant Europe, with Coryate repeatedly relating incidents that bear witness to the 'extreme hatred betwixt the Milanois and the Spaniards' (p. 105), the occupying power in the region.

There is a parallel architectural conversation taking place in the pages devoted to Venice. Coryate had carried with him a jesting letter of introduction from Richard Martin to his old friend, Wotton, who was one of the foremost English authorities on art and architecture, and in regular correspondence with Prince Henry. Coryate cultivated links with Wotton's secretariat in Venice – he formed a close friendship with George Rooke, who introduced him to his circle in Venice, and accompanied him to Padua (p. 128). Wotton showed Coryate the architectural sights of the city, on one occasion directing him 'to take speciall obseruation' of figures decorating the wall of the Ducal palace (p. 190). Coryate's deftness in artlessly conveying the comic aspect of many of his adventures means that his precise attention to architectural and topographical detail is often overlooked. Hence, critics frequently recall Coryate's jocoserious encounter with the rabbi or his visit to the Venetian courtesan, but pay less attention to his other observations which, as Edward Chaney points out, 'contain some of the best early descriptions of architecture in the English language'.[28] We do need to take Coryate at his word when he says that the truly distinctive feature of his observations is the detailed attention to antiquities and architecture. One could surmise that the conversations between Wotton and Coryate, as Wotton showed him the memorable sights of the city from his gondola, provided Coryate with a valuable lesson in architecture, enhancing his already keen interest in this area. Chaney suggests that it was Wotton who inspired Coryate 'to describe Palladio's buildings with unprecedented thoroughness'. The great English Renaissance architect, Inigo Jones, Henry's surveyor of works, also placed a mock-encomiastic verse before the *Crudities* and, as we shall see, was part of a convivial society that included Coryate. Wotton and Jones also corresponded on architectural matters. Jones was to set out on his own tour of Italy in 1613 in the entourage of Thomas Howard, Earl of Arundel, and spent his time studying Italian architecture.[29]

Coryate's architectural descriptions can thus be seen as part of a wider dialogue on matters of art and architecture between men, such as Wotton and Jones, and their patrons – the Earl of Arundel, Robert Cecil, Earl of Salisbury and Prince Henry.[30] Coryate draws his own 'Mecoenas' (and Prince Henry's chancellor), Sir Edward Phelips, into the conversation. He compares the paving of St Mark's Square in Venice with that in the hall of Phelips's country house, Montacute, remarking that the latter is superior because it is 'paued … with diamond pauier made out of free stone', also typical of other 'halles of some of our great Gentlemen in England' (p. 175). Such comparisons of architectural detail are not unusual in the *Crudities*. Elsewhere, he compares water features in gardens in Verona to those in Sir Francis Carew's gardens in Beddington, Middlesex.[31] Henry was also busy with building projects and so eager for news of the best examples of foreign architecture. In 1611 he was discussing plans for his palace at Richmond with the Florentine architect Constantino de' Servi. Henry employed the Huguenot hydraulic engineer and garden designer Salomon de Caus at Richmond, who had served as his architect since the creation of his household in 1610.[32] Coryate devotes a lengthy section to Fontainebleau, Henri IV's recently completed royal showcase, presumably of especial interest to Henry at a time when he was designing his own royal palace. Attention is devoted to objects and ornamental detail as Coryate walks about recording precisely what he sees in the gardens and courts of Fontainebleau: statues, iron railings, fountains and other water features, especially the decorative details, the workmanship of the garden, and the King's collection of exotic birds, which included storks and ostriches (pp. 38–42). He is writing for an audience with a very practical interest in garden design and building works and one which, like the Prince, was employing methods and craftsmen from Europe in the construction of their own great houses.

Coryats Crudities draws attention to the way that travel and travel writing increasingly concerned itself with 'virtuoso' interests that combined pleasure and recreation with learning and profit, and concentrated its attentions on art, antiquities, architecture and other rarities. Ambassadors, like Wotton in Venice and William Trumbull in Brussels, not only kept Prince Henry and other patrons informed of political wranglings but also acted as art agents, seeking out paintings, sculptures and other curiosities for their clients at home. John Finet wrote to Trumbull in early 1612 about an 'Italian gentleman' who wanted to sell his perspective glasses to the Prince.[33] The *Crudities* is a pivotal travel book in that it records the transition from what Coryate called 'statist' discourses and practices of travel, which emphasized the political education of the nobility at princes' courts, to virtuoso travel, which directed the reader's attention to the aesthetic pleasures to be derived from seeing and studying the architectural and artistic splendours of European cities.[34]

Seeing France, 1608–1611

To find contemporary politics writ large on the topography of Europe in *Coryats Crudities* we need to shift our attention from Venice and turn to the start of Coryate's travels, to France. England shared with its closest neighbour a long history of allegiances, conquest and migration. When Coryate landed in Calais he immediately set about marking out the Anglo-French history of the region in his observations of its architecture and topography, identifying

English landmarks in order to define France's political topography and make it comprehensible to an English audience. He describes the tomb of an English gentlewoman in a church in Calais, recalls the story behind the naming of the town's fortress 'Ricebank' around 1540 – 'Calais being in the hands of the English' (pp. 4–5) – and the fortified wall built around Boulogne 'which was made by our English men, after they had conquered the same, but whether in the time of *Edward* the third or *Henry* the eight I know not' (pp. 7–8). For the English, as Richard Hillman argues, France was 'simultaneously strange and familiar, foreign and domestic, hostile and hospitable, an ambiguous middle ground – and newly so in religious terms, insofar as it buffered England, precariously and contingently, against Europe's unequivocally Catholic South'. From the brutal civil wars which began in the 1560s – and took on horrible proportions with the St Bartholomew's Day massacre of Huguenots in 1572 – to the assassination of Henri IV in 1610, Anglo-French relations loomed large on the English political stage.[35]

The period between Coryate's travels in France in 1608 and the publication of the *Crudities* in 1611 was a critical time in Anglo-French politics. In 1608 when Coryate crossed the Channel to Calais the situation of the Huguenots in France was uncertain. Elizabeth's government had supported the Huguenots militarily and financially from the first of the French religious wars in 1562. The Huguenot cause at court was helped by the close friendship between Robert Devereux, Earl of Essex, and the leading Protestant nobleman, the duc de Bouillon. When Bouillon fled France in 1602 after he was charged with complicity in the conspiracy of the duc de Biron, Elizabeth continued to give him her support. On his accession, James broke ties with Bouillon. Rather than seeking military alliances with Huguenots, his policy to keep some type of balance of power in the region was to exploit the hostilities between Spain and France. The situation changed again in 1610. Bouillon was restored to Henri IV's favour, and his old friend, Sir Thomas Edmondes, the ambassador in Paris from May 1610, lobbied effectively for closer relations with Huguenots at the English court, finding an eager ally in Prince Henry.[36]

The mutual admiration between Henri IV and Prince Henry is well known. Henri IV, as Strong argues, 'deliberately cultivated the Prince from a very early age'; Henry, in turn, publicly adopted Henri IV, the warrior king, as his princely *exemplum*.[37] The assassination of Henri IV in May 1610 was thought by Protestants to be part of a wider Catholic conspiracy and sparked fears of a revived Catholic League that would quickly move to persecute French Protestants. The Huguenot Jean Loiseau de Tourval, who had been living in London since the accession of James I, described those 'black soules' behind the assassination as the 'infamous remnants of the League, infernal matches of our ciuill fires' in a pamphlet addressed to Prince Henry.[38] Attention turned to Henry to take on his royal namesake's mantle, and negotiations began in 1611 for a Protestant marriage alliance between his sister, Princess Elizabeth, and Elector Palatine Frederick V.[39]

Jean Loiseau de Tourval placed a French mock-encomiastic poem before the *Crudities*. His involvement with the volume draws Coryate into the ambit of the Huguenot community in London and Paris and foregrounds the points of 'Commerce and Correspondence', in the words of Peiresc, between English and French Protestants. It also suggests that Coryate's observations of France are a strategic intervention in the political conversations between Huguenots and their English sympathizers. Born in Paris of an English mother, Tourval sought to fashion an Anglo-French identity through his translations and his religion. He speaks of applying 'my selfe, my studies, my life, and best endeuours to the seruice and benefit … of this noble Kingdom, my second and substitute *Country*' to the extent that 'growne by habitude to such a poynt of bewitching, as euen I content my selfe to forbeare my right *Countrie* and *Kindred*'.[40] He was employed by James I as one of his agents: he carried letters from Paris for the king, translated James's *Apologie for the Oath of Allegiance* into French in 1609, and supervised its printing in Paris. Tourval lodged with Raphael Thorius in 1606, a close friend of Isaac Casaubon and Peiresc. When these men visited Thorius in the early seventeenth century, Tourval took part in their circle. He continued corresponding and exchanging books and other material with Peiresc when he returned to Provence.[41] Coryate had visited Casaubon in Paris in 1608. Once Casaubon arrived in England in late 1610, Coryate 'had the happinesse to enioy his desiderable commerce' (p. 32) on at least one occasion, and therefore had the opportunity to meet other Huguenots at his lodgings, including Casaubon's old friend, Tourval. It is more than likely that these conversations included discussion of the current state of France, particularly since Casaubon had just left Paris at a time when fears of renewed persecution of Huguenots were running high following the assassination of Henri IV.

In 1611, the same year that he took part in the literary gathering of wits before the *Crudities*, Tourval wrote to Henry of his 'most speciall and holy zeale to your Princely seruice', possibly offering to act for Henry as translator and agent in Paris as he had done for his father. As early as 1608 he had translated a work by Henry's chaplain, Joseph Hall, into English. However, although Tourval says that he has aspired to serve Henry since his arrival in England in 1603, he also admits that this has yet to be realised.[42] There was a substantial Huguenot presence at Henry's court, including the architect Salomon de Caus and the miniaturist Isaac Oliver. Tourval's association with the *Crudities* seems to be part of a campaign to bring himself to the attention of the Prince, whom he clearly saw quickly maturing into a key player in European politics. He appears to have been successful, as his name appears in a 1612 list of the Prince's pensioners, receiving £20.[43] Tourval encouraged Henry to embrace the role of general of the Protestant forces in Europe and avenge the murder of Henri IV in his *The French herald summoning all true Christian princes to a generall croisade, for a holy warr against the the great enemy of Christendome, and all his slaues*. This tract was a rallying cry for holy war against the Jesuits and Spain, the king-killers and 'rauenous Wolues' that he believed, along with many Protestants, were behind Henri's assassination. Dallington's earlier *View of Fraunce* had argued that the civil wars were the direct result of Spain's imperial ambitions and waged by its agents amongst the French nobility and clergy: 'Traitors falsly hearted, or Frenchmen truly Spaniolized, complotted how to bring in their Patron & Benefactor the King of Spaine' (sig. F2r). It was a political reading still current at Henry's court in the early 1610s, and implicitly advocated strong royal leadership in order to advance the cause of international Protestantism against Spain and the Jesuits. Tourval called on Prince Henry to head 'our Christian Army' whose ultimate aim was not simply to curtail the ambitions of Spain and to rid Europe of the Jesuits, but to renew the energies of the Reformation and to reform Rome itself, thus putting an end to religious conflicts between Huguenots and 'Leaguers'.[44]

The observations of France in the *Crudities* took part in these political conversations that engaged Henry's court in 1610/11. They were part of a wider political dialogue that was taking place not only at court but across London – in Huguenot circles, the diplomatic secretariats, and the London taverns. Coryate frequented meetings of a convivial society, the Sirenaical fraternity which met the first Friday of the month at the Mermaid tavern on Bread Street in the first decades of the seventeenth century.[45] A number of these convivial wits contributed to the 'Panegyricke Verses' – John Donne, Lawrence Whitaker (secretary to Sir Edward Phelips), Sir Robert Phelips, Lionel Cranfield, Inigo Jones, Hugh Holland, and the lawyers Richard Martin, John Hoskyns and Christopher Brooke. There are clear associations between this tavern society and Henry's court. The pivotal figure is Sir Edward Phelips, senior member of the Middle Temple, Speaker in the House of Commons, and chancellor to Prince Henry.[46] Phelips thus acted as the point of contact between Henry's court and the London tavern companies, which, in turn, were closely connected to Inns of Court circles and the secretariats of official households. Brooke's brother, Samuel, was Henry's chaplain, Inigo Jones, as we have seen, his surveyor of works, and Sir Robert Phelips, a gentleman of the Privy Chamber, while Richard Connock, who is listed among those present at the merry banquet at the Mitre tavern, sat on Henry's Council of Revenue alongside Sir Edward Phelips.[47] I want to look to one side of this group, to John Sandford, who took the pseudonym 'Glareanus Vadianus' in the 'Panegyricke Verses' before the *Crudities*.[48] Sandford contributes six macaronic and nonsense poems in Latin, Greek, French, Italian, Spanish and English (sig. g6v-h3r). His presence among the wits gathered at the front of the *Crudities* takes us once more to the Mermaid tavern, and provides a link between the Sirenaics, Henry's court and the secretariat of Thomas Edmondes, a crucial figure in Anglo-French diplomacy in this period.

Jean Beaulieu, the Huguenot secretary to Edmondes, wrote to his friend and fellow secretary, William Trumbull, in November 1609: 'Yesterday all the "holy crew" together with Mr. Monger, Mr. Calvert and us three champions of this house had a meeting at the '*Mayre Made*' in Bread Street to celebrate your health'.[49] Edmondes, together with his household, had returned to London in autumn 1609 in the hope of securing the office of ambassador to the court of Henri IV – he did not leave London to take up this post until April 1610. Mr Calvert was

presumably Samuel Calvert, clerk of the Virginia Company; his brother, George, was the secretary to Salisbury. James or Jacques Monger was a London merchant, possibly a Huguenot or
Walloon, who acted as agent for Edmondes and Trumbull, providing bills of exchange, ex-
porting goods, and passing on news to Trumbull in Brussels.[50] One of the other three champions of this house was almost certainly John Sandford, who had been Edmondes's merry
chaplain at Brussels. Sandford had returned with him to London, and stayed in his household
until Edmondes left for Paris. The company at Brussels, or this 'knavish crew' as Beaulieu once
laughingly described them, adopted jesting pseudonyms – Sandford at one time seems to have
taken the name 'Prester John'.[51] There were close contacts between the households of
Edmondes and Prince Henry. Trumbull, as we have seen, acted at an agent for Henry, and he
had other contacts at Henry's court, including the brother of a member of his own
household.[52] This web of interconnections functioned as a vector for commerce and correspondence not only within London, between royal and diplomatic households and other
circles, such as the tavern societies, but also between England and Europe. Jacques Monger,
for example, regularly passed news, along with money and household goods, between
London and Trumbull's household in Brussels.

Evidence would suggest that Coryate and the Sirenaics were holding convivial meetings at
the Mermaid at the same time as the 'Holy Crew', the company affiliated with Edmondes's
household. Sandford's involvement with the *Crudities* provides further evidence for the links
between Coryate and his tavern associates and the 'Holy Crew'. In February 1612, three years
after this Mermaid meeting at which he had been present, Samuel Calvert sent a letter to
Trumbull containing 'a Banquet of the Wits by Hoskins of the Temple'. This was a copy of the
'Convivium Philosophicum', a Latin poem supposedly celebrating a banquet held at the Mitre
tavern in 1611 which was attended by a number of Sirenaics including Coryate.[53] The satiric
table talk at this gathering turned to Prince Henry, who was said to be frustrated by his inability to prove himself on the battlefield: '*Princeps nescit otiari,/ Cupiens materiam dari/ Propriae virtuti*'
('Prince Henry cannot idly liuen,/Desiringe matter to be giuen/To prove his valour good').[54]
The talk in London in 1611 was of how Henry could 'prove his valour good'.

Coryate travelled through France two years before Henri IV's assassination in May 1610,
leaving England in May 1608. But his observations were clearly compiled in the shadow of this
event, as his remembrance prompted by a painting at Fontainebleau suggests, '*Henry* the 4.
King of France and Nauarre, lately slaine by that butcherly *Rauilliacke*' (p. 20). Throughout his
observations of France, Coryate was careful to draw attention to the marks the religious wars
of the preceding century had left on the French landscape. In doing so, he reads and writes
French topography with a historical sensibility, endowing natural features and architecture
with political memories. The memorable histories that he relates in his observations of France
are predominantly those of the civil wars which raged in France from the 1560s to 1598. At
Calais, he recalls the recent civil wars of 1596, when the Spanish took control of the town

under Archduke Albert, and the forces of Henri of Navarre failed to regain it until peace was concluded in 1598 (pp. 5–6). In Amiens, he gives the recent history of the town during the wars that began in 1597 when the Spanish took the city – this history ends with Henri's routing of the Spanish.

Fynes Moryson had travelled through France in May 1595, soon after Henri IV had been anointed King and had entered Paris. Moryson observed a landscape still ravaged by the wars. His experience of travel is shaped by profound and justifiable anxieties. Constantly warned of the threat from soldiers returning home, who would murder travellers for their goods, he changes his identity, disguising himself 'in poore apparrell', and later passes himself off as the servant of a Dutch merchant – he is not successful in this instance, and falls prey to a band of soldiers on the way to Paris. His travels are punctuated by 'the cries of the Country people, driving their cattell to fortified places' to escape the 'scattered troopes of Soldiers'. The landscape of the province of Champaigne is deserted; fertile fields 'now in the time of Civill warres, … lay unploughed, and the Husbandmens houses were fallen to the ground', the sole inhabitant is an old woman who refused the travellers hospitality.[55] Moryson, not surprisingly, did not linger; in all, he spent less than a fortnight moving through France.

Coryate arrived in France thirteen years after Moryson, and a decade after the end of the civil wars. Yet the way that he sees the topography of France often echoes Moryson's sense of horror at the destruction. Like Moryson before him, he admires the fertility of French soil, its 'faire meadows, and fruitfull corne fields' (p. 10). These fertile fields make a poignant counterpoint to images of a land ravaged by religious wars. Around Boulogne, Coryate sees the ruins of churches and monasteries (pp. 7, 9); later journeying from Amiens towards Paris, he observes 'a village exceedingly ransacked, and ruinated, by meanes of the ciuill warres' (p. 18). Coryate no doubt did see ruins; yet by turning these ruins into landmarks he was giving the geography of France specific ideological contours. One effect of these tragic landmarks is to dispel the sense that he is writing from a '"safe" distance'.[56] The wars of religion are not a distant memory but still present in the political landscape he travels through. His observations are part of a politicized process of remembering and memorializing that seeks to validate the place of the Huguenots in French history and enshrine their history in the very landscape of France in a way that challenges the sovereignty of the Catholic majority. Just outside Paris, he comes across a memorialized landscape marked by 'seuen faire pillars of free stone erected by an equall distance from each other' (p. 19–20), symbolizing a miracle said have occurred during the martyrdom of St Denis – a 'miracle too great to be true', the Protestant Coryate ruefully observes. This discredited Catholic memorial is displaced in the landscape by an alternative Protestant memorial, this time to a Huguenot martyr:

> A little on this side Paris, euen at the towns end, there is the fayrest Gallowes
> that I euer saw, built vpon a little hillocke called Mount Falcon, which consis-

teth of fourteene faire pillars of free-stone: this gallowes was made in the time
of the Guisian massacre, to hang the Admirall of France *Chatillon*, who was a
Protestant, *Anno Dom.* 1572' (p. 20).

The foundations of these 'faire pillars' which mark the murder of the Huguenot hero,
Châtillon, unlike those memorializing St Denis, are said to be firmly historical rather than re-
liant on a dubious Catholic miracle.

Yet history is being rewritten and re-imagined in mythic terms in this passage. In fact, the
gallows not only long pre-dated the murder of Châtillon during the St Bartholomew's Day
massacre, but he was not executed at this site; instead he was murdered in the Louvre – the remains of his body after being dragged through the Paris streets for three days were then hung
at Mont Faucon.[57] The reader sees this Protestant monument at a key moment in the narrative, just at the point when Coryate records his approach to Paris, the primary scene of the
massacre – Coryate calls it the 'Guisan massacre' after the duc de Guise, the leader of the
Catholic League. Soon after observing the castle of the duc de Guise in Lorraine, Coryate had
seen another set of gallows and 'a very dolefull and lamentable spectacle: the bones and
ragged fragments of clothes of a certaine murderer remaining on a wheele … the bones were
miserably broken asunder, and dispersed abroad vpon the wheele in diuers places' (p. 48). The
sight of gallows in France frequently attracts Coryate's attention. His pity seems to be aroused
in this instance by the traces of extreme violence, of bodies torn apart and dispersed, exemplifying state cruelty not bound by the limits of compassion and mercy. In Paris, religious difference increasingly determines Coryate's experience of social space and his sense of the
humanist community. He observes the Corpus Christi procession 'perambulating about some
of the principall streets of Paris', before which 'all the spectators prostrated themselues most
humbly vpon their knees'. The account gives a very clear sense that such a performance is
compelling not in itself – it is not comprehended in terms of a notion of religious awe – but
because of the absolute power it embodies, which requires the submission of both mind and
body. This prompts Coryate to speculate on the fate of those who would resist the spectacle,
according to their conscience: 'If any Godly Protesta[n]t that hateth this superstition, should
happen to be amongst them when they kneele, and forbeare to worship the Sacrament as they
doe, perhaps he may be presently stabbed or otherwise most shamefully abused' (p. 29).
Memorable spectacles within Paris are infused with images of religious persecution. Coryate is
moved by a 'spectacle very pittifull' during this procession of shaven-headed 'prety innocents
punies … so egregiously deformed by those that had authority ouer them' (p. 28). The intense
pathos of this scene recalls the image of the murdered innocent that had figured prominently
in representations of the horrors of the St Bartholomew massacre.

In Paris, within a cityscape viewed through the lens of violent religious persecution,
Coryate sought out the company of fellow Protestants. The internationalist ideal of the

commonwealth of learning structures much of the *Crudities*. And it takes on a distinctly Protestant aspect in Paris. After mocking 'the truth and certainty of Papasticall reliques', Coryate immediately proposed an alternative community of knowledge which functions to bear witness to papist tyranny. He recalled his stay at the house of Monsieur de la Roy, a 'French Protestant in the suburbs of St Germans, who in the ciuill warres fought against the Papists, and was most grieuously wounded, who shewed me his wounds' – the witnessing of these Protestant wounds subtly imitates those of Christ, and sets up an alternative martyrological repertoire to Catholic reliques. Coryate then recalled his joy at 'the sight and company of that rare ornament of learning *Isaac Causabonus*, with whom I had much familiar conuersation at his house, neare vnto St. Germans gate within the citie', and provides a brief catalogue of Casaubon's library, 'set forth, to the great benefite and vtility of the Common-weale of learning'. Coryate takes it upon himself to publish Casaubon's plea for a hagiography of Elizabeth I to stand 'as a liuely patterne for other Christian Princes', and more particularly to boost the morale of England's Protestant allies (pp. 31–33).

Coryate's observations of Paris, like the Huguenot tracts dedicated to the Prince, were designed to rally royal support for the Huguenots. The Parisian Huguenots are imagined as an embattled, yet triumphant 'Common-weale of learning', whose vulnerability is emphasized through their location within a cityscape structured by spectacles of ongoing religious persecution. The vigorous and vigilant Protestant gaze that comes to the fore in Coryate's account of Paris is not his usual mode of observation in the *Crudities*. Arguably it is triggered in this instance by the crisis in France in the immediate aftermath of the assassination of Henri IV. It is the case that Coryate's observations of France do not directly dabble in 'matters of policie', and instead are in keeping with the impressions of a 'priuate man' (sig. b5v). At the same time, his perspective as he travels through France, acting as the eyes of the Prince, is not neutral, rather memorable spectacles and histories are carefully selected and presented in order to excite the attention of a politicized readership intensely concerned with the plight of Protestants in France.

Travel was a vital mode of commerce and correspondence between England and Europe. Travellers abroad, whether diplomatic, military or private, like Coryate, provided Prince Henry, confined to the safety of England, with often eyewitness accounts of the unfolding events in places that held Henry's interest, such as Venice, France, and the Low Countries. That said, travellers and the travel book increasingly supplied other kinds of information and other modes of visual experience, including the skilled observation of art, architecture and antiquities. *Coryats Crudities* is remarkable for the way that it incorporates and frequently combines these variant modes of observation and thus provides us with an excellent guide to the way travel writing acted as the eyes of the Prince.

NOTES

1 Sir Thomas Palmer, *An Essay of the Meanes how to make our Trauailes, into forraine Countries, the more profitable and honourable* (London, 1606; Amsterdam, 1972), sig. A2r–v. Palmer's son, Roger, was Henry's cupbearer. I am indebted to Tim Wilks for this information.

2 Thomas Coryate, 'The Epistle to the Reader', *Coryats Crudities* (1611), intro. William M. Schutte (London, 1978), sig. b5r. All other references to this work will be provided in parentheses in the main text. I use 'Coryate' rather than 'Coryat' following the spelling given in his entry in the *ODNB*.

3 See the letter to Sir Michael Hicks, secretary to the Lord Treasurer, William Cecil, Earl of Salisbury, pasted into the back cover of Prince Henry's copy of *Coryats Crudities* (British Library, G 6750); see 'A Petition made to the Prince shortly after the death of the last Archbishop of Canterburie, concerning the printing of the Booke of my travels', *Coryats Crambe, or His Colwort twise Sodden, and now serued in with other Macaronicke dishes, as the second course to his Crudities* (London, 1611), sig. A1r–v.

4 See his letter to Hicks, *Coryats Crudities*, BL G 6750.

5 Dallington's *View of France* was first published in 1604, and republished a year later in his *A Method for Travell* (London, 1605). His *Survey of the Great Dukes State of Tuscany* was also published in 1605 by the publisher Edward Blount. Although it was not dedicated to Henry, it was presumably known and read at his court. On this text, see Edward Chaney, *The Evolution of the Grand Tour: Anglo-Italian Cultural Relations since the Renaissance* (2nd edn; London, 2000), chapter 5.

6 On Coryate's place in the development of the virtuoso traveller, see Randall L-W. Caudill, 'Some Literary Evidence of the Development of English Virtuoso Interests in the Seventeenth Century, with particular reference to the literature of travel', unpublished D. Phil thesis, Oxford (1976), pp. 115–16; Albert Meier, *Certain briefe, and speciall instructions for gentlemen, merchants, students, souldiers, marriners, &c. employed in services abrode*, trans. Philip Jones (London, 1589), pp. 17–18.

7 Roy Strong, *Henry Prince of Wales and England's Lost Renaissance* (London, 1986), p. 75; David Norbrook, '"The Masque of Truth": Court Entertainments and International Protestant Politics in the Early Stuart Period', *The Seventeenth Century*, 1 (1986), pp. 89–90.

8 Coryate claimed to be Essex's fourth cousin, *Coryats Crudities*, pp. 64, 239. Strong, *Henry, Prince of Wales*, pp. 42–43.

9 T.V. Wilks, 'The Court Culture of Prince Henry and his Circle, 1603–1613', 2 vols., unpublished D. Phil. thesis, Oxford (1987), I, p. 56.

10 Sara Warneke, *Images of the Educational Traveller in Early Modern England* (Leiden, 1995), pp. 174–79.

11 Robert Dallington, *A Method for Travell* (London, 1605), sig. B1r.

12 Sir Balthazar Gerbier, 'Project for an Academy Royal in England', in *Collectanea Curiosa*, ed. John Gutch, 2 vols. (Oxford, 1781), I, p. 213.

13 Wilks, 'Court Culture of Prince Henry', p. 56.

14 Palmer, *An Essay of the Meanes*, p. 43.

15 Palmer, *An Essay of the Meanes*, see the table on p. 1.

16 Strong, *Henry Prince of Wales*, pp. 46–47; D.J.B. Trim, 'Sir Horace Vere in Holland and the Rhineland, 1610–12', *Journal of Historical Research*, 72 (1999), pp. 336–37, 344–46, 350.

17 Giovanni Botero, *The Magnificence and Greatness of Cities*, trans. Robert Peterson (London, 1606; Amsterdam, 1979), p. 65.

18 E.J. Lefroy, 'Isaac Casaubon, 1559–1614', *Proceedings of the Huguenot Society of London*, 20:6 (1964), pp. 593–97.

19 Cited in Peter N. Miller, *Peiresc's Europe: Learning and Virtue in the Seventeenth Century* (New Haven and London, 2000), p. 2.

20 Alison Clarke, 'Jean Loiseau de Tourval: a Huguenot translator in England, 1603–31', *Proceedings of the Huguenot Society of London*, 20, 1 (1958), pp. 37–38.

21 Meier, *Certain briefe, and speciall instructions*, pp. 17–18

22 Hadfield, *English Travellers in Europe*, pp. 66–67.

23 Markku Peltonen, *Classical Humanism and Republicanism in English Political Thought, 1570–1640* (Cambridge, 1995), pp. 206–07.

24 Walter Raleigh, 'Observations Concerning the Royal Navy and Sea-Service'; see also his essay 'A Discourse of the Invention of Ships, Anchors, Compass, &c … ', which includes a study of the importance of commanding 'the sea, and thereby the trade of the world itself', *The Works of Sir Walter Ralegh, Kt.*, ed. Thomas Birch and William Oldys, 8 vols. (Oxford, 1829), VIII, pp. 350, 331.

25 Strong, *Henry Prince of Wales*, pp. 57–60.

26 Strong, *Henry Prince of Wales*, p. 77.

27 Robin Gwynn, *Huguenot Heritage: The history and contribution of the Huguenots in Britain*, 2nd rev. edn (Brighton, 2001), pp. 21–23.

28 Chaney, *Evolution of the Grand Tour*, pp. 13, 171. Barbour, in his brilliant study of Coryate and the 'Invention of Tourism', is the most recent critic to see the 'ocular' dimension of Coryate's observations encapsulated by his encounter with Margarita Emiliana, the Venetian courtesan: *Before Orientalism*, pp. 126–30.

29 Chaney, *Evolution of the Grand Tour*, p. 171.

30 Chaney points to the significance of Jones's friendship with Coryate: 'The publication in 1611 of Coryate's accounts of these and other Palladian buildings, including the Villa Capra, was still more significant, as it must have encouraged his friend Inigo Jones to visit them – Palladio's *Quattro libri* in hand – two years later' (*Evolution of the Grand Tour*, p. 208).

31 See *Crudities*, pp. 316, 329. On Carew's garden, see Roy Strong, 'Sir Francis Carew's Garden at Beddington', in *England and the Continental Renaissance. Essays in Honour of J. B. Trapp*, ed. Edward Chaney and Peter Mack (Woodbridge, 1990), pp. 229–38. De Tourval had described this garden in 1603 as '*le plus curieux de toute l'angleterre*': Clarke, 'Jean Loiseau deTourval', p. 57.

32 Strong, *Henry Prince of Wales*, pp. 88–110.

33 *Historical Manuscripts Commission: Report on the Manuscripts of the Marquess of Downshire*, Papers of William Trumbull the Elder (London, 1936–38), III, p. 238; Trumbull may have also been attempting to interest the Prince in a 'witty and worthy invention' for cataloguing a cabinet of curiosities (p. 239).

34 Randall Caudill points out that 'Coryat displayed virtuoso tendencies before the heyday of virtuosity', in 'Some Literary Evidence of the Development of English Virtuoso Interests in the Seventeenth Century, with particular reference to the literature of travel', unpublished D.Phil thesis, Oxford (1976), p. 116.

35 Richard Hillman, *Shakespeare, Marlowe and the Politics of France* (Basingstoke and New York, 2002), pp. 7, 2.

36 S.L. Adams, 'The Road to La Rochelle: English Foreign Policy and the Huguenots, 1610–1629', *Proceedings of the Huguenot Society of London*, 22 (1975), pp. 415–18.

37 Strong, *Henry Prince of Wales*, pp. 72–73.

38 Jean Loiseau de Tourval, *The French herald summoning all true Christian princes to a generall croisade, for a holy warr against the great enemy of Christendome, and all his slaues* (London, 1611), p. 15.

39 Adams, 'The Road to La Rochelle', pp. 418, 428–29.

40 Jean Loiseau de Tourval, 'A Preface of the Translator', Henri de Feynes, *Voyages faict par terre depuis Paris jusques à la Chine* (London, 1615).

41 Alison Clarke, 'Jean Loiseau de Tourval: a Huguenot translator in England, 1603–31', *Proceedings of the Huguenot Society of London*, 20 (1958–64), pp. 36–41.

42 Loiseau de Tourval, *The French Herald*, sig. A2v.

43 Thomas Birch, *The Life of Henry, Prince of Wales* (London, 1760), p. 467.

44 Loiseau de Tourval, *The French Herald*, sig. A2r–v, pp. 12, 28–29, 33, 38. He published a more measured lament for Henri IV in the same year, *Three Precious Teares of Blood, Flowing from the wounded harts of three great French Ladies* (London, 1611), dedicated to the Countess of Derby.

45 See his letter to Lawrence Whitaker, High Seneschal or Steward of this company, in *Thomas Coriate Traveller for the English Wits: greeting From the court of the Great Mogul* (London, 1616), p. 37. On this society, see my *English Wits: Literature and Sociability in Early Modern England* (Cambridge, 2007).

46 Rebecca Weeks More, 'The Rewards of Virtue: Gentility in Early Modern England', unpublished PhD thesis, Brown University (1998), pp. 189–92; Wilks, 'Court Culture of Prince Henry', I, pp. 11–17, 127–29.

47 Wilks, 'Court Culture of Prince Henry', pp. 16–17, 127, 129.

48 Brandon S. Centerwall, 'Identifying "Glareanus Vadianus" as John Sanford', *Cahiers Elisabethains*, 55 (1999), pp. 35–37.

49 *HMC Downshire*, II, pp. 182–83.

50 *Ibid.*, pp. 16–17, 100, 108, 129, 161, 163, 233–34, 340, 347, 404, 408.

51 *Ibid.*, V, XVIII, pp. 10–11, 14–15, 29–30, 32–33, 212.

52 *Ibid.*, p. 402.

53 *HMCDownshire*, III, p. 250.

54 The English translation is by John Reynolds, a fellow of New College who died in 1614; BL Harl. MS. 4931, fol. 17r, p. 25.

55 Fynes Moryson, *An Itinerary: Containing His Ten Yeeres Travell through the Twelve Dominions of Germany, Bohmerland, Sweitzerland, Netherland, Denmarke, Poland, Italy, Turky, France, England, Scotland & Ireland*, 4 vols. (Glasgow, 1907), I, pp. 397, 398, 401.

56 See Hillman's reading of Moryson and the *Crudities* in his *Shakespeare, Marlowe and the Politics of France*, pp. 28–29.

57 Michael Strachan, *The Life and Adventures of Thomas Coryate* (London, 1962), pp. 18–19.

4| 'To the Most High and Excellent Prince': Dedicating Books to Henry, Prince of Wales

John A. Buchtel

Henry, Prince of Wales received the dedications of 110 printed books during his brief career as one of early seventeenth-century Britain's leading patrons.[1] The essay which follows explores the dedication of books to Prince Henry from three vantage points. The first part provides an overview, using the dedications offered to Prince Henry during this period as case studies in the roles printed dedications played within an individual court culture. The second part offers a detailed quantitative analysis of the printed dedications offered during a single year, 1612, when Henry's court reached its apogee. The third section briefly contextualizes the results of this analysis within a broader analysis for the four-year period 1609–12.

Book dedications and the culture of patronage

The study of book dedications cannot limit itself to the study of literary patronage alone. Literary patronage forms only one piece of a much larger game, in which dedications themselves play only one small role. A total of 110 printed dedications, almost all received in a span of only ten years, is a large number – comparable with the number of dedications received over an entire lifetime by the Earl of Leicester, the leading non-royal patron of the preceding generation. Yet from another perspective, for a patron with a household numbering some 400 members, such an amount might seem proportionate. Of these, only a portion demonstrably partook of the assignment of place, appointment of livings, or other material remuneration. Nonetheless, book dedications were one of the most broadly dispersed and widely available cultural forms by which the reputation and courtly magnificence of a patron were distributed. The purpose of this essay is to explore some of the ways dedications relate to the other pieces and players in the game.[2] Dedications participate in a complicated system of patronage which functioned largely on a basis of personal alliances and unspoken conventions, as Timothy Wilks demonstrates in detail in his dissertation on Prince Henry's court circle.[3] There were always dedications whose rhetoric makes it plain that the writers are outsiders with no personal knowledge of the Prince or his circle. Such contributions might operate as a gamble, betting on the outside chance of attaining enough notice to gain entry into the household, but they more likely ended in small rewards if any, as evidenced by Prince Henry's surviving privy purse accounts: 13 December 1609: 'To a stranger who presented a booke to his highnes £4'; 3 January: 'To a poore scholler who presented a booke to his highnes £2'.[4]

Unlike these anonymous dedicators, most writers relied heavily upon the interpersonal networks of family relationships and regional proximities and loyalties, even though such connections provided no guarantee of results. Patronage was always subject to the individual whims of those dispensing it. It was a rule-based system whose rules might become clear only in their violation – and which even then might remain obscure to the patron-seeker. George Chapman's apologetic tone in his sonnet to the Earl of Arundel at the end of his twelve-book *Iliad*, for example, indicates that he guessed that he might offend Arundel when he failed properly to respect the Earl's place in the order of precedence of the Jacobean nobility. Yet this did not stop Chapman from trying his luck, and he was not certain that his decision was a mis-step until after his book had been published and Arundel's anger forced him to change the sonnet for the next edition.[5] The process of dedicating a book in hopes of a specific reward was often subject to uncertainty; witness the failure of John Donne's presentation of *Pseudo-Martyr* to Prince Henry, one of several recipients of presentation copies of the book, to bear any tangible fruit.[6] Richard Robinson in his *Eupolemia* (the fullest extant account of the relative success of an author's œuvre in achieving financial reward in the patronage system) complains about the parsimony of certain patrons relative to the effort he put into his presentation copies.[7]

The language of dedications is replete with sometimes implicit and often overt pleas for and anxieties over what the writer hopes to receive at the hand of the dedicatee: direct remuneration or other less direct means of financial support (a seat at table, a place in a household, placement in a church living), advancement or a recommendation toward advancement with another patron, political or religious protection, shelter from critics, endorsement of an idea or a policy, commercial endorsement on behalf of the sales of a book or, after the advent of subscription publication, subscriptions to it; in short, 'encouragement', in several senses of the word. Familiar dedications, in which books are dedicated by a social equal or superior as a token of love or re-spect and without the above considerations, are less common in this period. Even some of the obvious examples, such as James I's dedication of the *Basilicon Doron* to Prince Henry, are more complicated – in this case because of political associations – than simple expressions of paternal affection. Sir Philip Sidney's dedication of the *Arcadia* to his sister, though a pure example of the kind, was not intended (at least ostensibly) by Sidney to see print.

What did a patron expect to receive in return – and were such expectations met? Some expectations clearly involved a direct *quid pro quo*: service in return for financial support, loyalty in return for advancement, ready access to skilled pens for propagandistic purposes; increased glory of reputation. Works of literature frequently promise immortality in return for support, and history has borne this out: the support of a great poet can raise even the initials of an otherwise uncertainly identified patron to lasting fame, as in the case of Shakespeare's 'W.H.'.

Gift exchange theory has refined Early Modern rhetoric with another way of describing the less direct returns on the investment: an increase in 'cultural capital' as a result of the help given the conventionally starving artist.

The tendency to separate the study of the dedication of books from its context in the larger operations of the patronage system obscures the dedication's actual role. A book dedication may not itself always have been the place-seeker's primary instrument for requesting advancement. Some dedications instead functioned as gifts on behalf of the place-seeker in a socially unequal gift-exchange. The writer might re-articulate requests that have already been made, or might remind a patron of promises that have already been given – perhaps even already fulfilled. A writer might thus recall the patron's attention to favours pledged or dispensed by the act of re-presenting a printed book that might already have been presented (in manuscript) as a gift.[8] The book might even serve as a token in the process of one individual making suit on behalf of another.[9]

Many of these features of the patronage system are all well-known and in some cases well-documented.[10] Much more difficult to recover is the degree to which books that had been dedicated themselves influenced patrons in positions of power. Did dedicatees read the books dedicated to them; indeed, did they read the dedications presenting the books to them? Did writers expect them to read either? (While the anonymous author of *The Fierie Tryall of Gods Saints* expresses a hope that Prince Henry will read his book, he neatly gives the Prince an out, if not: 'Deigne (Sir) to reade this little Booke, / at least with milde aspect to looke / Upon't.') Did patrons learn from the books dedicated to them, or did the books pass directly into their libraries, where other members of their households might use and peruse them? To what degree did access to libraries – one of the most significant benefits for clients in the system of early modern patronage – lead to indirect infusion of ideas, first into a household, then into its leader?[11]

The influence of Prince Henry's court culture

To begin to answer such questions, to the degree that they can be answered, we must examine carefully the surviving evidence from specific patrons and the books dedicated to them, bearing in mind that what is true for one patron may vary according to the circumstances of another. Prince Henry's situation was substantially different from that of other patrons in several respects. As heir apparent, particularly after his investiture as Prince of Wales in 1610, he held more power, commanded more resources, and garnered more attention than was the case with most if not all the peers, let alone lesser patrons. Prince Henry's very youth factored strongly in the nature of the books dedicated to him, lending itself to attempts by writers to influence him in matters ranging from morals to statecraft. Indeed, many books dedicated to the Prince seem to have formed deliberate components of a programme of education. As

Wilks observes, 'Henry was the receptive object of unrelenting and painstaking instruction … The urge to provide a multi-disciplined education for Britain's Renaissance prince created the passionate climate of instruction within which the literary effusions occurred.'[12] Some of the books dedicated to the Prince appear to have been directed if not dictated by those in charge of his formal education. In some instances the Prince intervened himself. Other books appear to have been offered as supplements or alternatives to his formal education, sometimes from within his circle and in accordance with his predilections; and sometimes from outside his court culture and perhaps seeking either to enter into it, or to counter it.

As with all dedications, there is always a dual audience: the dedicatee himself, and other potential readers. Joshua Sylvester shows a pointed awareness of this when he writes to Prince Henry in the dedication of his translation of the *Quadrains* of Guy de Faur, Lord of Pibrac:

> And, though You want not these weake helpes of ours,
> To consummate your Selfe in Excellence:
> Yet may those Subjects, which shall once be Yours,
> Draw vertuous Wisedome, and all Dutie hence:
> If you but daigne with your deere Name to grace it,
> Which (Load-stone-like) shall draw them to embrace it (sig. 2Y2).[13]

Sylvester deploys the modesty topos with uncharacteristic delicateness to graft the Prince's own need for instruction on to the needs of his future subjects. The panegyric impulse, which denies the writer the latitude to state openly that the dedicatee is already anything less than perfect, operates not exactly disingenuously, but rather on the basis of understood convention, to state the opposite of what is meant. Of course Sylvester wants Prince Henry to 'draw vertuous Wisedome, and all Dutie' from his work, as his implication that Henry has not yet consummated himself in excellence suggests. At the same time, Sylvester's explicit request is merely that Henry design to grace the work with his name. The colourful simile of the magnetic power of a prince's endorsement reflects not only a desire that other readers will benefit from the book, but also a tacit hope that they will have purchased a copy in order to do so. In 1605, when the book was published, Sylvester was already writing from a position of some security, having managed to win the first pensioned appointment of poet in the Prince's household.

Some of the supplementary efforts embodied in books dedicated to Prince Henry, including Sylvester's translation of the *Quadrains*, were encouraged from within the Prince's circle. Wilks remarks that

> a failure to penetrate the court life which surrounded Henry leads inevitably to
> the mistaken conclusion that the great weight of literary addresses represent

no more than a predictable vogue. In fact, the literary response ... provides innumerable indications of the important national movement that was being
generated within Henry's court (p. 54).

The dedication of books to the Prince was not merely haphazard. This is not to insist that the
books dedicated to Prince Henry constitute a consistent or thorough propaganda campaign,
but rather to suggest that Henry, his advisers, and the very tone of his court culture tended to
shape the kinds of works he received. There is evidence that at least some books dedicated to
Prince Henry were commissioned or otherwise encouraged by his leading officers, and often
there are personal connections or communications between the writers of dedications to the
Prince and members of his household. Yet one can also overemphasize the role that books
dedicated to the Prince – especially those of a literary nature – played in shaping Henry's
court culture. As Wilks points out,

> Williamson's belief that literature was the fountain-head of the court culture
> would probably have been supported by some of the professional writers in
> Henry's service .... Yet ... the literary output inspired by Henry [was], essen-
> tially, a response to an observed court culture.[14]

In such cases, the influence is less direct, though nonetheless significant.

The role of the Prince's senior advisors should not be underestimated. Literary patronage
at the higher levels was never a matter of a patron interacting alone with isolated individual
writers. A number of books were dedicated to Prince Henry's officers, for instance, even as
those same servants themselves dedicated books to the Prince. Sir David Murray of Gorthy received the dedication of William Cowper's *A Preparative for the New Passeover* (STC 5933) in 1607,
with special mention in the dedication of Murray's privileged position as 'speciall Gentleman
of the Prince his bed-chamber', and of Murray's dual responsibility as both servant of Christ
and servant of the Prince. Cowper likely hoped his book would find its way from Murray's
hands to the Prince himself.[15] From this standpoint, any consideration of dedications to a
patron at the higher, particularly royal, levels needs to take account of dedications to that
patron's ranking servants. A dedication to an advisor must frequently be taken as a petition
for the advisor to use his influence with the greater patron.[16] It may be that Cowper's dedication to Murray paved the way for Cowper's dedication of part of one of his books to the Prince
himself in 1609.[17]

Cowper's works are concerned with the practical application of biblical doctrine in the
spiritual lives of his readers. His desire for his words to reach the Prince serves as a reminder that many of Prince Henry's contemporaries in Protestant Britain considered practical or 'experimental' theology to be a signal part of the education of a Protestant

Renaissance prince. Cowper's dedication asserts the divine's concern for the future monarch's spiritual well-being (and by extension, Cowper must have hoped that the future monarch's reception of a spiritual treatise would cause it to be received more readily by a more general audience):

> By which that same God who hath called you to be an apparant Heyre of the most famous Kingdomes on earth, doth also call your Grace to a more certaine inheritance of a better Kindome in heaven, which cannot be shaken: whereby above other Princes, and Rulers of the earth yee are blessed, if so be yee an-swere your Calling (sig. 2D5ᵛ).

Cowper might have hoped for an appointment as one of the Prince's twenty-four chaplains, who rotated into service in pairs each month, or he may already have held some similar posi-tion in the household. Cowper does not appear in Wilks's list of Prince Henry's servants, in-cluding the chaplains,[18] but he does sign his dedication 'Your Graces humble Servant and daily Oratour', which suggests not only that he was known to the Prince, but that he may have held a position, most likely as a chaplain, for at least some period of time in the Prince's service. Regardless of his actual position relative to the Prince, a divine like Cowper was as likely to see appointment as chaplain to the Prince as genuine spiritual service to God and to Britain, bringing the Word of God to the future ruler of England and Scotland, as to view it as a means of personal advancement.[19]

Both dedicatee and dedicator, Sir David Murray presented Prince Henry with the dedica-tion of one of his literary efforts, *The Tragicall Death of Sophonisba* (STC 18296), in 1611. Murray's book is a very slight octavo, unlike the substantial tome imposed in quarto bearing Cowper's dedication to the Prince. The size and heft of Cowper's book seems calculated to demand at-tention, whereas Murray's appears unconcerned about it. Murray signs his dedications 'Your Highnesse most loyall and affectionate servant': his book seems designed to act as a small, even familiar, token from a courtier secure in his position with his patron. Where Cowper's book begs for a place in a library, and to be used as an object of study, Murray's looks to be slipped into a pouch or pocket, to be savoured in brief moments of leisure.

Other officers in Prince Henry's household dedicated books of similar size and status. If the STC is correct in identifying the George More, Esq. who dedicated *Principles for Yong Princes* (STC 18068) to Prince Henry in 1611 as Sir George More of Loseley, the book is of a piece with Murray's.[20] More held the positions of Receiver-General and (for a time) Treasurer in Prince Henry's household,[21] and in size his book, a tiny duodecimo, generates much the same sensi-bility as Murray's *Sophonisba*. A book of practical advice for a future ruler, it fits into the same 'advice for princes' tradition into which Francis Bacon's *Essays* falls. Had the printed text of Bacon's 1612 *Essays* been dedicated to the Prince as had been planned, the book, imposed in octavo and little bigger than Murray's *Sophonisba*, would have aspired to the company of these books dedicated by prominent members of the Prince's household, and designed to be kept close at hand and, one might suppose, close to heart. Sir George More was one of Henry's earliest officers;[22] Sir David Murray came with Prince Henry from Scotland and served as Prince Henry's Keeper of the Privy Purse and Keeper of the Robes.[23] Wilks applies the adverb 'ruefully' to Bacon's observation from outside Prince Henry's court circle that 'The masters and tutors of [Prince Henry's] youth also (which rarely happens) continued in great favour with him'.[24] The implication is that Bacon saw himself in competition with such figures – and, by extension, with their books.

Francis Bacon and the dedication of the Essays

An attempt to work out who Bacon's 'competitors' were in 1612 has led to the following case study, which focuses on books dedicated to the Prince bearing the imprint of a single year, comparing in detail not only the rhetoric of their dedications, but also employing quantitative analysis of their production, genres and other factors. In 1612 Prince Henry was at the height of his power, influence and popularity even despite the death of Salisbury and its consequences in terms of Henry's diminished direct access to the government and affairs of state. In seeking to understand a society for which book dedications operated as critical rhetorical performances, it is important to read dedications with the same attention and consideration with which we study other performances, both theatrical and rhetorical. Book dedications provide an under-utilized and much-misunderstood window into the purposes to which early modern writers intended their books to be put. By setting Bacon's dedication to Prince Henry in the context of other writers' dedications to the same patron, this study seeks to provide a model for further inquiry regarding the relationship between book dedications and actual and projected patronage.

Sometime between 1610 and 1612, Francis Bacon took up the task of revising his *Essays*, originally printed in 1597 and dedicated to his now-deceased brother Anthony.[25] Bacon's objective was to present the revised version to Prince Henry, as witnessed by the unique manuscript copy of Bacon's dedication to the Prince. The Prince's untimely death evidently frustrated Bacon's plans, for the manuscript seems never to have reached the Prince's hands, and Bacon instead had the book printed in 1612 with a dedication to his brother-in-law, Sir John Constable.[26] The dedication of the 1612 *Essays* was the only printed book dedication Constable would receive, unless one counts the inclusion of his name in the Minsheu subscription list.[27]

Michael Brennan uses the successive dedications of the *Essays* to demonstrate that 'changes of patron were commonplace', though he omits the near-dedication of the 1612 edition to Prince Henry.[28] Change of patron may in fact have been rather less common than is sometimes assumed. Williams's list of changes of patron, which covers the entire period 1475–1641 and includes the death of the patron among several different motivating factors, takes up only a few pages of his *Index* (pp. 243–54). Only six works originally dedicated to Prince Henry – less than 5% of the total number of printed titles dedicated to him – were rededicated to other patrons following Prince Henry's death.[29]

In addition, there was a handful of works that had not yet been printed but were intended for dedication to Prince Henry. These include Bacon's revised *Essays* and Sir Walter Raleigh's *History of the World* (which in the end bore no dedication). A few of the books dedicated to Prince Charles in late 1612 and in 1613 may originally have been intended for Prince Henry, although it is not always possible to document this. In some cases, manuscript presentation copies to Prince Henry survive, or other evidence indicates they were written for Henry. Among the most notable examples is Sir Robert Dallington's *Aphorismes Civile, and Militare … out of Guicciardine*, for which a 1609 presentation manuscript to Prince Henry survives. When printed in 1613, the book bore a dedication to Charles.[30] Similarly, Sir John Hayward's *Lives of the iii Normans, Kings of England* was written for Henry but printed, again in 1613, for Charles; the dedication to Charles records a conversation between Hayward and Prince Henry on the subject of history.[31] Other examples are less certainly identifiable, such as the rare dedication to Prince Charles of Barnaby Rich's *Opinion Deified* (1613), which may at first have been intended for Prince Henry; it is more commonly dedicated to Sir Thomas Ridgeway.[32] This does not pretend to be an exhaustive list of such books, although it is probably safe to say that there are not many more than a dozen examples.

A second category consists of books whose original printed dedications to Prince Henry were redirected to other dedicatees for new editions after the Prince's death in 1612 – most of them long enough after his death that the dedicators seem generally not to feel compelled to mention Henry in their new dedications. Williams notes six titles.[33] Samson Lennard shifted the dedication of his translation of Pierre Charron's *Of Wisdome* from Henry (1608?) to his eponymous kinsman, Samson Lennard, Esq. (1615?).[34] Lennard starts the new dedication with a discussion of the loss of his former patron and of the problem of decorum in choosing a patron of an appropriate rank. Thomas James rededicated his *Catalogus Librorum* of the Bodley library (1605) to the King, Prince Charles, and the benefactors of the Bodleian (1620).[35] James replaces the prose dedication to Henry with epigraphic dedications consisting of the names, titles and superlative virtues of the dedicatees, but without any epistolary text or any mention of Prince Henry. Gervase Markham redirected his *Cavelarice* (1607) to Prince Charles (1617),[36] while Barnaby Rich rededicated *Faultes Faults* (1606) to Lady St John in 1616.[37] The Rider/Holyoke dictionary (originally dedicated to Prince Henry by Francis Holyoke in 1606)[38] carries new dedications in several later editions. Finally, Andrew Willet changed the dedication of his *Harmonie upon Samuel* (1607) from a personal one to Henry to an institutional one, to Christ's College, Cambridge (1614).[39] There are additionally a few books whose new editions seem as if they ought to carry a dedication to a new patron, like Chapman's 1616 *Whole Works of Homer*, but instead retain the old one to the deceased patron.[40]

Dedicating books to Prince Henry in 1612

The sudden and unanticipated death of Henry, Prince of Wales in November 1612 sent shockwaves throughout the patronage system of Stuart Britain. Writers great and low scrambed for sure footing. Francis Bacon hastily rededicated the *Essays* to a kinsman; George Chapman desperately sought fulfilment of Prince Henry's promised reward for his yet unfinished translation of Homer's works; Sir Walter Raleigh weighed the consequences of dedicating the *History of the World* to a new protector, and opted instead to leave the work 'without a Maister' (sig. E4v). In 1612, the year of his greatest promise and power as present patron and future king, Prince Henry received the dedications of sixteen printed books – more than he had received in any single previous year, and more than three times the number of dedications addressed to his father, James I, in that same year.[41]

A close examination of these sixteen dedications helps to set the context for the high hopes surrounding the Prince's patronage, as well as to gain some insight into the operations of the patronage system generally. A quantitative analysis of these dedications to Henry as artifacts, in terms of the composition and presswork involved in the production of the books, sheds some light on the possible motives their writers may have had, upon Prince Henry's practices as a patron, and on the place book dedications had in the broader contexts of early modern print culture.

Quantitative analysis in the humanistic disciplines must be handled with care. It can be slippery, for instance, to try to sort works into tidy subject categories, yet among the sixteen books dedicated to Prince Henry in 1612, some fairly straightforward groupings emerge.[42] Five of these works are primarily literary in nature. Of these, four seem to fall into the categories of *belles lettres*: Michael Drayton's *Poly-Olbion*; Francis Herring's *Poemata Miscellanea*; John Owen's *Epigrammatum … Libri Tres*; and Henry Peacham's emblem book, *Minerva Britanna*. Another of the works, intended as a school text, borders between the literary and educational. Thomas Farnaby's heavily annotated edition of Juvenal and Persius starts off with commendatory verse by no less a classicist than Ben Jonson. The book's subtitle clearly advertises its use as a text for study: '*cum annotationibus ad marginem, quae obscurissima quaeque dilucidare possint*': this is not unlike the covers of today's undergraduate paperback editions of Shakespeare vaunting the extensiveness of their footnotes. This was the first published work of a rising schoolmaster who would go on to become a bestselling author of school texts and one of the most widely respected classicists in Europe. Farnaby was about thirty-seven at the time of the dedication to Prince Henry (*Oxford DNB*).

Three of the works fall into the category Gants labels 'information', which includes 'works on language, business training and skills, education, husbandry, popular science and medicine'. The Puritan John Brinsley's *Ludus Literarius: or, the Grammar Schoole* is 'a detailed manual for country schoolmasters' (*Oxford DNB*). It presents a joint or shared dedication to Prince Henry and Prince Charles petitioning them to support more or less universal education.

Benvenuto Italian's *Il Passaggiere, The Passenger,* a set of dialogues in facing-page translation by a Mr King, plies the border between language aids and travellers' phrase books, incorporating as it does such incisive conversations as 'But how like you Parsenep rootes?' or 'This same Turnep pleaseth my taste very well'. William Sparke's philosophical work, *Vis Naturae et Virtus Vitae Explicatae, Comparatae, ad Universum Doctrinae Ordinem Constituendum,* might be a poorer fit for this oversimplified categorization. William Bellenden's *Ciceronis Consul,* a royalist work on statecraft, would probably most accurately be categorized with Law/Politics, though it could be considered alongside conduct books and works in the 'advice for princes' tradition as more informational in nature. Bellenden's is the only book among the sixteen to have been printed on the Continent.[43]

The seven remaining works are religious. Two of these are devotional. Joseph Hall's *Contemplations upon the Principall Passages of the Holie Storie* takes a largely contemplative approach to retelling the Genesis narrative. Lewis Bayly's *Practise of Pietie* would become one of the most popular works of Puritan piety of the seventeenth century.[44] The rest of the religious works are controversial texts, all of them written from an anti-Catholic outlook: William Fennor's *Pluto his Travailes, or, the Divils Pilgrimage to the Colledge of Jesuites*; John Gordon's *Antibellarmino-tortor, sive Tortus Retortus* (part of the pamphlet war with Robert Bellarmine); George Hakewill's *Scutum Regium. id est, Adversus omnes Regicidas et Regicidarum Patronos*; Samson Lennard's translation of Philippe de Mornay's *The Mystery of Iniquitie: that is to Say, The Historie of the Papacie*; and an anonymous translation of Edmond Richer's *A Treatise of Ecclesiasticall and Politike Power,* which argues for the limitation of papal authority and urges recusants to take the Oath of Allegiance.

In addition to these sixteen printed books, Prince Henry received presentations of several manuscripts in 1612. As mentioned above, a manuscript copy of Francis Bacon's *Essays* with a dedication to Prince Henry survives. Though it is uncertain if this copy in fact reached Prince Henry, it seems clear that Bacon planned to offer a manuscript to the Prince in advance of a new printed edition with a dedication to the Prince. The Prince's death intervened, and Bacon instead dedicated the printed edition to his kinsman, Sir John Constable.[45] Bacon's *Essays* was not the only manuscript book presented or prepared for presentation to Prince Henry in 1612, but determining precise dates or clear identifications for manuscript presentations is not always possible. One dedication which found itself in the same situation as Bacon's was Ben Jonson's dedication to Henry of *The Masque of Queenes,* which was entered in the Stationers' Register only weeks before Prince Henry's death.[46] A panegyric on Prince Henry addressed to the Duc de Lesdiguières, by James Cleland, tutor to Sir John Harington (later 2nd Baron of Exton), appears to date from 1612. More than one copy survives, so it would not be unreasonable to suppose that a copy might have reached the Prince.[47] A payment to Esther Inglis for one of the five manuscripts she dedicated to Prince Henry, a book of Psalms, occurs in Prince Henry's Privy Purse accounts for 1612.[48] Other manuscripts presented to Prince Henry possibly in 1612 include a collection of poetry in classical languages by Winchester schoolboys, Joshua Mene's *De Unionis Firmitate*, and Phineas Fletcher's satirical poem on the Gunpowder Plot, '*Locustae vel Pietas Jesuitica*'.[49] A manuscript on Church government by William Laud presented to Prince Henry may also date to 1611 or 1612, though its dedication or presentation inscription no longer survives.[50]

While there is much to be said for the argument set forth by Harold Love, Arthur Marotti and others that the circulation of manuscripts constitutes a significant form of publication well into the Early Modern period, there remains a fundamental difference between the act of presenting a manuscript copy and dedicating a printed edition of a text. The eccentricities of the manuscripts described in just the one paragraph above underscores the unusual character of many such gifts. The concentrated handiwork that went, for instance, into the presentation manuscripts of an Esther Inglis or Sir John Harington of Kelston sets itself against the multiplication of copies effected by the printing press.[51] It is this relationship, between the multiplicative effect of printing and the widely disseminated nature of printed book dedications, as opposed to the unique character of presentation copies, with which the present study is concerned.[52] The manuscript dedications of Bacon's revision of the *Essays* or the book of Psalms prepared by Esther Inglis are not without interest, of course, but for present purposes manuscripts must be omitted from the analysis in order to permit an evaluation of the broad cultural impact of the dedications of printed books.

The following analysis of printed books dedicated to Prince Henry in 1612 includes an overview of the books' formats, a rough comparison of the amount of composition and presswork involved in their production, and several other factors. While this analysis is exhaustive for books dedicated to Prince Henry in 1612, the number of books involved provides too small a sample upon which to rest definitive conclusions for patterns in a single individual's patronage, let alone for the study of book dedications generally. In a limited data set such as this, one very large book (such as Lennard's translation of Du Mornay's *Mystery of Iniquitie*) can skew the averaged results, as can the chance survival of more than the usual number of particularly small books (as, for example, Herring's exceptionally rare *Poemata Miscellanea*[53]). This study is meant to be suggestive rather than conclusive, a demonstration of methodology and a venue in which to raise questions and begin testing hypotheses rather than to determine hard and fast rules.

The most significant tool for this analysis is the edition sheet, a unit of measure which allows for comparison of the production output of handpress-period printers. Title counts are not sufficient. To say that Prince Henry received the dedications of sixteen books in 1612 does not account for the fact that some titles were tiny octavo pamphlets, while others were hefty folios. Comparing books simply by numbers of pages independent of format leads to apples-and-oranges results: Gordon's *Anti-bellarmino-tortor*, for instance, has twice the number of pages as Sparke's *Vis Naturae et Virtus Vitae*, but because Sparke is an octavo while Gordon is a quarto they turn out to have involved comparable amounts of presswork, at 7.5 edition sheets each. In other words, each copy of each book was made up from the same number of sheets.[54]

The edition sheet, as the term is used here, refers to 'the number of sheets in an exemplar volume used as a measure of the relative amount of work required to produce the complete run of that volume,' without reference to the number of copies in the complete run of the edition.[55] Each edition sheet is printed from a pair of formes of set type, each forme containing a number of type-pages dependent upon the format of the book in question. A pair of folio formes contains four type-pages, so that a single printed folio sheet contains four pages of text, two on each side. A quarto sheet contains eight pages, an octavo sheet 16 pages, a duodecimo sheet 24. The number of edition sheets in a book may be determined by dividing the total number of pages by the number of pages per sheet for the book's format: for instance, an octavo pamphlet of 32 pages, divided by 16 pages per octavo sheet, consists of two edition sheets.

As a unit of measure, the edition sheet is approximate. It cannot fully account for the variation among books according to the differing sizes of the sheets of paper from which they were printed, or of the relative sizes of type used in printing. Full precision would require the correlation of these data, as well. For comparison's sake, the use of the edition sheet requires something of a 'legal fiction' in which the editions under consideration are assumed to have seen roughly equivalent print runs; but of course this was not always the case. A devotional work like Bayly's *Practise of Pietie* would undoubtedly have been printed in many more copies than Drayton's *Poly-olbion*. This does not negate the utility of the edition sheet as a measure of comparison, but does serve as a reminder that the figures should be handled with caution.[56] Despite such limitations, the edition sheet provides a valuable rough measure of the amount of work that went into the production of a particular book, and from a relative standpoint, of the cost that might have gone into its production. The edition sheet in the absence of more involved measurements and archival evidence provides a valuable and quick preliminary tool for measuring these attributes relative to other books.

The use of the edition sheet as a unit for comparison is of particular value when considering the relative proportion of formats in which different groups of books were imposed.[57] Format, especially as combined with edition-sheet totals, may indicate some sense of the relative dignity to which the books dedicated to a particular patron aspired, the relative regard in which the writers held the patron, and the relative hopes the writers had for patronage. Only two folios were dedicated to Prince Henry in 1612. Drayton and Lennard's folios, two of the three largest books in number of edition sheets, respectively represent an ambitious nationalistic literary work of epic proportions (Drayton; 80 edition sheets, plus a number of finely engraved plates) and a major work of anti-papist Church history (Lennard's translation of du Mornay; 171 edition sheets). These two books together account for almost half (46%) of the total press output for the year in number of edition sheets of books dedicated to the Prince.

Of the sixteen books bearing a 1612 imprint dedicated to Prince Henry, three-eighths (six titles) are quarto in format. The quartos include several smaller, slighter works, like Fennor's *Pluto his Travailes* (four edition sheets). Fennor's title-page contains a cartoonish woodcut, and it was the only book dedicated to Prince Henry in 1612 to be printed in black letter: clear signs of a more popular target reading audience. The quartos also include weightier and more pretentious works like Benvenuto's *Passenger* (83 edition sheets). The average size of a quarto dedicated to Prince Henry in 1612 is 30 edition sheets. Taken together, folio and quarto account for almost four-fifths (79%) of the total output of books dedicated to Prince Henry in 1612.

The remaining 21% of the year's output – eight more titles – were imposed in smaller formats: six octavos and two duodecimos. The octavos range in edition sheet size from Francis Herring's little panegyric (1.5 edition sheets) to Joseph Hall's *Contemplations* (24 edition sheets). In terms of sheer number of titles, one would clearly be wrong to suppose that little books in octavo were perceived as beneath the dignity of the royal family. But in terms of the average number of edition sheets, at 13.5 per octavo book, one might safely speculate that octavo tended generally to be used for the dedication of less 'weighty' works. In other words, the ideal of decorum, of presenting things in a fitting manner, appears to have operated in the printer's or author's choice of format as it did in other aspects of early modern culture.[58]

A complicating factor in drawing conclusions from comparison of printed books in terms of edition sheets is the inclusion of engraved plates in such books as Drayton's *Poly-olbion*. The standard practice of descriptive bibliography is not to include plates in collation formulas, because copperplates would have been printed in a separate shop on different equipment, and would have been inserted into the book by the binder, not always in the same place in the book. Insofar as a collation describes the physical structure of an 'ideal copy' of a book, plates are something of a wild card. Historians of fine art prints have tended to ignore or at least downplay prints in books. And because the discipline of descriptive bibliography was developed by textual scholars such as W.W. Greg and Fredson Bowers, very little serious bibliographical work has been done on the production of copperplates for books, apart from a recent provocative article by antiquarian bookdealer Roger Gaskell.

Gaskell points out that surviving archival evidence for the operations of engravers is even spottier than the handful of Early Modern firms for which letterpress records remain. What can be deduced for sure is that it was slower and more expensive to print engravings. Gaskell observes that for one late seventeenth-century press, 'the … figures suggest that it cost about the same to machine one plate as three letterpress sheets for an edition of 500 copies. That is one plate per 24 pages of a quarto, 48 pages of an octavo.' While cautioning that his figures are 'probably not generally applicable', Gaskell writes, 'A standard assumption is that paper accounted for half the production costs of a book at this time, so that leaving aside composition and engraving, we can see that adding a plate to a quarto of 30 sheets (240 pages) in an edition of 500 copies is like adding three sheets, it adds 10 per cent to the machining costs or 5 per cent to overall production costs'.[59]

Since the edition sheet as a unit of measure is essentially a way of estimating machining costs, it might be possible (though this has not been done here) to develop a calculus by which to gain a more accurate picture of the production effort that went into a book like *Poly-Olbion*, perhaps by increasing the figure for the book in number of edition sheets by three sheets per plate, if one posits Gaskell's figure as generally applicable. This necessarily ignores several factors, including the cost of hiring the artist to create the drawing, of hiring the engraver to transfer the drawing to copper, and the higher cost of the better-quality paper typically used for engravings. The figure might have to be altered somewhat according to such variables as the size of the image being engraved and printed (a series of small plates might be printed several plates to a sheet, thus reducing the machining costs to some extent, whereas a very large plate might take a great deal of extra preparation for each impression). Not to mention the impossible-to-quantify sense in which a picture is worth a dedication of a thousand words, in terms of gaining the interest and attention of a patron who might or might not otherwise read a given book.

The larger the work, in number of edition sheets, the more likely its dedicator seems either to have been in the Prince's service or to have had prior success seeking the Prince's patronage. Of the eight largest books – those comprising more than twenty edition sheets – prior patronage from the Prince can be documented for five of the authors. Some of these are recorded in documentary sources. Drayton received a pension out of the Prince's privy purse, 'w^thout anie graunte in wrytinge', according to a document drawn up after the Prince's death.[60] It is tempting to speculate about the enjoyment the Prince might have taken from the elaborate double-page engravings with which Drayton's verse is illustrated and which might have influenced his receipt of a pension. Others can be documented in Prince Henry's household; Bayly and Hall, for instance, were chaplains to the Prince.[61]

Finally, the situations of some of the writers can be deduced from internal evidence in their books. Lennard reports prior success (with his translation of Charron's *Of Wisdome*) in his dedication. Similarly, the Prince had previously accepted Peacham's manuscript book of emblems, and Peacham records his gratitude to the Prince in the dedication to *Minerva Britanna*. Strong proposes that Peacham might have held some minor post with the Prince; but opportunities to serve in the Prince's household of course went beyond direct service to the Prince. Each of the Prince's young noble attenders, for instance, brought his own tutor, and Wilks proposes that Peacham held such a post with Sir Edmund Ashfield, one of the members of the Prince's Privy Chamber and dedicatee of Peacham's *Graphice*. It may be possible to draw inferences for some of the others as well. Bellenden's dedication of *Ciceronis Consul* had been preceded by the dedication to Prince Henry of his *Ciceronis Princeps* (Paris, Chappelain, 1608). Repeated dedications to the same individual are not proof of a receipt of prior patronage any more than the act of dedicating a book is by itself proof of a quest for reward in the first place. But it does indicate an increased likelihood. Nevertheless, living as he did in France, Bellenden's relationship to Henry may have been something more like that of a member of Henry's developing network of Continental informants than of a member of his court.

Of the eight lesser books (all under fifteen edition sheets, and six under ten), only one author is certain to have received anything from the Prince, and possible connections of some kind can be suggested for only three more. John Owen of Caernarvonshire, who had included short poems addressed to Prince Henry in earlier books of epigrams, is listed with Drayton as the recipient of a pension, and Wilks notes the 'high favour' Owen received as the Prince's 'latyn poett'. Fennor, whom Strong describes as a 'hack poet,' declaimed before the royal family shortly before the Prince's final illness, and it may be that his dedication to Prince Henry was somehow connected with the opportunity to do so. Herring had previously dedicated to Prince Henry the second edition of his *Pietas Pontificia*, an octavo in 5.5 edition sheets containing Latin verse on the Gunpowder Plot (1609) – probably though not necessarily evidence of prior patronage.[62] The dedication to the anonymously translated *Treatise of Ecclesiasticall and Politike Power* (eight edition sheets) is signed δ. The delta might, as Wilson suggests, be the mark of the same writer who signs the dedication of *The French Herald Summoning All True Christian Princes to a Generall Croisade* (1611) with a Maltese cross within a triangle. The online ESTC identifies the author of the latter work as Prince Henry's pensioner, Jean Loiseau de Tourval, who, as a French Protestant, would make a likely candidate for authorship of the *Treatise*.[63] None of the other dedicators of small books appears in the household lists, nor do Prince Henry's biographers report on any known ties between them and the Prince apart from the dedications of their books. All the same, none of the sixteen dedications declares its author to be unknown to Prince Henry, a rhetorical move that occurs occasionally in dedications of the period.[64]

In considering the difference between the smaller and larger books dedicated to the Prince, it is worth considering the amount of time a work like Lennard's translation of Du Mornay might have spent in the press. It is seldom possible to determine the actual length of time taken to print particular books. Nonetheless, archival research and painstaking bibliographical analysis can enable the reconstruction of likely norms for average work rates. Peter Blayney estimates 'that while a single press could produce 300 [edition] sheets a year, the annual production of a continuously-operated printing house would in practice be more like 200 sheets per press'.[65] We begin to get a sense of the weight a writer like Lennard might have given his decision regarding the dedication of a massive book like the translation of Du Mornay, at 171 edition sheets. If the book were to be in the press for the greater part of a year, its author would want to ensure as confidently as possible that the book's dedication would secure a reward commensurate with the effort involved. Even if the edition size were smaller than the print run Blayney posits in his calculations (and thus would not have tied up as many resources in the printing house for quite so long a period of time), Lennard's book would still have taken months to print: a substantial investment of time and paper, either way. An author would have hesitated to dedicate a book of this size speculatively.[66]

The printed books dedicated to Prince Henry in 1612 include three translations into English (Lennard, Benvenuto, and Richer) – one-fifth (19%) of the titles, but at 262 edition sheets, fully half (49%) of the total press output dedicated to the Prince that year. Seven of the books are in Latin – nearly half (44%) of the titles but merely one-eighth (13%) of the total press output, at 71 edition sheets. All the books over 20 edition sheets per book are in English, with the exception of the Continent-printed Bellenden and the Italian half of Benvenuto – printing in English accounts for four-fifths (79%) of the total output, at 427 edition sheets. These results might indicate, among other things, an expectation on the part of writers dedicating books to the Prince that, while their young patron could read Latin, he was much more comfortable in his own vernacular: not exactly earth-shattering findings, but a useful hypothesis to confirm, nonetheless.

According to the genre assignments made above, religion accounts for seven titles, for a total of 252 edition sheets: 44% of the titles, 47% of the total output. Literature also accounts for five titles, for a total of 127.5 edition sheets: one-fourth (24%) of the total output. The three titles categorized under Information account for one-fifth (19%) of titles and, at 136.5 edition sheets, one-fourth (25%) of total output. Law/Politics makes up 6% of titles and 4% of output. History is not represented in this sample. Even with figures pulled from such a small sample, these proportions correspond roughly to those reported in David Gants's analysis of the London booktrade from 1614 to 1618.[67]

Of the sixteen books dedicated to the Prince in 1612, five mention their dedicatee on the title-page: Richer, Owen, Gordon, Bellenden, and Benvenuto. If the dedicatee's name were routinely expected to assist in selling a work, one accustomed to modern Madison Avenue tactics might expect the name to appear more frequently on the title page, especially given the practice of Early Modern printers of printing extra copies of their title-pages to post as advertisements. The present data sample is too small to detect any patterns, except to say that the printing of the patron's name on the title-page seems to be relatively uncommon – only about a third (31%) of the sixteen titles in the present sample.

Another level of detail which could make for a useful augmentation of this study would be an analysis of the various books in light of the printers and publishers involved in their production.[68] Such analysis would have relatively little meaning, however, outside the context of a fulsome study of the other publications of the various printers, publishers and booksellers, and since such detail is well outside the scope of this project, this study has stopped short of dealing with this question. Moreover, if any meaningful patterns are to emerge relating, say, to the affinities of a particular stationer for particular kinds of books or types of authors, the data would have to be expanded to cover this information from year to year. Yet even within a single year, one thing that can be commented upon meaningfully here is the number of *different* stationers involved in producing books dedicated to one patron in a single year, with ten different printers for fourteen works: a substantial portion of all the London trade.[69] Three printers' names appear twice in the list (Humphrey Lownes, William Stansby, and Nicholas

Okes), and one appears three times (Richard Field). Except for Lownes, the books dedicated to Prince Henry produced by these printers were all under fifteen edition sheets: all of them slight in terms of the amount of presswork involved. Among publishers, only John Budge's name appears more than once in the list.

One can only speculate as to the significance. Perhaps the printers who appear more frequently simply had too few jobs in hand, or were taking smaller jobs, or had more presses to work with. Perhaps the publishers all had capital tied up in other projects and so couldn't handle more than one Henry-related project. Perhaps such considerations did not even occur to them. Michael Brennan's study of William Ponsonby suggests that at least some stationers worked with their patron's goals in mind. If this was true for Prince Henry, a larger data sample would be necessary to prove it; the evidence from 1612 by itself suggests a broad distribution rather than a tight concentration of Henry's influence. At any rate, the question is worth asking, and the imprints are worth analyzing for whatever tale they might hint at. In 1612, Prince Henry received the dedications of printed books totaling nearly 540 edition sheets (an average of 34 per book) – the equivalent of the total annual output of two to three presses. Prince Henry's patronage accounted for a not inconsiderable proportion of the total London booktrade in that year.[70]

There are other areas which an expanded version of the present study would usefully include. The first would be a detailed analysis of the books dedicated to Prince Henry in the context of the total output of the writers who dedicated books to him. To how many other patrons did each dedicate books? How many other books did each publish? Did the writer tend to use the same or different publishers? Where biographical data are available, do any patterns emerge according to the relative age of the writers at the time of dedication? Did younger writers tend to dedicate shorter works, as we might suspect? Similarly, it would be useful to be able to analyze the dedications to Prince Henry in the context of dedications to all other dedicatees during specified periods. What was the total output of the English booktrade in 1612? How many of those books bore dedications? How many other dedicatees received more than ten dedications? How do the percentages of works in various genres to other dedicatees compare to those among books dedicated to Prince Henry?

This kind of research can be done by hand on a limited basis, but only with a full-scale, comprehensive bibliographical database can this sort of investigation be conducted expansively. An ambitious new bibliographical initiative, the Early English Booktrade Database, which aims at a comprehensive augmentation of precise data for books covered by the English Short Title Catalogue, will make it possible to apply some of the methods of quantitative historical research to Early Modern English books on a much larger scale. In addition to enabling quantitative description of the workflow involved in publishing and printing by means of such measures as the edition sheet, the relative responsibility of the publishers involved, and the proportions of particular genres to total output, the database will enable sorting and comparison based on books' dedications and other paratextual features.

In anticipation of the database, and by way of an attempt to confirm the results of the more detailed analysis of books dedicated to Prince Henry in 1612, I have extended that analysis to cover books dedicated to Henry in the period 1609–12 (see tables 1–5). During 1609, as he formed his household, looking forward to his investiture as Prince of Wales in June 1610, Prince Henry began to achieve his greatest measure of independent control over his affairs. It should come as no surprise that nearly half (44%) of the printed books dedicated to Prince Henry – forty-eight of one hundred and ten titles – were printed during the last four years of his life, 1609–12. In studying Prince Henry's patronage, this is the most important period upon which to focus.

The 48 titles dedicated to Prince Henry over the course of this four-year period amount to a total of 1768.5 edition sheets. The Prince received an average of twelve titles (amounting to 442 edition sheets) each year; each year he received an average of two folios, six quartos, and four smaller books. Of the forty-eight titles, eight were imposed in folio and twenty-three in quarto, while twelve titles were imposed in octavo and five in duodecimo. Folio and quarto thus together comprise just over three-fifths (65%) of titles and fully seven-eighths (87%) of presswork for books dedicated to Prince Henry during these four years, whereas the smaller formats together account for slightly over one-third (35%) of titles and a mere one-eighth (13%) of presswork. The relative proportion of genres during this four-year period is also similar to that of 1612 by itself, as is the proportion of languages and the distribution of printers and publishers.

The analysis undertaken here, which anticipates the development of the Early English Booktrade database, is intended to be suggestive on a small scale of the kinds of results and further questions this type of contextualization may produce. When we begin to answer such questions on a scale larger than the study of individual authors and patrons – valuable as such studies are – we will begin to have a better understanding of the overall operations of early modern patronage.

Table 1: Books dedicated to Prince Henry, 1609–12: Summary

Format	# of Titles	Edn Sheets	% of Titles	% of Edn Sheets	Avg # of Titles/ yr	Avg edn Sheets / yr
Folio	8	775.5	17%	44%	2	193.9
Quarto	23	761	48%	43%	5.75	190.3
Octavo	12	173.375	25%	9.8%	3	43.3
Duodecimo	5	58.67	10%	3.3%	1.25	14.7

Table 2: Books Dedicated to Prince Henry, 1609

Dedicator (STC no.)	Format / Pages		Edn sheets	Other dedications / Notes	Language	Genre	Imprint
[Marcelline] (17310)	12°	98	4	Text and dedication to Prince Henry translated into English in 1610 (STC 17309; Jaggard for Budge)	French	Law/Politics	A Eleutheres [i.e., printed abroad]: Année embolismale, pour la Papauté
Jonson (14778)	4°	42	5.25		English	Literature	Okes for Bonian and Wally
Chapman (4976)	4°	44	5.5		English	Literature	H. L[ownes] for Bonian and Walley
Herring (13245)	8°	88	5.5	Blanket dedn to Pr Henry; part dedns to John Harington and jointly to James and Henry. English translation dedicated to Princess Elizabeth (1610; STC 13246)	Latin	Religion	13245: Excudebat Windet 13245a: ex officina Macham
Cowper (5919.5)	4°	64	8	Part dedication to Prince Henry, sigs 2D5-2D6. Complete work: 476 pp. 59.5 edn sheets. Other part dedns to James & Anne	English	Religion	Snodham for Firebrand and Budge [Budge's pt. ass'd to C. Knight 21 February 1609 (STC)]
Ferrabosco (10827)	2°	38	9.5	(with letterpress music)	English	Literature	Snodham for Browne
Lydiat (17041)	8°	352	22		Latin	Information	Felix Kyngston
Owen / Eudes (10561)	4°	252	31.5		English	Religion	Stansby for Fetherstone. Entered to L. Morrant; ass'd to Fetherstone 7 August [1609]
Hall (12696)	4°	272	34		English	Religion	[by J. Windet] for: 12696: Iohn Legate 12697: Eleazer Edgar 12697a: Sam. Macham
Erondelle (15491)	4°	328	41		English	Literature	[Printed by Eliot's Court Press] impensis Georgii Bishop
Morgan (18105)	4°	372	46.5	Secondary dedication to Prince Henry follows primary dedication to James I	English	Information	[Allde] for White
Chapman (13633)	2°	236	59	Publication date conjectured by STC	English	Literature	[H. Lownes] for Macham
Cotton / Calvin (4396)	2°	736	184		English	Religion	Kyngston, to be sold by W. Cotton

Table 3: Books Dedicated to Prince Henry, 1610

Dedicator (STC no.)	Format / Pages	Edn sheets	Other dedications	Language	Genre	Imprint
Davies (5118)	4°	28	3.5		English	Literature	[Stansby] for I. B[rowne]
Blenerhasset (3130)	4°	32	4		English	Information	Allde for Budge
Princes Prayers (12582.24)	12°	400	16.67	2nd edition; 1st lost	English	Religion	Windet for Chorleton
Niccols (13446)	4°	206	25.75	Part dedn to Prince Henry covers sigs 2O3 - 3E1; complete work: 896 pp; 112 edn sheets	English	Literature	Felix Kyngston
Price (20292)	4°	384	48		English	Religion	Oxford: Joseph Barnes
Morton (18183)	4°	468	58.5		English	Religion	[Stansby at Eliot's Court Press] for John Bill
Wright (26020)	4°	672	84		English	Information	Felix Kingsto[n]
Willet (25689)	2°	540	135		English	Religion	[Cambridge]: Cantrell Legge

Table 4: Books Dedicated to Prince Henry, 1611

Dedicator (STC no.)	Format / Pages	Edn sheets	Other dedications	Language	Genre	Imprint
Murray (18296)	8°	72	4.5		English	Literature	[Eld] for Smethwick
[Loiseau de Tourval] (11374)	4°	56	7		English	Law/politics	E. Allde for M. Lownes
More (18068)	12°	192	8		English	Information	Okes
[Burton?] Fierie Tryall (24269)	4°	82	10.25		English	Religion	P[urfoot] [and Creed] for A. Johnson
Hainricus, Salcolbrigiensis (Not in STC)	8°?	198	12.375		Latin	Religion	Oppenhemii: Typis Hieromymi Galleri, aere viduae Levini Hulsii
Burhill (4118)	8°	320	20		Latin	Religion	Barker
Tooker (24119)	8°	448	28		Latin	Religion	Excudebat G. Eld. impensis Nath. Butter, & R. Mab
Caus (4868.7)	2°	136	34		French	Information	[Field, and J. Mommart (Brussels)] for Barker. STC 4869: Variant: for Norton
Abbot (54)	4°	424	53		English	Religion	Stansby for Garbrand
Peake / Serlio (22235)	2°	412	103			Information	[Stafford and Snodham] for Peake. Variant: "Printed for Robert Peake" blacked out (STC).
Coryate (5808)	4°	942	117.75		English (primarily)	Literature	S[tansby for the author]

Table 5: Books Dedicated to Prince Henry, 1612

Dedicator (STC no.)	Format / Pages		Edn sheets	Other dedications	Language	Genre	Imprint
Herring (13248.2)	8°	24	1.5		Latin	Literature	Barker for Jones
Fennor (10785)	4°	32	4		English	Religion	Okes for Hunt
Owen (18988)	12°	142	6	Tp; part: throughout	Latin	Literature	Okes for Waterson
Gordon (12055)	4°	60	7.5	Tp dedn; "for" James	Latin	Religion	Field
Sparke (23028)	8°	120	7.5		Latin	Information	Field
Richer (21024)	4°	64	8		English	Religion	Stansby for Budge
Farnaby (14889)	8°	176	11		Latin	Literature	Field for Welby
Hakewill (12618)	8°	222	13.875		Latin	Religion	Stansby for Budge
Bellenden (Not in STC)	8°	376	23.5		Latin	Law/Politics	Paris: Jean Corbon
Hall (12650)	8°	378	23.625	Part dedications: 4	English	Religion	Bradwood for Macham
[Bayly (1601.5)]	12°	576	24	Later rededicated to Prince Charles	English	Religion	W. H[all] for Iohn Hodgets?
Peacham (19511)	4°	232	29	Part dedns: throughout	English	Literature	Dight
Brinsley (3768)	4°	368	46	Shared (with Charles)	English	Information	H. Lownes for Man
Drayton (7226)	2°	320	80	Engraving of Henry w/ descriptive poem	English	Literature	H. Lownes for M. Lownes et al.
Benvenuto (1895/1896)	4°	664	83	Tp dedication to Prince Henry	English/ Italian	Information	Snodham/Stepham for Redmer
Lennard (18147)	2°	684	171	Secondary, shared by two bishops	English	Religion	Islip

NOTES

1 This essay is revised and expanded from parts of Chapter 1 of my 'Book Dedications in Early Modern England and the Literary Patronage of Henry, Prince of Wales' (unpublished PhD diss., University of Virginia, 2004). A portion of this essay was presented at the Renaissance Society of America annual convention, University of Cambridge, England, 8 April 2005. I wish to thank Timothy Wilks, Michael Ullyot, Terry Belanger, Nicolas Barker, David Vander Meulen and David L. Gants for their suggestions, criticisms and encouragement at different stages.

2 While it has become customary to describe patronage as a system, this word must be used with the *caveat* that its modern connotations of machine-like precision do not necessarily apply in the Early Modern context.

3 An excellent example of the kinds of networking involved in place-seeking appears in a letter of Sir Dudley Carleton to Sir William Fleetwood, in which Carleton congratulates Fleetwood on his position in Prince Henry's service, then proceeds to discuss introductions to more highly ranking members of the Prince's household and to the Prince himself (December 1610?; printed in Timothy Wilks, 'The Court Culture of Prince Henry and his Circle, 1603–1613' [unpubl. D.Phil. diss., University of Oxford, 1988], Appendix II, 280). Private letters tend to provide more direct and detailed discussions of patron-seeking than do book dedications. But archival documentation for patronage is scarce, and the challenge is to find appropriate inductive ways to admit the conventionalized panegyric language of dedications as evidence.

4 Leila Parsons, 'Prince Henry (1594–1612) as a Patron of Literature,' *Modern Language Review* 47 (1952), p. 504.

5 For a fuller discussion, see my 'Book Dedications in Early Modern England,' pp. 139–42.

6 R.C. Bald, *John Donne: A Life* (Oxford: Clarendon, 1970), pp. 221–22; Wilks, p. 14.

7 George McGill Vogt, 'Richard Robinson's *Eupolemia* (1603),' *Studies in Philology* 21 (1924), pp. 635, 638.

8 Spareness of evidence requires this statement to be treated with caution. It is difficult to say, for instance, whether Henry Peacham's manuscript emblem book, followed by the printed *Minerva Britanna*, was typical or exceptional (see my 'Book Dedications in Early Modern England,' p. 167). Even when a manuscript survives, it is not always clear whether the manuscript was first presented before the patron gave approval to the printed dedication. A complication that must also be considered is a more performative version of pre-publication presentation, in which the book to be dedicated is shown and perhaps read to the patron, but in which the manuscript does not necessarily change hands. Chapman's *Tears of Peace* seems to indicate that Prince Henry saw the translation of the *Iliad* in draft form, just as the Prince's purported command to have Ben Jonson coordinate the commendatory verses for *Coryat's Crudities* suggests that the Prince saw that work in progress (Elkin Calhoun Wilson, *Prince Henry and English Literature* [Ithaca: Cornell UP, 1946], p. 103 n. 63). On a probable presentation manuscript by William Browne of Tavistock, see Wilks, p. 76.

9 This seems to have been the case in Francis Bacon's relationships with his elder brother Anthony and the Earl of Essex in the 1590s.

10 Among the various studies of literary patronage, studies of individual patrons containing the most useful information on the roles played by book dedications include Eleanor Rosenberg, *Leicester: Patron of Letters* (New York: Columbia UP, 1955); Michael Brennan, *Literary Patronage in the English Renaissance: The Pembroke Family* (London: Routledge, 1988); and especially L.A. Knafla, 'The 'Country' Chancellor: The Patronage of Sir Thomas Egerton, Baron Ellesmere,' *Patronage in Late Renaissance England. Papers Read at a Clark Library Seminar, 14 May 1977* (Los Angeles: William Andrews Clark Memorial Library, 1983).

11 One of the terms of Thomas Lydiat's appointment as Prince Henry's chronographer was permission to use his library (Parsons, p. 503 n. 6). See Wilks's fascinating account of the requests made by members of Prince Henry's household of Thomas James for use of the resources of the Bodley Library (pp. 49–50). James dedicated his catalogue of the library to Prince Henry in 1605 (STC 14449).

12 Wilks, p. 55.

13 Guy de Faur, Lord of Pibrac, *TETRASTICA, or The Quadrains*, trans. Joshua Sylvester (1605; sigs 2Y–3A8 of STC 21649, *Bartas: his Deuine Weekes and Workes*, with separately dated title-page; register and pagination continuous).

14 Wilks, p. 55.

15 Presumably because the first dedication was a successful one, Cowper dedicated another book to Murray a few years later, probably first in 1610: *A Most Comfortable and Christian Dialogue, betweene the Lord, and the Soule*, with Murray again styled 'speciall gentleman of the Prince his bedchamber'. One copy only of the 1610 edition (STC 5928.5) is listed in ESTC, and has not been microfilmed, so the quotation is from the 1611 second edition (STC 5929). Of the nine dedications to Murray listed in Franklin B. Williams, Jr., *Index of Dedications and Commendatory Verses in English Books before 1641* (London: The Bibliographical Society, 1962), three were offered during Prince Henry's lifetime, and four were offered following Prince Henry's death among the flood of elegiac and memorial publications. The other two came a number of years later.

16 Another example of the complications presented by the various levels of patronage at work in the Prince's household is William Barlow's *Magneticall Advertisements*, a manuscript dated 1609, written while in service of the Prince, and dedicated not to the Prince, but to Sir Thomas Chaloner, Henry's chamberlain. (It was printed after Prince Henry's death [in 1616; STC 1442], with the dedication shifted to Sir Dudley Digges.) In addition to Chaloner and Murray, other members of the Prince's household, including Sir John Holles and Sir Edward Phelips, received the dedications of one or more printed books, with mention of their relationship to the Prince. Prince Henry's household officers had the potential to have become even more significant brokers of patronage had the Prince survived to become king.

17 'The Glorification of a Christian,' the third of the *Three Heavenly Treatises upon the Eight Chapter to the Romanes* (1609; STC 5919.5). Cowper dedicated his book's first two treatises respectively to King James and Queen Anne. The dedication to the Prince appears on sigs 2D5–2D6v.

18 Appendix I, pp. 275–79. Wilks's list covers the period after 1608. Cowper does not appear in Thomas Birch, *The Life of Henry, Prince of Wales, Eldest Son of King James I* (London: A. Millar, 1760); J.W. Williamson, *The Myth of the Conqueror: Prince Henry Stuart, a Study in 17th Century Personation* (New York: AMS Press, 1978); or in Roy Strong, *Henry, Prince of Wales and England's Lost Renaissance* (London: Thames and Hudson, 1986). Wilson notices Cowper's dedication to Prince Henry and his position first as minister at Perth and later as a bishop, but does not mention Cowper's earlier dedication to Murray or his claim to be a daily orator to the Prince (p. 72).

19 The frequent extracurricular tutelage the Prince encountered through the regular attendance of sermons and the reception of devotional and theological works must be considered in any account of his education.

20 The Folger Shakespeare Library copy of *Principles for Yong Princes* has the feathers of the Prince of Wales giltstamped on its covers, on vellum over boards. Henry's badge possibly identifies the book as More's presentation copy to the Prince or at least as a copy that circulated in Henry's household (call number STC 18068).

21 Wilks, p. 12.

22 Wilks, pp. 12, 13 n.2.

23 Wilks, p. 30.

24 Wilks, p. 29.

25 Francis Bacon, *The Essayes or Counsels, Civill and Morall*, ed. Michael Kiernan (Oxford: Clarendon, 1985), p. LXXIV.

26 Throughout this chapter, I have followed the traditional assumption that Bacon changed his dedicatee because of Prince Henry's death, but it is worth at least mentioning other possibilities. It is conceivable, if unlikely, for instance, that Bacon re-dedicated to Constable not because Henry died, but because Henry rejected the dedication. In the case of Bacon's *Essays*, a more precise date for the printing (based, for instance, on the composition patterns involved in the printing house that produced the book) relative to Prince Henry's death might assist in these determinations.

27 Williams, p. 44.

28 Brennan, p. 4.

29 Similarly, of the 110 printed titles dedicated to Prince Henry, only five had previously been dedicated to someone else: Clapham, *A Briefe of the Bibles Historie* (STC 5333); Edmondes, *Observations* (STC 7490); Herring,

Pietas Pontificia (STC 13245); Wilcocks (trans. of Mornay), *A Worke Concerning the Trunesse of Christian Religion* (STC 18151); Weever, *An Agnus Dei* (STC 25222); and Wright, *Certain Errors* (STC 26020). Williams, pp. 243–53.

30 STC 6198; Strong, p. 31.

31 Strong, pp. 145–46.

32 STC 20994; Williams, p. 242.

33 Williams, *Index of Dedications*, appendix, pp. 243–54.

34 STC 5051 and 5052. Williams lists the undated STC 5051 under 1612, but the online ESTC proposes a date of 1608. The later date seems less likely insofar as Lennard's 1612 dedication of *The Mysterie of Iniquity* acknowledges Prince Henry's prior acceptance of the earlier book.

35 STC 14449 and 14450.

36 STC 17334 and 17335.

37 STC 20983 and 20984.

38 STC 21032.

39 STC 25678 and 25679.

40 The retention of Chapman's dedication to Prince Henry is discussed in my 'Book Dedications and the Death of a Patron: The Memorial Engraving in Chapman's *Homer*,' *Book History* 7 (2004), pp. 1–29.

41 See appendix. Williams gives fifteen dedications to Prince Henry in 1612, one of which (STC 5051) was probably printed between 1606 and 1608 according to the online English Short Title Catalogue. Williams does not record the dedications from Bayly or Bellenden. James I, though recipient of the most dedications overall during his reign, received the dedications of only five printed books in 1612, in addition to panegyric material in a couple other publications (Williams, pp. 93, 105).

42 While recognizing both the ambiguity of many Early Modern works especially where religion is concerned, and the disparate nature of some materials within categories, I follow here the broad genre categories suggested by David L. Gants in the explanatory essay for the Early English Booktrade Database: Literature, Religion, History, Law/Politics, Information, Official Documents, and Ephemera <http://www.lib.unb.ca/Texts/Gants/EEBD/> (accessed 30 January 2007). Such a broad category as 'Literature,' for instance, risks oversimplification, embracing as it does both study texts of classical verse like Farnaby and the epic-like stature of an original work like Drayton. The term is used here without either assuming the Romantic construct of high literature or denying early modern ideas about the didactic utility of imaginative writing.

43 Two additional works have been excluded. Henry Peacham's *Graphice* (1612; STC 19507) contains a woodcut of Prince Henry's badge (sig. B1v), which could be considered a dedication of sorts. Since the book is otherwise dedicated to Sir Edmund Ashfield (the only dedication Ashfield received, according to Williams), it has not been counted here as a book dedicated to Prince Henry. Salomon de Caus's *La Perspective, avec la Raison des Ombres et Miroirs* was first dedicated to Prince Henry in 1611 (STC 4868.7); the version dated 1612 (STC 4869) is merely a variant issue. The dedication to Prince Henry does not change, so it has not been counted with the 1612 dedications. On de Caus, see the essay by Alexander Marr in this volume.

44 STC and Strong, p. 53. The first edition is no longer extant; its existence and its dedication to Prince Henry can only be deduced from the second (STC 1601.5, which itself survives in only a single copy, at Lambeth Palace), whose dedication to Prince Charles begins 'This second Epistle I now write …'. While this has generally been assumed to indicate the existence of a prior printed edition, it is also possible that the dedication to Prince Henry survived only in manuscript or that it was printed for this edition but cancelled. The Lambeth Palace copy of the second edition has not been microfilmed; Bayly had already altered the text of the dedication to Charles again by the time the third edition was printed in 1613.

45 For an extended discussion of Bacon's abortive dedication to Prince Henry, see my *Book Dedications in Early Modern England*, pp. 73–85.

46 British Library MS. Additional 4259, according to Wilson, p. 116.

47 Wilson, pp. 51–53. The copy at Lambeth Palace Library (MS 822) was presented to Archbishop Abbott 'as a new year's gift in 1612' and contains a military equestrian portrait of Prince Henry in pen and ink, as well as a dedicatory letter addressed to the Prince (Wilson, p. 53 n.144). British Library MS Royal 16 E. XXXVII (or possibly XXVIII, the number given by Wilson), the parent manuscript, may or may not have been presented to the Prince. Cleland's panegyric apparently never saw print.

48 Mark Evans (ed.), *Princes as Patrons: The Art Collections of the Princes of Wales from the Renaissance to the Present Day: An Exhibition from the Royal Collection* (London: Merrell Holberton, 1998), p. 35. See also Georgianna Ziegler, 'Hand-Mai[i]de Books: The Manuscripts of Esther Inglis, Early-Modern Precursors of the Artists' Book,' *English Manuscript Studies 1100–1700* (2000), pp. 73–87, and "More than Feminine Boldness': The Gift Books of Esther Inglis,' in Mary E. Burke *et al.* (eds.), *Women, Writing, and the Reproduction of Culture in Tudor and Stuart Britain* (Syracuse, NY: Syracuse UP, 2000), pp. 19–37.

49 Respectively, British Library MS. Royal 12 A. XXVIII and MS. Royal 12 E. XXIV (Wilson, pp. 114–15 n. 92); and British Library MS. Eg. 2875 (formerly owned by Bertram Dobell). Yet another work offered by one of the Spenserian poets, Fletcher's dedication to Prince Henry is printed and translated in Phineas Fletcher, *Locustae vel Pietas Iesuitica*, ed. and trans. Estelle Haan (Leuven: Leuven UP, 1996), pp. 120–22. Haan dates the dedication to 'between March 1611 and 6 November 1612' (p. LXXIX).

50 William Laud, untitled manuscript on civil and ecclesiastical authority, Pierpont Morgan Library MA 226. The fine goatskin binding is richly gold-tooled and blocked with the arms of Prince Henry. The text is ruled in gold over red ink, and the handsome script is embellished throughout in gold ink: it is clearly a text intended for royal presentation. The initials 'WL' are to be found at the top of the final leaf, verso. The manuscript starts abruptly on its first leaf with the first section heading, 'A distribution of the bookes conteyned in the Bible,' and there are trace remnants of what may have been a title leaf, which almost certainly would also have included a presentation inscription or dedication. The binding is illustrated in *A Collection of Facsimiles from Examples of Historic or Artistic Book-binding* (London: B. Quaritch, 1889), no. 35.

51 Jason Scott-Warren comments that the highly individuated character of Harington's manuscripts encodes a 'complex transactional significance': 'The diversity of Harington's output becomes comprehensible if we bring back into the picture the material forms in which his works were embodied .... Harington devoted extraordinary quantities of time, energy, patience, and money to the task of customizing individual copies of his books for presentation to particular individuals. (*Sir John Harington and the Book as Gift* (Oxford: Oxford UP, 2001), p. 21.'

52 The tendency to concentrate on eccentric figures such as Inglis and Harington reflects a broader contemporary preoccupation with the marginal over against the typical. The practices of such figures take on even richer textures when set against a fuller picture of the usual workings of the patronage system. Compare Debora Shuger's observation that 'recent scholarship has focused on heterodoxy, whether sexual, political, literary, or religious, often remaining content to presuppose the contents of "official" belief' (Debora Kuller Shuger, *Habits of Thought in the English Renaissance: Religion, Politics, and the Dominant Culture* [Toronto: U of Toronto Press, 1997; first edition 1990], p. 3). The practice of creating elaborate presentation manuscripts was of course by no means limited to figures outside the mainstream, as William Laud's presentation copy of his treatise on civil and ecclesiastical authority bears witness (see above).

53 ESTC records only three locations for Herring (as of October 2006). Bayly's *Practise of Pietie* has been included in the analysis even though it can only be assumed that the non-extant first edition was the same format and length as the second.

54 Gordon collates 4°: A–G⁴ H². Sparke collates 8°: A–G⁸ H⁴ (not counting two folding letterpress tables).

55 David L. Gants, 'A Quantitative Analysis of the London Book Trade 1614–1618,' *Studies in Bibliography* 55 (2002), p. 186.

56 Because of the dearth of publishing records, it is seldom possible to determine the number of copies printed in any given edition in the early handpress period. Most editions ran to about 1,000 copies, though large

specialist works might be printed in only 500 copies, and small guaranteed sellers such as almanacs might run to 2,000 copies, after which point the economy of scale made reprinting later more economical. Counts of surviving numbers of copies are a wholly unreliable indicator of original print runs, since works printed in the highest numbers tend to survive in the fewest copies. See Philip Gaskell, *A New Introduction to Bibliography* (New Castle, DE: Oak Knoll, 1995; first edn 1972; corr. edn 1974), pp. 160–63.

57 The most accessible discussions of format are Philip Gaskell, pp. 78–109; and Terry Belanger, *Anatomy of a Book: Format in the Hand-Press Period* (Charlottesville, Va.: Book Arts Press, 1991 [videocassette], 2003 [DVD]).

58 Richard Robinson divides his list of his writings and receipts by format. His doing so probably reflects a general contemporary awareness of the significance of format, from an author's perspective, in the context of book dedication (Vogt, *passim*).

59 Roger Gaskell, 'Printing House and Engraving Shop: A Mysterious Collaboration,' *The Book Collector*, 53 (2004), p. 222.

60 Parsons, pp. 504–05.

61 Wilks, p. 277.

62 Herring's *Pietas Pontificia* is translated by Estelle Haan in *Humanistica Lovaniensia*, XLI (1992), pp. 251–95.

63 The work was formerly attributed to George Marcelline (STC).

64 Prior permission or at least some kind of introduction seems to have been usual, if not an absolute requirement, for dedications to members of the royal family at this date.

65 Blayney based his figures on D.F. McKenzie's study of the Cambridge University Press (cited on the 'Project Methods' page, Early English Booktrade Database, by David L. Gants, whose own figures are comparable in his 'Quantitative Analysis,' *passim*). Complicating factors, some of which would slow, and some of which would speed production, should also be noted. Printers rarely worked their way through a single book *seriatim*; they typically had several books in concurrent production, sometimes on multiple presses. Allowances need also to be made for interruptions for bread-and-butter job printing – and even for closures owing to the plague. Large projects were also sometimes farmed out among several printing houses. For a detailed study of concurrent production, see Charlton Hinman, *The Printing and Proof-reading of the First Folio of Shakespeare* (Oxford: Clarendon Press, 1963) and the excellent summary by Peter Blayney in *The First Folio of Shakespeare* (Washington: Folger Shakespeare Library, 1991). The First Folio was in the press from about February 1622 until after October 1623, and it shared the press with four other books in folio (Blayney, pp. 5–7).

66 From this perspective, Sir Walter Ralegh's decision in 1614 not to replace the planned dedication to Prince Henry with another for *The History of the World* – at 394 edition sheets – gains added poignancy. Ralegh had well over a year, and perhaps more than two, to contemplate (and solicit) potential dedicatees while the book was being machined (STC 20637).

67 Gants reports the following average outputs in terms of editions sheets for the five-year period: Religion, 52%; Literature, 15%; Information, 12%; Law/Politics, 11%; History, 7% ('Quantitative Analysis,' p. 190).

68 The term 'publisher' should be handled cautiously in describing early modern book production; I use it simply to mean an individual laying out the costs of the publication insofar as that can be determined ('printed for' so-and-so), without necessarily implying the sharper delineation of roles that obtains in modern publishing.

69 Gants notes that there were roughly twenty master printers in London at any given point during the early seventeenth century ('Quantitative Analysis', p. 188).

70 Gants calculates an average of 7616 edition sheets per year for the entire London booktrade during the years 1614–18 (*ibid.*, p. 187).

Appendix: Printed Books Dedicated to Prince Henry, 1609–12

The books dedicated to Prince Henry have been listed within each year alphabetically by dedicator. Unless otherwise noted, the source for each reference is Williams, *Index of Dedications*. Some titles have been abbreviated. The place of publication is London unless otherwise indicated. I have regularized i/j, u/v, and w/vv according to modern usage.

1609

Chapman, George. *Euthymiae Raptus; or the Teares of Peace*. STC 4976.

Chapman, George, trans. *Homer Prince of Poets*. [1609?] STC 13633.

> Dedication reprinted in STC 13634, *The Iliads of Homer*, 1611 (with new dedicatory acrostic sonnet added to preliminaries), and STC 13624, *The Whole Works of Homer*, 1616.

Cotton, Clement. Translation of John Calvin, *A Commentary upon the Prophecie of Isaiah*. STC 4396.

> Not in Williams. Wilson 72. Dedication shared with Princess Elizabeth

Cowper, William. *Three Heavenly Treatises upon the Eight Chapter to the Romanes*. STC 5919.5 (formerly STC 5935).

> Part dedication to Prince Henry of third treatise, 'The Glorification of a Christian,' sigs. 2D5-2D6. First part (possibly covering whole work) dedicated to King James; second part dedicated to Anne of Denmark. Dedication to Prince Henry reprinted in STC 5920, *Heaven Opened*, 1611; and STC 5909, *Works*, 1623.

Erondelle, Pierre. *Nova Francia*. Translation from Marc Lescarbot, *Histoire de la Nouvelle France*. STC 15491. Dedication to Prince Henry not reprinted in subsequent editions.

Ferrabosco, Alfonso. *Ayres*. STC 10827.

> Nine airs set to poems by Ben Jonson, and one each to words by John Donne and Thomas Campion (ESTC).

Hall, Joseph. *The Peace of Rome*. STC 12696.

Herring, Francis. *Pietas Pontificia*. STC 13245. Part dedications to 1) Henry (Williams lists it as a part dedication, but owing to its placement I have treated it as a blanket dedication covering the entire book); 2) John Harington (first Baron of Exton, not the second, according to Williams); 3) James and Henry. First published in 1606 with dedication to James only (STC 13244).

Jonson, Ben. *The Masque of Queenes*. STC 14778. Dedication to Prince Henry not reprinted in subsequent editions.

Lydiat, Thomas. *Emendatio Temporum Compendio Facta ab Initio Mundi ad Praesens usque*. STC 17041.

1612

Bayly, Lewis. *The Practise of Pietie*. London 1612? (No extant copy known). Not in Williams. The second edition (1612; STC 1601.5) is described in ESTC as 12° collating A-2A¹² and entered in the Stationers' Register on 11 January 1612.

Bellenden, William. *Ciceronis Consul, Senator, Senatúsq; Romanus*. Parisiis: apud Ioannem Corbon, 1612. 8°: ã⁸ A-Z⁸ 2A⁴. Not in Williams; not in STC. Reprinted in William Bellenden, *De Statu Libri Tres* (London 1787).

Benvenuto, Italian. *The Passenger*, with facing-page English translation by a Mr King. STC 1895. (Variant: STC 1896).

Brinsley, John. *Ludus Literarius: or, the Grammar Schoole*. STC 3768.
    Dedication shared with Prince Charles.

Drayton, Michael. *Poly-Olbion*. STC 7226.

Farnaby, Thomas. *Iunii Iuuenalis et Auli Persii Flacci Satyrae*. STC 14889.

William Fennor. *Pluto his Travailes, or, the divils Pilgrimage to the Colledge of Jesuites*. STC 10785.

Gordon, John. *Anti-bellarmino-tortor, sive Tortus Retortus*. STC 12055.

Hakewill, George. *Scutum Regium. id est, Adversus Omnes Regicidas et Regicidarum Patronos*. STC 12618.

Hall, Joseph. *Contemplations upon the Principall Passages of the Holie Storie*. STC 12650. Dedication reprinted in STC 12706, *A Recollection of Such Treatises*, 1615; and STC 12635, *Works*, 1625.

Herring, Francis. *Poemata Miscellanea*. STC 13248.2.

Lennard, Samson. *The Mystery of Iniquitie*. STC 18147. Translation of Philippe de Mornay, seigneur du Plessis-Marly, *Le Mystère d'Iniquité*. One of the copies in the Folger Shakespeare Library has the arms of Prince Henry on its binding (STC 18147 Copy 3).

Owen, John. *Epigrammatum … Libri Tres*. STC 18988.
    Dedication shared with Prince Charles. Also part dedications in STC 18987, *Epigrammatum Libri Tres* editio quarta, which was 'also issued as part 1 of his *Epigrammatum … Libri Decem*, 1612 (STC 18988.5)' (ESTC).

Peacham, Henry, the younger. *Minerva Britanna, or a Garden of Heroical Devises*. STC 19511.

Sparke, William. *Vis Naturae et Virtus Vitae Explicatae, Comparatae, ad Universum Doctrinae Ordinem Constituendum*. STC 23028.

[Tourval, Jean Loiseau de?]. *A Treatise of Ecclesiasticall and Politike Power*. STC 21024. Anonymous translation of Edmond Richer's *De Ecclesiastica et Politica Potestate* (Paris 1611). Dedication signed 'δ' (possibly Jean Loiseau de Tourval? STC).

5 | Prince Henry as Chapman's 'Absolute Man'

Gilles Bertheau

Published from 1598 to 1624, Chapman's translation of Homer[1] occupied the major part of his literary career and was regarded by him as the divine mission of his life.[2] Among the three aristocratic dedicatees of the different instalments of the translation of the *Iliad* and the *Odyssey*, Prince Henry stands out as the most prominent figure. To him – and his royal mother – Chapman dedicated *Twelue Bookes of the Iliads* in 1609, which was reprinted with the dedicatory Epistle in 1611. In 1616 – four years after the 'most disastrous death' of the Prince – Chapman published *The Whole Works of Homer,* dedicated to Robert Carr, Earl of Somerset, but containing also the dedicatory Epistle to Henry, to which the poet added memorial verses. These dedicatory texts – together with the prefaces, the addresses to the reader and Chapman's *Epicede* on the death of the Prince – make up a portrait of the young Prince as an example of what the poet calls the 'absolute man', the central heroic figure of his French tragedies.

Through the study of the introductory texts to his Homeric translations, it will be possible to understand how the poet creates a correspondence between the epic poetry of Homer, 'Prince of Poetts', the Homeric reader he deserves, and Henry as a 'Prince of Men'. This phrase enables Chapman to connect his patron with the concept of 'natiue noblesse',[3] developed in *The Tragedy of Bussy D'Ambois* (1607) and *The Conspiracy and Tragedy of Byron* (1608), which is central to the definition of the 'absolute man'. The Prince is therefore considered a model worthy of imitation, a 'matchless' hero, resembling the fictional Byron and the historical Essex, whom he admired.

At the end of the sixteenth century, it was high time an English poet set about to translate Homer's *Iliad* and *Odyssey*.[4] Highest in the hierarchy of genres in the Renaissance, epic poetry was regarded as fit to instruct and inspire rulers and princes and Homer as the best of poets. George Chapman, who gave him the title of 'Prince of Poetts' in his 1616 edition of Homer's poems,[5] belongs to this tradition. In a text prefixed to his 1611 edition of the *Iliad* – 'Of Homer' – Chapman writes: 'For his respect amongst the most learned Plato in Ione calleth him … *Poetarum omnium et præstantissimum et divinissimum*', that is to say 'the most prominent and divine of all poets'.[6] In his dedicatory epistle to the Earl of Somerset his *Twelve Bookes of the Odyssey* (1614), Chapman called Homer 'the most wise and divine Poet'.[7] Homer is the first of poets, never imitated since: 'all Homer's bookes are such as have been presidents ever since of all sortes of Poems, imitating none, nor ever worthily imitated of any',[8] and Chapman further said that 'not onely all learning, government and wisedome [is] deduc't as from a bottomlesse fountaine from him, but all wit elegancie, disposition and judgement'.[9] Here, beyond its moral

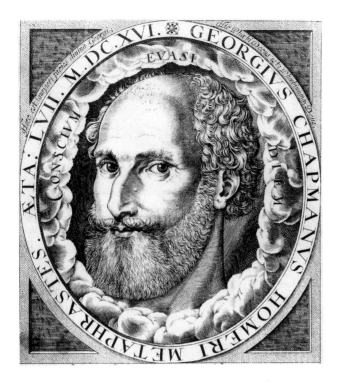

Fig. 1 Portrait of George Chapman by William Hole
in George Chapman, *The Whole Works of Homer* (1616)

and intellectual values, the *Iliad* is presented as a handbook of government, which is peculiarly becoming for a dedicatee such as the heir to the throne, the future ruler of Great Britain. This notion of political *exemplum* is developed in the same text:

> Nor can it [my paper] be reputed an unworthy incitement to propose the true image of all virtues and humaine government (even in the hart of this tumultuous season) to your other serious affaires, especially since it contaynes the true portraite of ancient stratagems and discipline of war, wherein it wilbe worthie little lesse than admiration of your apprehensive judgement to note in many thinges the affinitie they have with your present complementes of field – the orations, counsailes, attempts and exploits not to be exceeded by the freshest brains of this hote-spirited time, the horror of arms endlessly thundering, piety, justice, valour and royaltie eternally shining in his soule-infused verse.[10]

The translator especially emphasizes the 'Achilleian'[11] and martial virtues of Homer's teachings ('the true portraite of ancient stratagems and discipline of war') and their direct relevance to his own time ('the affinitie they have with your present complementes of field'). In a way, he justifies the interest of his translation of Homer for his contemporaries, and most particularly for the most promising person of James I's elder son. From this point of view, Homer is considered by Chapman – who belonged to the circle of the Prince as sewer-in-ordinary[12] – a most pertinent part of Henry's princely education. It is as if, in 1598, he prepared for his necessary change of dedicatees – after the Earl of Essex's execution in 1601 – by insisting on the analogy between the epic personnel of the poem ('Kings and Princes') and the princely dedicatee of 1609, when he presents Homer as 'this President of all learning, virtue, valour, honour, and societie, who (with his own soule) hath eternizde Armies of Kings and Princes; whose imperiall Muse, the great Monarch of the world would say effected more of his Conquests than his universall power'.[13]

Homer as a mirror for princes was already an opinion expressed by Sir Philip Sidney, who, in his *Defence of Poetry* (written around 1580, published posthumously in 1595), wrote: 'Alexander left his schoolmaster, living Aristotle, behind him, but took dead Homer with him. … the chief thing he was ever heard to wish for was that Homer had been alive. He well found he received more bravery of mind by the pattern of Achilles than by hearing the definition of fortitude', the English poet putting forward the superiority of the mimesis of Homer's works over mere rhetorical discourse.[14] The example of Alexander already showed with whom the readers of Homer could compare, which was well understood by Chapman, who, in 1609, explained that, for Homer's life,

> *Alexander* would haue giuen
> One of his kingdoms: who …
> Kept as his Crowne his workes; and thought them still
> His Angels; in all power, to rule his will;
> And would affirme that *Homers* poesie
> Did more aduance his Asian victorie,
> Than all his Armies (21–22; 25–29).[15]

As a matter of fact, George Chapman's conception of readers in general, and of the readers of his Homer in particular, confirms that they were to be special persons. As early as 1598, when his first translations appeared in print, the poet addressed the 'Reader' as a learned, intelligent and virtuous person. In the *Seaven Bookes of the Iliades,* Chapman wrote a preface 'To the Reader', which began as follows: 'I suppose you to be no meare reader since you intend to reade Homer, and therefore wish I may walke free from their common objections that can onelie reade.'[16] Reading Homer's 'soule-infused verse' requires more than mere literacy. This is reasserted again in *Achilles' Shield*, in which Chapman is even clearer insofar as he addresses not the reader but 'the Understander': 'You are not every bodie: to you (as to one of my very few friends) I may be bold to utter my mind',[17] and in the rest of the text he defends his previous dedicatory epistles and reasserts the qualities of Homer's poetry. Thus, the flattered reader

Chapman addresses belongs to a very select and intimate community; something Chapman emphasises further by prefixing to his translation an epistle to one of the cleverest men of the age, Thomas Harriot.[18] We may notice that the definition of the ideal reader expounded in these lines is not at variance with what Chapman stated in his dedication to Matthew Roydon of *Ovids Banquet of Sences* in 1595: 'The prophane multitude I hate, & onelie consecrate my strange Poems to these serching spirits, whom learning hath made noble, and nobilitie sacred'.[19] The natural consequence of this notion is already expressed in 1598: 'Onely kings and princes have been Homer's Patrones, amongst whom Ptolomie would say, he that had sleight handes to entertayne Homer has as sleight braines to rule his common wealth',[20] Therefore, the foremost presence of a reader and a dedicatee such as Henry in the opening pages of the 1609, 1611 and 1616 Folios becomes self-evident.

In 1609, the fifteen-year old Prince lived at St James's Palace surrounded by a select group of artists and a very large household of over four hundred.[21] Chapman was a recognized poet and playwright who had already published two French tragedies, *The Tragedy of Bussy D'Ambois* and *The Conspiracy and Tragedy of Byron*. The execution of his former patron, the Earl of Essex, had left him in a precarious financial situation and forced him to look for a new protector. Naturally enough, he turned towards the young Prince, acting as his voluntary sewer-in-ordinary from soon after the time of his arrival in England, always hoping Henry would become his 'Gracious and sacred Mœcœnas'.[22]

The 1609 Folio of the *Twelue Bookes of the Iliads* comprehends an Epistle to Henry, an anagram on 'Henrye, Prince of Wales', a sonnet to Queen Anne, an address 'To the Reader', 'The Preface to the Reader' and sixteen sonnets to noteworthy aristocrats of the time (one notices that the only great personage to be missing in the list of dedicatees is King James I himself).[23] The dedication begins with the following words: 'TO THE HIGH | BORNE PRINCE OF | MEN, *HENRIE THRICE | Royall inheritor to the vnited kingdoms | of Great* Brittaine, &c.' More than his official title, Chapman highlighted rather Henry's natural noblesse, encapsulated in this phrase 'prince of men', the meaning of which he developed in the first lines of the Epistle:

> Since perfect happinesse, by Princes sought,
> Is not with birth, borne, nor Exchequers bought;
> Nor followes in great Traines; nor is possest
> With any outward State; but makes him blest
> That gouernes inward; and beholdeth theare,
> All his affections stand about him bare;
> That by his power can send to Towre, and death,
> All traitrous passions; marshalling beneath
> His justice, his meere will; and in his minde
> Holds such a sceptre, as can keepe confinde

His whole lifes actions in the royall bounds
Of Vertue and Religion, and their grounds
Takes in to sow his honours, his delights
And complete empire – you should learn these rights
(Great Prince of men) by Princely presidents;
Which here, in all kinds, my true zeale presents
To furnish your youths groundworke, and first State … (1–17).[24]

The poet uses the political metaphor in an ethical perspective: 'perfect happinesse' and 'complete empire' can be achieved only through a complete control of passions and an absolute sovereignty over the mind. Homer fulfils a specular function ('To furnish your youths groundworke, and first State') for the prince, who must, before he becomes king, prove a true 'Prince of men'. Although the phrase does not sound dashingly original – it can be parallelled with the phrase used by the translator to designate Agamemnon, 'king of men'[25] – it sends us back to a concept closely associated to that of the 'absolute man': that of the 'natiue noblesse' of man.

The concept can be traced in his first two tragedies, *The Tragedy of Bussy D'Ambois* and *The Conspiracy and Tragedy of Byron*. In the former, King Henri (Henri III of France) rebukes the Duke of Guise for his anger at Bussy's vehement exposition of his notion of true noblesse:

- Cosen Guise, I wonder
Your equall disposition brookes so ill
A man so good, that only would vphold
Man in his natiue noblesse, from whose fall
All our dissentions rise … (III, II, 88–92).

The king supports Bussy's claim that true noblesse, 'natiue noblesse', has nothing to do with the notions put forward by Monsieur to defend Guise – 'titles'(III, II, 73), 'blood' (III, II, 77) and birth (III, II,76) – but everything to do with inner 'merit' (III, II, 78). Henri further explains:

Kings had neuer borne
Such boundlesse eminence ouer other men,
Had all maintain'd the spirit and state of D'Ambois;
Nor had the full impartiall hand of Nature
That all things gaue in her originall,
Without these definite terms of Mine and Thine,
Beene turn'd vniustly to the hand of Fortune:
Had all preseru'd her in her prime, like D'Ambois;
No enuie, no disiunction had dissolu'd,

> Or pluck'd out one sticke of the golden fagot,
> In which the world of Saturne was compris'd,
> Had all beene held together with the nerues,
> The genius and th'ingenuous soule of D'Ambois (III, II, 95–107).

This speech stresses the original noblesse of all men at the time of the Golden Age (104)[26] – also evoked by Sir Fulke Greville in his *Treatise of Monarchy* (I, 1–2) – the fall from which caused power to be wielded by princes. Bussy takes this stance to extremes when he declares:

> since I am free
> (Offending no iust law), let no law make
> By any wrong it does, my life her slaue:
> When I am wrong'd and that law failes to right me,
> Let me be King my self (as man was made)
> And doe a iustice that exceedes the law …
> Who to himselfe is law, no law doth neede,
> Offends no King, and is a King indeede (II, I, 194–99; 203–04).

In spite of the fact that the king's assimilation of Bussy with this prelapsarian 'ingenuous' man is problematic, in Chapman's mind there can be no doubt as to the positive connotation of this notion of 'natiue noblesse' (another way of saying goodness), opposed to the deceptive appearance of titles and outward greatness. The corollary of this same idea is expressed by Tamyra, when she says that 'Man is a name of honour for a King: | Additions take away from each chiefe thing' (IV, I, 48–49). If a man is naturally royal, then a king can be called a man without any blemish to his reputation and honour, and Henry 'Great Prince of Men'.

This is one of his dearest thematic threads, since it can again be found in *The Conspiracy of Byron*, where the Duke of Savoy alludes to the 'first royalty' of man (II, I, 72). Byron himself speaks of 'the free-borne powers of royal man' (III, I, 31) and later declares – very much like Bussy – 'I will be mine own King' (V, I, 137).

The haughty attitude of these two tragic characters, who claim what Jonathan Dollimore calls an 'essentialist autonomy',[27] is buttressed by a set of references that enable Chapman to carve his 'absolute man' into Greek mythology. First and foremost, both Bussy and Byron are compared to the demi-god Hercules (also called Alcides). When Bussy dies, the ghost of Comolet pronounces the following lines, which make him a demi-god: 'Farewell braue relicts of a compleat man: | Looke vp and see thy spirit made a star, | Ioine flame with Hercules' (*Bussy D'Ambois*, V, III, 264-66).[28] In *The Conspiracy of Byron*, the Duke of Savoy declares that 'Fortune to [Byron] was *Iuno* to *Alcides*' (II, II, 93), and the marshal compares himself to Hercules when he says: 'I haue *Alcides*-like gone vnder th'earth | And on these showlders borne the weight of

France' (*The Tragedy of Byron*, III, I, 151). The heroic stature of both characters is furthered by comparisons with Atlas. For example, the Count of Montsurry asks his wife to go to court along with him to 'see great D'Ambois / (Fortunes proud mushrome shot vp in a night) / Stand like an Atlas vnderneath the King' (*Bussy D'Ambois*, III, I, 99). In *The Tragedy of Byron*, Captain Vitry comments on the way the count of Auvergne bears his imprisonment, as compared with the Duke of Byron: 'See how he beares his crosse, with his small strength, / On easier shoulders then the other Atlas' (IV, II, 304). Last but not least, it is clear that the playwright has given Byron 'Achilleian' features. This is the case in *The Conspiracy of Byron*, when the hero pompously declares: 'like *Pelides* in *Scamanders* flood, / Vp to the eares in surges, I will fight, / And pluck French *Ilion* vnderneath the waues' (II, I, 151–53). In *The Tragedy of Byron*, Henri says that the Spaniards 'found him still, / As an vnmatcht *Achilles* in the warres, / So a most wise *Vlisses* to their words, / Stopping his eares at their enchanted sounds' (I, I, 77–80), Chapman combining Achilles with Ulysses, the *Iliad* with the *Odyssey*. These observations show how Chapman is hoisting his 'absolute man' to a status equivalent to that of Homer's heroes: beyond the strength of Hercules, he has the *virtù* of Achilles and the wisdom of Ulysses and in his person gathers physical, intellectual and moral qualities.

Like Chapman's tragic heroes (Bussy and Byron at least), whose characterization owes much to mythological heroism, Henry stands as this exceptional man the poet is addressing in his Homeric paratexts. He too possesses the intellectual qualities required by Chapman of his readers, as is confirmed by his early biographer, John Hawkins, who mentions the Prince's 'love of Learning, to the Muses, to all the Learned who any way did excel'.[29]

The unique personality of the Prince is asserted in *An Epicede or / Fvnerall Song: / on the most Disastrous Death, of the, / High-borne Prince of Men, HENRY / Prince of WALES* (1612). Described as his 'most deare and Heroicall Patrone' in the dedication to Henry Jones, the Prince is said to have been

> One that in hope, tooke vp to toplesse height
> All his great Ancestors …
> Vanisht without the end; for which he had
> Such matchlesse vertues, and was God-like made? (45–46; 49–50)[30]

The 'matchlesse vertues' of the Prince and his heroism are combined in the 1616 edition of Homer's *Whole Works*, which contains memorial verses addressed by the poet 'To the Imortall Memorie, of the Incomparable Heroe, *Henrye* Prince of Wales',[31] in which 'matchless' is Latinized and the Prince's 'Heroicall' stature clearly reasserted.

The poet went even further by transforming the Prince's death into an apotheosis:[32] 'Blest yet, and sacred shall thy memory be, / O-nothing-lesse-then-mortall Deitie, / Thy Graces, like the Sunne, to all men giuing (116–18).[33] This metamorphosis very much reminds us of Bussy's changing into an equivalent of Hercules at the end of the tragedy (see above) and enables the

poet to transfer on to the son the father's claim to a divine right of kings, an idea expressed –
among so numerous other instances – as early as in the sonnet of the *Basilicon Doron*, precisely
written for the young Henry (1598): 'God giues not Kings the stile of *Gods* in vaine' (1).[34]

In Chapman's corpus, the Prince shares this uniqueness with illustrious personages such
as Queen Elizabeth I, whom Henri III speaks of in the following terms, when he decides to
send the felonious Byron to England:

> And now for England you shall go, my lord,
> Our lord ambassador to that matchless queen;
> You never had a voyage of such pleasure,
> Honour, and worthy objects; there's a queen
> Where nature keeps her state, and state her court,
> Wisdom her study, continence her fort;
> Where magnanimity, humanity,
> Firmness in counsel and integrity,
> Grace to her poorest subjects, majesty
> To awe the greatest, have respects divine,
> And in her each part, all the virtues shine (*The Conspiracy of Byron*, III, II, 274–84).

Whereas the rest of the play is written in blank verse, this particular passage rhymes, most of
the time by couplets. By reading the last five rhymes, which are masculine, vertically, one can
– this is my interpretation – find a definition of the 'absolute man': a royal man ('humanity'
and 'majesty'), of superior moral valour ('integrity') and God-like created ('divine') outshining
all the others ('shine').

Besides, the eulogy of Elizabeth I's ideal kingdom (characterized by 'wisdom', 'continence',
virtue and order) can be taken as an oblique comment on James I's inability to live and reign
up to this standard, while the character of Henri IV – the Prince's godfather – is trying to establish, through these words, a parallel between her and him. This also points to Chapman's
usual tendency to exalt Henry the expense of his father, as Jean Jacquot remarked.[35]

The same adjective is used by the playwright to set up another and most significant parallel, between Byron and Essex. When Roncas, the ambassador of Savoy in France, presents
Marshal Byron to his master, he declares: '… he is a man / Of matchless valour and was ever
happy / In all encounters' (*Conspiracy*, I, I, 61-63). In *The Tragedy of Byron*, it is Byron himself who
uses the same word to describe the Earl of Essex: 'The matchless Earl of Essex, whom some
make, / In their most sure divinings of my death, / A parallel with me in life and fortune …' (*The
Tragedy of Byron*, IV, I, 133–35).

Therefore, Chapman establishes a triple comparison: between Prince Henry, Byron and
Essex. In his death, the Prince assumes the status of a hero, like Essex and Byron. Moreover, this

association between Henry and Essex is not simply literary: we know that the young Prince was a fervent admirer of the Earl, and tried to revive his chivalric spirit in the tournaments and barriers he was fond of: 'In one sense, by casting himself as the hero of tilts and tourneys Henry was taking upon himself even more forcefully the role played by Elizabeth's favourite, Robert Devereux, 2nd Earl of Essex, in the nineties: that of popular idol and hero of Accession Day Tilts'.[36] This also corresponds to the rehabilitation of the Devereux family under James I, who himself chose the 3rd Earl of Essex as a suitable friend for the heir to the throne.[37]

Therefore, Chapman's dedicating to Henry the same work as he dedicated to the Earl of Essex is, beyond obvious practical reasons, extremely meaningful. Chapman himself summed up the substance of the *Iliad* in these terms: 'the Body's fervour and fashion of outward Fortitude to all possible height of Heroicall Action'.[38] The same spirit breathes through another French tragedy, *The Revenge of Bussy D'Ambois* (1613), in the dedication of which Chapman wrote that such a play was to be considered 'as contayning matter no lesse deseruing your reading, and excitation to Heroycall life'.[39]

The Prince, succeeding Essex as a dedicatee of Homer's *Iliad*, also inherits the Earl's qualities. Through the figure of Achilles, the *Iliad* works as a mirror to its princely dedicatees, so much so that Chapman directly addressed Essex as Achilles:

> Most true Achilles (whom by sacred prophecie Homere did but prefigure in his admirable object and in whose unmatched virtues shyne the dignities of the soule and the whole excellence of royall humanitie), let not the Pessant-common [*i.e.* base, mean] polities of the world, that count all things servile and simple that pamper not their own private sensualities, burying quick in their filthie sepulchres of earth the whole bodies and soules of honor, virtue and pietie, stirre your divine temper from perseverance in godlike pursute of Eternitie.[40]

These 'unmatched' virtues – the adjective completing the comparisons already mentioned – are the mirror of the excellence of the soul – even martial virtues like valour – and courage on the battlefield, and as such they deserve and need to be defended from those base enough to indulge in 'their own private sensualities' and who consider such virtues as 'things servile and simple' and who therefore murder the 'whole bodies and soules of honor, virtue and pietie'. The adjectives 'servile and simple' refer to an anti-Machiavellian practice of politics. In *The Tragedy of Chabot Admiral of France* (published posthumously in 1639), when Chancellor Poyet wants to talk Constable Montmorency into taking part in the plot against Admiral Chabot, he tells him not to care about equity: 'Come, be not Sir infected with a spice / Of that too servile equitie, that renders / Men free borne slaves' (I, I, 181–83). François I also asks Montmorency (who has just made a flattering portrait of the admiral): 'Stand you firme on that sweete simplicitie?' (I, I, 132).[41] This anti-Machiavellian feature – only hinted at in this dedication – cannot be separated from the other – more heroic – qualities of the 'absolute man'.

And thanks to Hawkins's testimony, we know that Henry was devoid of any Machiavellian trait of personality: 'Dissimulation he esteemed most base, chiefly in a prince, not willing, nor by nature being able to flatter, fawne, or use those kindly who deserved not his love'.[42] He also insisted on the heroic nature of the Prince – already present in the title: 'of a fearlesse, noble, Heroicke, and undanted courage, thinking nothing unpossible, that ever was done by any'.[43] Finally, Hawkins cannot imagine that the Prince might be criticized, except by Machiavellian traitors: 'I dare sweare, none will thinke an ill thought, much less speake an ill word of him, unlesse it bee some *Ianus*-faced Machivillian, or hollow hearted Gunpowderers, who as they would have blowne up King, Progeny, and State, cannot choose now but barke against him.'[44]

Therefore it is with due reason that we can apply to Henry what the poet said of his reader:

> You are not every bodie: to you (as to one of my very few friends) I may be bold
> to utter my mind – nor is it more empaire to an honest and absolute man's suf-
> ficiencie to have few friends than to an Homericall Poeme to have few com-
> menders, for neyther doe common dispositions keepe fitte or plausible consort
> with judiciall and simple honestie, nor are idle capacities comprehensible of an
> elaborate Poeme. [45]

Henry was therefore this 'honest and absolute man' worthy of reading Homer, the 'Prince of Poets', and death striking so young and promising a prince in November 1612 seems to have illustrated these lines pronounced by the Duke of Guise before Bussy's tragic murder

> Nature workes at randome …
> But with as much decorum she may make
> A thing that from the feete vp to the throat
> Hath all the wondrous fabricke man should have,
> And leaue it headlesse for an absolute man,
> As giue a whole man valour, vertue, learning,
> Without an end more excellent than those,
> On whom she no such worthie part bestowes (V, III, 29-36).[46]

The 'absolute man' is left symbolically 'headlesse', in a sense that he cannot survive in a world unwilling to accommodate his high virtue and matchless personality. Like Byron – and his English counterpart Essex who was literally beheaded – Henry's life was shortened, although his death was natural and obviously not the result of high treason, as though he could not survive in an age lost to Homeric ideals of heroic chivalry.

NOTES

[1] Roy Strong writes that Chapman may have started his translation at the request of Henry; see *Henry, Prince of Wales and England's Lost Renaissance* (London, 1986), p. 134.

[2] George Chapman, *The Teares of Peace* (75–85), in *The Poems of George Chapman*, ed. Phyllis Brooks Bartlett (New York, 1941), pp. 174–75.

[3] Cf. *The Tragedy of Bussy D'Ambois*, III, II, 91. All references to George Chapman's tragedies are to Holaday's edition: *The Tragedies, with Sir Gyles Goosecappe* (Cambridge, 1987), vol. 2 of *The Plays of George Chapman*, 2 vols., ed. Allan Holaday (Cambridge, 1970–87).

[4] Chapman wrote to Henry in his Epistle dedicatory: 'All Realmes but yours / Are honor'd with him [Homer], and hold blest that State / That have his workes to reade and contemplate,' in George Chapman, *Chapman's Homer: The Iliad*, 1611, ed. Allardyce Nicoll, Bollingen Series 41 (Princeton, 1998), p. 4.

[5] Cf. *The Whole Works of Homer, Prince of Poetts, in his Iliads, and Odysses* (London: Nathaniel Butter, 1616).

[6] Chapman, *Chapman's Homer: The Iliad*, 'Of Homer', p. 20.

[7] George Chapman, *Chapman's Homer: The Odyssey*, 1614, ed. Allardyce Nicoll, Bollingen Series 41 (Princeton, 2000), dedication to Somerset, p. 6.

[8] Chapman, *Chapman's Homer: The Iliad*, dedication of *Achilles' Shield* to the Earl of Essex (1598), p. 544.

[9] *Ibid.*, p. 544. The image of the fountain applied to Homer can already be found in *The Boke Named the Governour* by Sir Thomas Elyot (1531): '… noble Homer, from whom as from a fountain proceeded all eloquence and learning. For in his books be contained, and most perfectly expressed, not only the documents martial and discipline of arms, but also incomparable wisdoms and instructions for politic governance of people, with the worthy commendation and laud of noble princes; wherewith the readers shall be so inflamed that they most fervently shall desire and covet, by the imitation of their virtues, to acquire semblable glory', quoted in Brian Vickers (ed.), *English Renaissance Literary Criticism* (Oxford, 1999, pp. 57–58). This idea of Homer as the fountain of all eloquence and learning ultimately comes from Quintilian, *Institutes of Oratory*, x, I, 46 and XII, XI, 21.

[10] Chapman, *Chapman's Homer: The Iliad*, dedication of the *Seaven Bookes of the Iliades* to the Earl of Essex (1598), p. 508.

[11] Cf. Chapman's dedication of the *Seaven Bookes of the Iliades* to the Earl of Essex (1598), 'To the Most Honored now living Instance of the Achilleian vertues eternized by divine HOMERE, the Earle of ESSEXE, Earle Marshall &c.', *Chapman's Homer: The Iliad*, p. 503.

[12] For Chapman's uncertain status in Henry's court see Timothy Wilks, 'The Court Culture of Prince Henry and his Circle, 1603–1613' (unpublished doctoral thesis, University of Oxford, 1988), pp. 10, 74, 251–54.

[13] Chapman, *Chapman's Homer: The Iliad*, dedication of the *Seaven Bookes of the Iliades* to the Earl of Essex (1598), p. 504.

[14] Quoted in Vickers, pp. 373–74. It was precisely because of Homer's use of the mimesis that Plato chose to exclude him from the Republic, which Chapman did not seem to understand: 'Why therefore Plato in another place banisheth him with all other Poets out of his Common-wealth, dealing with him like a Politician indeed – use men and cast them off – though Homer he thinks fit to send out crowned and anointed, I see not, since he maketh still such honourable mention of him and with his verses (as with precious Jemmes) everie where enchaceth his writings', in *Chapman's Homer: The Iliad*, 'Of Homer', p. 20.

[15] Chapman, *Chapman's Homer: The Iliad*, Epistle dedicatory to Prince Henry (1609), p. 3.

[16] Chapman, *Chapman's Homer: The Iliad*, 'To the Reader', p. 507.

[17] *Ibid.*, 'To the Understander, p. 548.

[18] Harriot seems to have provided Henry with some instruction in mathematics (see his exercises in London, British Library, Add. MSS. 6783, 6784), though Chapman's friendship with him undoubtedly pre-dated the Prince's court, and was probably formed within Raleigh's circle.

[19] Chapman, *The Poems of George Chapman*, p. 49.

[20] Chapman, *Chapman's Homer: The Iliad*, Epistle dedicatory to the Earl of Essex, p. 546.

[21] Strong, *Henry Prince of Wales*, p. 12.

[22] Chapman, *The Poems of George Chapman*, p. 389.

[23] These sonnets are addressed to the Duke of Lennox, the Lord Chancellor (Thomas Egerton, Lord Ellesmere), the

Lord Treasurer (Robert Cecil, Earl of Salisbury), the Earl of Suffolk (Thomas Howard, father to Frances, Lady Essex), the Earl of Northampton (Henry Howard), the Earl of Arundel (Thomas Howard), the Earl of Pembroke (William Herbert), the Earl of Montgomery (Philip Herbert), Lord Lisle (Robert Sidney, brother to Philip), the Countess of Montgomery (wife to Philip Herbert), Lady Wroth (Mary Wroth, daughter to Lord Lisle), the Countess of Bedford, the Earl of Southampton (Henry Wriothesley), the Earl of Sussex (Robert Ratcliffe), Lady Arbella (Arabella Stuart) and Lord Wotton (Edward Wotton). One can remark that Chapman, always desperate for subsidies, directed his efforts in many, even contradictory, ways, as it is well known that, 'apart from the young Thomas Howard, Earl of Arundel, and Charles Howard, Earl of Nottingham, the hero of the Armada, members of the Howard clan found no favour at the Prince's court and certainly he avoided its two most powerful and malignant members, the Earls of Suffolk and Northampton', as Roy Strong writes in *Henry, Prince of Wales*, p. 12.

24 Chapman, *Chapman's Homer: The Iliad*, Epistle dedicatory to Prince Henry (1609), p. 3. For another analysis of these lines, see Jerry Wayne Williamson, *The Myth of the Conqueror, Prince Henry Stuart, A Study in 17th Century Personation* (New York, 1978), p. 86.

25 Chapman, *Chapman's Homer: The Iliad*, I, 6, p. 23.

26 Chapman translated *The Works of Hesiod* in 1618.

27 Jonathan Dollimore, *Radical Tragedy: Religion, Ideology and Power in the Drama of Shakespeare and His Contemporaries* (Brighton, 1984), p. 186.

28 See George Richard Hibbard, 'Goodness and Greatness: An Essay on the Tragedies of Ben Jonson and George Chapman,' *Renaissance and Modern Studies*, 11 (1967), p. 34.

29 Sir Charles Cornwallis [assigned to], *The / Life and / Death of ovr / Late most Incomparable / and Heroique Prince, / Henry Prince of Wales. / A Prince (for Valour and / Vertue) fit to be Imitated in / Succeeding Times* (London: Nathanael Butter, 1641, p. 97). The true author of this work is now recognized as John Hawkins, who wrote the manuscript 'Life' in 1613; see Strong, *Henry Prince of Wales*, p. 227.

30 Chapman, *The Poems of George Chapman*, p. 255.

31 *Ibid.*, p. 388.

32 Although we can acknowledge a part of flattery in such conventional writings as elegies and dedications, Chapman was not 'servile' enough to flatter lords he did not admire, as his enduring (but problematic) fidelity to Somerset, even when the Earl was in prison, testifies.

33 Chapman, *The Poems of George Chapman*, p. 256.

34 James I, *The Political Works of James I, 1616*, ed. Charles Edward MacIlwain (Cambridge, MA, 1918), p. 3.

35 'L'Epicidium exalte trop le fils au dépens du père pour être bien accueilli. Chapman fait allusion aux efforts de Jacques en faveur de la paix. Mais il vante longuement les qualités guerrières du prince. Bien plus, il fait de lui l'ennemi des flatteurs, le régénérateur possible d'une société corrompue; de sa maison le lieu d'attraction des hommes vertueux', in Jean Jacquot, *George Chapman (1559-1634), sa vie, sa poésie, son théâtre, sa pensée* (Paris, 1951), p. 47.

36 Strong, *Henry, Prince of Wales*, p. 141.

37 *Ibid.*, p. 20.

38 Chapman, *Chapman's Homer: The Odyssey*, dedicatory epistle to Somerset, p. 4.

39 Chapman, *The Revenge of Bussy D'Ambois*, ed. Robert J. Lordi, dedication to Sir Thomas Howard, *The Tragedies of George Chapman*, p. 442.

40 Chapman, *Chapman's Homer: The Iliad* 504.

41 Reference can be made to Innocent Gentillet's use of the term to counter-attack Machiavelli's 'impiety', when he speaks of 'simple loyalty'. See, for example, *Anti-Machiavel*, ed. C. Edward Rathé (Les Classiques de la pensée politique 5, Geneva, 1968), III, Maxim 19, p. 438.

42 Cornwallis, p. 94.

43 *Ibid.*, p. 94.

44 *Ibid.*, p. 101.

45 Chapman, *Chapman's Homer: The Iliad*, 'To the Understander', p. 548.

46 Chapman, *The Tragedy of Bussy D'Ambois*, ed. John Hazel Smith, *The Tragedies of George Chapman*, p. 168.

6 | 'And when slow Time hath made you fit for warre': The Equestrian Portrait of Prince Henry

Gail Capitol Weigl

When *Henry, Prince of Wales, on Horseback* (fig. 1), the great picture now hanging in Parham House, Sussex, was cleaned in 1985, the removal of extensive overpainting revealed a hidden figure. Only then did it become obvious that it was the work of Robert Peake the Elder – not Isaac Oliver, to whom it had long been unsatisfactorily attributed. Reports by the restorers of the Hamilton Kerr Institute in Cambridge, and a flurry of perceptive, though brief, comments from Sir Roy Strong, revising his own earlier opinions, followed.[1] Now, more than twenty years later, this picture – the earliest large equestrian royal portrait in English art – deserves reconsideration with regard to its sources, altered design, meaning, commissioning and early ownership.

The portrait depicts Henry astride a spirited and amply proportioned white destrier. The Prince turns toward the viewer to disclose the calm oval face of a young man whose curved brows, large eyes, long slender nose and upturned bow mouth conform to the face-pattern Peake employed with only slight variation for all Henry's youthful portraits. It scarcely differs in feature, glance or expression from the face of the nine-year-old in Peake's hunting scene: *Henry, Prince of Wales, and Sir John Harington*, which bears the date 1603,[2] and the version in which he is shown with Robert, 3rd Earl of Essex (fig. 2), or from the assertive image of him delivered to the court of Savoy.[3]

Henry wears tilt armour with gilt embossed beading,[4] a lace collar of the type fashionable in the first Jacobean decade, and a white, felt hat with jewelled band and ostrich plumes.[5] A sheathed rapier with a jewelled pommel and S-shaped quillons is suspended from a magnificent sling adorned with serpentine pearl, and geometric sapphire and ruby motifs descending from the Prince of Wales's three-feather badge. This ornate and precious sword is clearly not intended for the seventeenth-century battlefield.[6] Henry's riding skirt matches his horses's caparison, on both of which his embroidered *impresa* or device is repeated.[7] Henry raises a switch in his right hand. He is self-aggrandized and self-possessed; a future king whose private self is entirely subordinated to his public persona; a living icon of chivalric disposition.

Stirrup and bit show discernible figures in relief; the former, a standing figure in a niche that resembles Henry VIII (fig. 3); the latter, a figure of Jupiter armed with two handfuls of thunderbolts, which he is hurling down from the clouds, astride the eagle that has delivered them (fig. 4). The bit is further embellished with sunburst patterns around the circumference.

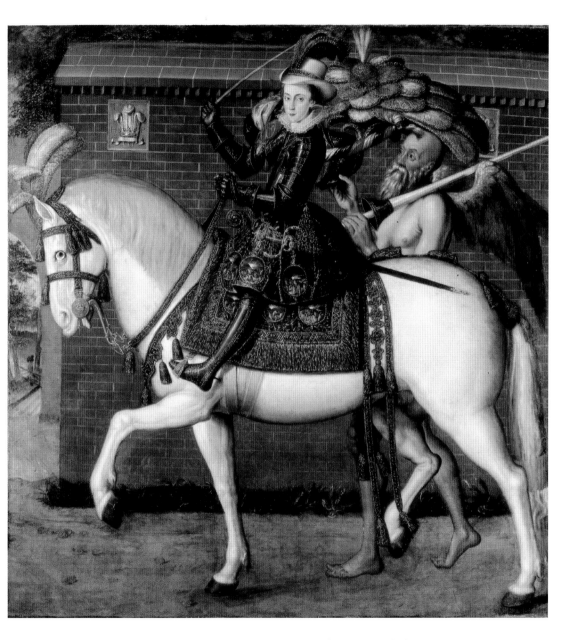

Fig. 1 Robert Peake the Elder, *Henry, Prince of Wales, on Horseback*
Parham House, Sussex

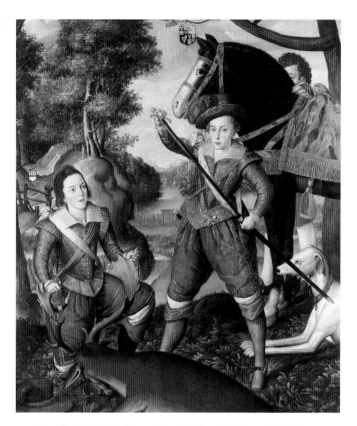

Fig. 2 Peake the Elder, *Henry, Prince of Wales and Robert, 3rd Earl of Essex*
Hampton Court Palace

The representation of the great Tudor king (and the Prince's namesake) shows Henry's readiness to match himself to figures of supreme authority drawn from both mythology and history. Dazzling effects are achieved in the details of costume and accoutrements: fringe and tassels of straw, blue and deep ochre, as if shot through with gold; sword sheath, pommel, caparison, harness and reins all embellished with geometric gold interlace, pearls and square-cut rubies and sapphires in simplified settings; white lace collar of threadlike delicacy; skirt and blanket of a gold-embroidered willow pattern, with sewn-on, oval *imprese* edged with luminescent pearls (fig. 5).

A scarf of Henry's red, white and blue colours billows from his raised arm, and twists behind to firmly tie the forelock of an otherwise bald Father Time. This long-legged ancient, acquiescing in the role of squire, lopes along bearing Henry's lance and tilting helmet, its prodigious plumes also of the Prince's colours, which are repeated in the dyed hairs of the horse's tail. These incongruous figures are constrained within a shallow foreground by a red brick wall bearing moulded plaques that display the triple ostrich feathers and 'HP' (Henricus Princeps) monogram. To the viewer's far left the wall ends, where may be seen an archway, and beyond it a tree-lined bank, an expanse of water and a distant bank with leafy

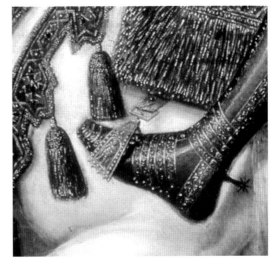

Fig. 3 Detail of stirrup from *Henry, Prince of Wales, on Horseback*

Fig. 4 Detail of bit from *Henry, Prince of Wales, on Horseback*

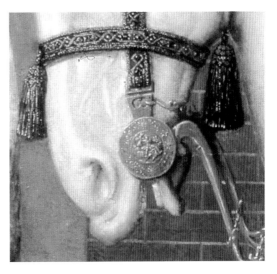

trees in full blossom. Again, this is reminiscent of the background in the 'Richmond Palace' portrait, where the view is taken to be of the Thames and the distinctive islands or eyots adjacent to Richmond Palace. Though Peake is fond of the summer landscape, he does not provide a Renaissance window on to a geometrically ordered world; only an Elizabethan, neo-medieval vision in which the picture plane remains inviolate, determining the disposition of line and colour across its surface.[8] Though these may signify mass, space and movement, the imagery remains essentially static and heraldic.

In early Jacobean England, the portrait was patronized, exchanged, circulated and displayed on a complex scale that testifies to its centrality in matters bearing little relationship to issues of personality in the modern epistemological sense.[9] These portraits impressed upon the viewer the status of the sitter, and were also intended to instruct posterity.[10] It was incumbent on the artist to allude to the sitter's past accomplishments, or in Henry's case, to his presence and his promise. His gaze, therefore, transcends time, and rider and horse are set against a wall that blocks any distracting view, proclaiming only Henry's immediacy with its repeated 'HP' plaques. The wall signifies Henry's firmness and resolve – allusion again preferred to Renaissance naturalism.[11]

Today, the portrait is susceptible to misinterpretation as a strident call to arms, but any contemporary would have seen at once that Henry is equipped not for the battlefield but for the tilt-yard or riding school. Though there is the promise of great things to come, the Prince is neither immediately threatening nor alarming; he raises neither weapon nor baton of command but a switch, a realistic observation indicating mastery of his powerful mount. Henry remains a youth engaged in exercises, and while the painting strikingly conveys his energy and assertiveness, it would not have seemed particularly bellicose to an early seventeenth-century viewer. His sword is sheathed and his felt hat has the curious effect of making his otherwise armoured image unthreatening.[12] There is no suggestion of imminent battle, as, for example, in the daunting equestrian portrait of Henry's uncle, Christian IV of Denmark painted some years later by Karel van Mander.[13]

It was after Peake had already settled on a relatively simple equestrian composition that the allegorical figure of Father Time, the lance and the plumed helmet were added. This constituted a major intervention, as these features were painted over the top of the brick wall, sacrificing the clarity and harmony of the original composition.[14] The Prince's head and upper body, once starkly set against the background, are crowded and less distinct after the addition of the billowing and twining favour and the profusion of plumes. Moreover, the figure of Father Time is wholly extraneous to the preconceived grid composition carefully worked out by Peake. Youthful prince and elderly companion combine in a rising and falling flutter of hands and arms, feathers and wings, switch and lance, creating a zigzag of forms that does little to impart a sense of general forward movement. Articulation and anatomical drawing are less than elegant. Father Time holds the Prince's helmet with a hand that appears unattached to its right arm and shoulder, and is as flaccid as the smaller hands within each *impresa*. This revision suggests the preferences of someone (presumably, the purchaser of the picture) more familiar with the literary than the visual Renaissance. It has ceased to be a temporal record of Henry, as he is now lifted from his actual martial exercises – familiar to all who frequented his court – and safely deposited in an allegorical world of hopes and dreams.

Though wild-eyed and moist-mouthed, Henry's horse fails to be animated by Peake's soft, fibrous brushwork; its bland, milky tones are no less convincing of weight and texture than its cautiously explored contours. Similarly, wing feathers, helmet plumes, the Prince's hair, grasses and plants are handled with a generalized brushwork and consistent lighting that does little to achieve convincing texture, while the modelling of Henry's features so subtly along the contour fails to suggest real structure and substance.[15] And yet, *Henry, Prince of Wales, on Horseback* presents all the qualities of the Elizabethan-Jacobean costume piece: pure, glowing colour unsullied by *chiaroscuro*, and line exploited to the full in the rendering of embroidered and jewelled textiles, lace collars and cuffs, and expensive accoutrements. Peake's assemblage of independently observed and meticulously rendered details results in an image that is peculiarly English in its linearity. This kind of portraiture was all about personhood constructed out of multiple parts.[16] Luxurious and allusive trappings denote rather than reveal the sitter, and the Prince's detached gaze, the avoidance of depth and the use of symbolism mark *Henry, Prince of Wales, on Horseback* as, essentially, an icon.[17]

In its first state, the portrait attempted little more than to claim Henry's right to be represented within the very potent iconographic tradition of the classical equestrian portrait. It was all the more imposing for its simplicity. Though its formal composition was wholly derivative, it agreed, nonetheless, with the familiar spectacle of Henry's regular schooling of the great horse, and his practising for tournaments. As an image of chivalry that accorded well with actual experience of Henry the portrait presented a prince already possessed of great authority and determination, but of intentions as yet undisclosed.

Peake still adhered to the stylistic and narrative principles of Elizabethan portraiture, presenting a world-picture that was nearing its end, without a new aesthetic comfortably in place to succeed it. This is a work embedded in the late sixteenth-century climate of chivalric virtue and Christian Providence, harking to a medievalism already long past even when Elizabeth reigned, but still of appeal to Henry and the aristocracy of his generation, even though they knew of, and were interested in the likes of Palladio and Galileo. While Henry patronized or sought to patronize cosmopolitan artists such Inigo Jones, Isaac Oliver, Salomon de Caus and Costantino de' Servi, he by no means abandoned Peake, who was given the huge task of painting histories in the cabins of his warship, the *Prince Royal*, while efforts were being made to persuade the celebrated Dutch portraitist Michiel Jansz van Miereveldt to visit the court. Peake, in fact, continued to paint large-scale portraits of his patron until Henry's death.[18] It is well known that Peake responded to the growing interest in Italian Renaissance theory by arranging the translation and publication of Sebastiano Serlio's *Four Books of Architecture, entreating of Geometric, Perspective, Antiquities, and Rules for Masonry or Building* (1611), which he dedicated to Henry, though intending it:

> … to benefite the Publicke; and convey unto my Countrymen (especially
> Architects and Artificers of all forts) these Necessary,Certaine, and most ready
> Helps of *Geometrie*: the ignorance and want whereof, in times past … hath left
> us many lame Workes, with shame of many Workmen ….[19]

There were already a few English *virtuosi* playing a significant role in the aesthetic education of England's future king – men such as Sir Henry Fanshawe, Sir Henry Wotton, and Thomas Howard, Earl of Arundel – capable of judgement and censure.[20] While Peake knew only one way to paint, he was, as a mature artist, still able to glean from Serlio the geometry that would enable him to arrive at theory-based compositions and possibly escape the 'shame' of which he wrote. As the restorers of the Hamilton-Kerr Institute have revealed, Peake put theory into practice. He subdivided the originally square dimensions of the painting into 16 x 16 squares, each measuring five and three-quarter inches, and drew a series of triangles and quadrangles on this grid to control his composition and achieve classical proportion and harmony.[21]

The most appropriate questions to ask of such a portrait are not those relating to its truth to nature, but to its meaning and reception. Peake adhered to the Elizabethan notion that the purpose of a painting was to communicate a precisely calculated set of meanings according to certain iconographic and symbolic conventions. His work shows he shared Nicholas Hilliard's conviction that while some shading along the contour might be appropriate for large

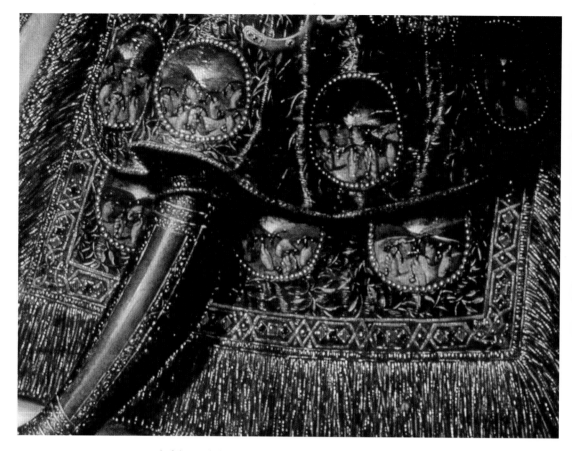

Fig. 5 Detail of skirt and blanket with *imprese* from *Henry, Prince of Wales, on Horseback*

paintings viewed at a distance, 'shadowing' was actually a form of deception. In his equestrian portrait, Peake, therefore, effectively concealed Henry, the person – or failed to find him – beneath an accumulation of visual clues to a predetermined idea of the Prince.

With *Henry, Prince of Wales, on Horseback* Peake persists with an image he had begun to fashion soon after Henry set foot in England. Henry's portrait had to conform precisely to a socially constructed identity, reinforcing and perhaps to some degree determining the social construct itself. It is entirely consistent with what Richard Brilliant has called the portrait as a 'social artefact' in which no 'uniquely private kernel of being' is suggested.[22] Peake presents a cult image that conflates the transcendent (hence timeless) presence of the religious icon with the narrative, time-bound aims of history painting; its power derives from the existence of the historical person, idealized beyond mere physical reality.[23] His adopted schema 'derived from the distillation of common experience and subsequently loaded with significance'[24] proclaimed Henry's identity. Indeed, Peake's way of seeing, though soon to be superseded, was that commonly shared by the English in the first decade of the seventeenth century. This portrait is an icon in the Tudor mould, in which the artist makes 'no attempt to suggest inner, psychological presence but allows his sitter's resolute exteriority to carry the full burden of signification',[25] and is, furthermore, an icon that presents 'the royal body that belongs to the state'.[26] As in the case of Elizabeth I, Henry's image makers understood that the 'most obvious embodiment of a national image … is the iconography of its figurehead'.[27] Peake, however, is able to present a far more activist image than had ever been possible with the late Queen Elizabeth or could ever be with King James. In this sense, his work may represent the reinvigoration, rather than the end, of a tradition.[28] Henry Stuart rides forth in arms to claim his destiny as heir to Elizabeth's England – his future realm no less mythical than Arthur's Britain.[29]

The impresa

Repeated, possibly as many as eighteen times in two rows on his skirt and matching caparison, Henry's *impresa* takes the form of an oval medallion edged in pearls, containing up to seven hands couped at the wrist, emerging from a mint-green ground (not water),[30] each hand holding a black anchor; in the distance the sun appears as a bright flash in the crotch of blue, blue-green and blue-grey hills. Assuming that real trappings are depicted here, this constitutes an invaluable record of the work of Edmund Palmer, the Prince's embroiderer.[31] Henry's *impresa* obviously pre-dates the portrait, and, more significantly, it pre-dates the allegorization of the portrait. As it constituted an ineradicable presence in the portrait, it is possible that an internal semantic contradiction might have been created by the introduction of Father Time. Alternatively, old and new elements might have combined with powerful effect. Not just for its intrinsic meaning, therefore, does Henry's *impresa* warrant the closest scrutiny.

William Camden's standard definition of an *impresa* emphasizes the mutual dependence of image and word.[32] For Camden, without the motto to provide a counterpoint to the picture, preferably in witty language 'neither too obscure, nor too plain', the device is without soul, and rendered so unreadable as to be without meaning, even for those learned intimates to whom it was directed. William Drummond of Hawthornden also emphasizes the importance of the words to carry the uniquely personal, ambiguous and learned character of the *impresa*,[33] but concedes that *imprese* can be of two sorts, either with or without words, and that the most ancient were in fact 'wanting words'. For him, the most necessary feature of the *impresa* is not the words, which taken by themselves have no determinate sense, but the clarity, perspicacity and brevity of the figures.[34] Ben Jonson, author of two of the court masques created for Henry's investiture, declared in his earlier *Masque of Blackness* (1605), 'A hieroglyphic was not accompanied by a motto or word. An *impresa*, however, was usually, though not always.'[35]

Many of the tournament *imprese* composed for *Prince Henry's Barriers*, the court celebration on 6 January 1610 that opened the year in which Henry would become Prince of Wales, bore mottos only. The shields of the Earl of Pembroke and Sir Thomas Howard, for instance, carried the mottos *Hinc color atque valor* (Hence beauty and valour) and *Per augusta palebit* (Through consecrated paths it will be revealed) respectively.[36] On this occasion, Henry also bore a motto without picture: *Fas est aliorum quaerere regna* (It is right to seek for the kingdoms of others),[37] a most provocative declaration, given the political tensions then prevailing in Europe. Tournament *imprese* represented not only lineage, but also the knight's personal qualities and policies, resulting in 'impresa-like devices' charged with meaning.[38] If Henry rode in the Barriers tilt with the skirt and caparison depicted in Peake's equestrian portrait, we would be justified in reading, just as onlookers would have, the *impresa* together with the motto.

The hands within each *impresa* serve the common function in emblematic texts of holding an object connoting the moral. As examples one might cite Whitney's image of a hand bearing a sword upright over a fire, with the motto, *Pietas in patriam* (patriotism in one's country),[39] or the vertical staff surmounted by an appalmed hand bearing the motto, *Fiducia concors*, and in English, 'We trust or hope all one thing', from one of Whitney's sources, *The Heroicall Devises*.[40] Lionel Cust, one of the first scholars to consider the equestrian portrait in modern times, in identifying it as a portrait of Prince Charles at his creation as Prince of Wales, suggested the hands holding anchors represented the 'numberless hopes of the nation' fixed on the young Charles after the grievous death of Henry.[41] It is an explanation that might still be applied to the elder brother. Certainly, the anchor is a familiar Christian symbol of hope and steadfast faith.[42] In one of Isaac Oliver's miniatures an anchor is seen hanging below the collar of Henry's mother, the Catholic Queen Anne; something surely not intended as a mere show of support for the navy.[43] That symbolic imagery of this kind was also acceptable in Protestant circles is clear from Protestant emblem books, where we find didactic explanations that echo theologians' acceptance of those images that served as reminders of religious truths, while condemning those that fostered worship or idolatry.[44] Calvin, for example, believed that 'God expresses his covenant with men visually, in 'signs … as a reminder of his promises', and defined a sacrament as an 'outward sign', to aid in the 'remembrance' of Christ.[45] During a period of iconoclastic sentiment such 'unabused' or 'memory' images, were justified by emblem writers in similar language.[46]

Both Thomas Palmer (Emblem 66)[47] and George Wither (Book 2, Emblem 72)[48]created emblems of an anchor entwined by a dolphin, based on Emblem 144 from Andreas Alciatus's *Emblemata*. Their verses differ significantly, but these three together present a range of moral admonitions that shed significant light on the symbolism of Henry's *impresa*. Palmer, emphasizing faith as the ground of hope, gives the motto, 'God is our refuge in adversitie.' Wither's motto, on the other hand, emphasizes that hope must be joined with steadiness if aims are to have good success: 'If Safely, thou desire to goe, Bee nor too Swift, nor overflow', and his verse reads, in part: 'An Anchor, they did figure, to declare *Hope*, *stayednesse*, or a *grave-deliberation*.' Alciatus's emblem: 'On a Seashore, an upright anchor encircled by a downward pointing dolphin with its head to the right. Seascape with ships, town on hilly coast at right' presents the Prince in the role of saviour on Earth. The Motto reads, 'The prince vouchsafing the safety of his subjects'; the Subject is, 'The benevolent prince'; and the Epigram explains:

> Whenever the Titan brothers, the Winds, are disturbing the sea then an anchor
> cast overboard aids the wretched sailors. The dolphin, devoted to men,
> embraces it, so that it may be fixed more securely in the lowest depths. How
> fitting it is for kings to bear these signs, being mindful that what an anchor is to
> sailors, they are to their own people.[49]

Here, we see the anchor as a symbol of one of the necessary constituents of rule, as all were reminded in the praise given Henry as he entered London for his investiture ceremony: '… Plato termeth Magistracy, to be the *Anchor, Head*, and *Soule* of any Citty…'.[50] For lack of water, the dolphin had no place in Henry's *impresa*, but the anchor, held aloft, continues to speak of hope rooted in faith, of steadfastness in pursuit of a goal, and of the responsibilities of the ordained ruler.

Henry was hailed from birth by preachers and poets as the hope of a nation. To the poet Samuel Daniel, Henry is the 'm'st hopefull Prince not as you are,/ But as you may be', in whom Daniel places 'the hope of you, that you one day/may grace this now neglected har-monie/ which set unto your glorious actions may/ Record the same to all posteritie'.[51]; in *Tethys' Festival*, Daniel's masque written in celebration of Henry becoming Prince of Wales, he is '… the Lord/ And Prince of th'Iles (the hope and the delight,/ Of all the Northerne Nations)…'.[52] Michael Drayton, dedicating *Poly-Olbion* 'To the High and Mightie, Henrie, Prince of Wales … the hopefull Heyre of the kingdoms of this Great Britain …' exhorted, opposite William Hole's engraving of Henry with the pike: 'Britaine, behold here portrayed to thy sight, Henry, thy best hope, and the world's delight.'[53] For the epigrammatist John Owen, the Prince is 'Great Britaines Hope, son of so great a Sire,/… in rare Parts/Follow'd by few, belov'd in all mens hearts …'.[54]

The ground from which the hands rise is surely the same ground alluded to in Daniel Price's second sermon preached after Henry's death, taken from Matthew 26: 31: 'The Sheepe of the flocke shall be scattered', in which the congregation were informed:

> A Scholiast upon Nazianzene expoundeth those
> Green fields to be the church, the grasse the Word….[55]

Proceeding from this, it is possible to read the anchor-bearing hands as Truth, as in Psalm 85: 12: 'Truth springeth out of the earth; And righteousness hath looked down from heaven.'

As early as 1521, as Fritz Saxl noted, Johann Knoblouch of Strasbourg chose as his printer's mark,

> … an illustration of a text from the Psalms (LXXXV.12) *Veritas de terra orta est* ('Truth Springeth out of the earth') …. Time is not represented in the cut; but the inscription promises that Time will bring Truth to light. There can be no doubt that this work alludes to the coming reform of faith.[56]

Insofar as Time is the destroyer of lies and hypocrisy, there is reason to associate him with Truth,[57] and it is thus that he appears in a woodcut inserted into the frontispiece of William Marshall's *Goodley Prymer in Englyshe*. Published in 1535, at the time of Henry VIII's break with Rome, the woodcut depicts 'the daughter of tyme' assaulted by 'hypocrisy', liberated from the cave of calumny and envy by a winged and bearded 'Tyme (who) reueleth all thynges' and bears the epitaph: 'Nothying is covered that shall not be discovered. And nothying is hydde, that shall not be revealed.'[58] Again, Saxl: 'The drawing stands for the liberation of Christian Truth (as seen by Protestant reformers) from her captivity under the monster of Roman Hypocrisy.'[59]

It only remains to interpret the burst of light at the crotch of the mountains; a task relatively easily dispatched. The 'rising sun' can only be understood as Henry, as his father was so designated when Queen Elizabeth lay dying:

> … she had heard some whisperings, and had also been advertised by the French King, that many of the Nobility did by underhand Letters and Messengers seek to curry Favour with the King of *Scots*, that they adored him as the rising Sun ….[60]

This sentiment was echoed in George Wither's elegies on Henry's death: 'Thy Father both a Sunne, and Phoenix is,/ Prince Henry was a Sunne and Phoenix too ….'[61]

The allegorization

As Strong (relying on Panofsky) elucidates, Henry seizes Time in the form of Opportunity (*Kairos*).[62] While not conforming to the antique image which Panofsky describes as a winged and swiftly moving youth bearing the attribute of a scale suspended at times from a shaving knife,[63] Time does bear the essential attribute of the forelock 'by which bald-headed Opportunity is seized'. His aged appearance shows the accepted fusion from antiquity of the Greek *Chronos* (Time) and the elderly senior deity of the Roman pantheon *Kronos* (Saturn). This benign, aged figure merged with the nude female personification of *Occasio*, or Fortune, in the emblematic art of Andreas Alciatus, where she bears the forelock, and sometimes the attributes of *Kairos*, balanced on a sphere in a landscape; from Alciatus, this image became standard in the emblem books of Renaissance Europe, most notably in Geffrey Whitney's *A Choice of Emblems* (1586), where, however, she balances on a wheel floating on the sea.[64] Alciatus's Epigram, in the form of a dialogue, reads in part: 'Who are you?' and the response: 'A moment of time ensnared, conquering everything'. Cato, the source of the idea of *Occasio* with seized forelocks, was widely used in Elizabethan and Jacobean grammar schools,[65] and, therefore, the image of Henry seizing Time by the forelock would have been instantly recognizable to educated viewers.

That 'Truth the Daughter of Time' could be widely adopted as a metaphor for the fulfilment of prophesy, and the working out of God's plan, is clear from the ways in which Mary I and Elizabeth I freely adapted the theme to their personal iconography and religious convictions.[66] Just as the male figure of Time merged with the female personification of *Occasio*, so might Peake have conflated the conventional female image of Truth, the Daughter of Time, with the future Henry IX. It is Henry who will seize the opportunity as prophesied by Ben Jonson soon after the boy prince first arrived in England:

> And when slow Time hath made you fit for warre,
> Looke over the strict Ocean, and thinke where
> You may but lead us forth, that grow up here
> Against a day, when our officious swords
> Shall speake our action better than our words.[67]

Jonson gives no direction to Henry, rather inviting him to 'think where/ You may lead us forth'. Whereas, by the time of his death others were less reserved, lamenting he had not lived to destroy 'Romes damned fiends'.[68] For others, he was, while he lived, a second Alexander the Great, hailed as such by Henry Peacham in his manuscript emblem books based on James I's *Basilicon Doron*. 'Advance, O Britain' is one motto (translated out of Greek) while its accompanying Latin epigram looks to Henry for deeds that will match those of Alexander:

> Bravo! For your courage, O glory and nurturing hope of the Britons,
> Second Alexander, outstanding for your [heroes], whether the
> Spaniard challenges you, or the Turk, or the rebellious Irish,
> Or the destitute German attacks you from the rear.[69]

Of the three extant versions, the last book, presented to Henry shortly after becoming Prince of Wales, is the only one with coloured pictures, and includes, to accompany the above epigram, a knight on horseback, meant to represent Henry. Peacham's 'good friend Mr. Peake'[70] probably saw this manuscript, while Peacham, a better scholar than artist, probably had occasion to admire the equestrian portrait in Peake's workshop.

The classical tradition and France

The classical tradition of European equestrian art stems from the Roman imperial portrait type, and principally from two statues that, remarkably, survived into the Modern era. These were the *Regisole* (3rd century C.E.), which stood in Pavia, and the bronze *Marcus Aurelius* (161–80 C.E.), which during Prince Henry's lifetime formed the centrepiece of Michelangelo's re-designed Piazza di Campidoglio in Rome. The *Regisole* not only influenced Leonardo's designs for his Sforza and Trivulzio monuments, but also Rustici's design for his equestrian statue of François I. It was, however, the *Marcus Aurelius* rather than the livelier *Regisole* that for the French School of the latter half of the sixteenth century became the prime source for the equestrian portrait in whatever medium. Indeed, Primaticcio, another of the Italian Mannerist masters who found patronage at the French court after the Sack of Rome, obtained a cast of the *Marcus Aurelius* for François I, thereby introducing this classical model to France in monumental form.[71]

These surviving examples (supported by the relatively recent Quattrocento masterpieces of Donatello's *Gattamelata* and Verrocchio's *Colleoni Monument*) served to underpin with classical authority the sixteenth- and early seventeenth-century chivalric obsession with horsemanship. This obsession was reflected in the enormous popularity of Federico Grisone's treatise *Gli ordini di cavalcare* (Naples, 1550), which appeared in new editions almost every year during the 1550s, and which, by 1558, was available in French, German and Spanish translations. Indeed, *haute école* even laid claim to the antique models, as the high-stepping trot of the *Marcus Aurelius* was fondly thought to resemble the *passage*, an exercise (illustrated in Grisone) that demonstrated the rider's complete mastery over his mount.[72] Henry's use of the switch and the pose of his horse are particularly reminiscent of Grisone's illustration of 'Refining the trot under saddle (and duress)', but what influence is here can only be indirect, in as much as any French artist thinking of attempting an equestrian portrait would have called to mind, *inter alia*, Grisone's familiar woodcut illustrations.[73] As for the switch, while Spanish commentators may have seen it as 'a symbol of the firm hand that must temper a ruler's kindness to his people (represented by a horse)',[74] English viewers are more likely to have seen in Prince Henry's raised arm a promising sign of his natural disposition to command rather than an indication that they were soon to be curbed by the whip hand of an absolute monarch.

François I's successor, Henri II, also desired an equestrian statue, and in his lifetime was represented 'victorious, on horseback, in bronze' in the courtyard at Oiron, the château of his Grand Equerry, Claude Gouffier.[75] It was in November 1559, however, a few months after his fatal injury (received while jousting), that his widow, Catherine de Médicis, wrote to Michelangelo to commission an equestrian monument of him. The ageing Michelangelo deputed Daniele da Volterra to execute the statue, but in 1566 Daniele died having made only the cast of the horse. Even so, the 'White Horse' as it became known, was set up in a courtyard at Fontainebleau, where it remained exposed to the elements, steadily deteriorating, until its removal in 1626.[76] Its influence upon those who saw it (these included many English visitors) during the sixty years it was on display was enormous.

We know Catherine de Médicis's commission deliberately referenced the classical tradition, as Antonio Tempesta's engraving of the 'White Horse' reveals its heavy debt to the *Marcus Aurelius*. That tradition in monumental form was resumed in 1604 by Marie de Médicis when she commissioned Giambologna (at one time Daniele da Volterra's assistant in Rome) to create an equestrian statue of Henri IV.[77] This statue, based on Giambologna's earlier magnificent *Equestrian Monument of Cosimo I* (1587–94) in the Piazza della Signoria in Florence, would be erected on the Pont Neuf in 1614.[78] It was intended to symbolize the absolute authority of the monarch, and once again it would demonstrate that the equestrian monument was central to French royal iconography. It should be borne in mind, therefore, that while Robert Peake designed and executed his equestrian portrait, the famed 'White Horse' stood on view at Fontainebleau, and in Florence the French crown's urge for an equestrian monument was again being pursued, though by 1610 the casting and chasing of the statue was in the hands of Giambologna's successor, Pietro Tacca. It was Tacca who would include two bronze horses (also after Giambologna) in a collection of cabinet statuettes presented in 1612 to Prince Henry by the Florentines.[79]

No sooner had Peake's portrait been cleaned than Sir Roy Strong recognized a French influence, concluding that the source for it 'must be either Clouet's equestrian portrait of Henri II in the Metropolitan Museum, New York, or another version of it'.[80] The work to which Strong refers, attributed to François Clouet and dated to the 1550s, shows similar poses of horse and rider, a foreground of grass and foliage, and a walled background. Like Henry, the French king carries a switch rather than the more standard commander's baton in his right hand. It is surely too confining, however, to point to a single, similar work without acknowledging the huge weight of the French equestrian portrait tradition (itself stimulated by the Italian revival) that impressed itself on the visual culture of the Jacobean court. More thought needs to be given to the kind of images to which Robert Peake would have had access.

It is not difficult to identify royal equestrian portraits painted prior to Strong's example in Metropolitan Museum, such as those portraits of François I in the Louvre and in the Uffizi that also exhibit certain features found in *Henry, Prince of Wales on Horseback*. Indeed, portraits painted by Jean (c. 1478–1541) and François Clouet (c. 1510–1572) and their followers established an iconographic formula that served for the equestrian portraits of all the Valois and Bourbon kings from François I (1494–1547) to Louis XIII (1601–1643). This tradition gained impetus during the reign of the excessively chivalric Henri II. In 1558, the poet and courtier Etienne Jodelle caused an equestrian portrait of this king to be painted for the Hôtel de Ville, which was much copied.[81] Other painted equestrian portraits of the Valois kings are now known only from drawings, such as that of *Charles IX lauré à cheval*, c. 1560, attributed to Antoine Caron, which may be a design for a painting once in the Room of the Emperors in Fontainebleau.[82] By the time a stream of young

Jacobean gentlemen and nobles were travelling to Paris to complete their education, many of them keen to ride at the famous Academy that was conceived by the riding master Antoine de Pluvinal as a 'school of the court',[83] a mass of royal equestrian images had accumulated over the previous half-century, which could not have escaped the notice of these visitors.

This branch of French royal iconography was exploited as never before during the reign of Henri IV, until his assassination on 14 May 1610.[84] We know, for example, that at Fontainebleau among the paintings in the Grand Galerie, at the doorway end, there was a portrait of Henri IV on horseback at the siege and surrender of Amiens, 'a painting of a grandeur without precedent', and in the Queen's Gallery, ten large paintings, five on each side of the room, commemorated Henri's victories, among them Ivry, Mantes and Vernon-sur-Seine.[85] From 1598, the bas-relief of *Henri IV on Horseback* created by Mathieu Jacquet for the Belle Cheminée in the Salle de la Comédie, the largest room in Fontainebleau, probably exerted more influence than any other work on subsequent equestrian images of the king. Henri IV intended the Belle Cheminée to surpass those chimneys François I and Henri II had constructed at Fontainebleau, and that it should dominate the great room created for Charles IX on the first floor of the eastern wing of the Fountain Court, adjacent to the Court of the White Horse.[86] Jacquet's life-size sculpture of the king, laurel-crowned and astride a trotting horse, maintains the balanced proportions of horse and rider and the management of the horse's limbs (raised left foreleg and right rear leg) characteristic of the Clouets' equestrian portraits, but introduces more emphatic movement, seen above all in the horse's tossing head and the king's flying scarf.[87]

Jacquet's equestrian sculpture gave even greater authority to an already established iconic tradition, which Henri IV used to create for himself an ambiguous identity as imperial warrior and peacemaker. Indeed, Henri IV was the first French king to make widespread use of his portrait to reinforce his status as 'legitimate and very Christian king' and to appease factions after the religious wars of 1589–94.[88] Though many of the painted portraits are now lost, they inspired a myriad of engravings, often issued in connection with specific events of Henri's reign and accompanied by verses underscoring the propagandist nature of the image 'that the hawkers were able to diffuse everywhere, even in the most humble cottages'.[89]

Print sources

Aside from close comparisons between the Belle Cheminée bas-relief and Caron's *Bataille de Marignan* from his 'Histoire des Rois de France' series executed between 1560 and 1570, certain mannered characteristics of Caron's horses are also seen in Jacquet's equestrian sculpture. These include prominently swollen veins and tense muscles that curiously turn around the limbs, stopping at the knees and at the angles of bulbous joints; and the way in which the left foreleg turns outward, showing the horseshoe beneath the hoof. The same is seen in Caron's drawings, and in engravings based on his designs,[90] such as the *Charles IX lauré à cheval*, which not only shows the turned out foreleg displaying the horseshoe, but also another feature characteristic of Caron's horses: the small, elegant head with ears pointing forward and mane sweeping in front.[91] Peake's treatment of the horse's musculature in his own equestrian portrait differs considerably from that of Jacquet or Caron, but a number of Caronesque details are to be observed in Peake's painting, namely the massive joints, the turned out left foreleg displaying the horseshoe, and the horse's ears pointing forward with mane sweeping in front. Prince Henry, we note, like the French king, wears a flying scarf (a feature also associated with Caron), though his is ingeniously twined into a rope and tied to Father Time's forelock.

A Caron drawing, *Henri III à cheval* (Musée Condé, Chantilly), provides a precedent for another distinctive feature of Peake's equestrian portrait: the French king, facing left in a three-quarter view astride a trotting horse, is placed, like Henry, against a wall with an archway at left. Another engraving, by Gisbert Voenius after a design by Caron (1600), shares with Peake's portrait the feature of a wall giving onto a distant scene, and also the flying scarf. Both examples, however, though essentially of the Clouet type, show kings laurel-crowned (which Henry is not), and both horses differ significantly from Henry's. A plumed hat-wearing Henri IV, scarf fluttering behind him, is to be found in an engraving by Caron's son-in-law, Thomas de Leu, dated 1596,[92] which, in other respects is reminiscent of the engraving by Voenius, and again, represents one of the dominant images of Henri's reign: the king astride a horse rearing to the left, placed high on a coulisse overlooking a massed battle below.[93]

Much closer to the compositional formula employed for the equestrian portrait of Henry are engravings by Léonard Gaultier (1561–1630) and Robert Boisssard (1570–1603?). Gaultier, like de Leu a son-in-law of Antoine Caron, created a number of engraved portraits of Henri III and Henri IV. One of these, dated 1610, depicts Henri IV as imperial conqueror being crowned with laurel, in a three-quarter view facing right, scarf fluttering in the wind, astride a white horse with a background battle scene (fig. 6); variants such as that by Johan van Haelbeck, show his horse trampling the arms of the defeated (fig. 7).[94] Of even greater interest as a model for Peake's portrait is a design by Boissard, which shows the king facing left, wearing a plumed hat, astride a trotting white horse with long leather thongs hanging from the horse's rear breeching. Like all the examples discussed thus far, here the king wears a sash across his breastplate, though the ends of the sash fall lightly over the horse's back; like the de Leu design, King Henri wears a sword at his left side while carrying a commander's baton in his right hand (fig. 8). Derivative versions exist which portray the king in chased armour, wearing a soft wide-brimmed hat with ostrich feathers, on a rock-strewn foreground against a blank ground.[95] An interesting variation is a design by Philippe Thomassin, dated 1596, that synthesizes the Gaultier and Boissard types. Thomassin's version, combining Gaultier's armour-strewn foreground above a distant battlefield with Boissard's escutcheon, depicts a bareheaded Henri IV facing three-quarters left on a trotting white horse, a commander's baton in his right hand, sword at his left side, his sash falling lightly.[96] It is clear, therefore, that

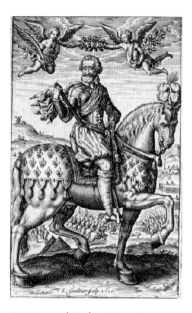

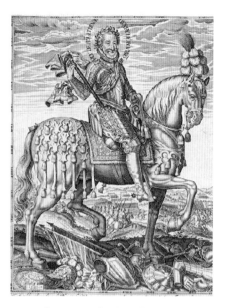

Fig. 6 Leonard Gaultier, *Equestrian portrait of Henri IV, King of France* engraving (1610)

Fig. 7 Johan van Haelbeck (Halbeek), *Equestrian portrait of Henri IV, King of France*, engraving (c. 1600)

there were two basic designs employed for equestrian portraits of Henri IV: the rearing and the trotting horse. With either of these, the king could be shown bareheaded or wearing either a laurel crown or a plumed hat. Both types may show a distant view of a battlefield and the king's horse trampling armour, or, as in the Belle Cheminée bas-relief and the engravings after Caron and Boissard, he may be placed against a wall or a blank ground. These stock features could be combined to provide a degree of variation within a highly conservative design tradition. Furthermore, the identity of the rider could be changed.

Such was the influence of French equestrian engravings, especially of Henri IV, that certain English engravings of contemporary heroes were highly derivative of them, and may be considered little more than variants, as was recognized over a century ago by Sidney Colvin. Thomas Cockson's Robert Devereux, 2nd Earl of Essex, dated 1599, closely corresponds to those Boissard engravings of Henri IV shown astride a trotting horse on a barren coulisse above a distant battle.[97] Essex, clad in armour with a scarf draped over his left shoulder and wearing a high broad-brimmed hat with plume and jewel, faces left and turns toward the viewer, sword at his side, commander's baton in his raised right hand. This work is one of four Cockson equestrian portraits, one of which, Charles Howard, Earl of Nottingham, is of a similar date; the others George Clifford, 3rd Earl of Cumberland and Charles Blount, Earl of Devonshire, both showing the horse rearing, being somewhat later, dated 1604.[98] Both Essex and Nottingham are treated in what Colvin describes as 'a quaintly symbolic or conventional way', each on land poised above a bird's-eye view of his martial and naval exploits, and

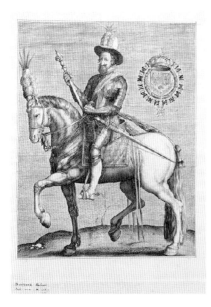

Fig. 8 Robert Boissard, *Equestrian portrait of Henri IV, King of France*, engraving (1603)

continues, 'The general treatment in both cases is adapted on an enlarged scale from the current engraved portraits by contemporary artists of the French king, Henri IV; the ponderous, comically rearing charger bestridden by Nottingham being indeed copied quite literally from that which occurs in a small portrait of the French king engraved by Leonard Gaultier in 1596'.[99]

Primarily concerned with the influence of continental prints on the decorative arts in Elizabethan and Jacobean England, Anthony Wells-Cole has found only a 'limited tally of borrowings from French prints', and speculates that they may have been 'relatively difficult to come by in England, or they simply may not have appealed to English tastes'; these tastes preferring Dutch 'Mannerist excess' to French 'classical elegance'.[100] French equestrian portrait prints, however, were certainly obtainable. Antony Griffiths, meanwhile, has found that 'equestrian portraits were not rare in London publishing in the late sixteenth and early seventeenth centuries',[101] and, though he refers here to English engravings, local production was stimulated by familiarity with French prints. Indeed, Boissard became directly involved in producing plates for the English market. In the printsellers' and stationers' shops in St Paul's Yard, Pope's Head Alley in Cornhill, and around Holborn (where Peake's premises were), Continental equestrian portrait prints would have been found alongside English ones.

We know that after Peake's conventional Clouet-Caron design was well underway on the canvas, and the first blocking-in done, that, in the words of the restorers, there was 'a decisive change in the character of the commission to the painter'.[102] At this stage, it appears that Peake referred once more to his print sources, in particular to the most famous and influential of all Albrecht Dürer's engravings, *Knight, Death and the Devil* (1513, fig. 9).[103] He may already have examined this engraving at the commencement of his work, as it shows a number of similarities in the composition of the horses and riders.[104] Both Dürer's and Peake's riders are set against a screen in the form of either mountain or wall, effectively restricting the rider to a grass-tufted foreground, and focusing attention on the horse's measured gait. Here, though, we might be detecting the powerful influence of Dürer through the intermediary print sources of the French School. Of new interest to Peake in Dürer's engraving would have been the attendant allegorical figures: Time, presented as Death, with a skull-like, noseless and snake-ringed head, wispy beard and raised hourglass; and, behind the Knight, the figure of

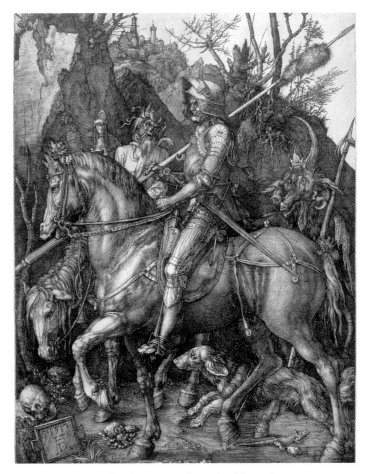

Fig. 9 Albrecht Dürer, *Knight, Death and the Devil*, 1513

the winged, swine-snouted Devil, his pick-axe raised like a lance. Taking this as a starting point for the revision, Peake may be seen to have retained a winged figure, carrying a poled weapon, and positioned behind the rider, who is no longer the Devil, nor even Time-as-Death, but Time-as-Opportunity. The Knight has been relieved of his lance and helmet, now carried by the figure of Time. Thus, the representation of the resolute knight pursuing his earthly course, refusing to be distracted by thoughts of death and damnation, becomes that of the knight who has full command of his destiny, with opportunity in his grasp. Central to this transformation is Henry's imperious, outward gaze toward the viewer, communicating awareness vastly different from the introspection of Dürer's Knight.

Wells-Cole suggests that another, as yet unidentified, print source might lie behind the figure of Time-as-Opportunity. Even more recently, Anthony Rooley claims to have found at least some inspiration for it in the title-page of John Dowland's *Firste Booke of Songes*

(London, 1597), which re-uses the engraving for the title-page of William Cunningham's *Cosmographical Glasse* (1559), showing a procession of figures, including a winged, bearded Time, with scythe held low and with goat's legs, followed by a bald, snow-bearded hermit. His fascinating argument, centring upon an identification of Sir Henry Lee as the deviser and commissioner of the portrait, and, indeed, model for the fugure of 'Time' is, though, not wholly convincing.[105]

Whenever Robert Peake was challenged to produce an unusual design for a portrait he tended to resort to prints. Though *The Procession Portrait of Queen Elizabeth I* (1600) has had its attribution to Peake challenged, it would be unwise to discount entirely Peake's involvement with it. He would, in any case, have known this ambitious work, and that its design was also derived from prints.[106] For *Prince Henry and Sir John Harington* (1603) he looked at *Turbervile's Booke of Hunting* (London, 1576).[107] Later, he found a model for his equally ambitious Turin portrait of Henry in Hendrick Goltzius's *Manlius Torquatus* from *The Roman Heroes* (c. 1586).[108] Even the inventive Isaac Oliver used an engraving found in *The Exercise of Arms* as a model for his drawing of Prince Henry practising with a pike. Such borrowing (or reference) was seen not as an indication of inadequacy but of erudition. It would, therefore, have been entirely uncharacteristic of Peake to neglect to look at prints when presented with an utterly unfamiliar commission: a large equestrian portrait in oils. Unlike many of his court clientele, whose increasing familiarity with art on the Continent made the arrival of the equestrian painted portrait in England an inevitability, Peake, for all we know, might never have visited France. A thriving London print market nonetheless offered numerous examples from the French School, which enabled him to produce a design that embodied the strengths of a powerful iconographic tradition. Those who saw themselves and their prince within the muscular Protestant tradition of Leicester, Sidney and Essex, remembered Henri IV also as the Huguenot king, Henri of Navarre. After his assassination, a transfer to Prince Henry of responsibility for leading the resistance to resurgent Catholic imperialism seemed to them the only course, and for those who knew of it, the migration of the royal equestrian portrait tradition to Prince Henry from its most recent exploiter must have seemed entirely appropriate.

NOTES

1 See Renate Woudhuysen-Keller, Sally Thirkettle and Ian McClure, 'The examination and restoration of *Henry, Prince of Wales on Horseback*', *The Hamilton Kerr Bulletin*, no. 1 (Cambridge, 1988), pp. 15–22; Ian McClure, 'Henry Prince of Wales on Horseback by Robert Peake the Elder' in Arthur Oddy, editor, *The Art of the Conservator* (London, 1992), pp. 59–62; Roy Strong, *The English Icon*, p. 364; *The Cult of Elizabeth: Elizabethan Portraiture and Pageantry* (London, 1977), pp. 187–91; *The Treasure Houses of Britain: Five Hundred Years of Private Patronage and Art Collecting* (Washington D.C., 1985) p. 132; *History Today*, vol. 36 (May 1986), p. 63; *Henry Prince of Wales and England's Lost Renaissance* (London, 1986), p. 115.

2 The Metropolitan Museum of Art, New York. For discussion of this painting see: E.E. Gardner, 'A British Hunting Portrait', *Metropolitan Museum of Art Bulletin* 3, no. 5 (January, 1945), pp. 113–17; Julius Held, 'Le Roi A La Ciasse', *The Art Bulletin*, XL, 2 (June, 1958), pp. 139–49; and Malcolm Warner and Robyn Asleson, *Great British Paintings from American Collections* (New Haven and London, 2001), pp. 49–50. For the painting and its pendant portrait of Henry's sister Elizabeth, see: Katharine Baetjer, 'British Portraits in the Metropolitan Museum of Art', *The Metropolitan Museum of Art Bulletin* (Summer, 1999), pp. 9–13.

3 Palazzo Reale, Turin. See Strong, *Henry, Prince of Wales*, pp. 114–15; John Peacock, 'The Politics of Portraiture', in Kevin Sharpe and Peter Lake (eds.), *Culture and Politics in Early Stuart England* (New York, 1994), pp. 199–228; Karen Hearn (ed.), *Dynasties: Painting in Tudor and Jacobean England 1530–1630*, (London: Tate Gallery, 1995), p. 187 (no. 127).

4 The elaborately embossed parade armour depicted in the portrait was of a kind not being made regularly by the end of the sixteenth century. In a personal communication, Claude Blair, former Chief Curator of the Royal Armouries at the Tower of London (to whom I am grateful for this information), has described the armour as of 'outstanding elaboration and quality, quite unlike anything else recorded in England'. There is no mention, either in the Prince's Wardrobe and Privy Purse accounts, or among recorded gifts to the Prince, of a similar suit of armour. As, however, Jacobean portrait painters saw it as a normal part of their task to create an accurate record of personal clothing and adornments, the possibility of the former existence of the portrait armour should not be entirely dismissed.

5 This may be one of the embroidered bands, perhaps the 'band embroidered with pearle', and 'plumes of feathers' itemized in the 'Extract from the Wardrobe Account of Prince Henry, eldest Son of King James I', *Archaeologia*, XI (London, 1794), p. 95.

6 This rapier seems to be that also depicted in Peake's 'Richmond Palace' portrait of Henry (National Portrait Gallery, London), and is very probably the gift given by Christian IV of Denmark in 1606 which according to the chronicler, Stow, together with its scabbard was worth 2000 marks. See: 'An Inventory of the Jewelles belonging once to the high and mightie Henrie Prince of great Brytane', *Archaeologia*, XV (London, 1806), p. 18; reprinted in Y. Hackenbroch, *Renaissance Jewellery* (London, 1979), pp. 408–09.

7 This can only be a faithful record of Henry's actual saddle and caparison, for which there is documentary evidence: 'By order dated 16th March, 1608. To Edmund Palmer, embroiderer to the Prince, the sum of 366 *l*. 13s. 4d, in full satisfaction and payment for a rich saddle', Frederick Devon (ed.), *Issues of Exchequer* (London, 1836), p. 90; Sir David Murray to Salisbury, from St James's, 4 February, 1609. Requests that Palmer may be paid 400 *l*. for a saddle bestowed a year and a half ago by the King on the Prince, who has ordered it to remain in his wardrobe till the poor man is paid. *Cal. S.P. Domestic, 1603–1610*, (61). NB these dates are *stylo vetere*, and therefore, according to Murray, the saddle had been delivered around the beginning of September 1608.

8 Erwin Panofsky, quoted in Lucy Gent, 'The 'Rash Gazer': Economies of Vision in Britain', in Lucy Gent (ed.), *Albion's Classicism: The Visual Arts in Britain, 1550–1660* (New Haven and London, 1995), pp. 383–84.

9 See Peacock, 'The Politics of Portraiture', p. 211.

10 See John Buxton, *Elizabethan Taste* (London, 1963), p. 111.

11 See David Howarth's observations on anti-naturalism as an element in Elizabethan portraiture, *Images of Rule: Art and Politics in the English Renaissance, 1485–1649* (Basingstoke and London, 1997), p. 110.

12 Cf. the straw-hatted St George in Pisanello's *Madonna with Two Saints* (National Gallery, London).

13 Though of a somewhat later date, *c.* 1643. Det Nationalhistoriske Museum på Frederiksborg, Denmark, A 2741.

14 For the evolution of the composition, see Woudheysen-Keller, 'The examination and restoration of *Henry, Prince of Wales on Horseback*', p. 18.

15 These characteristics, undoubtedly, are due to some degree to restorations and overpainting. See McClure, 'Henry Prince of Wales on Horseback by Robert Peake the Elder', pp. 60–72.

16 See David Piper: 'Each part has its significance; pose, costume and attributes establish the subject precisely in its rank, in its lineage, and in the centre its final individuality is differenced, as by a heraldic label, by the pale mask of the face', *The English Face* (London, 1957), p. 69.

17 Roy Strong, *The English Icon: Elizabethan and Jacobean Portraiture* (London and New York, 1969) is fundamental to the interpretation of the early English portrait as icon. See also Richard Wendorf, *The Elements of Life: Biography and Portrait-Painting in Stuart and Georgian England* (Oxford, 1990), who usefully points out: 'Portraits may be described as iconic not only when they resemble the static two-dimensional nature of religious or royal images, but also when they demand to be "read" in verbal or literary terms' (p. 69), and 'The combination of allegorical motifs with the static poses and inscribed legends of many Tudor portraits … produced representations that we would call over-determined; these paintings are so saturated with iconic devices that they are unable to suggest the character of the sitter except in hierarchic and formulaic terms (p. 89).

18 For the protracted and unsuccessful attempts to bring Miereveldt to Henry's court, see Timothy V. Wilks, 'The Court Culture of Prince Henry and His Circle', unpublished D. Phil diss., University of Oxford (November, 1987), pp. 93–98.

19 Robert Peake, *The first Booke of Architecture, made by Sebastian Serly, entreating of Geometrie. Translated out of Italian into Dutch, and out of Dutch into English*, (London, 1611), Prefatory epistle.

20 It has been suggested that the Serlio translation was part of Peake's response to Henry's inclination to patronize Continental artists such as Miereveldt and Costantino de'Servi. See Timothy Wilks, 'Forbear the Heat and Haste of Building', p. 59

21 See Woudhuysen-Keller, 'The examination and restoration of *Henry, Prince of Wales on Horseback*', p. 17.

22 Richard Brilliant, *Portraiture* (Cambridge, Mass, 1991), p. 12.

23 Hans Belting, *Likeness and Presence: A History of the Image before the Era of Art*, trans. Edmund Jephcott (Chicago and London, 1994), p. 10.

24 The term 'schema' is Brilliant's, and refers to the consolidation of 'socio-artistic conventions into specific verbal-visual images', which allow artist and viewer to 'categorize the person portrayed in general terms'. Brilliant, *Portraiture*, p. 37.

25 Elizabeth Honig, 'In Memory: Lady Dacre and Pairing by Hans Eworth', in Lucy Gent and Nigel Llewellyn (eds.), *Renaissance Bodies: The Human Figure in English Culture c. 1540–1660* (London, 1990) p. 71.

26 Brilliant, *Portraiture*, p. 102.

27 Maurice Howard, *The Tudor Image* (London: Tate Gallery, 1995), p. 62.

28 See Michael Leslie, 'The Dialogue Between Bodies and Souls: Picture and Poesy in the English Renaissance', *Word and Image* I, 1 (January–March 1985), p. 21.

29 Henry's wholehearted participation in the chivalric revival in court culture (which was by no means confined to England) was plainly compatible with the notion of him as King Arthur's heir; for an early example of which, see Walter Quin's 'Anagra: Henricus Fridericus Steuartus/Arthuriin Sede Futurus Crescis', in *Sertum Poeticum, in Honorem Iacobi Sexti Serenissimi, Ac Potentissimi Scotorum Regius* (Edinburgh, 1600). Henry's chosen name, Moeliades, for the Barriers of 1610 is that of an Arthurian hero born of a liason between Meliades, King of Lyonesse, and the Lady of the Lake. In his quarrel with the Pope, Henry VIII used King Arthur both as convenient precedent and as a model for his own kingship, having persuaded himself that the break with Rome was rooted in Arthur's conquest of Rome and declaration of himself as emperor; see David Starkey, 'King Henry and King Arthur', in James P. Carley and Felicity Riddy (eds.), *Arthurian Literature* XVI (Cambridge, 1998), pp. 171–72.

30 The setting has been variously interpreted: Lionel Cust, 'A Portrait Called 'Henry, Prince of Wales by Isaac Oliver', *Burlington Magazine* 24 (1914), p. 348, identifies it as ground and setting sun, as does J.W. Williamson, *The Myth of the Conqueror* (New York, 1978), p. 69. Woudhuysen-Keller, 'The examination and restoration of *Henry, Prince of Wales on Horseback*', identifies it as grass and rising sun (p. 15). Roy Strong, in an Arthurian interpretation of the impresa, has the anchors as substitutes for Excalibur and sees the hands rising from 'the waters' (*Henry Prince of Wales*, p. 115) or 'lake' (*History Today*, p. 63). Cf. *The Treasure Houses of Britain* (New Haven: Yale University, 1985), p. 132 (no. 56).

31 See above, note 7.

32 William Camden, *Remains Concerning Britain*, (London, 1674, facsimile edn London, 1870), pp. 366–67.

33 William Drummond, *The Works of William Drummond of Hawthornden* (Edinburgh, 1711), p. 228.

34 *Ibid.*, pp. 228–29.

35 In this Jonson was relying on Ieronimo Ruscelli, *Le Imprese illustri* (Venezia, 1584), p. 2, quoted in Allan J. Gilbert, *The Symbolic Persons in the Masques of Ben Jonson* (Durham, NC, 1948), p. 7.

36 Alan R. Young, *The English Tournament Imprese* (New York, 1988), pp. 71 (no. 164) and 101 (no. 319).

37 *Ibid.*, p. 64 (no. 127).

38 Neil Cuddy, 'Dynasty and Display: Politics and Painting in England, 1530–1630', in Hearn, *Dynasties*, p. 15.

39 Geffrey Whitney, *A Choice of Emblems and Other Devices* (London, 1586), no. 11, in Peter M. Daly (ed.), *The English Emblem Tradition*, I (Toronto, 1988), p. 203.

40 P.S. The Heroicall Devises of *M. Claudius Paradin* (London, 1591), no. 92, in Peter M. Daly (ed.), *The English Emblem Tradition*, 2 (Toronto, 1993), p. 63.

41 'A Portrait called "Henry, Prince of Wales" by Isaac Oliver', *Burlington Magazine*, XXIV (October–March, 1913–14), pp. 347–48.

42 See Louisa Twining, *Symbols and Emblems of Early and Mediaeval Christian Art*, 2nd edition (London, 1885), p. 132.

43 Diana Scarisbrick, *Tudor and Jacobean Jewellery* (London, 1995), p. 48.

44 Houston Diehl, 'Graven Images: Protestant Emblem Books in England', *Renaissance Quarterly* 39:1 (Spring, 1986), p. 56.

45 *Ibid.*, p. 59.

46 *Ibid.*, p. 57.

47 John Manning (ed.), *The Emblems of Thomas Palmer (the British Library Sloane MS 3794)* (New York, 1988), p. 71.

48 George Wither, *A Collection of Emblems, Ancient and Modern* (London, 1635), p. 60. See also, Book I, no. 39: a heart between an anchor and a bow and arrow, titled, 'Where strong Desires are entertain'd, The Heart 'twixt Hope and Feare, is pained'.

49 Peter M. Daly (ed.), *Andreas Alciatus I: The Latin Emblems* (Toronto, 1985), no. 144.

50 *London's Love to the Royall Prince Henrie, Meeting him on the River of Thames (at his return from Richmonde) with a worthie Fleete of her Cittizens, on Thursday the last of May 1610; &c.,* printed in John Nichols (ed.), *The Progresses of King James the First* (London, 1828), II, p. 316.

51 Samuel Daniel, *The Tragedie of Philotas* (London, 1607), sigs. A2, A3.

52 Stephen Orgel and Roy Strong, 'Inigo Jones, 'Tethys' Festival' in *The Theatre of the Stuart Court* (London, 1973), p. 194, ll. 35–38.

53 Michael Drayton, *Poly-Olbion* (London, 1613), Dedication.

54 John Owen, *The Epigrams of John Owen*, rendered into English by Thomas Harvey (London, 1677), Book 3, no. 7, p. 48.

55 Daniel Price, *Lamentations for the death of the late Illustrious Prince Henry and the dissolution of his religious Familie* (London, 1613), E3, p. 28.

56 Fritz Saxl, 'Veritas Filia Temporis', in Raymond Klibansky and H.J. Paton (eds.), *Philosophy and History: Essays Presented to Ernst Cassirer*, (Oxford, 1936), pp. 202–03, and fig. 3, p. 203. The discussion of Truth, the Daughter of Time is based on Saxl.

57 For the conflation of the Greek idea of Time leading Truth to light, and the Latin idea of Saturn as the father of Truth, see Saxl, 'Veritas Filia Temporis', pp. 199–200, and especially, footnote 1, p. 200.

58 *Ibid.*, p. 205.

59 *Ibid.*, p. 203.

60 William Camden, *The History of the most Renowned and Victorious Princess Elizabeth, Late Queen of England*, 3rd Edition (London, 1675), p. 244.

61 George Wither, *Prince Henries Obsequies or Mournfull Elegies Upon His Death* (London, 1613), Sig. B2, Elegy 8.

62 Strong, *Henry, Prince of Wales*, p. 115. Strong neglects to cite Panofsky in quoting his definition of Opportunity: 'that is, the brief decisive moment which marks a turning-point in the life of human beings or in the development of the universe': Erwin Panofsky, 'Father Time', in *Studies in Iconology: Humanistic Themes in the Art of the Renaissance* (New York, 1962), p. 71.

63 For an illustration of the ancient image of Time as Opportunity, see *ibid.*, plate XXI, fig. 35; for *Kronos* with a full head of hair, see Plate XXV, fig. 47.

64 Daly (ed.), *Andreas Alciatus I: The Latin Emblems*, no. 122: Motto: 'On Opportunity.' Picture: 'Naked Occasio, with a bald head, a long forelock, and a razor in her raised left hand, stands on a winged globe in a landscape. Her drapery is blown back over her shoulder like a sail.' Subject: Opportunity. Whitney, 'occasionem', based on Alciatus, no. 35, shows 'In Occasionem' ('On Opportunity') balancing on a wheel in the sea, holding a scarf in her left hand, Daly (ed.), *The English Emblem Tradition*, I, p. 280.

65 George Lyman Kittredge, 'To Take Time by the Forelock', *Modern Language Notes 8*; no. 8 (December, 1893), pp. 230–35. For examples of Elizabethan references to seizing Opportunity by the forelock, including those found in Shakespeare, see p. 232 and footnote 10. See also, R. Wittkower, 'Chance, Time and Virtue', *Warburg Journal*, I (1937–39), pp. 313–21.

66 Saxl, 'Veritas Filia Temporis', pp. 206–10; Donald Gordon, '"Veritas Filia Temporis": Hadrianus Junius and Geoffrey Whitney', *Journal of the Warburg and Courtauld Institutes*, III, nos. 3/4 (April–July 1940), pp. 228–40.

67 Ben Jonson, 'The Entertainment at Althorp', in C.H. Herford Percy and Evelyn Simpson, editors, *Ben Jonson*, VII (Oxford, 1941), p. 131.

68 George Wither, *Prince Henries Obsequies or Mournful Elegies Upon His Death* (London, 1613), Sig. D1, Elegy 39.

69 British Library: MS Royal 12A LXVI. Alan R. Young, editor, *The English Emblem Tradition 5: Henry Peacham's Manuscript Emblem Books* (Toronto, 1998), p. 197.

70 Peacham, *op. cit.*, p. 7.

71 See Francis Haskell and Nicholas Penny, *Taste and the Antique* (New Haven and London, 1981), pp. 252–55 (no. 55). For a full discussion of the channels by which the *Marcus Aurelius* and other equestrian monuments came to influence the equestrian monument in France and elsewhere, see Walter Liedtke, *The Royal Horse and Rider: Painting, Sculpture, and Horsemanship 1500–1800* (New York, 1989), pp. 61–73. NB many of the French interpretations place the horse's weight on opposite legs to those of the *Marcus Aurelius*. Fidelity to the original in this respect seems not to have been sufficiently important to take the trouble to counter the inevitable production of reverse images in the printing process.

72 Liedtke, *The Royal Horse and Rider*, p. 21.

73 From a Spanish emblem book, *Idea de un Principe Politico Christiano* (Munich, 1640), no. 38, given in Liedtke, *The Royal Horse and Rider*, p. 64.

74 Jean Adhémar, *Le Dessin Française au XVI siècle* (Lausanne, 1954), p. 131.

75 For the history of this commission and of the horse, see: Liedtke, *The Royal Horse and Rider*, pp. 68–69.

76 Abel Desjardins, *La vie et l'œuvre de Jean Bologne* (Paris, 1883), pp. 75–76.

77 Pierre Dan also tells us that in the 'Room of the Emperors', among the portraits of the Twelve Caesars, an equestrian portrait of 'Henri le Grand', helmeted, was centered above the chimney mantle, 'placed there as was due his virtues, as if there were in him alone the merits of all these great monarchs'. Implicit here was the propagandistic message that Henri was the new Caesar; see Pierre Dan, *Le Trésor des merveilles de la Maison Royale de Fontainebleau*, (Paris, 1642), II, pp. 144–45.

78 See Katharine Watson and Charles Avery, 'Medici and Stuart: a Grand Ducal Gift of 'Giovanni Bologna' Bronzes for Henry Prince of Wales (1612)', *Burlington Magazine*, cxv (1973), pp. 493–507.

80 Jackson-Stops, *The Treasure Houses of Britain*, p. 132. Cf., Strong, *Henry, Prince of Wales*, p. 115.

81 An anonymous drawing, *Henry II on Horseback, c.* 1550–1559 (Musée Condé, Chantilly), may be the design. (plate 54).

82 See Béguin, 'Tradition et Modernité dans les arts graphiques', in *Henri IV et la reconstruction du royaume* (Paris, 1989), p. 340.

83 J.W. Stoye, *English Travellers Abroad 1604–1667: Their Influence in English Society and Politics* (London, 1952), p. 57.

84 Sylvie Béguin cites a portrait, now in a private collection, by one Pierre du Plan, painter and valet du chambre to Henri IV around 1598, of the king on horseback, in armour, holding a letter in his gloved left hand, his scarf twisted around his cuirass and billowing behind in a manner that evokes Antoine Caron (*c.* 1520–1600); below in the background is a city wall encircled by soldiers. She refers to a similar picture in the Musée Carnavalet, Paris, but with a different background, and suggests these works might have been part of a series commemorating Henry IV's victories. See S. Béguin, 'Tradition et Modernité dans les arts graphiques', p. 340. Louis Dimier notes that François Clouet's nephew and student, Benjamin Foulon (or Foullon), also painter and valet du chambre to the king between 1588 and 1609, was summoned to Henri's camp in 1592 for two months, to work on several pictures 'the subjects of which are not known, but in view of the special commission must certainly have been battle pieces', *French Painting of the Sixteenth Century* (New York, 1904), p. 292.

85 Dan, *Le Trésor*, II, pp. 117–18, 149.

86 The room measured 10 m by 40 m. The chimney, 20 ft x 23 ft, so dominated the room, it became known as the 'Salle de la Belle Cheminée,' rather than by its original designation. Erected in two parts, the architectural framework, begun late December 1597, was completed in August 1598; the sculptural decoration, begun March 1600 was completed early 1601. For complete descriptions and illustrations of the Belle Cheminée, see Jean-Pierre Samoyault, 'Le Château de Fontainebleau,' in *Henri IV et la reconstruction du royaume*, exh. cat. (Paris, 1989), pp. 360–62, 370; Jean Ehrmann, 'La Belle Cheminée du château de Fontainebleau,' in *Actes du Colloque International sur L'Art de Fontainebleau* (Paris, 1975), pp. 117–24; Éd.-J. Ciprut, *Mathieu Jacquet, Sculpteur d'Henri IV* (Paris, 1967), pp. 55–62 and plates III–V, IX–X, and XII–XIII; Félix Herbet, *Le Château de Fontainebleau: Les Apartements, Les Cours, Le Parc, Les Jardins* (Paris, 1937), pp. 215–20; M.J.J. Champollion-Figeac, *Le Palais de Fontainebleau* (Paris, 1866) 2 vols., pp. 277–87; and Dan, Le Trésor, I, pp. 34–37, 139–41.

87 Jacquet seems to have responded to Giambologna's *Cosimo I*, widely known in Paris through reproductions, but continued to draw mainly from the long tradition of associating the Valois kings with the clement Roman emperor symbolized by Marcus Aurelius. A marble medallion of Charles IX (Paris, Musée du Louvre,), formerly identified as Henri III and attributed by Ciprut to Germaine Pilon, has recently been attributed to Jacquet, and should be compared with his marble bas-relief, Henri IV as a Roman Conqueror (Pau, Musée national du château). Geneviève Bresc-Bautier, 'Les sculpteurs parisiens,' in *Henri IV et la Reconstruction du royaume* (Paris, 1989), p. 382, no. 448. Both the medallion and the bas-relief share the same trotting, high-spirited horse trampling armour, their riders in Marcus Aurelius mode, riding bareback, bare or sandal-footed, arm raised in a gesture of clemency, in Roman armour with billowing scarf.

88 Cynthia Burlingham, 'Portraiture as Propaganda: Printmaking during the Reign of Henri IV,' in *The French Renaissance in Prints from the Bibliothèque Nationale de France* (Berkeley, 1994), p. 140.

89 Jean-Pierre Babelon, *Henri IV* (Paris, 1982), p. 195.

90 Jean Ehrmann, 'La Belle Cheminée du château de Fontainebleau' in *Actes du Collloque International sur L'Art de Fontainebleau, Etudes réunies et présentées par André Chastel* (Paris, 1975), pp. 118–22.

91 Ehrmann, 'La Belle Cheminée', p. 122.

92 Musée national du château, Pau. See Babelon, *Henri IV*, p.196, fig. 249b.

93 See A.P.F. Robert-Dumensil, *Le Peintre-Graveur Français* (Paris, 1868), X, p. 126 (417). Two versions of a very similar image of Henri dated 1596, designed by Léonard Gaultier and engraved by Jean le Clerc, are in the

Bibliothèque National, Paris, see André Linzeler, *Inventaire de Fonds Francais, Graveurs du Seizième Siècle* (Paris, 1932), I, p. 415 (227b). The British Museum also holds two versions of this design, both signed by Gaultier (B.M. 1848-9-11-614, and 1871-12-9-694). This same iconographic model, clearly one of the standard images of Henri IV, derived from Caron via de Leu and Gaultier, was also carried forward by Robert Boissard with his engraving (dated 1603) depicting, again, the horse rearing to the left, with a battle scene before a walled city below (Musée national du château, Pau), see Babelon, *Henri IV*, p. 193, fig. 249c. Cf. a very similar engraving by Carl de Mallery, dated 1599, see Ambroise Firmin-Didot, *Les Graveurs de Portraits en France* (Nieuwkoop, 1977), II, p. 170 (1420). Firmin-Didot also lists the de Leu, pp. 119–20 (1269).

94 Musée national du château, Pau (Babelon, *Henri IV*, p. 196, fig. 250d). The British Museum holds an identical print of this engraving, dated 1609, and signed *L. Gaultier Sculp.* and two similar versions, both published by Jean le Clerc (BM 1848-9-11-61. BM 1848-9-11-610). For an example of the Johan van Haelbeck version, bearing the name 'Hallbeeky', see (BM 1848-9-11-609). See also Babelon, *Henri IV* p. 198, plate 250c; also Ambroise Firmin-Didot, *Les Graveurs*, p. 279, no. 816.

95 Cf., Babelon, *Henri IV*, p. 196, fig. 250a; British Museum, BM 1865-7-8-104. Linzeler also identifies another version of this print in the Bibliothèque National, Paris as 'an anonymous print attributed to Robert Boissard by Le Blanc' (*Manuel de l'Amateur d'Estampes*, no. 38), *Inventaire*, I, p. 155.

96 See: *Le XVIe siècle Européen*, (Bibliothèque National, Paris), plate 38; Pierre de L'Estoile, *Les Belles Figures et Drolleries de la Ligue* (1589–1600) (Paris, 1877), pp. 331–32.

97 Arthur M. Hind, *Engraving in England in the Sixteenth and Seventeenth Centuries, Part I: The Tudor Period* (Cambridge, 1952), pl. 126.

98 Liedtke maintains that the most likely model for Cumberland's horse is Tempesta's *Titus* (plate 85A), while the mounts in the portraits of Devonshire and of Essex 'clearly were copied from Stadanus's Equile' (see plates 54A, *Equus Hispanus*, and 55B, *Brito*), *The Royal Horse and Rider*, p. 296.

99 Sidney Colvin, *Early Engravers and Engraving in England (1545–1695)*, (London, 1905), p. 60. NB an engraving sold by William Kip, Robert Devereux, Earl of Essex, showing the Earl on a horse rearing to the left, wearing armour and a plumed hat, an army and fleet in the background, titled in a cartouche at upper right, 'The most noble Robert Earle of Essex & Ewe…1600', is signed at lower left: *William Kip ex.: Robert Boissard*, (Hind, *Engraving*, I, p. 187 and pl. 109), which is clearly an adaptation of Boissard's 1603 engraving of Henri IV on horseback.

100 Anthony Wells-Cole, *Art and Decoration in Elizabethan and Jacobean England. The Influence of Continental Prints, 1558–1625* (New Haven and London, 1997), p. 42.

101 Antony Griffiths, *The Print in Stuart Britain, 1603–1689* (London, 1998), p. 46.

102 Woudhuysen-Keller, 'The examination and restoration', p. 18.

103 Dürer was particularly admired by Hilliard, who extolled the German artist as 'the most exclent Albert Dure … as exquisite and perfect … a painter and master of the art of graving on copper as ever was since the world began'. Hilliard also praised Goltzius as an artist who approached 'Albertus very near, most admirably imitating him', Nicholas Hilliard, *A Treatise Concerning the Arte of Limning*, R.K.R. Thornton and T.G.S. Cain (eds.) (Manchester, 1981), pp. 19–20.

104 Noted by McClure, 'Henry Prince of Wales on Horseback by Robert Peake the Elder', p. 69; Wells-Cole, *Art and Decoration in Elizabethan and Jacobean England*, p. 315, footnote 5. Mark Evans (ed.), *Princes as Patrons* (London, 1998), p. 24.

105 Anthony Rooley, 'Time stands still: devices and designs, allegory and alliteration, poetry and music, a new identification in an old portrait', *Early Music*, XXXIV, 3 (August, 2006), pp. 443–60. Rooley's contention that Sir Henry Lee, formerly Elizabeth's I tilt champion, 'was responsible for commissioning the painting and the designing of its allegory' requires firmer evidence. Rooley (p. 453) claims that Lee presented the Marcus Gheeraerts portrait of Henry that 'hangs in the National Gallery' (sic) to the Prince in 1608. It was, in fact, painted *c.* 1603, and Lee hung it at Ditchley Park; see Catherine MacLeod, *Tudor and Jacobean Portraits in the National Portrait Gallery at Montacute House* (London, 1999), p. 30. There is, therefore, no precedent for Lee

presenting a portrait of himself to Henry; though at the risk of providing a new argument for Rooley, there was a precedent for Lee commissioning such a portrait for his own collection, and, seven years on, an ardent supporter of Henry such as Lee might have desired an updated image. Yet, Rooley does not explain why Lee would have abandoned Gheeraerts, the painter he had long patronized, to turn to Peake. Identifation of Lee as the figure of Father Time based on Lee's ageing appearance in a succession of Gheeraerts portraits, ending with one dated *c.* 1602, i.e., one done as much as eight years earlier (for which, see Karen Hearn, *Marcus Gheeraerts II. Elizabethan Artist* (London, 2002), pp. 17–19), requires a degree of imagination, but it should not be altogether dismissed. Rooley surely goes to far in proposing that Lee 'played out the final scene' by actually leading Henry naked into the Barriers in January 1610, which would have caused a sensation and would have been reported, if only for the death of a septuagenarian courtier from cold. Rooley also misunderstands the nature of tournament combat, assuming the 10-foot high brick wall in the portrait to be 'the enclosure known as 'the Barriers'. He holds Lee responsible, moreover, for the *impresa* (p. 460), as if Lee had returned from retirement in the country to take over the entire visual programme of the Prince's court).

106 See David Armitage, 'The procession portrait of Queen Elizabeth I: a note on a tradition', Journal of the Warburg and Courtauld Institutes, LIII (1990), pp. 301–07; Wells-Cole, *Art and Decoration*, p. 208.

107 See Julius Held, 'Le Roi à la Ciasse', *The Art Bulletin*, XL, 2 (June, 1958), p. 145.

108 See Strong, *Henry, Prince of Wales*, p. 115.

6 II | *Henry Prince of Wales, on Horseback*: A note on patronage and provenance

Timothy Wilks

On 6 October, 1599, Thomas Platter of Basel visited Greenwich Palace, and noted in his diary, 'When we had made our way up into the royal palace we saw a very large picture of the king of France on horseback in one room'.[1] This was the portrait of *Henri IV of France on Horseback* that had hung at Greenwich since the latter years of Queen Elizabeth's reign. Fourteen years later, in the year immediately following that in which Prince Henry had died, it was seen in the same place by J.W. Neumayr von Rammsla, a gentleman from the court of Saxony.[2] It was still in the royal collection when Abraham van der Doort compiled his inventory, c. 1639, though he recorded that it had been moved elsewhere: 'itm te pictur on horsbak so big als te lijff king hnri te 4 auff franz his gentilman Wit a hed pis karing afor him this peece was in Greench before'.[3] The keeper's fractured English also reveals something of its composition: that the French king was attended by a gentleman carrying before him a head-piece, or helmet. This picture is likely to have been the only equestrian portrait of a royal subject hanging in the royal collection at the time Robert Peake painted his equestrian portrait of Prince Henry, and there could have been few, if any, such portraits elsewhere in Jacobean England. For this reason alone it is to be suspected that both Peake and the commissioner of the new work would have paid it close attention. The addition of a helmet-bearing attendant in Peake's revised composition, as discussed in Gail Weigl's essay in this volume, suggests that the influence of this portrait of the French king, whom Prince Henry was always encouraged to admire, may well have been significant.

Between 1610/11 and 1614 , not only *Henri IV of France on Horseback* but also *Henry, Prince of Wales, on Horseback* probably hung in Greenwich, separated only by half the width of the park, and their remarkable proximity provides the basis for a hypothesis for the commissioning of the later work. There are no known records of *Henry, Prince of Wales, on Horseback* during the sitter's lifetime, or any evidence to suggest that Henry commissioned or owned it. The earliest known record of 'a picture in large of Prince Henry on horseback in armes' is in the inventory of goods in the house in Greenwich Park belonging to Henry Howard, Earl of Northampton, taken after his death in June 1614.[4] Only one extant portrait of this description is known, and although its provenance does not extend into the seventeenth century it is probably safe to assume that the Parham Park portrait is that which formerly hung at Greenwich.

We are left to consider how this portrait came into the possession of the Earl of Northampton, a surprising fact as Henry and Northampton had been opponents in a bitter struggle over the running of the naval dockyards.[5] Both were present on 8 May 1609 at the

King's examination of the master shipwright Phineas Pett, a sworn servant of the Prince, over alleged deficiencies in the building of Henry's huge, three-decker warship, the *Prince Royal*. At the moment of Pett's vindication, Henry cried out, 'Where be now these perjured fellows that dare thus abuse his Majesty with these false informations, do they not worthily deserve hanging?'[6] He was referring to the expert witnesses clustered around Northampton, and though the Earl had not given evidence himself, and had, therefore, not been included in Henry's condemnation, it must have been plain to the vast crowd of courtiers and citizens assembled in the Woolwich shipyard that Henry blamed Northampton for instigating the proceedings.

Henry knew better than publicly to criticize or abuse one of his father's privy councillors, but he could be freer with his opinions among his own following. After his death, the diarist Sir Symonds D'Ewes (1602–1650) recalled that the Prince 'had formerly expressed his distaste against Henry Earl of Northampton'.[7] D'Ewes's source of information was almost certainly his admired friend, Sir Robert Cotton, who had a fair claim to have been within the Prince's circle of advisers.[8] Yet, Cotton was also close to Northampton, often acting as his private secretary, and had been chiefly responsible for the gathering of evidence for the 1608 commission of inquiry into abuses in the administration of the navy.[9] Cotton was regarded as a scholar and antiquary rather than a courtier, and this status seems to have allowed him to move freely between hostile huoseholds. If D'Ewes had been told by Cotton that Henry had spoken ill of Northampton, there can be little doubt this had also been reported to the Earl. As one of the Catholic Howards, Northampton's difficult early years had left him highly sensitive to the slightest word uttered against him. When, on 8 June 1609, a month after the Woolwich judgment, the findings of the formal inquiry into abuses and malpractice in naval administration began to be heard at Greenwich Palace, Northampton opened the proceedings by complaining to the king that Phineas Pett and his associates now 'traduced him in every tavern and ale bench. To his great dishonour'.[10] On that pretext, he sought to have the specific investigation into the construction of the *Prince Royal* re-opened. The King, however, angered that his judgment had not been taken as final, would have none of it. At the conclusion of the three-day hearing the King issued only the mildest of admonishments, and the naval yard stayed under the control of the complacent Lord Admiral, Charles Howard, Earl of Nottingham, and his principal clients, Sir Robert Mansell, the Treasurer of the Navy, and, Sir John Trevor, the Surveyor of the Navy, all of whom were favoured and trusted by Prince Henry. It amounted to a second frustrating rebuff for Northampton; one that he had never anticipated, having believed the mass of evidence gathered by Cotton would be damning.

If Northampton could be unsettled by tavern talk, then to receive confirmation from informants that Henry detested him must have been unendurable. He could not feel easy again until he had regained Henry's favour, which for him was also a matter of political necessity. Like the rest of the nation, Northampton had no intimation that this vigorous prince might die prematurely, nor of his own death within eighteen months. While many fervently hoped that Henry's precocity would, with the attainment of manhood, harden into decisive leadership, Northampton feared such a development, and he was reported to have declared – but only after the Henry was safely in his tomb – that the Prince would have become a tyrant.[11] While Henry lived, however, Northampton needed to make a show of his fidelity.

Opportunities for Northampton to make amends began to appear in 1610, as the court began to enjoy a series of celebrations anticipating Henry's creation as Prince of Wales. Northampton must have witnessed *The Barriers* on 6 January, since attendance was *de rigueur* for the entire court-attending peerage of England. On the following night he probably also attended the 'magnificke Feast at his Highnesses's house at St. James's, at which his Majestie, his Brother and Sister, with all other Earles, Lords, and Knights of the court were present'.[12] On 4 June, the day of the creation ceremony, Henry was supported by none other than the two antagonistic Howard earls: Northampton and Nottingham. All three robed together in the Court of Wards and then processed into the Parliament Chamber for the act of creation. There were other senior earls whom James I could have been chosen without any grave disruption of protocol, but the selection of the Howards was typical of a king who liked to see demonstrations of reconciliation, always preferring to believe they were sincere. For the next three years, Northampton attempted to mollify Henry and persuade him of his support. The acquiring and displaying of *Henry, Prince of Wales, on Horseback* may be seen as part of the Earl's pragmatic response to Henry's rapidly growing authority.

Northampton's hopes for Henry are partly disclosed by the toils of his devoted assistant, Cotton. His tract, 'An Answer to such Motives as were offered by certain Military Men to Prince Henry Inciting him to affect arms more than Peace', ostensibly written at the joint commands of James I and Henry, could only have been prompted by Northampton.[13] As a crypto-Catholic, his worst fear was that Henry would lead England into war with the Catholic powers of Europe, which would bring still less tolerable conditions for English Catholics than those which they had endured since the Gunpowder Plot of 1605. His desire to avert a war of religion was compatible with his support for an alliance with another state, to be sealed by the marriage of the Prince, that would preserve the continental balance of power. Tuscany fitted the bill well. '*Felice successo, felice ministro*' were the words an unctuous Northampton offered Ottaviano Lotti, the Tuscan Resident in London in 1611; words seized upon and immediately reported to the Florentine court.[14] Northampton was referring to Lotti's efforts to bring about a match whereby Henry would marry Caterina de' Medici, the sister of Grand Duke Cosimo. As the Lord Privy Seal, Northampton was a leading member of James I's Privy Council, and therefore one of the few real policy-makers of the early Jacobean years. His enthusiasm together with that of Salisbury, the Lord Treasurer, and the Queen, Anne of Denmark – an unusual combination – seemed to give the match a real prospect of success. Prior to Savoy's emergence as a late contender in 1612, the only prospect of an alliance with a rich and relatively independent Catholic state that would divert Henry from commitment to the northern Protestant states was that with Tuscany.[15]

If Northampton and his acolyte Cotton were bent on attempting to dissuade Henry from becoming a warrior prince, it may be asked why they would have had any interest in a portrait showing him on a warhorse wearing full armour. Yet, as Gail Weigl demonstrates, this portrait of Henry poised on the brink of leadership could be variously interpreted. That it was recognizably influenced by the image of the admired Henri IV would have pleased Henry and Salisbury, while any thought of Henri IV would have set a crypto-Catholic to musing upon the paradox that the French king's victory over the Catholic League permitted his subsequent conversion to Catholicism. Northampton could have gazed without dismay on *Henry, Prince of Wales, on Horseback*, dominating an end wall of his gallery and flanked by a collection of Venetian pictures, as it presented an eager young prince, whose future direction was by no means set. It, therefore, also presented Northampton with a challenge; that of gaining Henry's confidence.

Any suggestion that Northampton commissioned Peake requires that some thought be given to opportunity. At the very time Northampton was seeking to restore himself in Henry's favour Peake was engaged in work on the *Prince Royal*.[16] It is unlikely that he worked much inside the ship throughout this period, as he probably brought finished panels to Woolwich from his London workshop by boat. He would still have been found there on many days during the summer months of 1610, but would not have been visited there by Northampton, who was *persona non grata* about the shipyard, the scene of his humiliation.[17] Summoning Peake to Northampton's house on the hill in Greenwich Park, though, would have imposed barely a ten-minute horse ride on the painter, and it was equally convenient for Peake to inspect the equestrian portrait of Henri IV in nearby Greenwich Palace.[18] The tight triangle of Northampton's lodge (where the equestrian portrait of Henry would hang), Greenwich Palace (where the equestrian portrait of Henri IV hung), and the Woolwich shipyard where Peake was working very close to the time he must have painted the equestrian portrait, is highly suggestive of a connection.

I argue here that Northampton was the sole owner of the portrait from the time of its emergence from Peake's workshop (*c.* 1610–11) until his death in June 1614. It may be objected that Northampton could have acquired the portrait from Henry's collection, but there is no record of Henry possessing such a portrait, or any record of such a portrait hanging in one of his his palaces after his death. In fact, none of Peake's extant portraits of Henry bears the 'HP' brand of Henry's ownership, while there is ample evidence that Peake regularly painted portraits of Henry for the Prince's admirers.

Northampton was unusually interested in pictures for an Englishman of his generation, and though he was a great man beset with state affairs, he may have wished to instruct Peake on the matter of the portrait directly. It would also have been an opportunity to draw from the painter things he had seen and heard both in the Woolwich dockyard and at the Prince's court. If, however, as in so many other aspects of Northampton's business, Cotton, as the Earl's agent, had been involved in obtaining or commissioning the portrait, it might explain why (as the 1614 inventory of Northampton's possessions reveals) he chose it, but foresook the chance to acquire any of Northampton's other pictures. Unlike Northampton, Cotton was not greatly interested in pictures, even though among his vast archive he owned some of the finest illuminated manuscripts in England. As for portraits, he is known to have hung a portrait of the antiquary William Camden in his library,[19] but he had little interest in being portrayed himself – the portrait that D'Ewes commissioned was 'the first & onlie excellent Representacion that was euer taken of him'.[20] It might be surmised that Cotton intended to display *Henry, Prince of Wales, on Horseback* as testimony to his former association with Henry. Indeed, genuine devotion probably lay behind his labours on the naval inquiry, and behind the writing of his tract advocating a peaceful foreign policy. If Cotton kept the portrait, if only briefly, it would have hung either in the Blackfriars property which he leased in 1614 (he had not then taken his famous house next to the Houses of Parliament) or in his country house at Conington in Huntingdonshire, where, at least for a time, he kept his coin cabinet and antique fragments.

Unfortunately, the provenance of the portrait is incomplete, and there is no known record of it after Cotton presumably removed it from Greenwich in 1614 until it emerged from Hengrave Hall, Suffolk, in the early nineteenth century.[21] As there seems to be no clear connection between the Gages of Hengrave Hall and the descendants of Sir Robert Cotton (who died in 1631), and as the furnishings of Hengrave Hall passed with ownership of the property by descent through the whole of the seventeenth and eighteenth centuries, it is to the early-seventeenth century residents of Hengrave Hall that attention turns for any indication of association or affinity with Prince Henry. Upon investigation, a very strong association is found.

Hengrave Hall was presided over throughout the entire reign of James I by Elizabeth, Lady Kytson (d. 1628), widow of the Marian minister and later recusant, Sir Thomas Kytson, the builder of the house. She was the elder sister of Henry's treasurer, Sir Charles Cornwallis (Henry's early biographer), who was also the Earl of Northampton's staunchest friend in his beleaguered, dying days. Lady Kytson's daughter and heiress, Mary, and her estranged husband Thomas, 3rd Baron Darcy of Chiche, were he parents of Thomas Darcy, their only son, who was prominent among the young nobility fired by Henry's chivalric example, and it was he who took the prize at *Prince Henry's Barriers* in January, 1610.[22] This young man on whom his family's hopes rested heavily, like the Prince, died unexpectedly, sometime in 1612.[23] His family would, therefore, have had good reason to desire to have *Henry, Prince of Wales, on Horseback* after Northampton's demise, as to them it commemorated an association between not one but two lamented youths of promise. With the revelation of this East Anglian, predominantly Catholic interest, Cotton appears more convincing in the role of procurer, and perhaps gift-giver, than that of new owner. Whether the portrait went first to the young gallant's grandmother, Lady Kytson, or to his father, Thomas, Baron Darcy of Chiche (d. 1640),[24] or to his mother, Mary, Lady Darcy (d. 1644), or to his surviving sister, Elizabeth (d. 1651) and her husband, Sir Thomas Savage (d. 1635), who had very probably been a Gentleman of the Prince's Privy Chamber,[25] it would eventually have come into the possession of the Savages's daughter, Penelope, wife of Sir

John Gage of Firle, upon whom Hengrave was settled by her great-grandmother.

The portrait was not necessarily taken into the country and obscurity as soon as it was re-moved from Greenwich. If Lord Darcy or the Savages kept it their London houses, we might look with some hope for its influence on later English royal portraits, not least in the work of Van Dyck, who took notice of pictures he encountered in England, particularly those in the royal collection, occasionally borrowing or reworking their designs. Peake's *Prince Henry in the Hunting Field*, of which there are two extant versions (there might once have been more), seems to have provided a challenge of sorts, to which Van Dyck replied with his superb *Charles I à la Chasse* of 1635 (Louvre, Paris).[26] His *Charles I on Horseback* of which the King owned two versions – the great picture (originally in the Prince's Gallery at Hampton Court; now National Gallery, London), and a *modello* (originally in the Chair Room at Whitehall; now Windsor Castle) – also has similarities with Peake's equestrian portrait, though these might be considered generic.[27] Though Bellori wrote that Van Dyck painted this work '*ad imitatione di Carlo Quinto espresso da Titiano*',[28] there was another possible source that was much more accessible to Van Dyck, offering a further opportu-nity to create a reference between one picture and another within Charles's collection. We return to the old portrait of Henri IV, newly appreciated by the connoisseur-king Charles I, and moved from Greenwich Palace to a place of much greater exposure in the First Privy Gallery in Whitehall. *Henri IV on Horseback*, like Van Dyck's *Charles I on Horseback*, showed an attendant figure bearing the king's helmet. Such a figure also appears in the near-contemporary *Charles I with M. de St Antoine*, for which Van Dyck chose to employ a head-on Rubensesque pose for horse and rider. Here, the attendant figure has always been known to be the King's riding master, the Sieur de St Antoine, who twenty-five years earlier had served Henry in the same capacity, having been sent to him by none other than Henri IV. There might even be a joke here for the *cognoscenti* of the Caroline court. Is the ever-faithful, greying and haggard St Antoine a substitute for the figure of Father Time in this updating of the Stuart equestrian portrait?

NOTES

I am grateful to Gail Weigl to allow me to append a section containing my thoughts on the ownership of the portrait, and on the Greenwich *Henri IV*.

1 Clare Williams, *Thomas Platter's Travels in England 1599* (London, 1937), p. 224.

2 W.B. Rye, *England as seen by Foreigners in the Days of Elizabeth and James I* (London, 1865), p. 164.

3 Oliver Millar (ed.), 'Abraham Van der Doort's Catalogue of the Collections of Charles I', *Walpole Society*, XXXVII (1960), p. 195. The information that Henri IV's helmet was carried by an equerry might suggest the scene is the eve of the Battle of Ivry (14 March, 1590), when the forces of the Catholic League were finally routed. On this famous occasion Henri removed his helmet, and told his troops, 'If your cornets fail you, rally to my white plume; you will find it on the path of honour and victory.'

4 See 'An Inventory of the Effects of Henry Howard K.G. Earl of Northampton, taken on his death in 1614, to-gether with a transcript of his will', *Archaeologia*, XLII (1869), p. 372. For the dispersal of Northampton's

pictures, see Timothy Wilks, 'Art collecting at the English court from the death of Henry, Prince of Wales to the death of Anne of Denmark (November 1612–March 1619)', *Journal of the History of Collections*, 9, no. 1 (1997), pp. 31–48.

5 Perrin, *Phineas Pett*, pp. 48–70; Linda Levy Peck, *Court Patronage and Corruption in Early Stuart England* (Cambridge, Mass., 1990), especially Ch. 5: 'Corruption and early modern administration: the case of the navy', pp. 106–33; R.W. Kenny, *Elizabeth's Admiral. The Political Career of Charles Howard, Earl of Nottingham, 1536–1624* (Baltimore, 1970), pp. 296–318.

6 Perrin, *Phineas Pett*, p. 62.

7 Hope Mirrlees, *A Fly in Amber* (London, 1962), p. 268.

8 See Kevin Sharpe, *Sir Robert Cotton, 1586–1631. History and Politics in Early Modern England* (Oxford, 1979), p. 120.

9 Though the erudite Cotton assisted many occasional inquirers backed by the resources of his unrivalled library, his assistance to Northampton was continual. A measure of Cotton's support is the fact that of the fifteen commissioners of the 1608 naval inquiry only he and Northampton attended all 53 sessions and countersigned all the depositions. Even Northampton made fun of Cotton's willingness to rush to his summons.

10 Perrin, *Phineas Pett*, p. 69.

11 Mirrlees, *A Fly in Amber*, p. 268.

12 J. Nichols, *The Progresses, Processions and Magnificent Festivities of King James the First* (London, 1828), II, p. 359.

13 Sharpe, *Sir Robert Cotton*, p. 120, who also notes another edition, *Warrs with Foreign Princes Dangerous to our Common-wealth or Reasons for Forreign wars answered* (1675).

14 J.R. Galluzzi, *Istoria del granducato di Toscana sotto il governo della casa Medici* (Firenze, 1781) III, p. 321.

15 For a discussion of the marriage question, see Roy Strong, 'England and Italy: the Marriage of Henry, Prince of Wales', in R. Ollard and P. Tudor-Craig (eds.), *For Veronica Wedgwood These Studies in Seventeenth-Century History* (London, 1986), pp. 59–87. Strong notes (p. 70) Northampton at the head of the (small) Catholic party in the Council declaring, 'Behold our prince turns to Tuscany for a match' (again reported by Lotti).

16 Pett recalled this phase of the work: 'Between Easter and Michaelmas [1610] … the ship began to be garnished' Perrin, *Phineas Pett*, p. 77. The accounts for this extremely lucrative work, by far the largest commission of Peake's career, are printed, *ibid.*, pp. 207–08.

17 Cf. Pett's incurring of 'great blame and a sharp check from the Prince's Highness' for cooperating with a survey of the Navy by Trevor's successor, Richard Bingley, in 1611. See Perrin, *Phineas Pett*, p. 92.

18 Woolwich and Greenwich are approximately three miles apart on the south bank of the Thames.

19 See Sharpe, *Sir Robert Cotton*, p. 74.

20 J.O. Halliwell (ed.), *The Autobiography and Correspondence of Sir Symonds D'Ewes*, (London, 1845), I, p. 303.

21 Information from the picture file at Parham House.

22 See N.E. McClure, *The Letters of John Chamberlain*, 2 vols. (Philadelphia, 1939), I, p. 293.

23 He died between 11 November 1611 and 7 January 1613; see *ibid.*, pp. 316, 402.

24 As the brother of Elizabeth, Lady Lumley, widow of the great Elizabethan collector, he had already come into possession of Lumley's house on Tower Hill, which contained 'marbles and pictures'. See M.F.S. Hervey, *The Life, Correspondence and Collections of Thomas Howard, Earl of Arundel* (Cambridge, 1921), pp. 55–57.

25 As Thomas did not succeed his father to the baronetcy until 1615, he may be the 'Mr Savage' appearing in the 1610 household lists, and the funeral lists (LC2.4 [6]). A Sir Thomas Savage, however, advanced a small suit on behalf of another to the Prince, probably in 1612. See BL Harleian MS 7009 fol. 8. For Thomas and Elizabeth Savage, later Countess Rivers, see now Lyn Boothman and Sir Richard Hyde Parker (eds.), *Savage Fortune: An Aristocratic Family in Early Seventeenth Century* (Woodbridge, 2006).

26 This suggestion is made persuasively in Howarth, *Images of Rule*, pp. 132–36.

27 For Howarth it also brings to mind Dürer's *Knight, Death and the Devil*, suggested by Weigl as also one of Peake's sources, but only for the abstracted gaze shared by Charles and the Knight, which Peake does not give to Henry.

28 Oliver Millar prefers 'a reinterpretation of Titian's famous equestrian portrait of Charles V in the Prado'.

7| The Pike Charged: Henry as Militant Prince

Timothy Wilks

On opening the first book of the great labour of Michael Drayton's career, the chorographical poem, *Poly-olbion*,[1] the reader is confronted with an engraved frontispiece bearing a striking full-length portrait of Henry, Prince of Wales, in profile, practising with a pike (fig. 1).[2] It is to Henry that the book is dedicated,[3] and on the facing page Drayton's offers his dedicatory verses to the Prince:

> BRitaine, behold here portray'd, to thy sight,
> Henry, thy best hope, and the world's delight;
> Ordain'd to make thy eight Great Henries, nine:
> Who, by that vertue in the trebble Trine,
> To his owne goodnesse (in his Being) brings
> These severall Glories of th'eight English Kings;
> Deep Knowledge, greatnes, long Life, Policy,
> Courage, Zeale, Fortune, awfull Majestie.
> He like great Neptune on three Seas shall rove,
> And rule three Realms, with triple power, like Jove;
> Thus in soft Peace, thus in tempestuous warres,
> Till from his foote, his Fame shall strike the starres.[4]

Though the first line plainly refers to the portrait opposite, Drayton does not aspire to any emblematic combination of text and image. Indeed, were it not for a possible allusion in the final line – Henry's fame springing from his *foot*; a slightly odd insertion in an otherwise conventional panegyric to the Prince that declares the virtues of all England's eight, previous, royal Henrys are also present in him, where they combine with his own 'goodnesse' – these verses might easily have been conceived without sight of *Prince Henry practising with the pike* at all, as they would be suitable accompaniment to any of the portraits of Henry. Here, though, our concern is not with the verse or, in fact, with any of the text of *Poly-olbion*, but solely with the image, which alone is sufficiently problematic but interesting to warrant the full attention of an essay.

 Henry stands with feet planted well apart; his muscled legs and braced torso provide firm support for his weapon. His pike is held perfectly level at shoulder height by the right arm

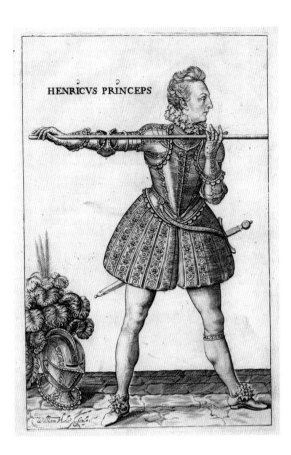

Fig. 1 William Hole, *Prince Henry practising with the pike*
engraving in Michael Drayton, *Poly-olbion*
(London: M. Lownes, L. Brown, I. Helme, I. Busbie, 1612)

drawn straight back, and by the right hand, which, by exerting downward pressure on the butt of the weapon controls its point (the full, sixteen-foot, length of the pike cannot be shown within the borders of the print). The Prince's left arm, with elbow dropped and fore-arm upright, provides a forward rest for the pike, which is held in a loose grip. Henry wears expensive armour, and more of it than normally worn by a pikeman, protecting his throat, torso, arms and hands;[5] the latter clad in gauntlets with segmented fingers, through which Henry would have sought to acquire a feel for his weapon. He wears at his side a sheathed, cross-hilted sword. The rest of Henry's attire consists of normal court dress: ruff, voluminous and embroidered cullions, Garter, hose, and shoes sporting lace rosettes. Henry practises bareheaded, though a plumed helmet rests on the paved ground behind him. The background is left blank.

Jacobeans readers, unaccustomed to seeing any portrait of a contemporary prince or king in the role of foot soldier, would have been arrested by such an image of their prince. The wide stance, at least, was reminiscent of Holbein's great wall portrait of Henry VIII, which for three-quarters of a century had confronted all those who entered the Privy Chamber at Whitehall, and had provided the model for the many portraits of that king which still hung in Jacobean long galleries.[6] Whereas Henry VIII's characteristic pose was determined by the great bodyweight his legs had to support, Prince Henry's pose, as we shall see, was determined by the precise requirements of military drill. In fact, *Prince Henry practising with the pike* owes nothing to the older portrait of Henry VIII, though in their very immovability both royal figures convey great steadfastness and resolve.

The *Poly-olbion* engraving bears the signature of William Hole, for whom we have scant biographical information, but his output of the 1610s alone is sufficient to indicate that he was part of the artistic and literary circle associated with the court of Prince Henry. Only a few months before *Poly-olbion's* publication he had been engaged on cutting most, and probably all, of the engravings that illustrate another book no less associated with that court: *Coryats Crudities*.[7] In the immediate aftermath of Henry's death Hole engraved the frontispiece for *Muses' Sacrifice* (1613) written by another of the court habitués, John Davies of Hereford, and he also engraved the musical notation for *Parthenia* (1613).[8] Even more rapidly, Hole produced 'The herse and representation of our late highe and mighty Henry Prince of Wales' for a pamphlet describing the funeral, which was quickly reissued with George Chapman's earlier *Epicede* to form a more substantial publication: *An Epicede or Funerall Song: On the most disastrous Death of the High-borne Prince of Men, Henry Prince of Wales &c. With The Funeralls, and Representation of the Herse of the same High and mighty Prince* (1613).[9] Chapman had served as an unpaid sewer-in-ordinary at Henry's court, and had long worked on his translation of the *Iliad* and the *Odyssey* at the Prince's command. When, in 1616, Chapman published the entirety of his Homeric labours as *The Whole Works*, Hole provided the portrait of the translator. He also provided a frontispiece for the *Sanctuarie of a troubled Soule* (1616) written by Henry's former historiographer, John Hayward.[10] Hole's obvious connection with Henry's court has been noted previously, by, among others, Roy Strong, who has suggested that Inigo Jones might have provided the designs for some of Hole's title-page engravings, including that for *Poly-olbion*.[11] Strong sees a knot of friendship binding Hole, Jones and Chapman together, and he might well be right. Yet, he also states that 'Henry cannot have been satisfied with Hole';[12] an assertion which pre-supposes Henry was his patron, though there is no evidence that the Prince ever took direct interest in the engraver.

Strong is, perhaps, over-keen to instil an impression that Henry was already a fine judge of art, and being impatient with the 'pedestrian' and 'provincial', was replacing English practitioners in his service with more sophisticated artists from the Continent: Cornelis Boel for Hole, Michiel Jansz van Miereveldt for Robert Peake, even Costantino de' Servi for Inigo Jones. This model, however, is too simple.[13] Hole's work certainly lacked the lightness of touch possessed by the best contemporary Dutch engravers, among them Boel (briefly in Prince Henry's service, *c.* 1611) and Crispijn de Passe, some of whose equally talented offspring came to work in England after Henry's death;[14] and for meticulousness it cannot compare with Renold Elstrack's, even though the latter was the busiest of all Jacobean engravers. None of this mattered when it came to engraving *Prince Henry practising with the pike*. Hole was a sufficiently competent engraver to enjoy regular work from the London book printers for a good decade, and, although it seems that Hole's commission owed much to his court contacts, it was just such work, i.e., a frontispiece, that now came to him in early 1612.

Hole was not even responsible for the design, his task being to copy from a supplied drawing. Such a procedure was still unusual for the period but not unknown. Elstrack, we know, worked occasionally from drawings supplied by Nicholas Hilliard, though the resultant portrait engravings defy facial recognition, being intended as representations rather than likenesses. The immediate source for *Prince Henry practising with the pike* would be entirely unknown were it not for an entry in the working catalogue of the collections of Charles I, maintained in several manuscript copies and updated and annotated by Abraham van der Doort, keeper of the king's cabinet room until his suicide in 1640. When a new cabinet room was built in Whitehall Palace to replace that in St James's Palace, Van der Doort took an inventory prior to the transfer of the many contents, which thereafter constituted an important section of the larger catalogue. Regarding the single entry we are concerned with, it is significant that three decades earlier Van der Doort had served Henry in a similar capacity, and could, therefore, draw upon his own memory of events at the earlier court. The catalogue entry records:

> Item a drawing in little of Prince
> Henry where he is playing wth a lance
> beeing side faced in a black frame
> with a shiver[15]

There is also a marginal annotation: 'Given to yo[r] Ma[ty] by M[r] Surveyor'. An earlier draft of the catalogue provides more accurate and more interesting information, though somewhat disguised by Van der Doort's fascinating Dutch-English:

> *…Wit a … pijck stading to a strijff … at lengt don bij isak oliffers vor a patron tu bi engraffen bij bin bot in blak and Wijt…*[16]

> [With a pike standing to a strife … at length done by Isaac Oliver for a pattern(?) to be engraven by being both in black and white …][17]

Oliver's drawing seems to have survived the Civil War and the sale and dispersal of the Royal Collection, only to perish in the disastrous Whitehall fire of 1698.[18] Van der Doort's entry, however, is surely reliable, and we may be confident that the drawing he is describing is that which served as the pattern for Hole's engraving. Van der Doort emphasizes the special purpose for which this drawing was done, and reveals that Oliver used a technique commonly employed in the Netherlands for such working drawings, i.e., line drawn with pen and a dark ink, followed by the application of washes and white highlights to serve as guides for the engraver when applying hatching strokes to the plate. Oliver had performed a similar task at least once before. In 1603 Hans Woutneel, a London-based print importer and publisher, engaged Oliver to provide a drawing of Queen Elizabeth to serve as a model for a plate that was then engraved by Crispijn de Passe in Cologne.[19] Those who now looked to Oliver to produce the design for the *Poly-olbion* frontispiece would have known this.

At some date after Hole had finished copying Isaac Oliver's drawing it was acquired, so Van der Doort informs, by 'Mr Surveyor': that is to say by Inigo Jones. Long since elevated to the Surveyorship of the King's Works by the time the catalogue was compiled, Jones had been Surveyor of the Prince's Works at the time of *Poly-olbion's* publication. As Henry's servant Jones was already greatly interested in drawing, and was attempting to improve his own drawing skills – possibly with some guidance from Oliver.[20] It is safe to say that Jones was perfectly placed to observe the progress of the project, though there is no indication of when he gained possession of the drawing, or of when he chose to present it to Charles I. It is conceivable that Isaac Oliver – acknowledged by his inclusion among the household mourners at Henry's funeral as having been one of the Prince's servants even though he was the Queen's and not the Prince's official 'limner' – retained the drawing of his late master until his own death in 1617. It is equally conceivable that Jones, having watched with interest the designing and execution of the *Poly-olbion* frontispiece, snapped up the preparatory drawing as soon as it had served its purpose. What is clear is that until Charles's death in January 1649 the drawing remained in the possession of those who had known Henry and continued to grieve for him, and that throughout the Oliver-Jones-Charles sequence of ownership the drawing, as much as for its artistic merit, was valued as a memorial by individuals who, though connoisseurs all, had also been close to him.

Though Van der Doort almost certainly did not mean 'patron' when he spelled that word in the phrase, 'vor a patron tu bi engraffen', we may safely assume that a patron did exist; in other words, the individual who paid Isaac Oliver for preparing the drawing for *Prince Henry practising with a pike*. As the drawing's prime purpose was to provide a striking frontispiece for *Poly-olbion*, it is to the book that one should look first for clues to the identity of this patron. Its author Drayton, however, should immediately be discounted, as he was a professional poet and perennially dependant on patronage. He was fortunate, however, in having his own Maecenas in the person of Sir Walter Aston of Tixall (1584–1639). As early as 1598 Drayton dedicated a work to Aston, and five more to him between 1602 and 1607. In 1603 Drayton, much to his pride, acted as Aston's squire when the latter was created a Knight of the Bath.[21] This patron-client relationship was so firm and enduring that, from the first moment of inquiry, Aston is to be strongly suspected as having paid for the drawing and, for that matter, the engraving. Significantly, Aston is the *only* person to whom Drayton acknowledges he is beholden in the *Poly-olbion* of 1612.

As plausible as this suggestion might seem given the strength of the Drayton-Aston relationship, one would hope for some contemporary record of contact between Aston and Henry to explain why Aston would have been eager to participate in the development of the Prince's image. Yet Aston's name did not appear on the lengthy list of members of the Prince of Wales's court when it was established in 1610 – a document which largely defined Henry's immediate following. Given Aston's age (turning twenty-six) and pedigree, it would have been entirely appropriate for him to be named a gentleman of the privy chamber or one of the carvers, cupbearers or sewers, but he was not among any of them.

Excluding the professional poets and students of the universities who satisfied a public need for lamentation, gentlemen tended to compose elegies only if they had known and loved the deceased well enough to infuse their work with genuine grief. Among Aston's manuscript poems, an unpublished elegy upon the death of Henry is to be found, indicating that, indeed, there had been some form of attachment sufficient for Aston to feel a sense of bereavement.[22] To this piece of evidence may be added Sir Simon Degge's recollection of something Aston had once told him. Aston sought merely to pass on to Degge an effective method of treating back pain, while the occasion upon which he injured himself was incidental to the story of his treatment by attendant physicians. Yet it is of great interest to us that the injury was sustained while playing tennis with none other than Henry – the casualness of this revelation only adds to its ring of authenticity.[23] It seems that Aston did become, perhaps late on, an intimate of the Prince and, therefore, one who would have been keen to participate in a significant development in the evolution of Henry's image. As confirmation of this, we find that in 1613, amid the scramble for places by those of Henry's servants who did not retire altogether from court, Aston was made a gentleman of the King's privy chamber, which the Earl of Pembroke told him was 'testimony of your [late] masters noble remembrance of you'.[24]

Shortly before drawing *Prince Henry practising with a pike* – a matter of a few months, possibly only weeks – Isaac Oliver drew Henry's head in profile, capturing for the first time his adult physio-gnomy, which exhibited the high, sloping forehead and long nose characteristic of all the Stuart-Oldenburg progeny. Henry's distinctive profile cried out for depiction, and, as Ben Jonson had Merlin tell him in *The Barriers* of January 1610/11, a certain resemblance to Henry V had been observed:[25]

> Yet rests the other thunder-bolt of warre,
> HARRY the fift, to whom in face you are
> So like, as Fate would haue you so in worth,
> Illustrious Prince …[26]

Strong draws attention to the significant fact that Henry V's image was known only in profile.[27] It is, nonetheless, obvious that classical examples also inspired Oliver.[28] Henry had recently purchased at enormous cost a coin and medal collection, which immediately stimulated pre-existing interest at court in the classical image, particularly in the profiles of Roman emperors as shown on coins and on intaglio- or cameo-cut stones.[29] Oliver, therefore, fulfilled what in the circumstances was an obvious requirement: a demand for an image of Henry as *princeps*. From late 1611, he produced several miniatures based on a single study that showed Henry in profile, set before an architectural niche, garbed as a Roman: tunic, square-cut below the neck with grotesque ornament around its border, and cloak thrown over the right shoulder, fastened with a great jewel or brooch. A few examples have survived; that in the Fitzwilliam Museum, Cambridge, is regarded as the finest, and possibly the original (fig. 2); that in the National Portrait Gallery, London, being an autograph copy (fig. 3); and that belonging to the Rijksmuseum, Amsterdam, being by Peter Oliver, Isaac's son, possibly produced after Henry's death for a former follower and admirer. A somewhat inferior version, currently bearing an attribution to Isaac, is in New College, Oxford (fig. 4).[30]

Once Isaac Oliver began to produce these miniatures, someone within the Prince's circle, possibly Oliver or another practitioner of the arts such as Jones, or a patron-courtier such as Aston, conceived the idea of lifting Henry's profile bust out of its classical setting and applying it to a full-length figure in a contemporary setting.[31] Whoever it was had something specific in mind, for he had clearly been studying the illustrations in a hugely influential Dutch manual of military drill that was first published in 1607 as *Wapenhandelinghe van Roers, Musquetten ende Spiessen*, and then quickly published in French, German, Danish and English editions. When the English version, *The Exercise of Arms for Calivres, Muskettes and Pikes*, appeared with the engraved Prince of Wales's arms, Henry joined a pantheon of dedicatees comprising northern Europe's foremost military commanders: the parent edition was dedicated to the great Stadholder, Maurits of Nassau, while the Danish edition, *Vaabenhandling om Rør, Musketter og Speder*, was dedicated to Henry's bellicose uncle, Christian IV of Denmark.[32] This extraordinary manual illustrated the drills that had evolved in the Dutch Protestant armies during many years spent fighting the Spanish, and which had enabled their mixed formations of pikemen and musketeers to manoeuvre and fight, both offensively and defensively, with great success on the battlefield. English and Scottish regiments stationed in the Netherlands, which as recently as 1610 had contributed 4000 men to the siege of Jülich under the command of Henry's mentor, Sir Edward Cecil, also adopted these drills. Now envisaging himself as a future field commander, Henry was keen to learn them. It was, therefore, very apt and not a little inspired to resort to *The Exercise of Arms* for the pose for Henry's new portrait.

Whether on his own initiative or under instruction, Isaac Oliver turned, therefore, to the 24th plate in the 'Pike Drill' section of *The Exercise of Arms* where a good full-length profile of the 'pike charged' was to be found (fig. 5).[33] His task was to substitute Henry for the bearded,

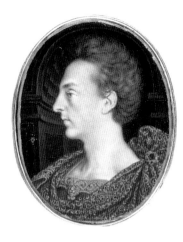

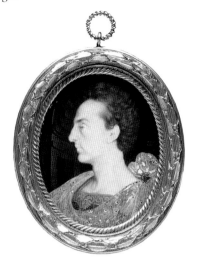

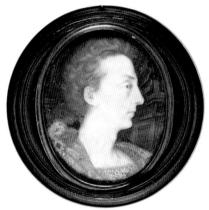

CLOCKWISE FROM TOP LEFT

Fig. 2 Isaac Oliver, *Henry, Prince of Wales*
Fitzwilliam Museum, University of Cambridge

Fig. 3 Isaac Oliver, *Henry, Prince of Wales*
watercolour on vellum, National Portrait
Gallery, London

Fig. 4 after Isaac Oliver, *Henry, Prince of Wales*
c. 1611, watercolour on vellum, New College,
Oxford

'combe-cap' or morion-wearing pikeman, the model for whom had been a certain Pierre du
Moulin, a captain in Maurits of Nassau's bodyguard. This position, one of many available
from the sequence of precise actions, seems to have recommended itself, as it was the stance
with which the enemy was actually engaged; hence Van der Doort's vivid phrase, 'standing to
a strife' – the pike-against-pike contest.[34] It was the highly regarded Jacques de Gheyn II
(1565–1629) who had provided the 117 drawings for the *Wapenhandelinghe* engravings. There is
documentary evidence that De Gheyn began work on the drawings as early as 1595/96, that is
to say a good decade before publication, at the behest and under the critical eye of Johan II of
Nassau-Siegen (1561–1623), a cousin of Maurits, the principal dedicatee.[35] Even at this date De
Gheyn was already moving away from the Mannerist style he had learned from Hendrick
Goltzius to a more realistic style that was well suited to the needs of the *Wapenhandelinghe* project. De Gheyn was also a proficient engraver, but left the work of transferring the drawings
on to copper plates to others, among them probably Andries Stock (*c.* 1580–*c.* 1648). None the

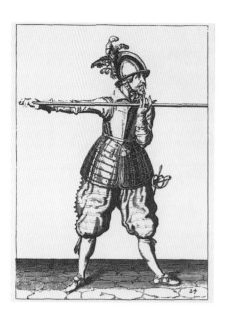

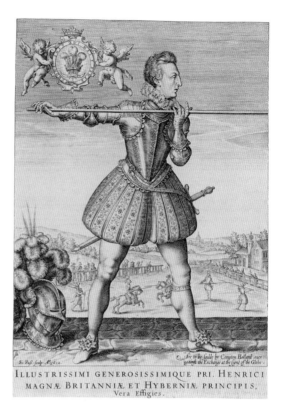

Fig. 5 'The Pike Charged', *The Exercise of Arms*

Fig. 6 Simon de Passe, *Prince Henry practising with the pike*, engraving

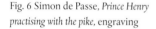

less, De Gheyn continued to oversee the work, and it is his name that appears on the title-page.[36] He also embellished with his own hand copies that Maurits of Nassau then presented to his allies. It was De Gheyn's style, therefore, if not his precise line, that Isaac Oliver now followed, albeit through the medium of an unidentified Dutch engraver. It is a matter for speculation as to how well informed Oliver was about the artistic endeavour behind this great Dutch publishing venture, though one suspects he was far from ignorant about it. Oliver's own line would subsequently be traced and cut by William Hole, whose work, in turn, would be copied by a succession of engravers in the years after Henry's death.[37]

It remains for the position to be established of another very similar engraving executed by Simon de Passe (fig. 6), which differs from Hole's in being considerably larger,[38] and having a background showing a military ground or military garden (not the old Banqueting House, where the Barriers was performed, or the Whitehall Tiltyard – Juel-Jensen refers to it as a tournament scene).[39] Both the William Hole and the Simon de Passe engravings of *Prince Henry practising with the pike* exist in several different states, but whether the Hole (in its first state) was done before the Simon de Passe (in its first state) or *vice versa* was a matter that until recently remained unresolved. A.M. Hind admitted, 'I find no certain clue as to the priority of the Van de Passe or the Hole, but the engraved lines are so close that they can hardly both have gone back to the original work'.[40] Hind lists three states for the Simon de Passe engraving: (I) Before artist's signature and imprint; (II) With the imprint: *Are to be soulde by Compton Holland ouer against the Exchange at the signe of the Globe*; (III) Signed in lower l. of subject: *S: Pass: sculp: A⁰ 1612*.[41]

If the year given on the third state of the Simon de Passe engraving to be a true dating of the work, only a matter of months or weeks during the course of 1612 could have separated the work of the two engravers. It might be thought unlikely that the finer work of de Passe could be based on the cruder work of Hole, as the quality of engraved work tends to deteriorate the more derivative it becomes; indeed, just such deterioration can be seen in the later seventeenth-century versions of this very image. This would allow the construction of a hypothesis in which Simon de Passe is seen as being engaged, perhaps only shortly before Henry's death, to produce a fine engraving suitable for the production of loose, collectors' prints. The Compton Holland imprint on states II and III provides confirmation that such prints were (at some time) produced. It fits well with the perception of a young prince who wasted no time in attempting to attract the best foreign artists to his court,[42] and of a court that was more sophisticated in its reception of the visual arts than any previous English court, where were gathered some of the earliest English art collectors.[43] To maintain the hypothesis it is necessary to assume that, in the meantime, Hole was allowed to engrave another plate from which the multiple impressions for the copies of *Poly-olbion* were to be derived; a secondary and inferior use for Isaac Oliver's design. It follows that the one major difference between the engravings – that concerning the background – has to be interpreted as a de Passe addition rather than a Hole omission. This was my reasoning twenty years ago, but my initial premise was wrong.[44]

We now know that, in fact, Simon de Passe never came to work for Henry – that he could not, therefore, have been the 'Duche graver sent for', who, as Alexander Marr persuasively suggests in his essay, was probably Cornelis Boel. Simon, a few months younger than the Prince, was still working in Utrecht for his father, Crispijn, and only in 1612 did he begin to sign and date his own plates. He did not arrive in London until 1616, and thereafter his work for a succession of publishers is very discernible.[45] How, then, may we account for the date of '1612' found on his engraving of Henry? Antony Griffiths makes the point that it was only added in the third state, and that the dating should be taken to refer to the year of Henry's death. It seems to me that this later addition might have been intended to signify a little more, that is, to date the image itself – reminding the viewer of the vigour and potential of Henry in his last year. However we interpret it, we now have to recognize it as a retrospective dating.[46]

The states of the Hole plate,[47] as with so many Early Modern copper engravings, reveal something of its working life and, in this case, something of the changing image of Henry both before and after his death. State I, included in the first issue of *Poly-olbion* (1612), bore only the signature; *William Hole sculp*: in the lower left hand corner of the plate. State II had the letters: *HENRICUS PRINCEPS* added in 1613 for the second impression of *Poly-olbion* (1613, fig. 1), and was used unaltered for a third impression (1622), though by this stage the plate was

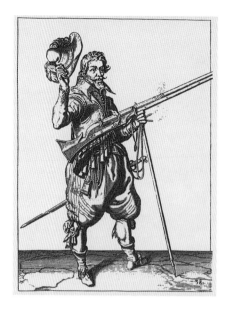

Fig. 7 38th plate of the Musket Drill section
Wapenhandelinghe

worn and producing far poorer prints than the brilliant first-state specimens. State III has the imprint: *William Ridiard excudit* instead of the old title, together with *ILLUSTR : HENRICUS PRINCEPS UUALLIAE* and the Prince of Wales's feathers within a garter and coronet. Juel-Jensen observes that these were probably copied from the engraving forming part of the collection of royal portrait prints published by the Holland brothers as *Baziliologia* in 1618. It appears, therefore, that at some point in the 1630s William Ridiard, the printseller, obtained the plate, and as well as making the above changes had it heavily retouched. As in the case of the de Passe engraving, the Hole engraving became increasingly embellished with lettering and heraldic flourishes intended to sustain the interest in, and the value of, an ageing plate.

To note breezily, as one scholar has done recently, that 'a copy of one of Isaac Oliver's royal portraits turns up as an engraving at the beginning of Michael Drayton's *Poly-Olbion*…'[48] is to overlook a complicated process of image construction, involving various courtiers and practitioners of the arts, by which Henry was adeptly integrated into an active tradition of northern European, Protestant militarism.[49] Such images did not simply turn up. Admittedly, the scholar in question is hastening to make his point that, via *Poly-olbion*, 'Henry had some success extending the preferred representation of his person beyond courtly drama into other media, offering James another source of distress', and this was undoubtedly the case.

As already noted, the prince-as-foot-soldier is a subject rarely found in the art of the Renaissance and Early Modern periods, though Henry's image had already been taken somewhat in that direction by Robert Peake's portrait in oils of Henry on foot and in the field, treading down a shield while boldly drawing his sword: a pose which Roy Strong recognized as having been taken from Hendrick Goltzius's engraving of Manlius Torquatus.[50] In that portrait, however, Peake dresses Henry in hunting green, and in spirit it has as more affinity with his earlier portraits of *Prince Henry and Sir John Harington in the hunting field* and the very similar *Prince Henry and Robert, 3rd Earl of Essex in the hunting field* (see Weigl, fig. 2) than with any military image. Precedents – at least any that might have been an influence upon Oliver and his friends within the Prince's circle – do not easily spring to mind, but three intriguing portraits of Henry's first cousins, princes of Denmark, and of only a slightly later date, bear comparison.

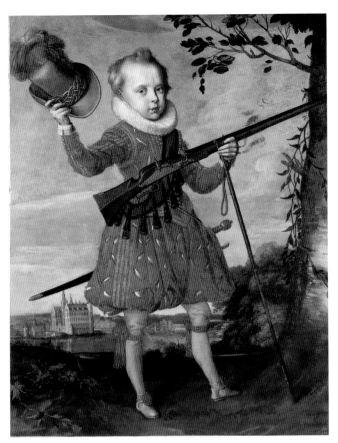

Fig. 8 Pieter Isaacsz, *Prince Frederik depicted as Musketeer*, 1615

The first, dated 1615, is of a six-year-old Prince Frederik (later Frederik III) depicted as a musketeer (fig. 8);[51] the pose also being taken from *Wapenhandelinghe* (or perhaps more accurately *Vaabenhandling*); specifically from the 38th plate of the Musket Drill section: 'Balance your musket in the rest with your left hand, leaving the right hand free' (fig. 7). The other two, a pair, depict Prince Frederik at a slightly older age, though still a youth, *c.* 1616–20 (fig. 9), and his younger brother, Duke Ulrik, *c.* 1618–20 (fig. 10).[52] In the later portrait of him, Prince Frederik stands in front of a cannon holding a pike upright in the 'ordered' position, though his pose is not taken directly from the corresponding De Gheyn illustration. Duke Ulrik stands in front of a mortar, performing the same drill as Prince Frederik in the 1615 portrait, i.e., balancing his musket, but he is viewed from the other (left) side; his pose, therefore, cannot be said to be copied from De Gheyn, though the painter must have referred to *Wapenhandelinghe* to ensure the handling of the weapon was shown correctly.

The painter of all three portraits was Pieter Isaacsz, one of the first of several Dutch artists to work at the court of Christian IV,[53] among them Simon de Passe; he did not arrive until 1624 and could not therefore have been the link. It seems more than likely that Pieter Isaacsz knew that a *Wapenhandelinghe* print was the source for an engraving of the recently deceased Prince of Wales, but if he had seen one of the English prints before beginning the first of these portraits it would have been one of William Hole's, as we now know Simon de Passe's engraving was done no earlier than 1616. We tend to underestimate the rapidity with which new designs and images spread among the artists and artisans of the Protestant Dutch diaspora, not least through the movements of the practitioners themselves. Even had Pieter Isaacsz remained in Denmark during these years he would have had contact with those merchants, some specializing in luxury items including prints, who regularly passed through the Sound on their Baltic

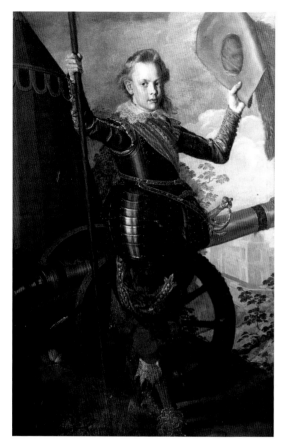

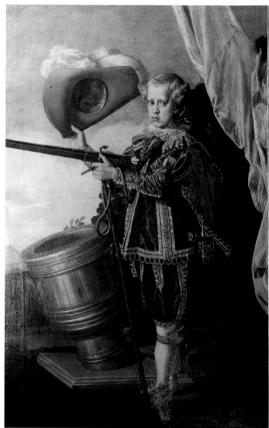

Fig. 9 Pieter Isaacsz, *Prince Frederik*, c. 1616–20   Fig. 10 Pieter Isaacsz, *Duke Ulrik*, c. 1618–20

circuit, and put in at Elsinore and Copenhagen. An inventory of the stock of a Scottish merchant who died at Malmö in 1617 even lists prints of Prince Henry's funeral, presumably Hole's *The herse and representation of our late highe and mighty Henry Prince of Wales*.[54]

The simple combination of prince and pike would immediately have struck contemporaries as both unusual and significant. Seventeenth-century royal commanders, we hardly need to be reminded, had good reason to remain on horseback during battle, for it enabled them to exercise tactical control and to remain as visible as possible to their own side. Shakespeare's audiences would have realized at once what the unhorsing of Richard III on Bosworth Field meant: his immediate reduction from a figure of command to one of inconsequence.[55] They also continued to lead cavalry charges, as Prince Henry's great well-wisher, Henri IV of France, had done at Vitry in 1599, and Henry's contemporary, Gustav Adolf II of Sweden, would do (with fatal consequences) at Lützen in 1632, two decades after he and Henry had exchanged their first letters as eager, young Protestant princes. Another decade on, Prince Henry's nephew, Prince Rupert, would lead the first cavalry charge of the English Civil War at Edgehill.

Why, therefore, place a pike in the hands of a prince? For a commander to practise with what at the beginning of the seventeenth century still remained the weapon of the infantry mass (though the pike was by then invariably used in combination with the musket) was to become more aware of the capabilities and limitations of one's forces, and so to become a better tactician. To take a position within the ranks, and to fight on foot in actual battle, has always been a prerogative of leadership, but done rarely and only with calculation. When, therefore, a prince or general practised with an infantry weapon it signalled his readiness to give up the saddle of command for another kind of advantage: that of shoulder-to-shoulder comradeship with his men. Again, it is Shakespeare who provides a memorable example from English history, that of Warwick the Kingmaker before the opening of battle at Towton:

> Then let the earth be drunken with our blood:
> I'll kill my horse, because I will not fly.[56]

One of the professional instructors who taught Henry, Joseph Swetman, in attempting to draw 'his Highnesse in bare colours', leaving 'the oily colours unto those which are learned', recalled:

> At a word hee had experience in all arts and sciences [of combat], thereby
> seeming as it were desirous to trust more to his owne valour, if occasion
> served, then to the goodness of his horse.[57]

Robert Devereux, 2nd Earl of Essex, provided a much more recent example than that of Warwick the Kingmaker. Even in death he retained many Jacobean sympathizers, not least James I, and was remembered by them, generously, as the most loyal of rebels. Following Robert Dudley, Earl of Leicester, and Sir Philip Sidney, he had, for a decade, headed in notably chivalrous fashion the cause of English nationalism, later to be laid before Henry. In 1589 Essex had raided Lisbon harbour, and before withdrawing his men to waiting ships he had thrust his pike into the closed gate of the city, and left it there embedded.[58] England's most recent chivalric hero had played the pikeman to demonstrate to his men that he was their comrade-in-arms; at their head when confronting the enemy, and the very last to leave.[59]

A few old soldiers had lived through it all. Samson Lennard, a veteran of Leicester's campaigns in the Netherlands, and a participant at the siege of Zutphen where, in 1586, the revered Sidney received his mortal wound, was still yearning to follow an English saviour-prince to final triumph a quarter of a century later. To Prince Henry he addressed the hope:

> That I may live to march over the Alpes, and to trayle a pike before the walls of
> Rome, under your Highnesse Standard.[60]

It is worth pausing to consider what Lennard's words 'to trayle a pike' meant to Jacobean readers.[61] Lennard's readership, even if they lacked direct experience of soldiering, had seen the militia often enough. After the trained bands were introduced in the early 1570s, Devon regularly assembled a thousand pikemen (besides musketeers and a dwindling number of bowmen); Hampshire half that number, and the rest of the English shires numbers proportionate to their populations.[62] In addition to the trained bands of gentlemen-led yeomen who would return to their farms after their occasional musters, more than 100,000 troops were raised for service abroad between 1585 and 1602.[63] Elizabethan England, therefore, though never invaded, had been very aware it was in a state of war, and was accustomed to the sights and sounds of its soldiers drilling.

Though Lennard was a gentleman, in fact a kinsman of that other Samson Lennard who fathered a new line of the Lords Dacre of the South, his preference for the pike was not odd for a man of his social station. C.H. Firth observed that the pike was regarded as the most honourable of arms on the field of battle, and that 'Roger Williams in his *Discourse of War*, published in 1590, devotes a chapter to proving this proposition, and Richard Elton writing sixty years later makes the same statement'.[64] The latter declares, '…it hath been the ambition of many Gentlemen, both in Holland, France, and in these late unhappy Wars in England, to trail Pikes with severall Commanders whom they shall thinke fit. And lastly, to conclude all, that the Pike is the more honourable Arms, it is so in respect of its antiquity…'.[65] Again, Shakespeare, in *Henry V*, has something to say on the matter (also not missed by the great Firth), capturing in a single, brief and witty exchange the snobbery that existed within late-Elizabethan and Jacobean soldiering;

> Pist.   Discuss unto me; art though officer?
>   Or art thou base, common, and popular?
> K. Hen.   I am a gentleman of a company.
> Pist.   Trail'st thou the puissant pike?
> K. Hen.   Even so. What are you?   [IV, 1,]

In 1620, as an English brigade assembled to reinforce the Palatinate, John Chamberlain observed, 'Sir George Smith his brother in law is come to a faire preferment (for a man of his rancke) to traile a pike in my Lord of Oxfords companie'.[66] As late as the Restoration period, the author of the mock-poem *Scarronides* referred to Æneas 'Gentleman-like' trailing a pike.[67] The antiquity of the pike, according to Elton, was 'many hundred years before there was any knowledge of the Musket, as in many Histories you shall finde'. Elton, clearly, was either unwilling or unable to provide references, but could probably have been reminded of Ælian's *De instruendis aciebus*, the well-known classical source for the organization, drilling and manoeuvring of the phalanx that elucidated the ancient use of the pike by the Macedonians.

Several Latin editions had been published in Italy since 1496, and the tract was known throughout Northern Europe even before the appearance of a Leiden-published Latin/Greek edition in 1613 and John Bingham's English translation, *The Tactiks of Ælian; or Art of embattailing an army after ye Grecian manner,* in 1616. Though the pike, like so many features of Renaissance society, was validated by a classical precedent, there was also a modern example which allowed the English and north European gentry and nobility to choose it without loss of honour, and that, whether they cared to admit it or not, was the Spanish *tercio;* easily the most successful formation on the battlefields of sixteenth-century Europe, which had been packed with the pikes of the sturdy and willing sons of Castile's aristocracy.[68] For the English, Scottish and Irish of good birth, however, the choice between cavalry and infantry always posed more of a dilemma.[69] Trailing a pike often bore (as if to compensate) connotations of humility and self-sacrifice, though to do so out of disillusionment or shame was an act that seems to have been more often imagined than enacted.

Lennard's vivid image of marching over the Alps, no doubt savoured by militant Protestants who bought his book in such quantities that it went to three editions, failed to recognize that Henry's interest in Italy did not run so far counter to James's satisfaction with his war of treatises with Cardinal Bellarmine as to embrace the destruction of the Papacy. Henry was fascinated by Italy's art and inventions, and was already sending for examples to display in his palaces. Edmund Bolton, the Catholic scholar who dedicated a work, *Tricorones* (1607), to Henry, expressed the hope that through his friend, Inigo Jones, the Prince's Surveyor of Works, 'all that is praiseworthy in the elegant arts of the ancients, may some day insinuate themselves across the Alps into our England';[70] a somewhat different aspiration for the outcome of Henry's transalpine forays. Henry might also have found a bride in Italy, as the two most attractive marriage matches proposed for him (taking into account strategic implications as well as dowry size) were those of Tuscany and Savoy. Lennard and many others of his persuasion might well have had to accept a Catholic princess alongside their beloved prince.[71]

Italy, we scarcely need to be reminded, was a source of endless fascination for Jacobeans, as it had been for Elizabethans; witness the number of plays set in Italy and the fond use of Italian names in them. Certain similarities between Giovanni, the prince in John Webster's *The White Devil* (first performed in early 1612) and Prince Henry have been noticed by Tristan Marshall, and he is surely right in suggesting they were intentional.[72] Indeed, Webster was taking no small risk in making his play such an obvious commentary on the deleterious effect of bad counsel and weak leadership on contemporary policy-making. The play includes a tart exchange between Giovanni and the supercilious Francisco:

> Giov.   Give me a pike.
>
> Fran.   What, practising your pike so young, fair cousin?
>
> Giov.   Suppose me one of Homer's frogs, my lord.[73]

Tossing my bulrush thus.
Pray, sir, tell me,
Might not a child of good discretion
Be leader to an army?

Fran.   Yes, cousin, a young prince
Of good discretion might.

Giov.   Say you so?
Indeed, I have heard, 'tis fit a general
Should not endanger his own person oft;
So that he make a noise, when he's a-horseback,
Like a Danske drummer, – Oh, 'tis excellent!
He need not fight, methinks his horse as well
Might lead an army for him; if I live
I'll charge the French foe, in the very front
Of all my troops, the foremost man (II, I, 120–23).

The image of Henry handling infantry weapons – pike included – was no conceit, but an oft-observed and recorded event. As early as October 1606, the French ambassador, Antoine le Fevre de la Boderie, listed 'tossing the pike' first among those active pursuits that Henry engaged in after his regular two hours of study each day,[74] and on one occasion, being asked by the same ambassador while watching him toss the pike whether Henry had a message for his master, Henri IV, the Prince replied, 'Tell him what I am now doing'.[75] We should not be surprised to find an ambassador present, as these exercises were also performances. Swetman, surely a fine judge, observed, 'his cunning in weapons … made strangers stand amazed to behold him'.[76] Henry's Treasurer, Sir Charles Cornwallis, similarly recalled that 'tossing of the pike' was among 'his princely sports' – vigorous activities that he balanced against his book-learning.[77] Robert Dallington, one of Henry's longstanding household tutors, made Gentleman of the Privy Chamber in Ordinary in 1610, saw Henry's exercises and studies as preparatory to an adult life that was to maintain a similar balance between generalship and statecraft. He touched on this essential combination (recommended in sixteenth-century treatises stemming back at least to Castiglione's *Il Cortegiano*) in *The View of Fraunce* (1604),[78] but such a spread was to characterize the whole of his *Aphorismes, civil and militarie*, a translation and amplification of Guicciardini's *Ricordi*, which, we are informed, Henry 'pleased favourably to entertaine, and often to reade over', but which Dallington published only some months after his master's death, offering the reader 'these his papers in his memory'.[79]

Henry, urged on by militants at court, so seriously threatened to disrupt this carefully conceived programme that, around 1609/10, a battle of tracts ensued.[80] First into Henry's hands came *Arguments for War*, which put forward a number of reasons including 'instructing our people in arms', which might seem to us to be a case of getting things the wrong way round. Yet, in the context of the age, perennial, or at least recurrent, limited war could be presented as a justification for the militarization of aristocratic society. It was certainly taken seriously enough for James to require the antiquary Sir Robert Cotton (most probably through Cotton's patron in the Privy Council, the Catholic Henry Howard, Earl of Northampton) to write a response, which remained in manuscript for a generation until it was published as *Wars with foreign Princes dangerous to our Commonwealth: Or Reasons for foreign Wars answered* (London, 1657), with a corrected version appearing as *An Answer to such Motives, as were offered by certain Military men to Prince Henry, inciting him to affect Arms more than Peace* (London, 1675).[81] The title of the latter displays a fine understanding of the relative nature of the argument, the key word being 'more' – it was never imagined that Henry would wholly adopt one course and wholly abandon the other.

Henry warned his childhood companion, Sir John Harington of Exton, at that time travelling abroad for his education, that 'When I see you (and let that be shortlie) you will find me your better at tennis and pike'.[82] This was penned in 1609, when Henry was practising more intensively than ever, in order to be ready for another Barriers performance (there had been one before, in 1606) on the coming Twelfth Night, designed for him to demonstrate his prowess before 'the Kinge and Queene, and the Ambassadours of Spayne and Venice, and of al the Peeres and great ladies of the land, with a multitude of others', in other words, before a good part of the political nation as well as foreign representatives, who would then report the qualities of the emerging Prince of Wales to the rest of Europe. On the great night, Henry, assisted by six others, took on fifty-six assailants (eight each), at push of pike and with single sword, in what was a managed – almost choreographed – spectacle that was minutely observed. Henry, according to his treasurer, Cornwallis, 'did admirably fight for his part, giving and receiving that night 32 pushes of pikes, and about 360 streakes of swords, which is scarce credible in so young yeares, enough to assure the world, that Great Britaine's brave Henry aspired to immortality'.[83]

Such prowess was to be gained through practice on the military ground or military garden, a kind of facility that sprang up throughout England in the first half of the seventeenth century, as in Bristol and Coventry, though by far the best known were the two situated on the outskirts of Westminster and London. Significantly, the military ground in Westminster had a traditional association with Prince Henry, maintained by London's antiquaries through several generations. Maitland writes, 'On the west side of Lord Newport's garden (where Gerard Street, &c., are now situate) was a Military or Artillery Ground, wherein were exercised the militia of Middlesex';[84] while Pennant writes, 'Behind Leicester House stood in 1658, the Military-yard, founded by Henry, Prince of Wales, the spirited son of our peaceful James. M. Foubert afterwards kept his academy for riding and other gentleman-like exercises, in the reign of Charles II. It is to this day a noted riding school'.[85] Earlier, Vertue had noted, 'where Gerrard Street is was the Artillery ground built by P. Henry for his exersice or a military garden'.[86] More informative and earlier still is the recollection of John Bagford (fl. 1650–1716):

> Prince Henry caused a piece of ground near Leicester-fields to be walled in for the exercise of arms which he much delighted in; a house was built at one end for an armory and a well furnished library of all such books as related to arms, chivalry, military affairs, incamping, fortification etc. the best that could be got in the kind in all languages, at the charge of the prince, who had a particular learned man for a librarian, whose name I have forgot [presumably Edward Wright]. It was called the Artillery Ground, and remained till the Restoration of Charles II; and then it fell into the hands of the Lord Gerard, who let the ground out to build on.[87]

Richard Elton in *The Compleat Body of the Art Military* (1650) refers to the same site as the 'Military Garden'; a curious term to modern ears, but one that had currency and was well understood in the seventeenth century, as in James Achesone's *The military garden, or instructions for all young souldiers and such who are disposed to learne, and have knowledge of the militarie discipline* (Edinburgh, 1629). Here, though, I use 'Military Yard' as a reminder that the site was enclosed by a high wall,[88] and also to distinguish it from the formal gardens of two great houses which later abutted it on the east and south sides: those of Newport House, built by Sir William Howard on land acquired in 1627, and of Leicester House, built by Robert Sidney, 2nd Earl of Leicester, between 1631 and 1635.[89]

The most authoritative account of the Military Company of Westminster and its Military Yard is to be found in *The Survey of London*.[90] We are informed that a petition was presented to the Privy Council for permission to establish the Military Company in December 1615, which was granted, and that it was 'modelled on the Artillery Company which exercised in Spitalfields'. The *Survey* acknowledges the strong tradition associating the Military Yard with Henry, even citing 'an old member of the company [who] affirmed in 1669 that he had heard that Prince Henry was "in his life time Captaine of ye said Military Company", but declares it 'false' on the grounds that the Company was founded some three years after Henry's death. Traditions, however, especially deep-rooted ones, should not be dismissed lightly. Moreover, there is a certain inconsistency in the information given on the Military Yard in different volumes of the *Survey*. In the volume concerned with the parish of St James, Westminster, we are further informed that a highway led eastward from the Haymarket to a gate leading into St Martin's Field, and that 'In 1613 this part of St. Martin's Field was bought for use as a military exercise ground and was known as the Military Garden or Yard; it was enclosed by a brick wall'.[91] We need not be troubled by references to military grounds being in both St Martin's Field and Leicester Fields, as they were one and the same. Strictly speaking, the Military Yard was in St Martin's Field, though the two fields lay next to each other. The earlier date of 1613 does, therefore, relate to the location we are interested in, and, if reliable, narrows the time gap between Henry's demise and the earliest confirmed use of the ground for military exercises.

As for any desire to emulate the Artillery Company, though there had been a long history of military training in Spitalfields, by the early years of the reign of James I the gunners of the Tower had effectively taken over the site, and seem to have been running weekly firing exercises in the fields not as private trials but as a money-spinning sideline. Precisely at the period of Henry's greatest influence, i.e., mid to late 1612, the Tower gunners and the Society (later Company) of Artillery, the latter composed of gentlemen of the City, both sought formal recognition of their claims to the ground. This wrangling is indicative of a general resurgence of interest in training for war.[92] It was not a little stimulated by the energetic example of Henry, though there is no record of Henry ever using Spitalfields, a site more convenient for the citizens of London than for those who lived in Westminster. St Martin's Field, however, was just one field away from St James's House, Henry's residence when in Westminster. In order to travel from one to the other, it was only necessary to ride up the lane (now St James's Street), to turn onto the old highway that led into London from the west (now Piccadilly), and then to follow it along the side of St James's Field until it crossed the Haymarket road. From there, it was but a short way up another lane (now Coventry Street) to the Military Ground – in all, a ride of only three-quarters of a mile (1200m).[93]

That the Company and Yard grew directly out of Henry's informal, if regular, military practising (in which he would have been joined by companions and instructors)[94] seems all the more likely when we note that one Thomas Holcroft was nominated by the petitioners and approved by the Privy Council to be captain of the Military Company. A 'Captain Thomas Holcroft', surely the same person, appears on the list of subscribers in the Second Charter of the Virginia Company of 23 May 1609 – a veritable roll call of Henry's supporters.[95] He was certainly no sleeping investor, for within the week he was sent to recruit more settlers from among the English living in the United Provinces,[96] while Sir Thomas Dale, another professional soldier patronized by the Prince, prepared to sail for Cape Henry to restore the Virginia Plantation to good order.[97] From this we may assume Holcroft had soldiered in the United Provinces and knew the English garrisons well.[98] Moreover, among the Gentlemen of the Privy Chamber Extraordinary of Henry's household we also find the name 'Mr Holcroft'.[99]

De Passe's background contains no feature that clearly identifies the location, though a building by the side of the practice area would appear to be an armoury. We know that such a building was built at the Military Yard, and the descriptions of it – a tile-roofed building with wings – are not inconsistent with what we see in the engraving.[100] There is, however, no sign of the Military Yard's distinctive wall, and as the building of a nine-foot high brick wall around a two-acre site must have been a long job, it might be explained by the engraving having been completed before the wall. There is a distant settlement, clustered around a church, also fields, trees and hills, but apart from the armoury there are no buildings close by. Such would have been the view from St Martin's Field until the Earls of Salisbury and Leicester allowed building on their land in the reign of Charles I. Perhaps we should conclude that the view is intended to be more typical than actual; more iconic than mimetic. We should not, therefore, attempt to identify these distant features or be concerned by what appears to be a waterway. Neither should we object that pike-against-pike contests, musketry and jousting are shown taking place all at the same time, as they are represented in order to show the variety of military exercises that took place. Yet the gentlemen lolling on the rails have an observed authenticity about them, and one recalls John Evelyn's diary entry: 'Mr Foubert having railed in a Manage & fitted it for the Academy, I went with my Lord Cornwallis to see the Young Gallants do their Exercise'.[101]

Paradoxical though it might seem, a growth of militarism is now perceived as having occurred during the reign of the pacific James I, and having continued into the reign of Charles I. Lawrence Stone's finding that the English aristocracy lost interest in soldierly pursuits during the early seventeenth century, until by the Civil War they 'no longer knew how to fight' has been called into question;[102] as has Mervyn James's contention that the importance of honour as both motivation and justification for action diminished at much the same time.[103] Though peace was concluded between England and Spain in 1604, the Dutch remained at war with the Spanish until 1609 and, even then, the Jülich-Cleves crisis soon brought soldiers back to the colours in the United Provinces, the Spanish Netherlands and France. Young English gentlemen in Paris prepared to abandon their studies to accompany Henri IV to the assembling of his army at the French border, while the standing English regiments in the United Provinces marched to their rendezvous at the great Rhine fortress of Schenkenschanz. Soon, gallants such as Lord Herbert of Cherbury would return to the English court with accounts of their bravery in the siege trenches beneath the walls of Jülich. In February 1612, a Danish ambassador arrived in London seeking aid in the War of Kalmar then being fought between the Danes and the Swedes. Only doubt as to who would pay for an English expeditionary force seems to have prevented the rapid raising of regiments under Lord Willoughby, Sir Edward Cecil, Lord Dingwall and the Earl of Clanricard – experienced soldiers all. Later the same year, German Protestant and Dutch nobility began gathering in England for the wedding of Henry's sister, Elizabeth, and Frederick, the Elector Palatine, though much of their conversation with English hosts would have been of the Evangelical Union and impending war. Though James I wished it otherwise, to be at war was still considered a more natural state of affairs than to be at peace.[104]

Voluntary training in arms by the nobility and gentry in the early seventeenth century, hugely encouraged by Henry's example, is a phenomenon under-regarded by modern historians, but which for many Jacobeans was as much a reminder of a resurgence of martialism as the farewells and homecomings of professional soldiers who served abroad, or the frequent allusions to soldiering in London stage plays.[105] Although we have no precise date for Simon de

Passe's engraving, we know it could have been done no earlier than 1616, the year of his arrival in London, and that it was very probably done in that same year, as from its second state it bore the imprint of de Passe's first publisher, Compton Holland, with whom he soon parted, shifting to the rival firm of Sudbury & Humble, for whom he worked almost exclusively throughout 1617 and 1618.[106] Its appearance, therefore, seems to have very closely coincided with the formalization of military exercises in St Martin's Field in 1616. I suggest there is a connection, and that the de Passe engraving, with its distinctive background scene, was an attempt to place Henry's posthumous seal of approval upon the activities there, and to claim, with some justification, that the Military Company could trace it origins back to Henry.

When we consider who might have conceived the idea of a fresh engraving of *Prince Henry practising with the pike*, we are not required to probe a tangle of friendships and patron-client relationships such as that surrounding the long-awaited publication of *Poly-olbion*. This was a much simpler undertaking: to produce an improved and enlarged version of Hole's engraving and to sell the prints of it separately. As these were to be retailed exclusively by Compton Holland, we should concentrate our attention upon him, and upon his business partner and brother Henry Holland.[107] It was they who persuaded the hugely talented Simon de Passe to move to London from Utrecht, a *coup* that enabled them to extend their business to portraits engraved and printed locally, beginning with de Passe's *Prince Henry practising with the pike*. It is not difficult to understand why the Holland brothers would have been keen to revive the image and specify a military garden for the background. Their connection to the late Prince is very clear, as the Haringtons of Exton were the patrons, friends and Warwickshire neighbours of their scholar father, Philemon Holland, the celebrated translator of Pliny the Elder, Plutarch, and Camden's *Britannia*. It was Sir John Harington of Exton (whom Henry had sought to surpass in prowess with the pike) who had been described to the Doge of Venice in 1609 as the Prince's 'right eye', with the prediction that he would one day rule England as Henry's first minister.[108] A few months after the Prince's death, we find Henry Holland attending Sir John's father, Lord Harington, as he escorted Princess Elizabeth, his former charge, on her journey to Heidelberg. As for the Holland brothers' military inclinations, we know little about Compton who died in 1622, but Henry was still active during the Civil War, and in 1643 served in the life guards of the Parliamentarian Basil Feilding, Earl of Denbigh, proud of the fact that he was the 'eldest man' of the troop (he was by then sixty); in 1647 he attested that he had formerly been 'one of the trained band charged with a corslet'. Here, surely, was a man who in his younger days had frequented the military grounds.

De Passe's striking portrait was but one example of a surge in publications relating to military training that occurred at the same time (1615/1616) as the forming of the company which developed the Military Yard in Westminster. The prolific Gervase Markham's *A schoole for young soldiers, containing in briefe the whole discipline of warre, especially so much as is meet for the captaine to teach, or the souldier to learne, that is, to trayne or be trayned* was published in

1615, with a further issue appearing in 1616. This was also the year in which Bingham's long-overdue English translation of *The Tactiks of Ælian* appeared. Even Thomas Dekker, languishing in debtor's prison, caught the mood, writing his poem *The Artillery Garden* in the same year. Europe, meanwhile, was generally peaceful – though it was the lull before the storm that would be the Thirty Years' War. If the year 1616 was remarkable for anything, it was for Charles's creation as Prince of Wales, to the accompaniment of a further surge of that expectation which had transferred to him after Henry's death, and this must largely account for the rash of military publications. Joseph Swetman, the professional instructor, having presented his *Schoole of the Noble and worthy Science of Defence* in manuscript to Henry, who, he informs the reader, 'earnestly perswaded me to print it', brought up the rear, achieving publication in 1617, predictably dedicating his book to Charles. Earlier, Robert Dallington had let the younger prince know what he faced, now that Henry was dead, though almost in the manner of a blessing:

> Sir, All eyes are upon you. Those your sweet graces of nature, and ingenuous dispositions to goodnes, makes men looke upon your worthy Brother in your princely self; holding you the true inheritor of his vertues as of his fortunes, and making full account that he had no oddes of you but in yeares. Your matchlesse Brother for these seven yeares to come, may take you by the hand, and leade you in the faire apprentisage of all honour and vertue.[109]

One might think it an unenviable inheritance.

The publication of the fine Simon de Passe version was not the end of the Hollands' interest in the portrait, as they would include it, newly engraved for both publications, for *Baziliologia* (1618) and *Heroologia Anglica* (1620), their innovative sets of the portraits of English kings and worthies; the former intended to be collected print by print, and wholly without letterpress, and the latter conceived as a book, with numbered pages of Latin text by Henry Holland, who devoted no less than seven pages to the late Prince, supported by three engravings, the middle one being *Prince Henry practising with the pike* (fig. 11).[110] This new engraving was done by either Willem or Magdalena de Passe in Utrecht, as were all the engravings for *Heroologia*, while the printing was done in Arnhem. Engraved on the foot of the plate are two sets of unrelated verses; Latin to the left, and English to the right, presumably sent in manuscript from London to be copied. The poorly spaced and occasionally misspelled English verses betray the engraver's unfamiliarity with the language, but, overlooking that, we have here sentiments that attempt to make sense of Henry's death, written possibly seven years after the event by someone who clearly had been close to the Prince's court. They are framed by a fine understanding of the essential concern in Henry's last months that the carefully constructed balance between the Prince's study and exercise, i.e., preparation for peace and war, might be tipped by his military enthusiasms:

Hee that the LIFE of this FACE ever saw
The MILDNESS in it noting, and the AWE
Will judge that PEACE, did either in her LOVE
So soone advance hem to hir STATE above
Or else in FEARE that HEE would WARRE preferre
Concluded with HIM HEE should LIVE with her.
To both, HIS aptnes fluentlie apeares;
In evrie SOLDIERS griefe SCHOLLERS teares.[111]

It is entirely possible that these verses were not composed by Henry Holland, as some other verses contained in *Heroologia* are certainly not. On the text page immediately preceding the plate, however, Holland's interpretation of the portrait is to be found. Here, there is no attempt to maintain any kind of balance; rather, it is a throwback to the kind of bombast directly aimed at Rome ('*quae est Antichristi indubia sedes*') that Samson Lennard fired off in 1612. Before all the princes of the Christian world, we are told, Henry would have scaled its walls in person, and we are invited to ponder over the image of him with the pike that he would have thrust forward: '...*intuemini enim illum hic graphice depictum & Lanceam suam in Romam vibrando intorsurum*'. Henry Holland's stridency was, no doubt, brought on by alarming news of the melting away of support on the Continent for the derided 'Winter King' Frederick and his consort Elizabeth (to whom Holland is likely to have had special affection due to his Harington connections), and by the sound and excitement of recruiting in London. For in March 1620, at the very time he must have been sending material to his Dutch engravers and printers, and receiving proofs, 'drummes went about the streetes to give notice to all voluntaries that wold serve the King of Bohemia to repayre to Westminster'.[112] Even in June it was reported 'Our drummes beat dayly about the streets for the raising of men for this new service'.[113] Eventually, in August, 2250 men under the command of Sir Horace Vere sailed for Holland, from where they proceeded down the Rhine to attempt to defend the Palatinate while its ruler and his wife (Henry's sister) awaited the advance of the Catholic League on Prague.

The companies making up the expeditionary force of 1620 were led by men of Prince Henry's generation, who had been well known to him, such as the Earls of Essex and Oxford, and Sir John Wentworth, a former Gentleman of the Prince's Privy Chamber and once, therefore, within the 'family' of Henry's household.[114] Another former Gentleman, Sir Peregrine Bertie, would also have gone to the Palatinate as a commander, but for a conceived slight to his honour; so also Edward Sackville (later 4th Earl of Dorset), who had been within Henry's circle.[115] A few, the more durable and fortunate, of this generation fought in the Civil War, but most of the combatants of the 1640s were of the next generation. These officers were the same languid courtiers whom Van Dyck had depicted in the

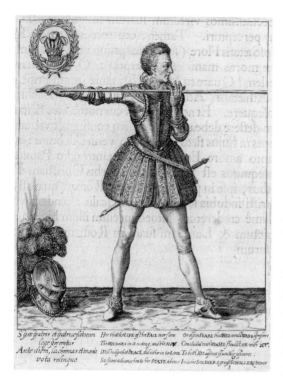

Fig. 11 Willem or Magdalena de Passe, *Prince Henry practising with the pike*, engraving, in *Heroologia Anglica* (1620)

1630s, but it had only taken the buckling on of their corslets to reawaken in them an old honour code.[116] Their faces – chapped by weeks of service in the field, drawn by fatigue, yet still resolute – as captured by Van Dyck's gifted Civil War successor, William Dobson, should be sufficient to prompt a severe questioning of Stone's assertion that 'the nobility were losing their nerve'.[117]

Sir Edmund Verney, formerly Henry's Sewer, and thirty years on, Charles's Standard Bearer at Edgehill, heroically 'broke the poynt of his standard at push of pike before he fell', as described by a survivor of the battle.[118] It had been the first, terrible clash of the pikes on English soil in the seventeenth century, and the first occasion on which many, trained in its use since their youth, had ever pushed the weapon home. Verney, four years older than Henry, had as a young man done what his first master was never able to do – visit the armies in the Low Countries, and he had probably been among those who practised arms with Henry.[119] Why, at the age of fifty-two, he contrived to be in the thick of battle at Edgehill is possibly explained by Elton:

> …they [the pikes] are the more honourable Arms, in respect the colours flying upon the head of them and upon the drawing up of the Company there is the most properest place for the Captain to be … If upon a Stand the Captain shall have occasion to engage against an Enemy, thither his Officers may repair unto him upon the head of the pikes….[120]

Facing Verney at Edgehill was the commander of the Parliamentarian army, Robert, 3rd Earl of Essex (painted with Henry when both were boys), and many others who had always cherished the memory of the late Prince, no doubt confident he had shared their beliefs, and that had he lived they would have stood with him, not against him. Meanwhile, in Westminster, the Military Yard stood deserted; its ordnance soon to be sequestered by order of Parliament. In June 1645 it was designated as a prisoner-of-war camp for royalists captured at the Battle of Naseby.[121]

NOTES

I am grateful to Edward Chaney for reading the typescript and for his helpful comments.

1 Michael Drayton, *Poly-olbion. Or A Chorographicall Description of Tracts, Rivers, Mountaines, Forests, and other Parts of this renowned Isle of Great Britaine, With intermixture of the most remarkable Stories, Antiquities, Wonders, Rarityes, Pleasures, and Commodities of the same* (London, 1612). The second part was not published until 1622.

2 Bent Juel-Jensen, in '"Polyolbion", "Poems Lyrick and pastorall", "Poems" 1619, "The Owle", and few other books by Michael Drayton', *The Library*, 5th series, VIII, No. 3 (1953), pp. 150–53, no doubt influenced by the entry in Van der Doort's catalogue (see below n. 15), fails to identify the weapon correctly, thereby missing its significance, calling the image: *The portrait of Prince Henry playing with a lance*. A.M. Hind, in his standard reference work, *Engraving in England in the 16th and 17th Centuries. II. James I* (Cambridge, 1955), no. 28, p. 258, corrects this to *Henry Frederick, Prince of Wales, with the pike*. However, the mistake is repeated by J.W. Williamson in his otherwise laudable *The Myth of the Conqueror. Prince Henry Stuart: A Study of 17th-century Personation* (New York, 1978), p. 66. Here, for succinctness and accuracy, I have decided to refer to the image in all its forms as *Prince Henry practising with the pike*.

3 'TO THE HIGH AND MIGHTIE, HENRIE, Prince of Wales. THis first part of my intended Poeme I consecrate to your Highness: in whom (beside my particular zeale) there is a naturall interest in my Worke; as the hopefull Heyre of the kingdoms of this Great Britaine: … … To your HIGHNESS, the most humbly devoted, MICHAEL DRAYTON.'

4 Drayton, *Poly-olbion*, sig. π3v.

5 See C.H. Firth, *Cromwell's Army*, 4th edn. (London, 1962), pp. 71–72.

6 See Susan Foister, *Holbein in England*, exh. cat., Tate Britain (London, 2006), nos. 103, 104.

7 Four plates are signed by Hole, while another four, unsigned, are also likely to be his work. See Michael Strachan, *The Life and Adventures of Thomas Coryate* (London, 1962), p. 123. Coryate's association with Henry's court is more fully considered by Michelle O'Callaghan elsewhere in this volume.

8 For Davies, see Chapter 2: 'John Davies of Hereford: a life of writing' in Brian Vickers, *Shakespeare, 'A Lover's Complaint', and John Davies of Hereford* (Cambridge, 2007), pp. 15–46.

9 *The Funeralls* may also have been issued separately. See STC 13157.

10 See Strong, *Henry Prince of Wales*, p. 130.

11 See Strong, *Henry Prince of Wales*, p. 130–31; also Margery Corbett and R.W. Lightbown, *The Comely Frontispiece. The Emblematic Titlepage in England, 1550–1660* (London, 1979), pp. 113–18.

12 Strong, *Henry Prince of Wales*, p. 131.

13 For a fuller discussion, see Timothy Wilks, ' "Forbear the Heat and Haste of Building": Rivalries among the Designers at Prince Henry's Court, 1610–1612', *The Court Historian*, 6, 1 (May 2001), pp. 49–65.

14 See Alexander Marr's essay in this volume.

15 Oliver Millar (ed.), 'Abraham Van der Doort's Catalogue of the Collections of Charles I', *Walpole Society*, XXXVII (1958–60), p. 153. Transcribed from Windsor MS., f.120.

16 *Ibid.*, p. 153. Transcribed from Bodleian MS. Ash. 1514, f. 144.

17 Juel-Jensen, 'Polyolbion', p. 150, and Strong, *Henry Prince of Wales*, p. 130, interpret the word 'patron' to mean 'pattern', which is probably correct. Of less consequence, Strong interprets 'bin' as 'him', whereas I suggest 'being'. NB also Karen Hearn (ed.), *Dynasties. Painting in Tudor and Jacobean England 1530–1630* (London, 1995), no. 84, where the entry for the Fitzwilliam miniature of Henry touches on its relationship with Oliver's drawing, but is misleading in as much as it describes the latter as a 'large miniature … the basis of portrait engravings by William Hole and Simon van de Passe'.

18 Both Juel-Jensen, 'Polyolbion', p. 150, and Hind, *Engraving in England*, p. 258, note that a print in the British Museum (now Library) bears an early inscription: 'from the original which was burnt at Whitehall'. Hind also notes that 'contemporary or early MS marginalia in certain copies of the *Heroologia* state that the print

was from a whole length at Whitehall'. He refers to Henry Holland's *Heroologia Anglia* (Arnhem, 1620), which contained a smaller, derivative version of the portrait by either Willem or Magdalena de Passe.

19 See Antony Griffiths with R.A. Gerrard, *The Print in Stuart Britain 1603–1689* (London, 1998), pp. 40–44.

20 Jones set about improving his drawing skills around 1605, an essential undertaking if he were ever to succeed in communicating his designs for the early masques. See Stephen Orgel and Roy Strong, *Inigo Jones. The Theatre of the Stuart Court*, 2 vols. (London, Berkeley, and Los Angeles, 1973), I, pp. 29–47, and the pre-1610 marginal annotations in his copy of *Le vite* alongside Vasari's comments on draughtsmanship belong to this phase (Jones re-taught himself in the 1630s). For the possibility that Jones was not self-taught, see Jill Finsten, *Isaac Oliver. Art at the Courts of Elizabeth I and James I*, 2 vols. (New York and London, 1981), I, pp. 141–45, and for Jones's ownership of Isaac (and Peter) Oliver drawings and possible meeting in Italy, see Edward Chaney, *Inigo Jones's 'Roman Sketchbook'*, 2 vols. (London, 2006), I, pp. 75–76.

21 See the entry for Aston in *ODNB*.

22 See Oxford, Bodley MS. Eng. Poet. C.37. The attribution is convincingly proposed in D.C. Kay, 'Poems by Sir Walter Aston, and a date for the Donne/Goodyer verse epistle Alternis Vicibus', *Review of English Studies*, XXXVII (1986), pp. 198–210.

23 Arthur Clifford (ed.), *Tixall Letters, or, the Correspondence of the Aston Family and their Friends during the Seventeenth Century*, 2 vols. (London, 1815), I, p. 78.

24 B.H. Newdigate, *Michael Drayton and his Circle* (Oxford, 1961), pp. 147; 154; also Tristan Marshall, 'Michael Drayton and the Writing of Jacobean England', *The Seventeenth Century*, 15 (2) (Autumn 2000), pp. 127–49.

25 Noted by Frances A. Yates, *Shakespeare's Last Plays: a New Approach* (London, 1975), p. 23; also Strong, *Henry Prince of Wales*, p. 118.

26 'The Speeches at Prince Henries Barriers', Nichols, *Progresses*, II, p. 278.

27 Strong, *Henry Prince of Wales*, p. 118. A portrait of Henry V, probably painted in the late fifteenth century, and one of a set of old kings which had hung in royal palaces since at least the reign of Henry VIII, was recorded by Van der Doort during the reign of Charles I as 'a Sidefaced picture without a beard in a black capp…' that was one of 'Nyne old heades', see Millar, 'Van der Doort', p. 27. Millar offers as a source the following possibilities: 'a medal, the effigy of the King in Westminster Abbey (from which the head was stolen in 1546) or a votive portrait in miniature or on the scale of life in which the King appeared as a donor', see Oliver Millar, *The Tudor, Stuart and Early Georgian Pictures in the Collection of Her Majesty the Queen*, 2 vols. (London, 1963), text vol., no. 6, p. 50. It is not infrequently conjectured that Henry V was depicted only in profile to hide a disfiguring scar, caused by an arrow at the Battle of Shrewsbury (in other words, for the same reason as Federigo di Montefeltro's portrayal in profile by Piero della Francesca).

28 Henry was not the only sitter whom Isaac Oliver limned in profile. Cf. *A Member of the Barbor Family* (V&A); *Anne of Denmark* (The Royal Collection); *Alice Stanley, Countess of Derby* (Estate of Lord Bearsted). There is also a portrait miniature of *George Villiers, 1st Duke of Buckingham*, attributed to Peter Oliver (Mauritshuis, The Hague), which appears to be inspired by the earlier *Prince Henry*, and is a late development of this Oliver type. There are also earlier precedents in English art, e.g. the large profile portrait roundels (the roundel chosen to emphasize the numismatic allusion), done by Holbein in England, such as *Simon George*, c. 1535, and Sir *Thomas Wyatt*.

29 See Strong, *Henry Prince of Wales*, p. 198; also J. G. Pollard, 'England and the Italian Medal', in Edward Chaney and Peter Mack (eds.), *England and the Continental Renaissance* (Woodbridge, 1990), p. 196. More work remains to be done on Henry's coin and medal collection, which was based upon at least two separate acquisitions. Only the cost of the first, bought in 1611 from 'Abraham van Hutton' (?Abraham van Hattem, Vassal of Culemborg and later Captain of the garrison of Deventer), who was paid £2200 in two instalments (NA. E351/2793), was taken into the reckoning when Henry's possessions were audited after his death. In April 1612, reference was made in an Exchequer warrant to 'the custom and subsidy of a cabinet of antiquities bought into this realm by Hans von Dirbige and sold to the Prince' (HMC *Salisbury XXI*, p. 352). It is possible that this 'Hans von Dirbige' (?van der Beeke) was the carrier for 'Abraham van Hutton', but it seems more

likely that he was an associate of one Christopher Fulke, who, in December 1616, petitioned the Privy Council for payment regarding 'divers peeces of gould and silver coynes and medalles of antiquity, which the late Prince Henry had from this peticioner to the valew of 600 li sterling', a claim supported by the confirmation of Adam Newton and Sir David Murray. It might be significant that the customs due on the 'Dirbige' consignment (£62 10s) was close to 10% of the figure stated by Fulke. See *Acts of the Privy Council of England, 1616–1617*, pp. 98–99. This petition has gone unnoticed by previous commentators. Strong links the 'Dirbige' cabinet to that formerly owned by the Delft antiquary, Abraham Gorlaeus (d. 1608), traditionally held to have come into Henry's possession.

30 See Roy Strong, *Artists of the Tudor Court. The Portrait Miniature Rediscovered* (London, 1983), no. 230; also Hearn, *Dynasties*, no. 84. NB the suggestion made there that the V&A keeps another version is mistaken.

31 Strong points out this link in *Artists of the Tudor Court*, no. 159, but, curiously, does not do so in his later *Henry Prince of Wales*, though the Oliver profile miniature and the Hole engraving are discussed there separately.

32 The full title being *Vaabenhandling onm Ror, Musketter og Spedser. Effter den Hoyb. Forstes Moritz, Printz aff Orianen, ordning bekreffuedt, figurlig affbildit* (see *Bibliotheca Danica* II, 336). Christian Kaaber, to whom I am indebted for information regarding the Danish-language edition (printed at The Hague), has drawn my attention to the survival of Jørgen Lunge's personal copy. Lunge (1577–1619) held the title of 'Rigsmarsk' (equivalent to England's Earl Marshal), and the fact that he owned a handsomely bound and gilt copy further underlines its indispensability to the commanders of the forces arrayed against the Habsburg threat prior to the Thirty Years' War.

33 There is very little difference between plates 19 and 24, as both exhibit the same position, i.e., the pike charged, though arrived at from different previous positions.

34 Cf. the study, *c.* 1605, by Robert de Baudous in pen and brown ink with grey wash for the 19th plate, reproduced in Kees Zandvliet (ed.), *Maurits Prins van Oranje*, exhib. cat. (Rijksmuseum, Amsterdam, 2000), no. 103, pp. 251–52.

35 See A.W.F.M. Meij (ed.), *Jacques de Gheyn II drawings*, exh. cat. Museum Boymans-van Beuningen, (Rotterdam, 1986), no. 19, p. 46.

36 See Zandvliet, no. 102, p. 251, where a hand-coloured title-page of *Wapenhandelinghe* is reproduced.

37 Juel-Jensen ('Polyolbion', pp. 150–53) identifies five separate plates that were cut before 1642, four of which are known in different states. Their relationships have yet to be fully clarified. The latest plate, that cut by William Marshall for *The Life and Death* (1641), is regarded as a small copy of an earlier plate in its third, retouched, state, as used to provide the frontispiece for Cornwallis's *Discourse* (1628), and used previously to provide a supplementary print of Henry to be included among the set of royal portraits gathered under the title *Baziliologia* (1618).

38 Hole's plate: 190 mm x 122 mm, approx.; de Passe's plate: 260 mm x 195 mm. The area of Hole's plate is, therefore, less than half that of de Passe's plate.

39 Strong (*Henry Prince of Wales*, p. 119) promises to discuss Simon de Passe's engraved portrait in connection with Oliver's drawing, but, regrettably, does not do so.

40 Hind, *Engraving in England*, p. 258. This statement is hard to understand, given the different sizes of the two plates. It is possible that Hind was thinking of a third plate, that done for the Holland brothers' *Baziliologia* (see above, note 38), which has octavo dimensions that are very close to those of Hole's plate, although in its second state it shows the military ground found in Simon de Passe's plate. Juel-Jensen ('Polyolbion', pp. 150–53) catalogues it as '2. Artist uncertain'.

41 Hind, *Engraving in England*, no. 28: 'HENRY FREDERICK, Prince of Wales, with the pike', p. 258.

42 Only a few prominent Englishmen, including Sir Dudley Carleton (1620) and George Villiers, 1st Duke of Buckingham (1626), as a consequence of having had their portraits painted in Delft by Miereveldt, became the fortunate subjects of Willem Jacobz. Delff, the finest northern portrait engraver of the first quarter of the seventeenth century. But neither Miereveldt nor his associate Delff could ever be induced to come to England, despite the efforts of Sir Edward Conway, English governor of the port of Brill, to persuade the

former to visit Henry's court at much the same time that Hole was working on his engraving of him. The correspondence is published partly in 'Vertue MSS. V', *Walpole Society* XXVI (1937–38), pp. 83–84, and partly in Birch, *Life*, pp. 485–7, 489, 491, 496.

43 Apart from Arundel and others who donated paintings to Henry's picture gallery, Sir Henry Fanshawe is of particular interest as an early print collector. His will of 1616 mentions 'Picktures, Prints, Drawings, medalls, engraven stones, musicall Instruments'; see H. Fanshawe, 'Abstract of the Will of Sir Henry Fanshawe of Ware Park', *Notes, Genealogical and Historical of the Fanshawe Family, IV, Fanshawe Wills, I* (1871), p. 48.

44 See Wilks, 'Henry', pp. 105–07. Also Strong, *Artists of the Tudor Court*, no. 259, pp. 154–55, assumed that if Oliver's drawing had contained the background shown by de Passe, then Van der Doort would have mentioned it. He concluded that Hole's engraving, therefore, had to be the earlier. In this, he has since been proved correct, but it does not confirm his assumption. It seems entirely possible that Van der Doort might have felt his catalogue entry was sufficient, whether or not there was a background (he makes no mention of the plumed helmet, nearly half the height of the figure, which we may be confident, was in the drawing). Juel-Jensen opined that 'the background … was very probably a feature of the original drawing' ('Polyolbion', pp. 150–53). If Isaac Oliver did give the portrait a background, he might have done so well after Hole had finished with it, and then either for his own satisfaction or for de Passe's requirements.

45 Griffiths, *The Print in Stuart Britain*, p. 56.

46 Griffiths (p. 56) notes another example in Simon de Passe's oeuvre: his engraving of *Charles, Duke of York*, where the date '1613' appears to have been copied from Crispijn de Passe's *Regiae Anglicae Maiestatis Pictura*.

47 For the following, I rely on the analysis in Juel-Jensen, 'Polyolbion', pp. 150–53.

48 Richard Badenhausen, 'Disarming the infant warrior: Prince Henry, King James, and the chivalric revival', *Papers on Language and Literature*, 31 (1995), pp. 20–37.

49 The literature is extensive, but see most recently David Trim, 'Calvinist Internationalism and the English Officer Corps, 1562–1642' *History Compass*, 4: 6 (2006), pp. 1024–48; Roger B. Manning, *Swordsmen. The Martial Ethos in the Three Kingdoms* (Oxford, 2003); Mark Charles Fissel, *English Warfare, 1511–1642* (London, 2001); Barbara Donagan, 'Halcyon Days and the Literature of War: England's Military Education before 1642', *Past & Present*, 147 (1995), pp. 65–100.

50 Strong, *Henry*, p. 114. See also Hearn, *Dynasties*, pp. 187–88.

51 See Steffen Heiberg (ed.), *Christian IV and Europe*, exh. cat. (Copenhagen, 1988), no. 95.

52 Badeloch Noldus and Juliette Roding (eds.), *Pieter Isaacsz (1568–1625). Court Painter, Art Dealer and Spy* (Turnhout 2007), nos. 22 and 23.

53 Pieter Isaacsz was born to Dutch refugees at Elsinore (Helsingør) and raised in Denmark, but trained as a painter in Amsterdam. He returned to Denmark, c. 1607/08; see the entry for Isaacsz in *The Grove Dictionary of Art*.

54 Thomas Riis, *Should Auld Acquaintance be Forgot. Scottish – Danish Relations c. 1450–1707*, 2 vols. (Odense, 1988), I, 79.

55 *Richard III*, Act V, Scene 4.

56 *Henry VI, Part III*, Act II, Scene 3, ll. 23–24.

57 Joseph Swetman, *The Schoole of the Noble and Worthy Science of Defence* (London, 1617), 'An Epistle unto the Common Reader'.

58 See Walter Bourchier Devereux, *Lives and Letters of the Devereux, Earls of Essex*, 2 vols. (London, 1853), I, 203–04.

59 The author [Anthony Wingfield?] of *A true coppie of a discourse written by a gentleman, employed in the late voyage of Spaine and Portingale* (London: Thomas Woodcok, 1589) does not mention the pike incident, but confirms that Essex was the last to withdraw: 'The next morning, seeing no performance of promise kept, he [General Norris] gave order for our marching away himselfe, the Earle of Essex and Sir Roger Williams remaining with the Stande that was made in the high streate, till the whole Armie was drawn into the field' (p. 38).

60 Samson Lennard, *The Mysterie of Iniquitie* (London, 1612), sig. 3v.

61 To trail the pike was to hold it just behind the head with the right hand at waist height. The shaft would,

therefore, trail out behind the holder, the butt resting on the ground. This was the least tiring standing position for the pikeman. It was also possible to walk with the pike at the trail, when, effectively, it would be dragged along. From the trail to the charged position, the pike would be palmed forward, hand over hand.

62 See Paul E.J. Hammer, *Elizabeth's Wars* (Basingstoke and New York, 2003), pp. 98–101.

63 *Ibid.*, p. 246.

64 Firth, *Cromwell's Army*, p. 70.

65 Richard Elton, 'Several Reasons Why the Pike is the More Honourable Arms', *The Compleat Body of the Art Military* (London, 1659), printed as Appendix B, Firth, *Cromwell's Army*, pp. 385–86.

66 Chamberlain, *Letters*, I, 314. The commander of his company was Henry de Vere, 18th Earl of Oxford.

67 'R.M.', *Scarronides: Or, Virgile Travestie, a Mock Poem* (London, 1665), ll. 476–77.

68 Arguably, Beaumont and Fletcher, in their comedy *The Spanish Curate* (1622), reveal some familiarity with this tradition in Ascanio's offer to trail a pike under the command of Don Jamie.

69 See Hammer, *Elizabeth's Wars*, p. 227.

70 Translated from the Latin in John Peacock, *The Stage Designs of Inigo Jones: The European Context* (Cambridge, 1995), p. 7.

71 See Roy Strong, 'England and Italy: The Marriage of Henry Prince of Wales', in R. Ollard and P. Tudor-Craig (eds.), *For Veronica Wedgwood These: Studies in seventeenth-century history* (London, 1986), pp. 59–87. Strong argues that a Savoy match had been concluded at the time of Henry's death. I have argued elsewhere that the advocates of a Florentine match pursued their cause to the end. See Wilks, '"Forbear the Heat and Haste of Building"', p. 59, note 48.

72 Tristan Marshall, ' "That's the Misery of Peace": Representations of Martialism in the Jacobean Public Theatre, 1608–1614', *The Seventeenth Century*, XIII; 1 (1998), pp. 1–21.

73 The reference is to the *Battle of Frogs and Mice*, 'Homerica'.(7th cent BCE).

74 Thomas Birch, *The Life of Henry, Prince of Wales* (London, 1760), p. 76. 'Tossing the pike' appears to have been a sport rather than a drill exercise, though one assumes only those well used to handling a pike would have been any good at it.

75 Lucy Aitken, *Memoirs of the Court of James the First*, 2 vols (London, 1822), I, 345.

76 Swetman, *Science of Defence*, 'Epistle to the Common Reader'.

77 For Cornwallis's summation of Henry's martial exercises, see *Discourse*, sigs C4v–D1v.

78 Noted by Manning, *Swordsmen*, p. 33, citing *This View of France* (sic) (1604), sigs S3r–4r; R4v–S1r. Its first publication lacked Dallington's permission, though manuscripts had been in circulation for several years.

79 Robert Dallington, *Aphorismes, civil and militarie, amplified with authorities, and exemplified with histories, out of the first quarterne of Fr. Guicciardine* (London, 1613), A4r. Cf. K.J. Höltgen, 'Sir Robert Dallington (1561–1637): Author, Traveler, and Pioneer of Taste', *Huntington Library Quarterly*, XLVII (1894), pp. 147–77.

80 See Birch, *Life*, pp. 186–87; Williamson, *Myth of the Conqueror*, p. 61; Kevin Sharpe, *Sir Robert Cotton* (Oxford, 1978), p. 120.

81 Published shortly after England had returned to peace following the Third Dutch War, when it had opportunistically sided with France against the Dutch. Now an alliance of German princes was mounting a futile resistance in the Rhineland (echoes of the defence of the Palatinate) to Charles II's subsidiser, the aggrandising Louis XIV.

82 Nichols, *Progresses*, II, 268.

83 *Ibid.*, II, 270.

84 *Notes & Queries*, 2nd series, XI, (25 May 1861), citing Maitland's *London*, p. 1335.

85 Thomas Pennant, *An Account of London* (London, 1790), p. 113.

86 'Vertue MSS. I', *Walpole Society*, XVIII, p. 136. See similarly, *Notes & Queries*, 2nd series, XI, (25 May, 1861), p. 401, citing 'Walpole, ed. Dallaway, v, 60'.

87 Published without attribution in *The Gentleman's Magazine*, LXXXVI, Part II (1816), p. 214, but cf. BL Ms. Harley 5900, fols. 44–52.

88 The distinctive shape of the site is apparent in: 'Military Ground, plan. Based on the Ordnance Survey, 1869–74 and a plan of 1660/1 in the Public Record Office (LRRO1/1830)', *The Survey of London*, XXXIV, p. 382, and also in Faithorne and Newcourt's map, *An Exact Delineation of the Cities of London and Westminster* (1658). See also 'Estate boundaries in the late-seventeenth century', *Survey of London* XXXIII, fig. 1, p. 21.

89 See *The Survey of London*, XXXIII & XXXIV, *The Parish of St Anne Soho*, ed. F.H.W. Sheppard, (London, 1966), pp. 1–19.

90 *Ibid.*, pp. 380–81.

91 *Survey of London*, XXXI and XXXII, *St James, Westminster, Part 2* (London, 1963), pp. 41–56. The source is C.L. Kingsford, *The Early History of Piccadilly, Leicester Square, Soho and Their Neighbourhood* (London, 1925), p. 57.

92 See Vimala Cleamona Pasupathi, 'Playing soldiers: martial subjects in Early-Modern English drama', 1560–1660', unpublished PhD diss. (University of Texas, 2005).

93 *Survey of London, St James, Westminster, Part 2*, pp. 41–56.

94 Henry's first instructor in arms appears to have been Richard Preston, Lord Dingwall, a Scot who appears to have been given this responsibility while Henry was only about seven years old, and while still in Scotland. Birch (*Life*, p. 21) cites Robert Johnston, *Historia rerum Britannicum*, I (Amsterdam, 1655), p. 383. Though I know of no contemporary record of Dingwall instructing Henry, he was among the many Scottish courtiers who followed their king into England in 1603, becoming a regular participant at the Accession Day tilts, and, for the March 1610 event, rode atop an elephant in a Mannerist 'howdah' designed by Inigo Jones. See Orgel and Strong, *Inigo Jones*, I, p. 177. Dingwall was also one of the six combatants chosen to support the Prince against all-comers at the Barriers in January 1610, which suggests that his supervision of Henry's military training had not ended. In April 1606, an order was issued confirming a writ of March 1603 appointing Charles Guerolt (presumably Guéroult) 'to attend the Prince, and instruct him in the science of defence', for which he received an annuity. See Frederick Devon, *Issues of Exchequer* (London, 1836), p. 34. Guerolt, however, was probably a pure fencing master. Joseph Swetman, noticed above, never claimed to be Henry's instructor, only to have been befriended and encouraged by him. The simultaneous rise of the 'schools of defence' was a phenomenon separate from the rise of the military grounds, though not entirely unconnected. See Jay P. Anglin, 'The schools of defense in Elizabethan England', *Renaissance Quarterly*, 37 (Autumn, 1984), pp. 363–410; also Markku Peltonen, *The duel in early modern England. Civility, politeness, and honour* (Cambridge, 2003).

95 Also among the subscribers was Sir Thomas Holcroft of Vale Royal, member of several Parliaments and sometime sheriff of Cheshire (NB Henry was Earl of Chester), who had a house in the Strand, where he died in 1620. (See Chamberlain, *Letters*, II, 291). An indication of his religion and loyalty is that he conducted Princess Elizabeth from Coombe to the safety of Coventry when there were fears of a Catholic uprising in Warwickshire following the Gunpowder Plot in November 1605. Sir Thomas had a son, also Thomas, who is to be strongly suspected as being our 'Captain Thomas Holcroft' (though it is acknowledged there were other Thomases of similar age in both the East Ham and Hurst branches of the Holcrofts). A Captain Jeffrey (Geoffrey) Holcroft was the third Holcroft who subscribed to the Virginia Company in 1609. He was a veteran of the Dutch wars, his company having been disbanded in 1608 after the Twelve Years' Truce was agreed. See David Trim, '"Fighting Jacob's Wars". The Employment of English and Welsh Mercenaries in the European Wars of Religion: France and the Netherlands, 1592–1610', unpublished PhD diss. (University of London, 2003), p. 437. I am grateful to Dr Trim for the reference.

96 For Holcroft's letter of instruction, dated 29 May 1609, see Alexander Brown, *The Genesis of the United States*, 2 vols. (New York, 1964), I, 317–18.

97 For summaries of Henry's support for the Virginia colony, see Williamson, *Myth of the Conqueror*, pp. 51–52, 165; Strong, *Henry*, pp. 61–62, 178.

98 John Chamberlain reported the loss of a Captain Holcroft as one of those of 'most marke' among the many English casualties suffered at Ostend in September 1601. Chamberlain, *Letters*, I, 131. David Trim, '"Fighting Jacob's Wars"', p. 437, identifies him as Henry Holcroft, probably also of the Vale Royal branch, who had served in the Low Countries since 1598. I am again indebted to Dr Trim for the reference.

99 NA. L.C. 2.4 (6).

100 For a description and plan of the Military Ground in 1661 showing the location of the armoury, see *The Survey of London, XXXIV*, pp. 381–82.

101 De Foubert, a Huguenot instructor, is said to have briefly used the Military Yard, but his later premises, to which Evelyn's diary entry of December 1684 refers, were nearby. See *The Survey of London, XXXI & XXXII, St James Westminster, Part 2* (1963), pp. 176–95.

102 See Lawrence Stone, *The Crisis of the Aristocracy, 1558–1641* (Oxford, 1965), pp. 265–67, which seems to be strongly influenced by Arthur B. Ferguson, *The Indian Summer of English Chivalry* (Durham, N.C., 1960). Ferguson maintains broadly the same position in his more recent *The Chivalric Tradition in Renaissance England* (Washington, 1986), while Manning, *Swordsmen* (2003), provides a revisionist analysis.

103 See Mervyn James, 'English Politics and the Concept of Honour, 1585–1642', *Past & Present*, Supplement no. 3 (1978).

104 See Paul C. Allen, *Philip III and the Pax Hispanica, 1598–1621* (New Haven and London, 2000), pp. viii–ix.

105 See Marshall, 'Misery of Peace'.

106 See Griffiths, *The Print in Stuart Britain*, p. 56.

107 The following biographical details of the Hollands are drawn from *ODNB*.

108 *Cal. S.P. Venetian, 1607–1610*, pp. 215–16

109 Dallington, *Aphorismes*, sig. A3r–v.

110 Holland, *Heroologia Anglica*, pp. 45–51. Henry's half-length portrait in an oval frame after the similar engraving by Cornelis Boel (*c.* 1612) appears on p. 45; two text pages follow; the pike portrait appears on p. 48; two more text pages follow; p. 51 has letterpress followed by an inferior copy of Hole's engraving of the hearse.

111 *Ibid*, p. 48. I have corrected two obvious mistakes: 'AVE' to 'AWE'; 'SCHOLLEES' to 'SCHOLLERS'. I thank John Buchtel for his comments regarding this plate.

112 Chamberlain to Carleton, 11 March 1620, *Letters*, II, p. 294.

113 *Ibid.*, 28 March 1620, p. 307.

114 See Charles Dalton, *Life and Times of General Sir Edward Cecil*, 2 vols. (London, 1885), II, p. 332.

115 Chamberlain to Carleton, 11 March 1620, *Letters*, II, p. 294. Sackville was a close friend and political ally of Henry's comptroller, Sir John Holles, whom he referred to as 'cousin', and of John Heydon whom Holles referred to as 'our one-handed Heydon'; he who had been maimed in an altercation while following Henry on progress. He served as Sackville's second in his duel with Lord Bruce in 1613. Sackville later (*c.* 1628) hung a posthumous portrait of Henry at Knole, his seat in Kent.

116 There was no single Renaissance idea of honour, or of how it related to virtue and heroism. See John. M. Steadman, *Milton and the Paradoxes of Renaissance Heroism* (Baton Rouge, 1987); Norman Council, *When Honour's at the Stake: Ideas of honour in Shakespeare's plays* (New York, 1973); Curtis B. Watson, *Shakespeare and the Renaissance Concept of Honor* (Princeton, 1960).

117 Stone, *Crisis*, p. 266. For Dobson, see, for example, *Colonel Richard Neville* (National Portrait Gallery); *Colonel John Russell* (Lord Spencer); *An Unknown Officer* (Tate Britain); and *An Unknown Officer* (Lord Sackville), which bears the inscription: *Ano. Dmi, 1642 / Aeta Suae, 50*, another, therefore, of Henry's generation (thought to be Sir Thomas Dallison). See Malcolm Rogers, *William Dobson*, exh. cat. (London, 1983).

118 Sir Edward Sydenham to Ralph Verney, 27 October 1642, quoted in Peter Verney, *The Standard Bearer* (London, 1963), p. 202.

119 Verney, *Standard Bearer*, p. 18.

120 Elton, from *The Compleat Body*, given in Firth, *Cromwell's Army*, p. 385.

121 *Journal of the House of Lords II: 1640–1643* (1802), pp. 961–63; *VII: 1644* (1802), pp. 442–49. The prisoners were, in the event, taken elsewhere, as it was concluded the arrangement would prove 'a great Annoyance' to the Yard's neighbours – the Earls of Leicester and Manchester, the former complaining that his garden would be trampled by the guards.

8| 'A Duche graver sent for': Cornelis Boel, Salomon de Caus, and the production of *La perspective auec la raison des ombres et miroirs*

Alexander Marr

It has long been recognised that the court of Henry, Prince of Wales, provided a fertile environment for the flourishing of the arts in early seventeenth-century England. Notables such as Isaac Oliver and Inigo Jones fashioned the young Prince's image through portraits, architecture and masques, setting the stage for a substantial transformation of visual culture. An important aspect of these artistic changes was a growing interest in geometry, which many considered a crucial ingredient in the foundations of modern art and architecture. However, geometry was a subject about which a great many British courtiers, artists and artisans were largely ignorant at the turn of the century. Robert Peake, Prince Henry's official painter, sought to help remedy this situation by translating into English Serlio's *First Book of Architecture*, in which he hoped to

> … convay unto my Countrymen (especially Architects and Artificers of all
> sorts) these Necessary, Certaine and ready helps of Geometrie; the ignorance
> and want whereof, in times past (in most parts of this Kingdome) hath left us
> many lame Workes, with Shame of many Workemen.[1]

Peake's translation was published in 1611, the same year as another important treatise concerned with the application of geometry to the visual arts: Salomon de Caus's *La perspective auec la raison des ombres et miroirs*. This justly celebrated, lavishly illustrated folio was the first full-length treatise on perspective to be published in England, and one of the earliest works on the visual arts issued (if only in part, as discussed below) by an English printer.[2] We need look no further than Prince Henry's picture collection in order to appreciate the significance of perspective for the arts at this time. [3] One of the few paintings certainly owned by the Prince was Hans Vredeman de Vries's *Christ in the House of Mary and Martha* (1566; fig. 1), in which the biblical subject is but a pretext for a virtuosic exercise in the depiction of a contemporary interior in single-point perspective.[4] Works such as this could only be fully appreciated if the viewer had mastered the necessary principles of perspective with which the picture is imbued.[5] Such an understanding of perspective was clearly considered an important accomplishment for Prince Henry, as de Caus, a French architect-engineer, was engaged as his tutor

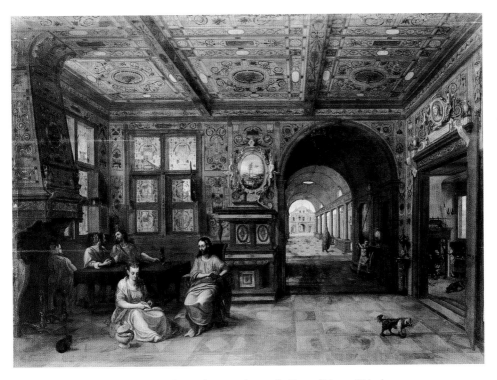

Fig. 1 Hans Vredeman de Vries, *Christ in the House of Mary and Martha*
1566, oil on copper, British Royal Collection

in this subject from about 1608.[6] In the 'letter to the reader' of *La perspective* de Caus informs us that the work was compiled from his lessons in perspective to Prince Henry, which he had been delivering 'for two or three years'.[7] As Luke Morgan has observed, 'the vagueness [of this statement] from an otherwise precise man is hard to understand'.[8] The letter is signed and dated 1 October 1611 from Richmond Palace, where de Caus was domiciled in his capacity as 'Ingenieur du serenissime Prince de Galles', as he is termed on the title-page of the book. As such, it seems that the Prince's instruction may initially have been by correspondence, for de Caus only moved to London from Brussels (where he was employed by the Archdukes Albert and Isabella) in September or October 1610.[9] Alternatively, it is conceivable that de Caus made occasional, fleeting visits to London in order to deliver his lessons in person and to evaluate the patronage opportunities available at court.[10] Once in England, however, de Caus was a prominent member of the Prince's circle, overseeing the production of water features for the garden of Henry's palace at Richmond as well as undertaking some engineering works for the gardens at Hatfield House.[11]

De Caus was undoubtedly a man of considerable technical skill, whose extensive practical knowledge of hydraulics and pneumatics proved welcome at Henry's polymathic court. An indication of the range of his wonder-working abilities is provided by his third published work, *Les raisons des forces mouvantes* (1615), a book filled with images and descriptions of

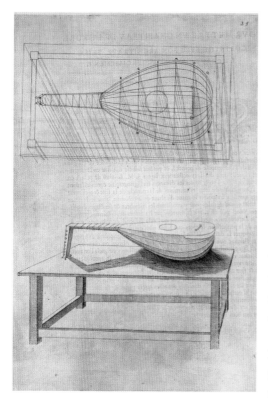

Fig. 2 Cornelis Boel, *Lute in perspective,* from Salomon de Caus, *La perspective* (Barker, 1611)

remarkable fountains and automata.[12] The designs for these devices were (according to de Caus) begun whilst in the service of Prince Henry in order to 'satisfy his noble curiosity [*gentille curiosité*] which always desires to see and to know new things'.[13] Certainly, the contents of this treatise conjour up the fascination for technical marvels that evidently formed a part of the cultural milieu at the Prince's court, which attracted technicians such as the Italian engineer Costantino de' Servi and Cornelius Drebbel of Alkmaar.[14]

De Caus's technical and gardening projects have tended to obscure his role as Henry's tutor in perspective, yet this was no less a contribution to the vibrant cultural world surrounding his young pupil. By educating the Prince in the principles of perspective de Caus inducted his patron into a hugely important artistic tradition that included authorities such as Piero della Francesca, Leonardo da Vinci and Albrecht Dürer.[15] Indeed, his lessons to the Prince almost certainly featured the sort of subject-matter contained in the numerous treatises on perspective that proliferated during the sixteenth and early seventeenth century. We are fortunate that de Caus chose to commit the content of his teaching to paper in the form of a printed treatise, even though it was not a groundbreaking work, drawing heavily on Dürer's *Unterweysung der Messung* (1525). In essence, *La perspective* is a practical (indeed somewhat pedestrian) book, proceeding from sound optical principles to applied examples of perspective, including methods to depict various objects perspectivally, such as globes, lutes, fortresses and so on (fig. 2).[16] Arguably, the work's greatest interest lies in its attitude towards the arts: a Vitruvian enthusiasm for 'fitness and arrangement in architecture' and a geometrical approach to design, reflecting the cultural aspirations of Prince Henry and his circle.[17]

However, the book's contents are by no means *La perspective*'s sole historical value and I do not seek to analyse them in the present essay. Nor do I wish to address de Caus's contribution (important though it may have been) to technological culture in the period. Rather, I am concerned here with the *making* of de Caus's treatise. Surprisingly little attention has been paid to the production and retail of de Caus's printed books, yet his published oeuvre represents a particularly rich source for the study of early seventeenth-century printing communities. Moreover, the production and distribution of *La perspective*, in particular, offers valuable insights into the international networks of authors, stationers and artisans connected to Prince Henry and his court, as well as presenting fresh perspectives on the social and intellectual world of the Early Modern architect-engineer, notably the ways in which court networks affected their publications.[18] Attending to the book-making process is particularly important for figures such as de Caus for whom little archival evidence survives, greatly assisting the reconstruction of his professional world while bringing into question certain assumptions about his published works. If, for example, de Caus's treatises were artefacts designed for presentational purposes for patrons such as Prince Henry, how were these expensive volumes funded? If the frontispieces to works such as *La perspective* reflect the 'conceits of the author, represented at the front of his book in visual symbols that he himself had chosen and designed as its most fitting emblems,' did the choice of engraver have any impact upon their design?[19] Did the backer or patron play any part in the distribution of a given book, thereby affecting its subsequent influence? These may seem modest issues, yet they constitute the fine grain necessary for a detailed understanding of those books that made such a vital contribution to the social, cultural and intellectual world of the Early Modern court. As such, the present essay offers an in-depth case study of the production of de Caus's *La perspective*, which, I argue, was deeply affected by its author's intimate association with Prince Henry and his circle.

Like many of his contemporaries, de Caus attempted to use print as a means of elevating his status and furthering his career.[20] In fact, *La perspective* is but one of five works published during his lifetime, all of which are in folio, produced to a high standard, and liberally illustrated. Each bears familiar dedications to current or prospective patrons, as well as carefully crafted textual and visual rhetorical programmes promoting the usefulness, liberal status and potential pleasure of the disciplines of which he treats.[21] Notably, however, in some cases the titles appearing on de Caus's books stress the status of both author and stationer. For example, the royal privileges held by his sometime publishers Barker and Norton (both King's Printers) are displayed on the title-pages to the first two issues of *La perspective*.[22] Thus, de Caus's self-fashioning built not only upon the credit of his own appointed position but also on that of his books' retailers, mutually enhancing the standing of both author and publisher. In an age in which, as Shapin and Johns have shown, the construction of trust was an important component in the production and consumption of knowledge, de Caus and his books play the status game to considerable effect.[23] Furthermore, the very fact that his books regularly appeared at the time he was seeking or attempting to consolidate patronage strongly suggests that they were conceived within the ubiquitous court culture of gift-giving articulated by Natalie Zemon Davis, Mario Biagioli and others.[24] Indeed, *La perspective*, dedicated to Prince Henry himself, appeared at a time when de Caus was potentially under threat from the appointment of a new architect-engineer to the Prince's service, the Florentine Costantino de' Servi.[25]

La perspective was published in one edition with three issues. The first issue appeared under the imprint of Robert Barker with the date 1611, the second bears the imprint of John Norton and is dated 1612.[26] The Hulsius firm published a third issue sometime before 1615, as I shall explain.[27] Given that *La perspective* was issued during de Caus's employment at the royal court, it is unsurprising that the King's printers Barker and (subsequently) Norton were involved in its publication. Barker was an important (not to mention wealthy) London stationer, holding the lucrative monopoly on Bible production.[28] Even so, de Caus's treatise clearly represented a significant venture in terms of both funds required and subject matter. As Henri-Jean Martin has shown, at the beginning of the seventeenth century London was still a relatively small centre of book manufacture and producing a fully illustrated folio was a costly affair.[29] For example, the 1610 inventory of the Parisian publisher Matthieu Guillemot lists some eighteen plates for 'Philostrate' (Beroalde de Verville's *Tableau des riches inventions* [1600]) valued at as much as 324 French *livres*.[30] By way of comparison *La perspective*, printed just one year later, featured more than eighty plates, the figurative examples of which (as opposed to the geometrical diagrams) were just as sophisticated as those illustrating Beroalde de Verville's book. Given the large capital outlay that would evidently have been necessary to finance a book of this type and scale, it seems probable that, rather than purchasing the plates outright, Barker was working in partnership with one or more additional backers.[31] Without further evidence it is impossible positively to identify these figures, though we should not rule out the possibility that the publishers and author were involved in the financing of *La perspective*.[32] Although it is unlikely (but not impossible) that Prince Henry himself was involved in supporting the work financially, *La perspective* was very much an 'in-house' production – written by the Prince's appointed tutor and engineer, published by the King's Printer and, as I will show, cut by an engraver in Henry's employ.[33]

Though identified in the imprint of *La perspective* as 'King's Printer', John Norton was not involved in the mechanical process of printing *per se*.[34] Rather, he was a stationer who facilitated the book-making process and whose main role lay in financing and selling books. Barker, however, ran the largest printing shop in London at the time, yet, somewhat surprisingly, it seems that *La perspective* was not printed on his own premises.[35] Instead, the printing work was undertaken jointly by Jan I Mommaert in Brussels and Richard Field in London. Evidence from the type and decorative woodcut borders indicates that Mommaert printed the majority of the book. Field printed the prelims, the letterpress of chapter ten of 'Ombres' (Livre II), and all (except the plates) of 'Miroirs' (Livre III).[36] The choice of Field as the London-based half of the printing partnership is unsurprising. Although, according to the bibliographical evidence in *STC*, he had not worked with Barker prior to *La perspective*, Field could boast considerable experience in the printing of foreign-language books.[37] His expertise may be attributable to his marriage, in 1588, to Jacqueline Vautrollier, widow of the French refugee bookseller, bookbinder and printer Thomas I Vautrollier (d. 1587).[38] In addition to acquiring, through his marriage, a set of type that included the accented characters necessary for foreign-language printing, the match suggests (more importantly) that Field's business would have included compositors who could read French, an important skill for this type of venture and of particular importance given that de Caus could not speak English.[39] It may be that, along with the printing house, Field inherited Vautrollier's Continental business contacts. However, as there is no evidence that Field worked with Mommaert before or after the production of *La perspective*, it may reasonably be assumed that the latter was employed through the agency either of the publisher, Barker, or the author, de Caus.[40]

The reason for employing a foreign printer in addition to the London-based Field is not immediately clear. As *STC* records, Mommaert (active as a printer from 1585) was responsible for the sections of *La perspective* which required the inclusion of engraved illustrations on the same page as letterpress. [41] Although the expertise of British printers could run to the incorporation of woodblocks with letterpress, the combination of engravings with letterpress on the same printed page was a task better suited to the more advanced techniques of Continental printers and, significantly, necessitated the use of a different type of printing press.[42] While letterpress could be printed using a conventional screw press, engravings were printed using a rolling press that applied the additional pressure necessary to squeeze ink into the lines of intaglio-cut copper plates. Why, though, was Mommaert chosen over the dozens of Continental printers with comparable skills? Although our first thoughts turn to the likelihood that de Caus had been acquainted with Mommaert's business while based in Brussels, it is still necessary to consider whether Mommaert's involvement was brought about by one of the other interested parties. The choice of printer for a given book in this period seems most frequently to have been determined by the publisher. Yet there is no evidence of a working relationship between Barker or Norton and Mommaert before or after the production of *La perspective*, and this is the only known instance of printing having been divided between Field and Mommaert. Moreover, while several of Mommaert's extant publications do feature engraved plates, these are generally of an inferior quality and rarely combined with letterpress – hence Mommaert could not boast a reputation for producing books equal in quality to *La perspective* that would have immediately recommended his skills to the publisher or letterpress printer.[43] In fact, it seems most likely that the choice of the Brussels printer derived, somewhat unusually, from the author himself.

We know that de Caus was employed as Henry's tutor in perspective whilst still retained by the court in Brussels. It is quite conceivable, therefore, that de Caus had begun planning the book before leaving the employ of the Archdukes Albert and Isabella. One possible explanation for the choice of Mommaert as printer is that de Caus has already contracted him to print *La perspective* before leaving for England, suggesting that he initially intended the treatise as a gift to Prince Henry, with the hope that his young pupil might offer him a permanent position at his London court. It may be the case that de Caus initially intended that Mommaert print the entire book and that the treatise was almost fully printed upon his move to England in late 1610. This would explain both Field's minimal involvement in the venture and why he was responsible for the letterpress of the latter part of the book and the prelims – normally the last part of a book to be produced. As discussed below, the copperplates of 'Miroirs' may have already been printed by the time de Caus arrived in England, or the plates may have remained with or been sent to Mommaert (or, as is more likely, a dedicated copperplate printer) in Brussels and the printed sheets returned to de Caus in London for incorporation with Field's letterpress. At the very least, even if the printing of the book was only begun once de Caus had settled in England, which seems improbable, it is likely that de Caus was acquainted with Mommaert prior to his departure for the Richmond court, and that on arrival in England he recommended the Brussels printer to his publisher, Barker.

De Caus's association with Prince Henry's court almost certainly accounts for the involvement of the King's Printers Barker and Norton in the publication of *La perspective*. Though neither was officially appointed to Henry, Norton was one of his principal suppliers of books.[44] As early as 23 January 1608/09 Norton was paid 100 marks for books ordered by the Prince, while after his death (and that of Prince Henry), Norton's nephew and executor, Bonham Norton, was paid the considerable sum of 456*l* 17*s* 8*d* for 'books delivered into the late Prince's library'.[45] John Norton (1556/57–1612) was one of the most important stationers of early seventeenth-century England, eventually rising, in 1603, to the position of Master of the Stationers' Company.[46] Before his death he was involved with the financing, publishing and printing of a prodigious number of books and, as John Barnard has recently noted, his role as a 'cultural broker and facilitator'[47] was entwined with his extensive business dealings, which included bookselling throughout England, Scotland and the Continent. Norton's Continental activities are particularly notable; from the beginning of the seventeenth century his firm began to displace the immigrant families who had previously monopolized the Latin book trade in London, and he is known to have bought and sold books at Paris and Frankfurt. Norton had French business dealings from at least as early as 1604 when his business partner John Bill was busily acquiring books on the Continent for Thomas Bodley's recently inaugurated Oxford library.[48] The Norton firm seems to have maintained a regular presence at the annual Frankfurt Book Fair which, as discussed below, was significant for de Caus's publishing ambitions.

Norton's strong links to the royal courts of both James I and Prince Henry included his appointment as 'Printer to the King's most excellent Majesty in Hebrew, Greek and Latin'. Indeed this imprint appears on one of his best-known publications, Abraham Ortelius's *Theatrum Orbis Terrarum* (London, 1606). It has passed unnoticed, however, that this imprint presents a significantly different title to that of *La perspective*: 'Jan. Norton Imprimeur du Roy de la grande Bretaigne, aus langues estrangeres'. For Ortelius's *Theatrum* Norton was not Royal Printer in *all* foreign languages, but specifically in ancient ones. It is not until 1612, the date of Norton's issue of de Caus's book, that a publication appears bearing an imprint similar to that of *La perspective*. James I's *Declaration … touchant le faict de Conradus Vorstius* bears the imprint 'A Londre,

Chez Iean Norton, Imprimeur ordinaire du Roy éslangues estrangeres'.[49] Significantly, *La perspective* is the only French text printed by Norton not to be an official declaration or work of King James himself, further suggesting that either Prince Henry or the King may have had a hand in its publication.

It would certainly have been difficult, given the state of the English book trade at the time, for de Caus to secure the services of a stationer willing to publish a foreign-language work on a subject for which there was no precedent (and hence no reliable market) in English publishing without high-status connections. Furthermore, if the printing of the book was initiated in Brussels it is unlikely that de Caus's patrons, the Archdukes, would have supported a venture designed to transfer their client to the service of another prince in a different country. As such, the Richmond court network seems to have been crucial in securing a publisher for *La perspective*.

Having accounted for the choice of printers and publishers for the book, the question remains as to who designed and engraved the treatise's many perspectival diagrams and elaborate figurative illustrations. The engravings of *La perspective* are amongst the finest and most sophisticated to be found in books bearing an English imprint from this period. Unusually for work of this quality, however, none of the plates are signed with an *invenit*, a *fecit* or a *sculpsit* in any of the three issues of the book. They are here attributed to the hitherto overlooked Flemish emigrant artist Cornelis Boel.[50] The engravings for *La perspective* (which, if my attribution is accepted, enlarge Boel's oeuvre by almost one hundred plates) range from simple geometrical diagrams to full-page illustrations of the Prince's lessons in perspective (clearly influenced by Dürer's depiction of a similar scene in the *Unterweysung der Messung*), to a large double-page plate of an elaborate architectural feature (figs. 3, 4 and 5).[51]

Born in Antwerp in *c*. 1576, Boel was most probably a pupil of Jan Sadeler, whose genre he adopted. Whilst in Antwerp, he engraved plates for works by Rubens's master, Otto van Veen, including *Amorum emblemata* (1608) and *Vita D. Thomae Aquinatis* (1610), both of which bear strong stylistic similarities to the illustrations in *La perspective* (figs. 6 and 7). It may have been *Amorum emblemata* that brought Boel to the attention of the English court, as van Veen prepared various editions of this work in a combination of different languages, including one with an English title-page dedicated to William Herbert, Earl of Pembroke, and his brother Philip.[52] However, it may be the case that de Caus himself introduced Boel to London. We know that Boel was in England by 1611, when he produced the title-page engraving for one of the most important books issued in England during the reign of James I – the Authorized Version of the Bible, published by none other than Robert Barker in 1611 (fig. 8).[53] The title-page of this work is clearly signed 'C. Boel fecit in Richmont', providing us with a useful *terminus post quem* for Boel's activities in England and linking him specifically with Prince Henry's circle.

Throughout his English period, Boel was particularly active in the construction of the royal family's image. He made portrait engravings of the King, Queen, Princess Elizabeth

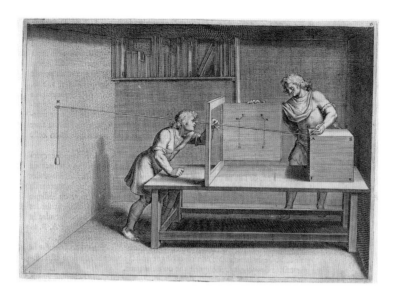

Fig. 3 Cornelis Boel,
Perspective lesson, from
Salomon de Caus,
La perspective (Barker, 1611)

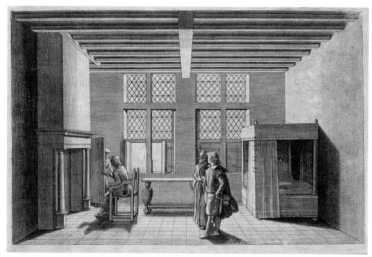

Fig. 4 Cornelis Boel,
Interior of a room, from
Salomon de Caus,
La perspective (Barker, 1611)

Fig. 5 Cornelis Boel,
Architectural feature, from
Salomon de Caus,
La perspective (Barker, 1611)

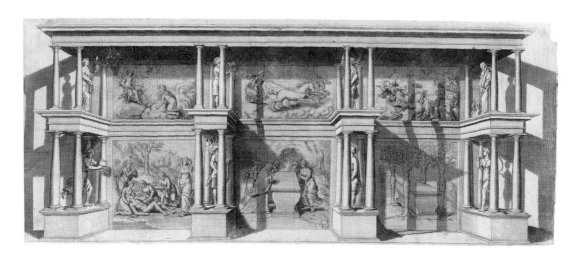

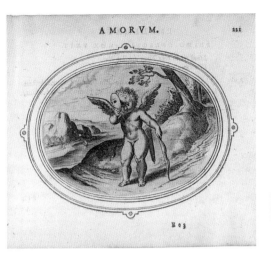

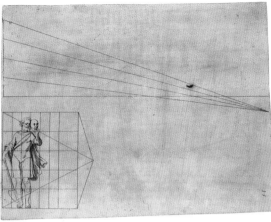

Fig. 6 Cornelis Boel, *Cupid with mask*, from Otto van Veen, *Amorum emblemata* (Van Veen, 1608)

Fig. 7 Cornelis Boel, detail of *Figure with mask*, from Salomon de Caus, *La perspective* (Barker, 1611)

(fig. 9) and Prince Henry himself. These portraits were considerably more accomplished and sophisticated than the majority of engraved portraits then being produced in England, whether by native or by immigrant artists. For example, a comparison between Boel's portrait of Princess Elizabeth and a double portrait of James I and Queen Anne (early 1610s; fig. 10) by the English engraver Renold Elstrack – described by Griffiths as 'the most prolific and competent of the few native-born engravers working in London during the reign of James' – demonstrates the quality of the Flemish engraver's work. Where in Elstrack's engraving the drapery is schematic, the *chiaroscuro* unsubtle, and the features of the sitters poorly observed, Boel's confident portraits exhibit a degree of refinement, quality of execution and mastery of form that far surpasses the English engraving. Indeed, Boel's portraits even compare favourably to the celebrated portrait of James I by Francis Delaram (fig. 11), executed in 1619, described as 'quite exceptional, not only in Delaram's work ... but in the entire production of English prints at this time'.[54]

Explanations for Boel's involvement in the production of *La perspective* are inextricably linked with the thorny issue of where and when the plates for the work were cut and printed. Either Boel cut the plates before his move to London, in or around 1611, or he cut the plates in London during his brief stay in Richmond, where he was employed informally at Prince Henry's court.[55] In the first scenario, de Caus must have known Boel before their respective London periods (they may have been introduced to one another by Mommaert), in which case it may be assumed that de Caus introduced the engraver to the court and Barker, who subsequently commissioned the frontispiece to the 1611 Bible from the Fleming. In the alternative scenario, Boel and de Caus first met in England, which would suggest that the engraver was commissioned to work on *La perspective* by virtue of his association with the court and his

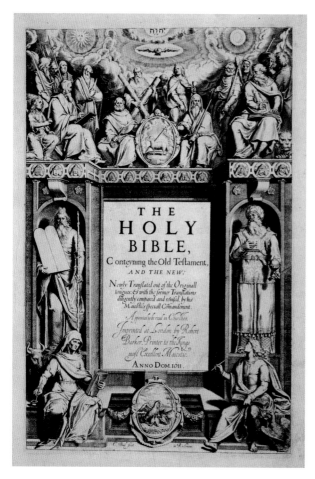

employment by Barker at the time. It should be noted, however, that we might well be dealing with a combination of both these scenarios. Boel may have begun the work for *La perspective* on the Continent and only completed it in England, following the author (who may have been his employer), de Caus. In any of these scenarios, *La perspective* provides compelling evidence for the importance of the artist-practitioner network in providing solutions – in terms of availability, skills and ability – to the needs of authors, the book trade and even princely patrons. Furthermore, the relationship between de Caus and Boel was almost certainly strengthened by, even if it did not originate from, the fact that by 1611 both artisans were resident at Richmond, living in the same quarters, in the service of the same prince (they were also probably both Huguenots).[56]

Regardless of whether or not the plates of *La perspective* were cut on the Continent, in London or both, it is almost certain that the book's illustrations were not printed in London, as printing of this type and scale was at this point beyond the expertise and capacity of English printers. While it is clear that Mommaert printed the majority of the letterpress of *La perspective* it is by no means certain that he printed the plates; he could not boast of experience in this type of printing.[57] Given the staggered nature of the production of *La perspective* – as evinced by Field's involvement during the latter stages – it is difficult to reconstruct precisely where and when the numerous plates of the book were printed, but there was evidently considerable movement of sheets between the Continent and England, where the book was completed and published. It is entirely plausible, for example, that de Caus brought with him to England sheets of letterpress (up to the beginning of 'Miroirs' [Livre III], excluding the prelims), printed by Mommaert in Brussels, containing spaces for the insertion of copperplates, which were cut by Boel and then returned to the Continent, along with the Mommaert sheets for printing. Once printed, these sheets would then be sent back to London and added to the prelims and the letterpress of 'Miroirs' (Livre III) printed by Field. Alternatively, the book was complete

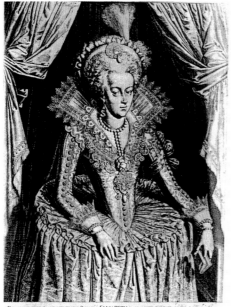

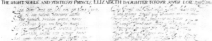

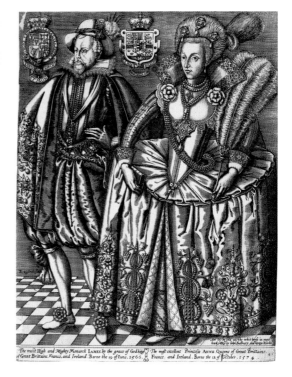

PREVIOUS PAGE

Fig. 8 Cornelis Boel, Title-page to the Authorized Version of the Bible (Barker, 1611)

CLOCKWISE FROM TOP LEFT

Fig. 9 Cornelis Boel, *Princess Elizabeth* (c. 1611)

Fig. 10 Ronald Elstrack, *King James I and Queen Anne* (early 1610s)

Fig. 11 Francis Delaram, *King James I* (1619)

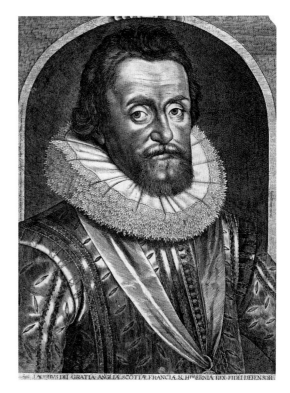

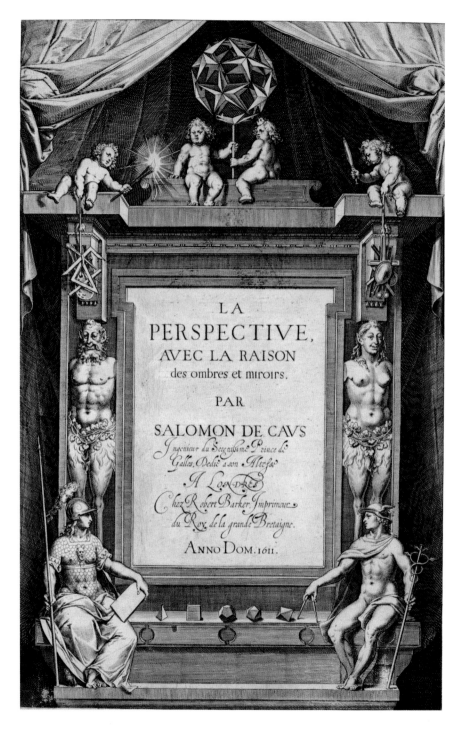

Fig. 12. Cornelis Boel, Title-page to Salomon de Caus, *La perspective* (Barker, 1611)

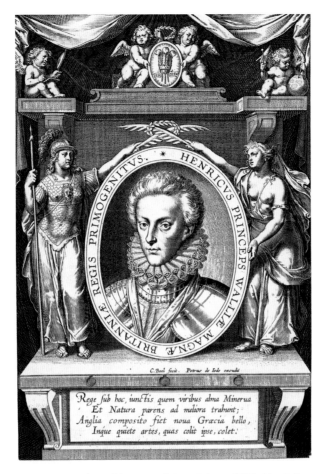

Fig. 13 Cornelis Boel, 'Portrait of Henry, Prince of Wales' (*c.* 1612)

(i.e. both letterpress and copperplates had been printed) up to the beginning of 'Miroirs' (Livre III) by the time de Caus reached England, and the few remaining sheets requiring copperplates were either returned to the Continent for printing or else printed in London by an English printer with a rolling press. It is unlikely that Field was responsible for any of the copperplate printing – as Nicholas Barker suggests, even the printing of mathematical tables in Francis Junius's works presented 'no small challenge to Field'.[58]

Regardless of which printing scenario is correct, a comparison between the title-page of *La perspective* (fig. 12) and those works that, until now, have constituted Boel's English œuvre clearly demonstrates that Boel was the engraver of the book's plates.[59] The positioning and style of the figures of Mercury and Minerva on the *La perspective* title-page recall the Evangelists St John and St Luke in the bottom right- and left-hand corners of the 1611 Bible title-page. More striking, however, is the comparison between the title-page of *La perspective* and Boel's portrait engraving of Prince Henry (fig. 13), which is in turn similar to Isaac Oliver's celebrated miniature of the Prince dated by Strong to late 1611 or 1612.[60] The *La perspective* title-page and Boel's portrait of the

Prince both feature near-identical *putti* and mathematical instruments at the tops of their respective architectonic frames, whilst the figure of Minerva, although differently positioned in the *La perspective* title-page, is clad identically to that of the Prince Henry portrait.[61] Made at around the same time, it is not certain which of these two engravings was produced first but they are clearly the invention of one artist. It should be noted that Boel's production of Henry's portrait reaffirms the importance of the artist-practitioner network at the Richmond court. Boel was probably working from a face pattern, in the form of a drawing, provided by Isaac Oliver and it is highly likely that Oliver and his fellow Huguenot, Boel, were acquainted with one another.

The extent to which Boel was involved with the design, as opposed to the actual cutting, of *La perspective*'s title-page and illustrations is uncertain.[62] Indeed, we do not know whether his skills extended to draughtsmanship as well as the actual cutting of copperplates.[63] It is worth noting, for example, that the term *fecit* as it appears on the Prince Henry portrait normally refers to the cutting, rather than the design, of the image. Somewhat surprisingly, this engraving is signed with an *excudit* by the Antwerp-based draughtsman, engraver and publisher Pieter I de Jode, suggesting that the portrait was published in the Low Countries (although the bulk of the print were probably imported back to England, where the biggest market would have been).[64] It is highly unlikely that Boel had a hand in the invention of the geometrical diagrams of de Caus's book; these would simply have been copied from the author's manuscript and required no stylistic interpretation. However, some of the larger, figurative illustrations – the title-page in particular – are so distinctively in Boel's style that the attribution of their invention to the engraver cannot be entirely ruled out. The matter is further complicated if we accept Strong's argument that Boel's 1611/12 portrait of Henry employs an iconographic programme 'deliberately compiled at Richmond', designed to present 'the vision of a Prince who through wisdom and learning will unlock, by means of science, the mysteries of nature'.[65] However, the creators of the iconography have not been identified and the involvement of the Antwerp-based de Jode suggests that the print may well have been a commercial venture rather than, as Strong suggests, a portrait conceived by courtiers intent on deliberate image-fashioning.

The fact remains, though, that the iconography of both the Henry portrait and the *La perspective* title-page are very similar and that both engravings would have been considered appropriate for the young Prince. Does this mean, then, that both engravings consciously employ similar iconography, and that neither de Caus nor Boel was responsible for their design? It must be remembered that while some title-pages and frontispieces of the period certainly were meant to be decoded, an equal, if not greater, number were decorative, with allegorical content that was sufficient to provide a veneer of learning but vague enough to inhibit elaborate interpretation. The figures of Minerva and Mercury and the curious *putti* of *La perspective*'s title-page are relatively standard for this period and could easily be an engraver's decorative – and, in the case of the *putti*, rather humorous – flourish, borrowed from an earlier design, rather than serious, purposeful iconographic features.[66] Indeed, this should sound a note of warning in relation to the interpretation of emblematic title-pages in general, particularly Corbett and Lightbown's well-known assertion that a frontispiece illustration represents the 'conceits of the author'. [67] It is not impossible, however, that de Caus had a hand in devising the iconography of both the engraved portrait of Henry and the title-page to his book. He was, after all, in the vicinity of London at the time the portrait was executed, and the incorporation of *putti* peering through lenses and measuring globes in both images reflects the Prince's lessons in perspective, as well as perhaps recalling the popular 'mirror for princes' genre of writing popular at the time. Given that *La perspective* was dedicated to Henry, the title-page's relationship to the dedicatee's portrait is entirely appropriate, the implication being that in receiving this book the Prince's mathematical knowledge is increased and his capacity to 'unlock the mysteries of nature' enhanced, all through the agency of his devoted engineer. Regrettably, without further documentary evidence the respective roles played by Boel and de Caus in the design and production of the portrait and the *La perspective* engravings must remain speculative, although the most likely scenario is some form of collaboration between author and engraver, which may have included contributions from other members of the Richmond court network, such as Isaac Oliver.[68]

The illustrations of *La perspective* were important not only for their demonstration of de Caus's perspectival theory, but also in making the book an object worthy of his princely patron.[69] In his study of the Henrician court, Strong questions whether more works than the five images then securely attributed to Boel might have been planned. Noting that 'engraving was a chief means of manifesting princely magnificence', Strong asks whether it might have been the Prince's intention to commission a *fête* book or the like to enhance his status through the production of a spectacularly visual printed work.[70] *La perspective* suggests that this may well have been the case. Though not a *fête* book *per se*, *La perspective* was doubtless visually magnificent. Moreover, it had the extra appeal of intellectual respectability through its foundations in geometry, and was especially applicable to those arts with which Henry's circle was increasingly enraptured, namely architecture, drawing and painting.[71] It may be that, upon his arrival in England, de Caus presented his patron with a selection of the printed sheets of the work (or, at the very least, a manuscript of the treatise), which captured the Prince's interest and cemented his patronage.[72] The appearance of a sophisticated, finely illustrated treatise on perspective would undoubtedly have been immensely appealing to those few courtiers and artisans at the Prince's court engaging with the most up-to-date visual arts and mathematical practices. For example, de Caus's treatise may be associated with the unfinished and projected mathematical instruments devised for the Prince by Edward Wright, such as 'An instrument of brasse to make a plat or any Geometricall figure smaller or greater in any proportion.'[73]

It is not clear how many copies of *La perspective* were distributed in England, nor is it known how many copies of the book were actually printed, although between 500 and 750 copies seems a reasonable estimate. It is possible that the single print-run was jointly financed by Barker and Norton and that the former agreed to take a relatively small proportion of the stock straight

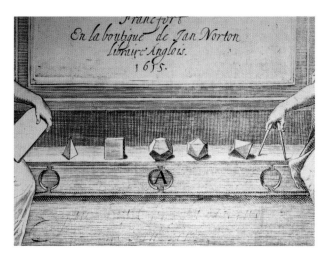

Fig. 14 Detail of Cornelis Boel, Title-page to Book II of
Salomon de Caus, *Les raisons des forces mouvantes* (Norton, 1615)

away to be sold under his own imprint (1611) with the latter taking the majority of the stock, sold with a variant title-page slightly later (1612). Although it is not known how many copies were re-tailed by either stationer, evidence from *STC* and the Hand Press Book database records more than three times as many surviving copies of Norton's 1612 issue of *La perspective* as Barker's, sup-porting the scenario described above.[74] It is likely, moreover, that Barker, whose bookselling activities seem to have been confined to the English market, catered for a local clientele in retail-ing *La perspective* whereas Norton, with his Continental contacts, was well placed to sell the book abroad. Despite the increasing popularity of the visual arts in Henry's circle, in the wider context of the Early Modern book trade the English audience for de Caus's treatise was still small, espe-cially given that a generously illustrated folio of this type, in French, would have commanded a high price.[75] We may be sure, however, that at least one copy of Barker's 1611 issue was presented to Henry. As such *La perspective* entered a library, or rather set of libraries, in which, given its numerous potential applications – artistic, military, technological, etc. – it would have been in good company. Not only had the Prince received a large portion of the Lumley library, rich in cosmological and geometrical literature, but he had also established a substantial collection of books on the military arts.[76] Furthermore, it seems highly likely that had the Prince not died in 1612, and the artists of his court dispersed, Boel would have been commissioned to undertake the engravings for an even more magnificent and ambitious book: de Caus's third treatise, *Les raisons des forces mouvantes*, alluded to in the dedication of *La perspective* as 'another work, already begun'.[77]

As suggested above, unlike Barker, Norton engaged extensively in the Continental book trade, and it seems likely that the number of copies financed and/or sold by him reflected the wider audience that these activities could command.[78] Interest in treatises concerned with the visual arts was generally more widespread on the Continent than in England at this date, and Norton was well positioned to take advantage of this market. In fact, Norton's Continental activities – particularly his presence at the Frankfurt Book Fair – may explain the existence of a third issue of *La perspective*. This issue bears both the Norton imprint of the 1612 issue and an additional imprint added to the sill at the base of the title-page, which reads *A Fran[c]fort chez la vesue de Hulsius*. It has been claimed that this issue was produced several years after the publication of *Les raisons* (published in 1615) – *STC* records the book as a variant issue, published sometime after 1619 by the Hulsius firm, i.e. by Anne van Hulsen, widow of the Frankfurt instrument designer, publisher and bookseller Levinus van Hulsen, or Levinius Hulsius (d. 1606).[79] The Hulsius firm had a history of publishing technological literature, particularly re-issuing (in somewhat cheaper versions) finely illustrated treatises of this genre.[80] For example, under Levinius Hulsius the firm published a number of books on instrumentation and mathematics, as well as an issue of Agostino Ramelli's famous book of machines *Le diverse et artificiose machine* (1601) which seems to have passed unnoticed by Teach Gnudi in her bibliographical study of the book.[81] One of Hulsius's most important publications was a low-quality edition of Tycho Brahe's seminal publication *Astronomiae instaurata mechanica* (Nuremburg, 1602).[82] The firm is an interesting example of a technological variety of a 'polyglot household', in which the book shop acts as a centre for material and intellectual exchange, though on a far smaller scale than Eisenstein's model examples. Levinius Hulsius had been a pupil of Galileo, and at his Frankfurt shop he manufactured and sold mathematical instruments as well as books and prints.[83] If de Caus was involved in brokering a deal to re-issue *La perspective* through the Hulsius firm, we are presented with an intriguing set of potential circumstances for the transfer of knowledge associated with mathematical practitioners through professional and social interaction mediated by the business of bookselling.

The engraved title-page of the second book of the first edition of *Les raisons* (1615) is clearly taken from the same plate as the Hulsius issue of *La perspective* and hence postdates it – traces of the Hulsius imprint can be made out at the base of the page where it has been erased with a burin (fig. 14).[84] It is clear, given the absence of a 'fingerprint' in the third issue, that the Hulsius version of *La perspective* is not a re-printing but, rather, that Norton (or perhaps his business partner, John Bill) sold surplus stock of *La perspective* to the Hulsius firm, who issued it under their own imprint. The re-use of the title-page in this way is of considerable interest as it shows the use of the same plate, not a copy, by a variety of publishers: Barker and Norton in London in 1611 and 1612, Hulsius (for *La perspective*) and Norton (for *Les raisons*) again in Frankfurt in 1615, Johann Theodore de Bry (for de Caus's *Hortus Palatinus*) in Frankfurt in 1620, and eventually Charles Sevestre in Paris, who used the plate for his enlarged 1624 edition of *Les raisons*. This raises the question as to who owned the title-page plate and, presumably, all the plates for the book. Two possible answers suggest themselves: first, that business transactions conferred the plates upon whichever stationer was financially backing de Caus's books for a given issue; second, that the plate was owned by the author himself and carried to whichever location his peripatetic career, dominated by the search for patronage, led him.[85] That this might be the case is suggested by the various privileges granted to de Caus for his books. Both the 1611 edition of *La perspective* and the two editions of *Les raisons* bear French royal privileges granted to the author, not the publisher, for the standard period of six years, prohibiting the reproduction of the text and images without the author's express permission, within the boundaries of the kingdom of France. The wording of the privileges is certainly consistent with the notion that de Caus retained ownership of the plates, granting the author permission

> … to print these works through the offices of whichever printer he deems fit, and to likewise offer them for sale through whichever people he should choose for the duration of six years from the first day that they are printed, during which time we prohibit all printers and booksellers of this our realm to print or have printed the said books ….[86]

It seems likely, then, that de Caus retained ownership of the plates for his book (perhaps implying that he contributed financially to its printing) and that the market for his work was sufficiently healthy for a Continental stationer, such as Hulsius, to take the not inconsiderable financial risk of publishing *La perspective* without the safety net of royal support.

The case study presented here has shown the extent to which a focus on the production, rather than the contents, of Early Modern printed books may reap valuable rewards. The production history of *La perspective* reveals a rich web of interactions between a wide variety of individuals, most of whom were connected to Prince Henry and his court. Indeed, the very way in which the court operated encouraged such interactions. The overarching figure of the Prince lent credibility to the author, encouraged the involvement of prominent stationers and helped to secure the services of talented artists and artisans. Indeed, it is clear that *La perspective* should be situated at the very centre of the artistic and intellectual aspirations that characterized the Prince's ill-fated court. The fact that, despite first being published in England, the work was written in French suggests that (initially at least) it was intended for consumption by a small, courtly elite, rather than being a commercial work that could be marketed to a wide audience. However, it is also clear that, through Norton and Hulsius, the second and third issues of *La perspective* reached the Continental market, although the exact particulars of its reception remain elusive. While further work must be undertaken on the distribution of books by de Caus (and authors like him) before a satisfactory account of the impact of works such as *La perspective* may be achieved, it is clear that by examining the role of stationers who procured books for royalty and courtiers (such as Barker and Norton) as well as the mechanisms of the book trade (most notably the Frankfurt Book Fair) we can edge closer to a more complete, accurate and useful image of the role such works played in the transformation of knowledge and the arts in the Early Modern period.

Perhaps most importantly, the case of *La perspective* casts the artist-practitioner network at Richmond in a fresh light. Specifically, it reveals that Cornelis Boel's work at Prince Henry's court was far more prominent and extensive than previously suspected. Generally, it illuminates the manner in which books and prints presented to Prince Henry were produced: through the agency of intricate relationships between artists and artisans, individuals drawn to England from abroad who shared a similar status and (most probably) common beliefs, and whose aesthetic and worldly ambitions created a dynamic, if short-lived, artistic community centred on Richmond palace and the figure of the Prince.

NOTES

This essay is a revised version of parts of Chapter 3 of my 'Architects, Engineers, and Instruments: Technology and the Book in Late Renaissance Europe', 2 vols, unpublished D.Phil., (Oxford, 2005). My work on de Caus has benefited greatly from conversations with Luke Morgan, whose doctoral dissertation 'Salomon de Caus and early seventeenth-century landscape design', Ph.D. diss. (Melbourne, 2004), is now the starting point for any serious assessment of de Caus's life and work. I am grateful to Ian Maclean and John Barnard for their thoughtful comments on the text and to Tim Wilks, especially, for his assistance in the analysis of watermarks and the distribution of printing responsibilities.

1 R. Peake, prefatory epistle in S. Serlio, *The first Booke of Architecture, made by Sebastian Serly entreating of Geometrie* (London, 1611), n.p.

2 The earliest was Richard Haydocke's translation of Lomazzo, *A Tracte Containing the Artes of curious Paintinge, Caruinge & Buildinge* (Oxford, 1598).

3 See R. Strong, *Henry Prince of Wales and England's Lost Renaissance* (London, 1986), pp. 184–200; T. Wilks, '"Paying special attention to the adorning of a most beautiful gallery": The Pictures in St James's Palace, 1603–49', *The Court Historian*, 10, no. 2 (December, 2005), pp. 149–72.

4 See L. Campbell, *The Early Flemish Pictures in the Collection of H.M. The Queen* (Cambridge, 1985), no. 83.

5 De Vries was, of course, the author of numerous treatises on perspective. See H. Borggrefe, T. Fusening and B. Uppenkamp (eds.), *Hans Vredeman de Vries und die Renaissance im Norden* (Munich, 2002). De Vries's published works were certainly known in England at this time, though the extent to which his treatises on perspective were read and digested in unclear. They were clearly considered important enough to be purchased for Thomas Bodley's library in the early years of the seventeenth century. See A. Marr, '"Curious and Useful Buildings": The 'Mathematical Model' of Sir Clement Edmondes', *The Bodleian Library Record*, 18, no. 2 (2004), pp. 108–50, Appendix 1.

6 For de Caus's life and works see the classic, but now out-of-date, study by C.S. Maks, *Salomon de Caus, 1576–1626* (Paris, 1935); Georg Müller, 'Salomon de Caus und die Wasserkünste des Coudenberg-Gartens in Brüssel', *Die Gartenkunst*, 3 (1991), pp. 159–74; B. Franke, '"… zur Lust und Zierde der Palläst und Gärten" – Salomon de Caus und die Grottenkunst', in U. Härting (ed.), *Gärten und Höfe der Rubenszeit im Spiegel der*

Malerfamilien Brueghel und der Künstler um Peter Paul Rubens (Munich, 2000), pp. 83–88; R. Strong, *The Renaissance Garden in England* (London, 1979), pp. 73–111; H. Vérin, 'Salomon de Caus, un mécanicien praticien', *Revue de l'art*, no. 129 (2000–03), pp. 70–76; Morgan, 'Salomon de Caus', *passim*.

7 It seems probable that de Caus was, like the mathematician Thomas Harriot, a 'guest tutor' of the Prince. Any lessons that de Caus provided to Henry would have been approved, and perhaps arranged, by the Prince's principal teacher, Adam Newton.

8 L. Morgan, 'Landscape Design in England *circa* 1610: The Contribution of Salomon de Caus, *Studies in the History of Gardens and Designed Landscapes*, vol. 23, no. 1 (2003), pp. 1–21 (p. 2).

9 Morgan has clarified that de Caus probably arrived in England in September or October of 1610, his final payment for work in Brussels being made for the period 14 February to 13 August 1610; Morgan, 'Landscape Design', p. 2 and n. 15. De Caus's decision to move to London was, apparently, occasioned by the destruction of one of his grottoes by the drunken Prince de Condé. He left the Archducal court in disgust after the Prince left the building, in de Caus's words, '*rompu et gasté*'. See Strong, *Renaissance Garden*, p. 74. It should be noted, however, that as the Prince de Condé left Brussels in the last days of February 1610 there was a significant time gap between the destruction of the grotto and de Caus's decision to leave the Archdukes' service. This suggests that what we are witnessing is the dimming of one source of patronage while another was growing steadily brighter, rather than a sudden break. For the Prince de Condé's movements see T. Sawyer (ed.), *Memorials of Affairs of State in the Reigns of Q. Elizabeth and K. James I. Collected (chiefly) from the Original Papers of … Sir Ralph Winwood*, 3 vols. (London, 1725), III, pp. 122, 129, 130, 135.

10 Theodore Turquet de Mayerne, a Huguenot like de Caus, did a similar thing, travelling to London from Paris several times (and even being appointed one of the Queen's physicians in 1606) before moving to London permanently in 1610. It is possible that, like Mayerne, de Caus initially considered Anne of Denmark a likely patron, perhaps hoping to contribute to her gardens at Somerset House, works for which were underway in the spring of 1609.

11 On de Caus's English period see, in addition to sources cited in note 6, T. Wilks, 'The Court Culture of Prince Henry and his Circle', 2 vols., unpublished D.Phil. (Oxford, 1988), I, pp. 143–47, and '"Forbear the heat and haste of building": Rivalries among the Designers at Prince Henry's Court, 1610–12', *The Court Historian*, vol. 6, no. 1 (2001), pp. 49–65.

12 It seems that *Institution harmonique* (1615), a treatise on musical theory, should be designated de Caus's second published work as in the dedication of this book the author notes that he plans to bring out a work on hydraulic machines (*Les raisons*) should the present work find favour. I am grateful to Luke Morgan for bringing this to my attention.

13 '*pour satisfaire a sa gentille curiosité, qui desiroit tousiours voir et cognoistre quelque choses de nouveau*'.
S. de Caus, *Les raisons des forces mouvantes tant utiles que plaisantes* (Frankfurt, 1615), 'A la tresillustre et vertueuse Princesse Elizabeth'. For the relationship of de Caus's works to the culture of curiosity and wonder in the late Renaissance see A. Marr, '*Gentille curiosité*: Wonder-working and the culture of automata in the late Renaissance', in R.J.W. Evans and A. Marr (eds.), *Curiosity and Wonder from the Renaissance to the Enlightenment* (Aldershot, 2006), pp. 149–70. For Henry's interest in mechanical contrivances of the sort illustrated in *Les raisons* see Wilks, 'Court Culture', I, pp. 201–03.

14 For de' Servi, see C. Pagnini, *Costantino de' Servi, architetto-scenografo fiorentino alla corte d'Inghliterra (1611–1615)* (Florence, 2006). For Drebbel, see L.E. Harris, *The Two Netherlanders. Humphrey Bradley, Cornelius Drebbel* (Cambridge, 1961).

15 For Renaissance perspective treatises in general, see M. Kemp, *The Science of Art* (New Haven and London, 1990). Publications on the visual arts in England at this time were few and far between. See L. Gent, *Picture and Poetry 1560–1620: Relations between Literature and the Visual Arts in the English Renaissance* (Leamington Spa, 1981).

16 Morgan provides a useful summary of the book's contents and contribution to perspective theory in 'Salomon de Caus', pp. 131–36, noting that de Caus's treatise shows evidence of the author's awareness of Keplerian optics as well as standard Euclidean geometry.

17 Wilks, 'Rivalries', p. 58.

18 For a bibliography of de Caus's printed works, with a discussion of the production of *Les raisons*, see A. Marr, 'Architects, Engineers, and Instruments: Technology and the Book in Late Renaissance Europe', 2 vols., unpublished D. Phil (Oxford, 2005), I, Chapter 3, and II, Appendix 2.

19 M. Corbett and R.W. Lightbown, *The Comely Frontispiece. The Emblematic Title-page in England 1550–1660* (London, Henley and Boston, 1979), p. 1. On Early Modern frontispieces in general, see W.B. Ashworth Jr., 'The Hapsburg Circle', in B. Moran (ed.), *Patronage and Institutions: Science, Technology, and Medicine at the European Court, 1500–1750* (Woodbridge, 1991), pp. 137–67; P. Burke, 'Reflections on the Frontispiece Portrait in the Renaissance', in A. Köstler and E. Seidl (eds.), *Bildnis und Image: das Portrait zwischen Intention und Rezeption* (Cologne and Vienna, 1996), pp. 151–62; V. Remmert, 'Picturing the Scientific Revolution: Frontispieces, their function and audience in the seventeenth century', in S. Kusukawa and I. Maclean (eds.), *Transmitting Knowledge: Words, Images and Instruments in Early Modern Europe* (Oxford, 2006), pp. 240–70.

20 See, by way of comparison, Adrian Johns's discussion of Tycho Brahe in *The Nature of the Book: Print and Knowledge in the Making* (Chicago and London, 1998), p. 14 and n. 21.

21 For a discussion of de Caus's rhetorical strategies, see Spriggs, 'Fabrique et discours'; Vérin, 'Salomon de Caus'; Marr, 'Gentille curiosité'.

22 On the office of King's Printer, see H.R. Plomer, 'The King's Printing House under the Stuarts', *The Library*, 2nd series, 2 (1901–02), pp. 353–75. It should be noted that Barker and Norton held different privileges despite both being King's Printers. I am grateful to John Barnard for bringing this to my attention.

23 See S. Shapin, *A Social History of Truth: Civility and Science in Seventeenth-Century England* (Chicago, 1994); Johns, *Nature of the Book*, esp. pp. 31–32, 187–88, 475–76, and 314–15; C. Muldrew, 'The currency of credit and personality: belief, trust, and the economics of reputation in early modern English society', in L. Fontaine *et al.* (eds.), *Des personnes aux institutions* (Louvain-la-Neuve, 1997), pp. 58–79.

24 On gift-giving in this period, see N.Z. Davis, 'Beyond the market: books as gifts in sixteenth-century France', *Transactions of the Royal Historical Society*, 5th series, 33 (1983), pp. 68–88, and *The Gift in Sixteenth-Century France* (Oxford, 2000); M. Biagioli, 'Galileo's System of Patronage', *History of Science*, 28 (1990), pp. 1–26, and *Galileo, Courtier: The Practice of Science in the Culture of Absolutism* (Chicago and London, 1993), pp. 36–54. On the role of patronage in Early Modern printing, see e.g. G. Parry, 'Patronage and the Printing of Learned Works for the Author', in J. Barnard, D.F. McKenzie, and M. Bell (eds.), *The Cambridge History of the Book in Britain, Vol. IV: 1557–1695* (Cambridge, 2002), pp. 174–88.

25 On which see S. Eiche, 'Prince Henry's Richmond: the Project by Costantino de' Servi', *Apollo*, vol. 148, no. 441 (November, 1998), pp. 10–14; Wilks, 'Rivalries', p. 58. Wilks compares de Caus's presentation of *La perspective* to Peake's publication of Serlio in the same year, although Morgan recently challenged this view in 'Landscape Design'.

26 A.W. Pollard, R.G. Redgrave, and K. Pantzer, *A short-title catalogue of books printed in England, Scotland & Ireland and of English books printed abroad, 1475–1640*, 2nd edn, 3 vols. (London, 1986–92), I, nos. 4868.7 and 4869 respectively (STC hereafter). It is important to stress that Barker's was the first issue, in 1611, as Norton's 1612 issue is usually cited as the earliest copy.

27 The second edition of *STC* lists the Hulsius issue as a variant issue, dated (incorrectly) in the *Addenda* to 1619 or later.

28 On Barker's professional activities see Barnard, *Cambridge History of the Book*, pp. 457–67.

29 Martin also notes, however, that London was to expand exponentially as a centre of book production from c. 1621–60. See H.-J. Martin, *The French Book: Religion, Absolutism, and Readership*, trans. P.H. and N. Saenger (Baltimore and London, 1996), pp. 4–5 and 21–23.

30 See H.-J. Martin, *Print, Power, and People in 17th-Century France*, trans. D. Gerard (Metuchen, N.J., and London, 1993), p. 254. See also the evidence on production costs for the Plantin publishing house presented in L. Voet, *The Golden Compasses: A History and Evaluation of the Printing and Publishing Activities of the Officina Plantiniana at Antwerp*, 2 vols. (Amsterdam and New York, 1969–72) and for the near-contemporary production of Mutio

Oddi's *Dello squadro*, on which see A. Marr, 'The production and distribution of Mutio Oddi's *Dello squadro* (1625)', in Kusukawa and Maclean, *Transmitting Knowledge*, pp. 165–92.

31 On the relatively common practice of joint publishing in the early seventeenth century, see Martin, *Print, Power, and People*, pp. 236–38 and 256.

32 A possible backer may have been Jacob le Maire, a French Huguenot (like de Caus) born in Antwerp and son of the extremely wealthy merchant Isaac le Maire. Jacob le Maire wrote the celebratory acrostic that appears at the beginning of *La perspective* (it is signed 'Jacques la Maire'). This, along with his confessional sympathy towards the author and his interest in the mathematical arts (such as navigation) suggest that he may have supported financially the production of de Caus's book.

33 The direct engagement of Early Modern patrons in this sort of project is not unheard of, and we should not rule out entirely the possibility that Henry contributed financially to the production of de Caus's book. To take just one example, Henri IV instructed his *Ingénieur du Roi*, Jean Errard, to produce a treatise on fortification, the celebrated *La fortification reduicte en art et demonstrée* (1600). A payment for 220 écus was paid to Errard for the production of 'un livre de l'art des fortifications que Sa Majesté luy a commandé faire' (quoted in D. Buisseret, *Ingénieurs et fortifications avant Vauban: L'Organisation d'un service Royale au XVIe–XVIIe siècle* (Paris, 2002), p. 74). A draft manuscript of the work, to the best of my knowledge not previously identified as such, is Bibliothéque Nationale de France, MS Fr. 663: 'Le Traittié que fist un tres sollemnel et notable chevalier, nommé maistre Jean Herard, touchant l'office d'armes'. On Errard, whose career bears some striking similarities to that of his countryman de Caus, see M. Lallemand and A. Boinette, *Jean Errard de Bar-le-Duc, premier ingénieur du très chrestien roy de France et de Navarre Henri IV, sa vie, ses œuvres, sa fortification (lettres inédites de Henri IV et de Sully)* (Paris, 1884).

34 He did, though, have books printed for him at Eton. See the entry for 'Norton, John I', in STC, vol. III.

35 As explained below, Barker probably did not undertake the work in-house due to the fact that the production of *La perspective* seems to have been begun and almost completed on the Continent and only finished in London.

36 The second edition of STC states that Field printed all of 'Miroirs'. As argued below, this seems unlikely since this part of the book features copperplates and there is no evidence (based on his other known publications) that he owned a rolling press.

37 As *STC* shows, Field (active between 1588 and his death in 1624) was a prolific printer. Numerous foreign language titles (mainly translations) are attributed to his printing house.

38 Following their marriage, Field succeeded to the Vautrollier London printing house, which had been managed by Jacqueline during Thomas I's visits to Edinburgh, where he ran a bookshop and printing house. See the entries for 'Field, Richard', 'Vautrollier, Jacqueline' and 'Vautrollier, Thomas I' in STC, vol. III.

39 While working for Prince Henry de Caus was given the services of a translator called Samuel Mercer. See Wilks, 'Rivalries', p. 57, citing PRO E351/3247.

40 Barker may have decided to employ Field rather than print the work in his own shop because throughout 1611 he was stretched to capacity by the production of the Authorized Version of the Bible, for which he held the privilege. See J. Barnard, 'The Financing of the Authorized Version 1610–12: Robert Barker and 'Combining' and 'Sleeping' Stationers', *Publishing History*, 57 (2005), pp. 5–52.

41 Jan I Mommaert was active as a printer from 1585, following his return from Salamanca where he may have worked as an apprentice in the atelier of Mathias Grast. His printing materials derived from Michiel van Hamont, the witness at his wedding to Jeanne Lodewij in 1585. Mommaert's second wife, Martine van Straeten, and his son, Jan II Mommaert (b. 1611), continued to run the publishing house following Jan I's death in 1627 or 1631. Though the date of Jan II Mommaert's death is unknown, he continued to publish until the late 1660s. See, for example, his 1662 edition of Cervantes' *Don Quixote*. See P-E. Claessens, 'Deux familles d'imprimeurs brabançons … les Mommaert et les Frieux, 1585–1777', *Brabantica*, 2 (1957), pp. 339–43 and (1958), pp. 205–11.

42 As Martin notes, 'ordinary printers rarely owned the special type of press used for printing plates', Martin, *Print, Power, and People*, p. 254.

43 Indeed, it is rather puzzling that Mommaert should have been approached to produce an illustrated book of this type. It may be the case (given Mommaert's lack of experience in the field) that the printing of the copperplates in *La perspective* was contracted out to another printer, who may or may not have worked in Brussels (see below).

44 On Prince Henry's association with books and printing, see Wilks, 'Court Culture', I, pp. 54–85; Parry, 'Patronage and the Printing of Learned Works', pp. 180–81.

45 F. Devon (ed.), *Issues of the Exchequer, being payments made out of His Majesty's Revenue during the reign of King James I* (London, 1836), p. 164, quoted in Wilks, 'Court Culture', I, p. 68.

46 On Norton's life and career, see J. Barnard, 'Politics, Profits and ?Idealism: John Norton and Sir Thomas Bodley', *The Bodleian Library Record*, vol. 17, no. 6 (2002), pp. 385–408.

47 *Ibid.*, p. 385.

48 See *ibid.*, *passim*. It should be noted that Norton's Continental contacts seem to date from his Edinburgh period onwards.

49 As Barnard notes, both Norton and Bill were instrumental in the 'propaganda wars' centred on James I's *Triplici nodo* of 1607. The Norton firm published and sold polemical works by James and his supporters, advertised in the Frankfurt Book Fair catalogues, as well as purchasing Continental responses from the other side of the debate. See Barnard, 'Politics, Profits and ?Idealism', pp. 396–97.

50 Surprisingly, given the quality of his engravings, little work on Boel has been undertaken to date. This may be due to the hitherto limited number of engravings attributed to Boel from his English period. See A.M. Hind, *Engraving in England in the Sixteenth and Seventeenth Centuries. A Descriptive Catalogue with Introductions*, 3 vols (Cambridge, 1952–64), II, pp. 57–60, 313–15; B.G. Vega, 'Cornelis Boel', in *Grove Dictionary of Art Online* (Oxford, accessed 2003). The fullest account to date is that in Strong, *Henry Prince of Wales*, pp. 118, 131–37.

51 Further work needs to be carried out on the sources for the numerous architectural images (including, in some cases, entire rooms) that appear throughout *La perspective*, as Boel or de Caus may have been inspired by the decorative schemes and room layouts of St James or Henry's long-vanished Richmond Palace. On Henry's residences see Strong, *Henry, Prince of Wales*, *passim*; Wilks, 'Court Culture', I, pp. 133–59.

52 See Griffiths, *The Print in Stuart Britain*, p. 18. Veen's insertion of various title-pages was a cunning way to personalise what was essentially a single edition into multiple patronage-seeking gifts. It is not clear how successful they were, however, as Griffiths notes that from the wording of the English edition it is clear that Veen did not know the Herberts and that his dedication was without permission.

53 See Strong, *Henry, Prince of Wales*, pp. 131–32. Boel's Bible title-page had an afterlife in William Hole's engraving for Thomas Lodge's translation of Seneca's *Workes* (London, 1614), which features copies of two of the evangelists and several attendant figures from Boel's image.

54 Griffiths, *The Print in Stuart Britain*, p. 54. Little is known about the life of Delaram (active 1615–24) beyond what can be deduced from his prints. See *ibid.*, pp. 53–56; Hind, *Engraving in England*, II, pp. 215–42.

55 Boel's attachment to Prince Henry seems to have been somewhat informal; he is not recorded in any of the household lists. Professionals attached to the Prince's household were, of course, allowed to take on private work. It may be that Boel's portrait of Prince Henry (see below) falls into this category.

56 Notably, a payment made to Boel refers to him as a 'Frenchman' ('A Frencheman that mad the Frontispiece of the Byble', PRO E.351/2794, Privy purse acts, Henry, Prince of Wales, 1610–1612), perhaps because at this stage he was so closely associated with de Caus. The reference to the Bible frontispiece does not necessarily imply that Henry paid Boel for the engraving. It may equally be a general reward for his attendance at the Richmond court. There is one other payment to Boel in the Prince's accounts, for the sum of £13, which probably paid for his crossing from the Low Countries ('A Duche graver sent for xiij li', PRO E.351/2794, Privy purse acts, Henry, Prince of Wales, 1610–12).

57 This notion is perhaps borne out by the evidence of watermarks, taken from a 1612 issue of *La perspective* currently in the possession of Prof. Edward Chaney. Whilst none of the watermarks have been positively identified, their distribution may help explain the apportioning of printing responsibilities. The sheets printed by

Field bear a 'grapes' watermark, while those printed by Mommaert (3 sheets of 9 gatherings) bear an 'H' inside a heart. However, at the beginning of the fifth of the Mommaert gatherings we find a different watermark, an elaborate armorial surmounted by a crown. This watermark also appears on a fold-out leaf inserted immediately after this sequence of gatherings and on the very last gathering, which is simply a folded sheet bearing a decorative illustration of an arm bearing a stellated dodecahedron. This distribution suggests that Mommaert sent out to a rolling press all the sheets on which he had printed letterpress on at least one page and which now required a plate or plates to be printed on them. But, in instances where plates were to be printed on otherwise blank sheets (i.e., where there was no letterpress on any of the four pages making up a single sheet which the imposition decreed would take one or more engravings), it made no sense for one printer to provide another with fresh paper for the job. As the 'crown' watermark suggests, in these instances the copperplate printer used sheets from his own stock. A complicating factor, however, is the fact that that the Hulsius issue of *La perspective* bears an additional 'eagle' watermark (personal communication from Houghton Library, Harvard). As such, the evidence of watermarks is not conclusive and further examination of multiple copies of the three issues of the book will clearly be necessary to illuminate the relationship between the supply of paper and the distribution of printing responsibilities.

58 N. Barker, 'Editing the Past: Classical and Historical Scholarship', in Barnard, McKenzie, Bell, *History of the Book in Britain*, pp. 206–27, 215. It should be noted that because *La perspective* was not reset for the Norton issue, and as the title-page is fully engraved (i.e., it does not incorporate letterpress), the 1612 issue could be produced entirely in England. All it required was the printing of an altered title-page.

59 Johnson, who lists the title-page as anonymous, notes '[the] engraved title can hardly rank as English; it was used by the author in other books printed at Frankfort'. A.F. Johnson, *A Catalogue of Engraved and Etched English Title-Pages Down to the Death of William Faithorne, 1691* (Oxford, 1934), p. 61.

60 For Oliver's miniature see G. Reynolds, *The Sixteenth- and Seventeenth-Century Miniatures in the Collection of Her Majesty the Queen* (London, 1999), no. 54; Strong, *Henry, Prince of Wales*, pp. 119, 132.

61 The term and herm figures flanking the title seem to be original to the *La perspective* title-page. The stellated dodecahedron, however, is copied directly from Wenzel Jamnitzer's famous *Perspectiva corporum regularium* (1568), where it appears as plate FV. As noted above, this shape also appears, enigmatically clutched by a hand emerging from a cloud, on the final sheet of *La perspective*, probably as a decorative flourish. I have been unable to identify the copy of Jamnitzer's book used by Boel/de Caus, although it may have been de Caus's personal copy. Jamnitzer's book was extremely rare in England at this date – no copy is listed in the Bodleian Library before 1620 or in the libraries surveyed in R.J. Fehrenbach, and E.S. Leedham-Green (eds.), *Private Libraries in Renaissance England: A Collection and Catalogue of Tudor and Early Stuart Book-Lists*, 5 vols. (New York and Marlborough, 1992).

62 See Strong, *Henry, Prince of Wales*, pp. 131–32.

63 For example, Tim Wilks has suggested, in a personal communication, that Boel may only have acted as cutter for the portrait of Princess Elizabeth, which may have been based on a studio drawing by Marcus Gheeraerts the Younger, possibly provided by Gheeraert's brother-in-law, Isaac Oliver, acting as intermediary. If Boel was not an accomplished draughtsman the question arises as to who designed the frontispiece for the 1611 Authorized Version of the Bible.

64 It is possible that de Jode was involved in the printing of the *La perspective* plates. The geographical proximity of Brussels and Antwerp certainly suggest that he could readily have acted as a collaborator with Mommaert.

65 Strong, *Henry, Prince of Wales*, p. 132. Strong persuasively suggests that the sources for the iconography are two engravings by William Rogers of the Elizabethan military heroes Essex and Cumberland.

66 Nonetheless, it should be remembered that the *putti* were (in English terms at least) highly accomplished and, in their relationship to the architectural features, provide a perspective lesson in themselves – they were technically beyond the competence of virtually all English artists at the time.

67 However, the proximity between aspects of de Caus's text and the frontispiece illustration for his second

published work, *Les raisons des forces mouvantes*, strongly suggests that, in this instance at least, the author was indeed the 'inventor' of the frontispiece image for his book. See Marr, *'Gentille curiosité'*, pp. 156–59.

68 In this particular case, collaboration is made more plausible by the immediate geographical proximity of Boel and de Caus, as well as their common emigrant status. Interestingly, the calligraphy of the imprint on the title-page to *La perspective* is particularly fine. It may be the case that the imprint was engraved by Boel after penmanship by a courtier associated with Prince Henry, such as John Davies of Hereford. I am grateful to Tim Wilks for this suggestion.

69 It should be noted, though, that appealing to the Prince was probably only one of several roles that de Caus planned for his book. By having the work printed, de Caus could potentially reach an audience outside his immediate court circle, fashioning an international reputation for himself – doubtless a calculated move given the mutable, unstable nature of employment at court.

70 Strong, *Henry, Prince of Wales*, p. 133. For the idea of 'magnificence' in the Renaissance see A.D.F. Jenkins, 'Cosimo de'Medici's Patronage of Architecture and the Theory of Magnificence', *Journal of the Warburg and Courtauld Institutes*, 33 (1970), pp. 162–70; R. Strong, *Art and Power: Renaissance Festivals, 1450–1650* (Woodbridge, 1984).

71 As de Caus notes in his dedication to Henry, *'entre les sciences qui despendantes des Mathematiques, celle icy est tant necessaire, qui est mal aisé ordonner bien les ouurages tant d'Architecture que de peinture'*. De Caus, *La perspective*, 'Au serenissime Prince de Galles'. On the prominence of drawing as a courtly pastime and useful practice in the Early Modern period see e.g. Gent, *Picture and Poetry*; A. Bermingham, *Learning to Draw: Studies in the Cultural History of a Polite and Useful Art* (New Haven and London, 2000).

72 Given the complexities of the production of *La perspective*, outlined above, it may of course equally be the case that de Caus had shown the Prince a manuscript or printed sheets of the books on one of his visits to London prior to the commencement of his employment on the gardens and waterworks at Richmond Palace.

73 See Wilks, 'Court Culture', I, p. 202. Wilks lists a number of other designs and unfinished instruments used in cartography and surveying, including the renowned 'Coelesticall Automaton', a universal instrument for use in 'Cosmography, Astronomy, Geography, Navigation, or in any other Arts subalternate to the part of Geometry concerning the Sphere'. Wilks, 'Court Culture', I, p. 203. De Caus hints towards the potential military application of *La perspective* by including a chapter on the manner of drawing fortifications in plan and perspective. De Caus, *La perspective*, Chapter 21 and plate 24.

74 For the problems of estimating print runs based on the evidence of surviving copies, see I. Maclean, 'The market for scholarly books and conceptions of genre in Northern Europe, 1570–1630', in G. von Kauffmann (ed.), *Die Renaissance im Blick der Nationen Europas* (Wiesbaden, 1991), pp. 17–31. For further evidence on print runs see Voet, *Golden Compasses*.

75 No copies of *La perspective* are recorded in the book lists assessed in Fehrenbach and Leedham-Green's survey of private libraries in Renaissance England, nor in the Bodleian Library catalogues of 1605 and 1620. On the audience for publications such as *La perspective* in England at this date see Marr, '"Curious and useful buildings"'; Gent, *Picture and Poetry*, passim.

76 The library was to include 'all such important books as related to arms, chivalry, military affairs, incamping, fortification, etc., that could be got in all languages'. See 'An account of the several Libraries, public and private, in or about London, for the Satisfaction of the Curious, whether Natives or Foreigners', *The Gentleman's Magazine*, vol. 86, no. 2 (1816), p. 214, quoted in Wilks, 'Court Culture', I, p. 62. For the Lumley library, see S. Jayne and F.R. Johnson (eds.), *The Lumley Library: The Catalogue of 1609* (London, 1956).

77 '… *esperant d'auoir dans quelque temps le loisir d'acheuer un autre oeuure ia commencé'*. De Caus, *La perspective*, 'Au serenissime Prince de Galles'. It should be noted that although the first issue of *Les raisons* appeared under the imprint 'A Francfort en la boutique de Jan Norten', by the year the book was published (1615) Norton had been dead for some three years. In fact, the book was published by Norton's business partner and successor, John Bill, who continued to operate a Frankfurt bookshop under the Norton name. See Marr, 'Architects, Engineers, and Instruments', I, chapter 3.

78 The 1612 issue of *La perspective* is listed in the Frankfurt Book Fair catalogue for Spring 1612 under *Libri pere-grine Idiomata*: 'Declaration du Serenissime Roy de la grand Bretaigne, sur ses actions devers les Estats Generaux de Pays bas vnis, touchant le faict de Conradus Vorstius, à Londres chez Iean Norton, in 4 and 8. La perspective avec la raison des ombres & miroirs, par Salmon de Caus Ingenieur du sereniss. Prince de Calles, *ibid.* ['à Londres chez Iean Norton'] in fol.', *Indicis generalibus continuatio, in quo continetur designatio libro-rum, qui nundinis Vernalibus Francofortensibus & Lipsensibus Anni 1612* (Frankfurt, 1612), sig. E4[a].

79 The involvement of women in the book trade is a relatively common occurrence in this period. See M. Bell, 'Women in the English book trade 1557–1700', *Leipziger Jarbuch zur Buchgeschichte*, 6 (1996), pp. 13–45.

80 It is not clear whether the Hulsius family were printers as well as publishers. Levinius Hulsius's skills as a metalworker (see below) certainly do not preclude this as a possibility.

81 This issue is not recorded in Teach Gnudi's bibliographical study of Ramelli's book. See A. Ramelli, *The Various and Ingenious Machines of Agostino Ramelli: A Classic Sixteenth-Century Treatise on Technology*, ed. and trans. M. Teach Gnudi (Aldershot and New York, 1976), pp. 24–40. The Hand Press Book database lists only two surviving copies of the Hulsius edition of Ramelli.

82 Given the importance conferred on Tycho's book production by both Eisenstein and Johns, a more thor-ough investigation of the Hulsius firm is a *desideratum*. See E. Eisenstein, *The Printing Press as an Agent of Change: Communications and Cultural Transformations in Early-Modern Europe*, 2 vols. (Cambridge, 1979), II, *passim*; Johns, *Nature of the Book*, pp. 18–19. For a brief account of the Hulsius firm see S. De Renzi, *Instruments in Print: Books from the Whipple Collection* (Cambridge, 2000), pp. 3–6. It is interesting to note that Prince Henry owned a copy of the 1602 Hulsius edition of the *Instaurata* (Wilks, 'Court Culture', I, p. 69).

83 Levinius Hulsius may have been related to the German goldsmith, engraver and painter Esaias Hulsius, al-though this has yet to be established conclusively. Esaias Hulsius, like de Caus, also worked on grottoes and fountains, although no connection between the two is known. See 'Esaias Hulsen' in *Grove Dictionary of Art Online* (Oxford, accessed 2003).

84 See, for example, the copy in the Houghton Library, Harvard, Typ 620.19.264 F. In addition to Harvard, copies survive in Folger, Newberry, Michigan, and Yale.

85 Given the weight of copperplates this would have involved considerable labour and expense. There is evi-dence to suggest that Early Modern authors actually transported copperplates of their publications them-selves. For example, a French author, Joseph de la Pise, financed his own plates for *Tableau de l'histoire des princes et principauté d'Orange* (The Hague, 1639) and then brought them from Orange to The Hague. In a diary-cum-account book of this trip (preserved in MS) he records that one of his three horses was packed with '*mes papiers et planches de cuivre pour mon livre*'. These concerned the huge engravings of, in particular, buildings, which he had commissioned from the French engraver Jean Bauguin. See M. Keblusek, *Boeken in de hofstad. Haagse boekcultuur in de Gouden Eeuw* (Hilversum, 1997), pp. 186–87. I am grateful to Marika Keblusek for bringing this example to my attention.

86 '*de faires Imprimer lesdicts Liures par tel Imprimeur que bon luy semblera & mesmes de le faire vendre & distribuer par telles personnes qu'il voudra choisir & ce durant le terme de six ans à compter du jour que lesdicts liures seront achevez d'imprimer pendant lequel temps nous defendons à tous Imprimeurs & Librarires de cestuy nostre Royaume de Imprimer ou faire Imprimer lesdicts Liures … '.* S. de Caus, *Les raisons des forces mouvantes* (Frankfurt, 1615), 'Privilege'. Notably, the privilege specified not only the book itself but also the engravings ('*les tailles douces des figures qui sont dedans*').

9| Calvinist Internationalism and the Shaping of Jacobean Foreign Policy

D.J.B. Trim

The quatercentenary of the death of Elizabeth I received much greater attention than the same anniversary of the accession of James I. That the Jacobean accession had its own separate commemorations, which did not, however, match the celebrations in honour of Gloriana, reveals the enduring taste of both academic and public history for Elizabeth over James[1] – and of both over Parliament, which had the 350th anniversary of its Cromwellian expulsion almost entirely ignored.[2] In addition, however, it also highlights that the passing of the Virgin Queen and the advent of the first Scottish King of England are seen as distinct events. This perpetuates an historiographical orthodoxy that emphasizes change, rather than continuity, in Tudor-Stuart England. This essay argues instead that, in the area of foreign policy, much remained the same in the first years of the Jacobean regime; change came after the deaths of Henry, Prince of Wales, and of royal ministers such as the Earl of Salisbury and Lord Chancellor Ellesmere who, like Prince Henry, preferred the Elizabethan approach to Continental Protestantism – and in particular to Continental Calvinism, which, before the expansion of the Thirty Years' War in the mid-1620s, was the form of Protestantism that was most endangered by Catholic and especially Habsburg arms.

This essay also stresses the importance of foreign events and foreign policy debates for the English body politic. It thus underscores Jonathan Scott's assertion that seventeenth-century English and British history makes sense only in the context of the 'wider European religious and political complex of which it formed only a part'; and supports the view, espoused by Simon Adams, Thomas Cogswell and Andrew Thrush, that domestic politics was greatly influenced by debates over foreign policy.[3]

*

In considering the early part of James VI's reign as James I it is impossible not to be struck by the haste with which he and his ministers obtained the successful negotiation of the Treaty of London with Spain, ending a war that had lasted eighteen years within seventeen months of the new Brutus's accession to the English throne.[4] This precipitate peace-making, together with James's ecumenical instincts, his later prolonged efforts to obtain a 'Spanish match' for his heir, and his refusal to intervene openly in the Thirty Years' War, even on behalf of his own daughter's family and in spite of sustained Parliamentary requests that he do so, produce an apparently clear picture of a regime that was, right from the start, in complete contrast to that which preceded it.[5] It has seemed evident to most scholars that James VI and I and the ministers he chose were always cool towards militant Calvinist internationalism and were, if not pacifistic, at least non-aggressive.

However, for the first third, if not half, of the reign of James I, he and his counsellors pursued foreign policy aims – and even means – largely similar to those of the Elizabethan government. Important change did eventually occur, but the attitudes and policies that are often seen as characteristic of the Jacobean regime really originated only during the years 1612–19. The Treaty of London is now a red herring, blinding us to continuity between Elizabethan and Jacobean policy, because it has generally been read in the light of subsequent events. Dr Adams has already argued for a shift in Jacobean foreign policy, which he dates to 1616.[6] This essay supports his contention that a shift occurred, but in addition it demonstrates that in the first decade of the new king of Great Britain's reign, James and his government supported the Dutch Republic and cause of international Protestantism far more than has previously been realised; this means that the policy shift of the middle years of the reign was far more significant than current scholarship acknowledges.

The Jacobean regime continued Elizabethan policy – effectively continued, too, a confessional struggle, despite formal peace with Spain – because there was a powerful consensus within the English polity that this should happen. This naturally raises the question of how a shift away from a Protestant foreign policy (broadly defined) affected politics within England.[7] This essay first addresses the issues which seem to point to a significant difference between the last Tudor and the first Stuart; it then demonstrates that the Jacobean policy stance was essentially similar to the Elizabethan one and was supported by a significant (perhaps even the greater) part of the English political nation; so that when Jacobean foreign policy ceased to be confessionally partisan the Stuarts were left substantially out of tune with a wide cross-section of the polity.

*

As James VI of Scotland, the King had enjoyed good relations with the States-General of the Netherlands and the Dutch commander-in-chief, Prince Maurits, and consistently exchanged cordial correspondence with both, especially, though not only, about the recruitment of Scottish mercenaries, which James facilitated.[8] The amicable relations between the King of Scots and the Dutch Republic were amply illustrated in 1594 on the birth of the Prince of Scotland, later Prince of Wales, when the Dutch embassy presented gifts that impressed an anonymous Scottish chronicler with their generosity, demonstrating, as he put it, 'thair forder benevolence towart the King, the prince and the cuntrie'.[9] These gifts included announcement of an annual payment of five thousand guilders to be made to the young Henry

– drawn, appropriately enough, from lands of the city of Ter Veere, where Scottish soldiers had fought in their first campaign in the Low Countries in 1572. The revenue of these lands was hypothecated to Prince Henry's pension, equivalent to some £500 sterling *per annum*, and the royal household benefited from the payment of this pension from the Prince's birth until his death.[10]

As James I of England, the King was constantly being advised of the importance for British security of preserving the Dutch state – a point of which he probably did not need much persuading, given the good relations he had enjoyed with the republic over the years. Much of this advice originated with people who had opposed peace with Spain in the first place and/or were trying to undermine the Treaty of London.[11] However, even counsellors and courtiers willing to support their sovereign in making peace with the Spanish nevertheless emphasized to the king the need not to abandon the Dutch to their possible fate.[12]

Indeed, the new King's chief minister was Robert Cecil, by 1605 created Earl of Salisbury. His late father, William Cecil, ennobled as Lord Burghley by Elizabeth, whose chief minister he was, had been personally devout and Calvinist in his theology and his mother, too, had been a notably godly Protestant.[13] Robert inherited their confessional view, consciously aligning himself with all 'that love the Gospell' in support of the United Provinces, against the forces of 'Idolatrie and superstition', as he characterized their enemies. While Cecil had supported peace talks with the Spanish in the late 1590s, attracting thereby the hostility of the Earl of Essex, he had supported *negotiations* – not peace at any price. Essex's mistrust of this position reflected his own problematic personality, rather than the reality of Cecil's commitment to the United Netherlands, or indeed to the Protestant cause in Europe more generally and in particular to the Calvinists who, at this point in history, were the Protestants chiefly threatened by Catholicism.[14]

How, then, do we explain the Treaty of London? The Dutch were undoubtedly unhappy about it and attempted to convince the new British monarchy to remain in the Eighty Years' War overtly. As will be shown, however, the Jacobean peace with Spain did not result in any lessening of English military commitment to the United Provinces: what actually happened was that the balance of financial responsibility shifted from the Anglo-British state to the Dutch Republic – or rather, completed shifting, for this was the culmination of a process that had begun at the end of 1598 when, by the terms of the York House Treaty, the Dutch took over the pay of the great majority of English troops in the Netherlands, excluding only the garrisons of the cautionary towns of Flushing and The Brill.[15] Thus, as Dr Adams has argued, James's move to make peace was not as dramatic a disjuncture with the policy of his predecessor as it appears on superficial inspection.[16]

Indeed, when English/British relations with the Spanish Monarchy and the United Provinces in the period 1604–10 are seen in long-term perspective, the impression of continuity, rather than change, is heightened further. The Elizabethan regime had only openly gone to war with Philip II in 1585, but throughout the late 1560s, the 1570s and the early 1580s, England had subsidized first the Huguenots and then the Dutch rebels-cum-Republic, had supplied their armies with victuals and munitions of war, and had supported them covertly (sometimes not so covertly) with privateers and mercenaries from England and auxiliaries from Germany.[17] Royal armies and fleets had not been deployed until the situation absolutely called for it, to stave off potential disaster in both France and the Netherlands. Elizabeth herself was not a Calvinist but, at least in the 1560s, she had been personally interested in aiding fellow Protestants; thereafter, while the government had sought to create an alliance incorporating Lutherans as well as the Reformed and while aid to Europe's Protestants had enjoyed ecumenical support among the English elite, Calvinists had been the driving force behind the consistent financial, logistical and military assistance provided to the Reformed in France, the Rhineland and the Netherlands.[18] But Calvinists were prepared to act independently to aid their confreres and the government knew it – indeed relied on it to some extent. By the late 1590s even Puritan Privy Councillors supported a return to the situation of 1585 and before, in which the Dutch and England's Reformed communities bore the burden of a war that had lasted without pause since 1572.

By the time James VI had succeeded Elizabeth as James I, Henri IV was secure on the French throne; the Dutch Republic was in a strong military position; and Lord Mountjoy's very recent victory over Irish and Spanish troops at Kinsale had effectively crushed Tyrone's rebellion. The time was thus propitious to negotiate a settlement with Spain, regardless of the identity of the English sovereign.

However, the contention of one scholar that 'the conflict in the Low Countries [was] steadily winding down' in 1603 is incorrect. The attempts by Philip III to gain the military victory that had eluded his father had foundered in Ireland but they were ongoing in the Netherlands.[19] There was thus still an imperative to aid the United Provinces – and circumstances in the Netherlands during and in the years immediately following the negotiation of formal peace with Spain during 1603–04 dictated that the necessity of aiding the Dutch was unchanged. In 1603 Ostend was still besieged, as it had been since late 1600 and would be until late 1604, and was the focus of such powerful Spanish military efforts that the town was widely called a new Troy. Its strategic location and the fact that it had been garrisoned by English troops for over fifteen years meant that, both for military operational reasons and for prestige, James – the so-called 'new Brutus' – and his Privy Council were just as committed to holding the 'new Troy' as were Maurits and the *raad van state* (council of state). After Ostend finally fell, the Dutch Republic was shaken in 1605 and 1606 by offensives conducted by the brilliant new commander-in-chief of the Spanish army of Flanders, Ambrogio Spínola.[20] As a result, neither in the negotiations for peace with Spain, nor in the decade following, did the Jacobean regime shrug off its allies in the Netherlands. Rather, it adopted the Elizabethan policy of supporting confessional allies – no longer at first hand or overtly, yet, as will be seen, still significantly.

*

It is striking that, immediately after the conclusion of the Treaty of London and probably partly in response to it, the States-General gave their agent in England (Sir Noel Caron – whose knighthood was English) the title of ambassador. Flush with the success of the Treaty of London, the Spanish plenipotentiary to the court of St James responded by trying to push what he doubtless perceived as the Habsburg advantage. He complained that accepting an envoy titled 'ambassador' from the Dutch dishonoured the Spanish king and was, furthermore, 'contrary to the league and friendship which was then betwixt them'. He requested that any Dutch representative who styled himself 'ambassador' should be denied access, 'as beeing sent from such persons as had traiterously fallen from their lord and soveraigne Prince: with many other bitter words, and full of spleen'. Instead, James, after consultation with the Privy Council,

> Thought it good to let [Philip III's ambassador] know that, by the contract of peace
> made with Spain, all neutralitie with the Netherlands was allowed him: saying
> moreover, that as he was no author of their separation from Spaine, so would he
> not breake the league and frendship, that … his kingdom [had] with them.[21]

The accession of a new king and negotiation of formal peace had not, after all, signalled a sea change in English foreign policy.

In fact, under James, the English government reverted to the practice and policy of the 1568–85 period, with which Robert Cecil was of course *au fait*, since Elizabeth's chief adviser had been his father. In 1604, rather than abandoning the preceding regime's position, the Jacobean regime actually reverted to Elizabethan type. After the Queen's death, Sir Walter Raleigh explicitly urged James to aid the Dutch using Elizabethan methods, suggesting he 'relieve the Netherlands underhand, as … her Majesty did in the Beginning of their Revolt'; and in fact, as we will see, the new king was to allow the States-General 'an underhand permission', as Salisbury put it, to raise English troops.[22]

This relieved the chief anxiety of the Dutch. Ideally, of course, they wanted England to continue as overt partner in a coalition war, but above all they wanted to be able to keep recruiting troops in James I's Great Britain, as they had in Elizabeth's England and Wales (and indeed in James VI's Scotland). The States-General, in their first communication to James after Elizabeth's death, diplomatically congratulated him on his accession to her throne and included prayers for his success, happiness, health and long life, but moved swiftly on to 'beseech' the king,

> Seeing it pleased the aforesaid Queene of famous memorie, in her latter dayes,
> to grant us leave to take up certaine souldiers in England, for to fill up and
> make compleat the English companies, that serve under us, as we likewise be-
> sought your Majestie to suffer us to doe the like in Scotland, for the Scottish

> companies: that it will now please your Majestie to grant us the effect thereof,
> that we may at this present take up the sayd souldiers both in England and
> Scotland, to be transported into the Netherlands, there to be imploied in our
> service, as the necessitie of our cause requireth … for [its] preservation.[23]

And when, shortly after, the Dutch embassy sent for his coronation arrived, upon meeting James 'they layd open unto him the estate of their affaires, and craved a supply of souldiers'. In his reply James clearly hinted that he would negotiate with the Spanish, but also promised 'with all friendly care and affection [that] hee would continue all love and friendship with them, as his predecessor had done'.[24]

This was not just diplomatic nicety. It was what actually happened. The claim, made on a celebratory medallion struck in 1604,[25] that peace with Spain would ensure 'prosperity and pure religion' must have seemed highly unlikely to those Englishmen and women committed to aiding Reformed brethren in the Netherlands, but turned out to be more than propaganda. 'Pure religion' in the Netherlands (not to mention Dutch independence) was preserved partly through British assistance.

The Treaty of London did not prohibit recruiting for the Dutch army. Even as the first negotiations commenced in the summer of 1603, two thousand English volunteers were recruited and sent to Ostend despite Spanish grumbling.[26] When peace talks began in earnest, the Habsburg ambassadors' demand that English soldiers henceforth be forbidden to serve the Dutch was refused by the King and Cecil, even though they risked a breakdown in the negotiations thereby. In order to obtain the peace settlement they were obliged to permit the King's subjects to serve the Spaniards, too – James agreed by Article 12 of the Treaty of London to 'forbid none to any side'. But Spain's agents were not permitted to recruit openly in England. It is true that, in order to maintain Britain's nominal neutrality, neither were those of the States-General. Open recruiting, by the 'stryking of Drummes and displaying of Ensignes', was reserved by James 'only to those as were to levy men for his own service'. However, Spanish recruiters who used such methods were often arrested, whereas captains in Dutch pay, as long as they were discreet, were able to raise troops with little difficulty, both in England and in Scotland. As Cecil wrote to Sir Ralph Winwood, the English ambassador in The Hague, the King by the Treaty of London promised 'neither to punish nor to stay, but only that he will not consent …. You know the latitude as well as I.'[27] When Ambassador Caron was 'denied [permission] to levy any new companies' in the winter of 1605–06, it was a necessary side-effect to the rejection of Spanish requests to recruit men for twenty to twenty-five companies in England and Ireland – and as a Spanish envoy observed, the Dutch had already raised troops in England anyway.[28] Later that year the Jacobean government moved to restrict Spanish recruiting further, in an episode illuminated by Pauline Croft.[29] Recruiting for the Dutch army could not be carried out openly, as it had before the Treaty of London, but it never faced similar sanctions.

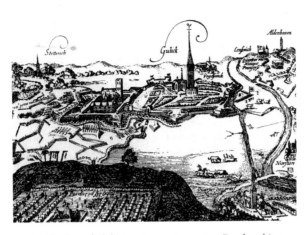

Fig. 1 *The Siege of Jülich*, 1610, in a contemporary Dutch etching

(The quarters of Prince Henry's later friend, Count Hendrik, are lower right, below Maurits's main camp.)

In fact, during the first eight years of the new reign (up to the end of the Jülich succession war of 1610) the numbers of English soldiers in Dutch employment increased. On average there were almost 5,000 English mercenaries in Dutch pay each year from 1604 to 1610 inclusive. Moreover, taking the whole of the period 1572–1610, English mercenaries, as a percentage of the total Dutch establishment, were at their greatest in 1601 (when they were almost a quarter), but every year from 1605 to 1610 inclusive they comprised at least fifteen per cent – a proportion rare in Elizabeth's reign. Furthermore, the English establishment within the Dutch army was at its greatest actual strength at any time in those forty-odd years in the crucial years of 1607 and 1608, after Spínola's great offensives momentarily had left the republic reeling.[30] Indeed, one reason Spínola was ultimately unsuccessful was the English and Scottish contingents serving the United Provinces; its English troops alone outnumbered all the Scots, Irish and English in Spanish pay. Although their numbers dropped after the agreement of the twelve years' truce between the Spanish Monarchy and the United Provinces in 1609, extra troops were raised in England in 1610 for the Jülich-Cleves succession war.[31] The Anglo-Scottish brigade in the Dutch army sent to take Jülich was commanded by Salisbury's nephew, Sir Edward Cecil.[32] As far as the Dutch were concerned, then, the Treaty of London meant that, though the English no longer contributed naval forces to the war against Spain, the number of English soldiers in the Netherlands actually increased!

Even on the seas the 1604 treaty gave the Spanish only reduced respite from Anglo-Dutch cooperation. Looking back after almost a decade of 'peace', Don Diego Sarmiento de Acuña (later Count of Gondomar), ambassador to England, complained to the Privy Council that England's naval war had not stopped – that on the contrary, since the treaty there had been 'brought into this kingedome more than three Millions of goodes, take from the kinge of Spaines subjectes, soe that soe much harme was not done to them in tyme of warr'.[33]

*

In the decade after the Treaty of London the British government did more than turn a blind
eye to Dutch recruiting and English privateering. King James's ambassador in The Hague
was, after all, a member of the *raad van state*, the body that directly oversaw the republic's
armed forces. Nor was there a standoffish relationship between the Jacobean regime and
the English, Welsh and Scottish soldiers in Dutch employ; rather, there were numerous intimate connections between court and camp. Men who fought for the Dutch were favoured
by the Jacobean establishment, leading members of which also avowed a Calvinist internationalist stance more generally.

And the King himself set the example! Among the first peers James created were Sir
Robert Sidney, Sir William Russell and Sir William Knollys: each had formerly been a soldier
in Dutch pay, each was a devout Calvinist and each was an advocate of helping Europe's
Reformed communities.[34] Sidney was, as he remained, governor of the cautionary town of
Flushing. After Sir Francis Vere, the Dutch Republic's celebrated English general, was forced
into retirement from the States-General's service by a disagreement with his employers, the
king made him governor of Portsmouth and gave him other subsidiary profitable offices in
that vicinity.[35] Vere was already governor of the cautionary town of Den Brielle; on his death
in 1609, James granted the governorship to his younger brother, General Sir Horace Vere –
and this was evidence of royal favour rather than natural succession, for both Sir Edward
Conway, the town's lieutenant-governor and Thomas, Lord Arundell of Wardour had also
actively sought the post.[36]

Of course, the allocation of such offices might have merely reflected a desire to maximize
existing military expertise, while when the King 'provided' Edward Cecil 'a court appointment', it might simply have been due to his distinguished connections.[37] But other former
mercenaries also benefited from the King's patronage. Sir Richard Wigmore was another
granted an important office at court, while James not only allowed one of his favourite
courtiers, Sir Henry Cary, to serve in the Netherlands – he ransomed Cary after the Spanish
captured him.[38] Later, in 1622, after Colonel Sir John Ogle had returned to England from the
Netherlands, he was considered for the post of Secretary of State; he was not, in fact,
appointed but in considering him for a post for which he really was barely qualified, the king
clearly did not hold his mercenary past against him.[39]

In addition, Sir Philip Pakenham, a serving lieutenant colonel in Dutch pay, seems to have
enjoyed the patronage of the queen.[40] And Prince Henry, who as Timothy Wilks has shown in
this volume, deliberately fashioned himself as a 'militant prince', was also an active patron of
military men. By 1609 the youthful Henry's clients already included Edward Cecil, Thomas
Dale, a Dutch-pay captain since 1603, Geoffrey Holcroft, a captain in Dutch employ from
1601–08, and Sir Henry Peyton, a Dutch-pay captain since 1604.[41] Sir John Holles, controller

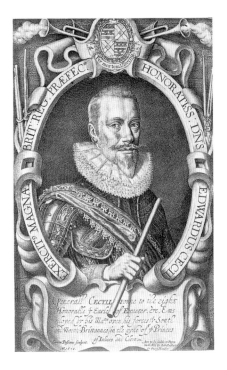

Fig. 2 Simon de Passe, *Sir Edward Cecil*, 1618

of the Prince's household, had been a gentleman volunteer in Dutch pay in 1599 and probably helped to raise extra troops for the campaign in Jülich in 1610 at his master's bidding. Sir John's younger brother George commanded one of the English regiments in that campaign and Prince Henry deliberately extended his patronage network in 1610 to include Sir Horace Vere; indeed, as Dr Murdoch suggests, it may well have been he who persuaded his father to make a military contribution to the Jülich campaign.[42] This would help explain the great number of 'our court gallants' and peers who flocked to join the army besieging Jülich.[43] Two months before his death Henry was still seeking to obtain a captain's commission in the Dutch army for one of his clients.[44]

Royal ministers, like their master, his queen and his son, also had personal, as well as general, connections to veterans of the Dutch army. Edward Cecil had been a Dutch-pay captain since 1599; he had relied on his uncle's patronage to rise in the Dutch army and continued to enjoy that patronage through to Salisbury's death.[45] Nor was Robert Cecil interested only in his kinsmen. One of his chief parliamentary 'men of business' was Sir Robert Wroth, whose second son, John, was a captain in Dutch employ until the autumn of 1603 and whose eldest son, also Sir Robert, married Robert Sidney's daughter.[46] Legislation proposed in the Commons by Sir Robert the elder, probably with Salisbury's permission or at his suggestion, included a 1604 bill for banning the export of iron ordnance, which was aimed at depriving the Spanish of munitions; and a 1606 bill that would have obliged all persons over the age of fourteen who went abroad to take the oath of supremacy, had not Wroth's death prevented its enactment.[47] The mercenary Cyril Tourneur, a client of Sir Francis Vere, was later patronized by Sir Edward Cecil and by Salisbury; in 1612 he wrote a panegyric of Salisbury that circulated widely in manuscript ('The Character of Robert Earle of Salesburye Lord High Treasuror of Englande') and was dedicated to Sir Edward Cecil's wife.[48] Lord Chancellor Ellesmere was a devout if moderate Calvinist, whose notes on his personal Bible-study reveals adherence to the internationalist view of Calvinism in which aiding fellow believers was essential.[49] Ellesmere's clients included Major Sir Thomas Panton and Captain Sir Thomas Dutton (both of whom were within Prince Henry's clientage network),[50] and Ellesmere maintained his patronage of both men, even though both men were active soldiers after 1604; indeed Panton, certainly, continued to recruit vigorously during the Twelve Years' Truce.[51] In addition, throughout the first decade of James's reign, royal ministers regularly intervened with local authorities on behalf of returned mercenaries to ensure they were paid the pension due veterans of the royal armies.[52]

Ecclesiastical, as well as temporal, ministers were also personally associated with the cause of militant Protestant internationalism. George Abbott, the Calvinist Bishop of London and later Archbishop of Canterbury supported 'an aggressive Protestant foreign policy' and in his sermons supported the presence of English troops in Jülich.[53] Thomas Morton, the moderate Puritan Bishop of Lichfield and Coventry, who circulated an 'appeal for financial aid to help Huguenot refugees in England … to [all] ministers' in his diocese, patronized William Fenner, a gentleman volunteer in the Dutch army from 1602, turned priest.[54]

Leading nobles not only patronized soldiers serving in the Netherlands – several of them also served in the Dutch army. William Herbert, 3rd Earl of Pembroke, had fought in the Nieuwpoort campaign of 1600; he seems not to have returned to serve in the Netherlands, but his illegitimate half-brother, Henry, fought for the Dutch until his death in 1605 or shortly thereafter. Thomas, Lord Grey de Wilton commanded a battalion of cavalry in the Dutch army in 1602. Lord Chandos, Lord Howard de Walden and Lord Rich all fought in the Dutch army during the Jülich campaign.[55]

*

That James I's early foreign policy continued to allow for active military assistance to the Dutch is not surprising when we consider the patrons of (and sometimes fellow participants with) English soldiers serving in the Netherlands. Even if James himself and his queen are discounted, Prince Henry, Salisbury, Ellesmere, Wroth, Abbott, Morton, Pembroke, Grey and Rich are all identifiably of 'the hotter sort of Protestants'. There was, then, a significant group within the Jacobean élite committed to aiding fellow believers on the Continent – and especially in the Netherlands, perceived as a bulwark against the Habsburgs and the Papacy. Their views were disseminated by their patronage and may well have reflected a wider enthusiasm in the political nation for war against Spain and the Catholic powers.

Ben Jonson was, of course, patronized by Pembroke, the leader of early Stuart political Puritanism, but though David Norbrook has suggested that 'Pembroke's influence may have something to do with the fact that Jonson did not satirize moderate Puritans who remained in the established church', this does not go far enough. Jonson did rather more than simply refrain from attacking moderate Puritans.[56] In his *Epigrammes*, published in 1616, he praises Pembroke and Lady Mary Wroth, but he also lauds a range of godly soldiers – for although Jonson mercilessly lampooned grasping but impoverished captains, living off whores, cheating at cards and not paying their bills, this was not his only verdict on soldiers.[57] A veteran of the Dutch wars himself, Jonson lauded what he calls 'true Souldiers', to whom he apologized for 'bring[ing] to view/Such as are misse-call'd Captaynes [and hence] wrong[ing] you'.[58] To Sir Henry Cary, who suffered financial disaster when captured by the Spanish, Jonson declares:

> Hee's valiant'st, that dares fight, and not for pay;
> That vertuous is, when the reward's away.[59]

Other commendatory verses went to Sir John Radcliffe, captain in Dutch pay from 1606 until at least 1610, two of whose brothers had died in the Low Countries and to Clemont Edmondes, translator of Cæsar's *Commentaries* and a former subaltern of Francis Vere.[60] And Jonson punningly declared Sir Horace Vere's deeds 'fit to be Sung by a Horace', hymning his 'fame … wonne/In th'eye of Europe, where thy deedes were done'.[61]

The dramatist and translator of Homer, George Chapman, himself a veteran of Dutch service, also celebrated Vere in verse.[62] Chapman's success as a playwright is, moreover, ascribed by his modern biographer partly to the popularity with 'Jacobethan' audiences of the figure of the soldier, fighting abroad for England and the Protestant religion.[63] Chapman was not the only writer to portray positively such soldiers, their employers or their cause. In 1605, Thomas Dekker, in his play *The Whore of Babylon*, a dramatization of Elizabeth's reign, has one of his characters praise the Dutch.[64] Samson Lennard, former soldier turned herald, and translator of Perrin's history of the Waldensians, expressed his desire to 'trail a pike' over the Alps in the assault he envisaged Prince Henry would lead on Rome.[65] In 1611 John Davies celebrated 'our renowned late English military Knights and Chieftaines' as 'Englands nine worthies'.[66] At least up to the death of Prince Henry in 1612 and probably for some years thereafter, the annual accession day tilts were important sites of political and cultural interaction. These tourneys, on which more money was spent 'than on any other form of public ceremonial', had 'a strongly Protestant colouring'. Because they were public ceremonials, they did not only represent the enthusiasms of the nobility and gentry; they were also eagerly consumed by the masses, at least in London.[67]

Some of these writers were not Calvinists, but the message they transmitted in their literary and dramatic works reinforced the views of those who were and were communicated to a wide audience. Calvinist internationalism was, indeed, not a concern only of the aristocracy. As we might expect given the Dutch ability consistently to recruit large numbers of soldiers in England and Wales, despite being unable to use conscription, there was widespread interest in, and enthusiasm for, war on behalf of Continental Protestants – especially against Spain. Ordinary citizens in London were greatly agitated by the 1603–04 negotiations with Spain when, it was reported of them that they 'much harken after' after a more aggressive policy. This statement occurs in a partisan tract, but the city of London's internationalist Protestant stance makes it credible. City merchants had underwritten the Elizabethan war against Spain (often without great hopes of reimbursement) and it is notable that the city of London refused to celebrate the Treaty of London, instead choosing pointedly to celebrate, at public expense, Maurits of Nassau's recapture of the Flemish port of Sluys.[68] Just over a decade and a half later, in 1621, the king's policy on 'affairs of Forein States' was subject, among the ordinary citizens of London, to such 'general liberty of discourse …; which King James could not bear', that he was driven to issue a proclamation declaring his policies on the religious wars in Germany, and on relations with the nations involved, 'no fit Themes or Subjects for Vulgar Persons, or Common Meetings'.[69] The same year, when James refused his son-in-law's appeals for troops in 1620, he nevertheless authorized 'a free collection … for the defence of the Palatinat'.[70] Although some contemporaries thought no more than £30,000 would be contributed,[71] in fact almost £35,000 was raised – and the city of London was the largest contributor, with a donation of £6,666 13s. 4d.[72] But not only Londoners were concerned by the fate of foreign Protestants; the town of Dorchester, for example, contributed £200 to the same benevolence; and the same year the justices of Somerset reported to the Privy Council widespread concern in the county about calamities in Germany.[73]

*

However, by 1621, the Jacobean regime's stance had changed and its commitment, whether covert or overt, to Continental co-religionists had become questionable. This was the fruit of a changed European political-grand strategic environment. The Edict of Nantes (1598) had (as it seemed) secured the future of the reformed religion in France. The Dutch Republic survived the renewed Spanish offensive under Philip III and secured, in the Twelve Years' Truce, effective acknowledgement of Dutch sovereignty. Then in 1614 the second Cleves-Jülich succession crisis, which caused the King and council 'to cast a vigilant and provident eye to the saftye' of Britain and order a 'generall Muster and survey' of England's militia – the first since 1599 – was (as it seemed) definitively and peacefully resolved after manoeuvring (by a Dutch army that, as in 1610, included a large English contingent), but no fighting.[74] The Protestant cause on the Continent thus seemed much safer in 1615 than at any time for forty years or more.

There were also other, materialistic factors. The United Provinces' (partial) repayment of the debts inherited from Elizabeth's reign, by redeeming the cautionary towns in 1616, removed one of the chief incentives for James to stay on amicable terms with the Dutch Republic and one basis for a strong Continental military commitment.[75] Dutch competition to English fishermen had been a cause of concern to English fishing towns throughout Elizabeth's reign, without resulting in any strain in relations between the respective governments, but 'in the early seventeenth century [Dutch] hegemony of the north sea fisheries became greater than ever' and, as contemporaries recognized, was a cause of 'controversie' between England and the United Provinces.[76] Dutch prosperity in general had resulted in expressions of envy in the Commons as early as 1604, but these were matched by expressions of support for the United Provinces. Yet by the end of the first decade of the century this envy, perhaps aggravated by tensions over the cloth export trade, was 'beginning to permeate English economic thought', or so Pauline Croft argues; traces of it may even be evident in one of Salisbury's memoranda to the King. This was probably not enough in and of itself to erase the traditional support for the Dutch – England's longstanding political allies and commercial partners. But it soured attitudes and was then to be exacerbated by the increasing Anglo-Dutch competition in the East Indies in the following decade. All this ultimately resulted in relatively widespread genuine hostility to the Dutch within the English mercantile community: even in the previously supportive City of London.[77] This, too, however, was a development of the second decade of the seventeenth century.

The shift in Jacobean policy was not necessarily sudden. As early as the summer of 1611 Englishmen in the Netherlands were apparently already becoming disenchanted with royal foreign policy, yet in 1614 Sir Ralph Winwood, ambassador to the United Provinces and of course pro-Dutch, was made Secretary of State. The same year Sir Fulke Greville was appointed Chancellor and Under Treasurer of the Exchequer: under Elizabeth he had actively supported a Protestant internationalist foreign policy, his concept of which under James is characterized by David Norbrook as 'apocalyptic', and in the 1610s he continued to advocate a strong commitment to the Dutch.[78]

However, the death in 1612 of both Prince Henry and the Earl of Salisbury removed the highest advocate of Protestant internationalism and the king's effective prime minister from his side. Salisbury was a vital link between Elizabethan and Jacobean. He not only had his father's papers, he had been one of the old queen's ministers; he both shared the concern for Continental co-religionists common to James's English subjects and had a good sense of what the political nation would support. After Salisbury's death James no longer had an obvious chief minister; certainly the royal favourites, Somerset and Buckingham, were, at least in the 1610s, virtually non-entities in foreign policy. Moreover, as Charles Giry-Deloison observes, the office of Secretary of State was downgraded after Salisbury's death, with fifteen secretaries holding the two posts in the next thirty years, in contrast to 'six during the forty-five years of Elizabeth I's reign'.[79] The death in 1617 of James's last Elizabethan minister, Lord Chancellor Ellesmere, truly marked a changing of the generational guard, for it removed another councillor with long experience in foreign policy – one prepared to regulate relations with foreign states by Protestant considerations.[80] Foreign policy was thus ever more the domain of James and James alone.

This mattered not least because of the influence that came to be exercised over James by Diego Sarmiento de Acuña, Count of Gondomar, Spanish ambassador to England from 1613 to 1618 and 1619 to 1622. The personable and charming Gondomar seemed, as many of James's subjects felt, to hold almost a spell over the King – one they judged malign.[81]

In any event, regardless of the reasons why a change occurred, it did occur. James's interaction with the Spanish and Netherlands' ambassadors was in 1604 entirely favourable to the latter, as we have seen, yet in 1619 the reverse was true. With the end of the Twelve Years' Truce drawing near and the outbreak of the Thirty Years' War in the Holy Roman Empire, the States-General sent ambassadors to 'the Kings of great Brittaine and France, their antient confederates, to reconfirme their alliance with them, and by this meanes to strengthen themselves against the king of Spaine and his adherents'. The French were quick to do so, but the Dutch envoys met with such 'controversie' at the court of St James, that, as a sympathetic chronicler recorded, they believed themselves to be victims of 'a Gondomarian plot or a project urged by some Spanioloized English'.[82]

Then, in the early 1620s James consistently refused actively to intervene on behalf of his own son-in-law, Frederick, Elector Palatine, and would-be king of a Protestant Bohemia, because it would imperil his cosy relationship with Spain. It was not, to be sure, that James was actually willing to let Continental Protestantism be wiped out, as his more extreme domestic opponents charged. But whereas James saw in the Spanish conquest of the Palatine only a particular policy issue, for men such as Pembroke it was part of a general struggle with an Antichristian enemy – a war which James and later Charles were eager to avoid, 'a war for religion', as Pembroke called it.[83]

In fact, the United Provinces faced no real threat to their sovereignty or even their territorial integrity until a sequence of military failures in the mid-1620s and then the prospect of concerted Habsburg action – a grand double envelopment – in the late 1620s. Indeed, the Jacobean policy of genuine rapprochement with Spain was only possible in a world where the Dutch Republic was not teetering on the brink of extinction. Although the state of Protestantism in Germany, too, would eventually seem endangered, before the Swedish intervention of 1631, that danger was by no means apparent in 1620. What did seem apparent, however, to many of James's English subjects was that, while he might not countenance the destruction of European Protestantism, he was quite content to accept the destruction of some Protestant states and the oppression of many European Protestants, in order to avoid the expense and disruption of war.

*

The decade after the deaths of Prince Henry and the Earl of Salisbury emerges, then, as a crucial period for the development of Jacobean policy; it was only then that the regime moved to a more firmly anti-war, anti-Protestant internationalist stance, open to overtures even from Spain. What also emerges is that this shift helped to poison James's relations with the domestic body politic in the last years of his reign.

As I have indicated, in pursuing a prudent yet pronouncedly Protestant foreign policy in the early years of his reign – in allowing Dutch recruiting, the operation of privateers, and encouraging men to fight against Spain by royal patronage of those men who did so – James I of Great Britain was reflecting not only Salisbury's sage advice and Prince Henry's preferences, but also the views of significant body of opinion within the political nation of England and Wales. James in these years was personally sceptical about the existence of an international Catholic league, disliked the subversive implications of Calvinism, and admired the Spanish. But these attitudes did not significantly affect English foreign policy and so had little English political relevance. In the first decade or so of his reign there was thus no 'distinct break with the past'.[84] That came in 1616–18 onwards, after which James's own attitudes determined his foreign policy – and the new policy, rejecting 'considerable enthusiasm for English intervention' in Europe's wars of religion, put him at odds with 'many of the most engrained of English political attitudes'.[85]

England's foreign policy in 1619 and the following years caused widespread unhappiness in the English political nation. This should not be overstated, given that there were also strong anti-Calvinist and overt Roman Catholic interests at the Jacobean court, which welcomed the new approach. But we can now see that it was a new approach, one quite different to the foreign policy James had originally pursued. This must have made it all the more bewildering, as well as disturbing, to the many Englishmen and women to whom the long-term, 'Jacobethan', policy of aiding embattled Continental Protestants was, in several senses, what they expected of an English monarch. The frequently bitter political disputes of the 1620s really make sense only with a full understanding of the shifts that occurred in Jacobean foreign policy.

The different stances of the King and many of his politically active subjects were embodied at Oxford University. Any visitor to the Bodleian Library (founded by a notable Calvinist internationalist)[86] can contrast Le Sueur's statue of Pembroke, depicted as a soldier, clad in three-quarter armour, which stands outside the library's modern entrance – directly opposite the Schools quadrangle's great gate, over which, high on the tower of the five orders (built between 1613 and 1619), James is depicted, underpinned by a Latin inscription that proclaims his status of peacemaker. How Prince Henry would have been depicted had he survived to become king we cannot know – but the essays in this volume indicate that almost certainly it would have been more like Pembroke than like his father. Similarly, though we cannot know how James would have reacted to the crisis in the Palatinate had Henry still been alive, and how Henry would have responded to developments in the Thirty Years' War had he, not his younger brother Charles, succeeded their father in 1625, all the evidence suggests that the hypothetical Henrician foreign policy would have been very different to the Jacobean reality. Even though Henry's death was clearly not the sole cause, nor even the occasion, for the change in direction of Jacobean foreign policy, that change might well not have taken place had the forceful, adult Henry, rather than the diffident Charles, been a factor in English politics – and it seems overwhelmingly likely that it would have been reversed on the accession of Henry IX. The confrontation of England's king with leading subjects (sympathetic to the cause of international Calvinism), which is embodied in the statuary opposition of Pembroke and James in the old Schools quad at Oxford, and which helped to destabilize both late Jacobean and then early Caroline England, would then, for good or ill, not have taken place or at least been quickly reversed.

What this would have meant for English history is the great imponderable! However, there can be no doubt that Henry's premature death, with the concurrent or subsequent deaths of other important early Jacobean counsellors, left his father free to follow his own instincts on foreign policy. The result was a course of action sharply at odds with the views of a significant portion of England's political elite and all the more controversial because it was also at odds with the policy followed by James throughout the lifetime of his eldest son.

NOTES

I am grateful to Barbara Donagan for reading and commenting on an earlier draft, and to Simon Healy, Ralph Houlbrooke and Andrew Thrush for valuable suggestions. I am also obliged to the History of Parliament Trust (hereafter HoP) for allowing me to read and cite the drafts of biographies of several Jacobean MPs. In addition, I gratefully acknowledge the award of a one-month Andrew W. Mellon Foundation Fellowship at the Huntington Library in 2003, during which I undertook much of the research on which this paper is based.

1 In 2003 Elizabeth was the subject of an exhibition at the Tate Britain; an exhibition and academic conference at the National Maritime Museum (see S. Doran (ed.), *Elizabeth: The Exhibition at the National Maritime Museum*, London, 2003); exhibitions plus lecture series at the Folger Shakespeare Library (see G. Ziegler (ed.), *Elizabeth I: Then and Now*, Seattle, 2003), the Huntington Library and Art Gallery, and the Newberry Library; and a travelling exhibition at public and academic libraries throughout North America, under the auspices of the American Library Association. The same year, James VI and I was the subject of two academic conferences, at the Universities of Hull and Reading, and a lecture at the British Academy, which also staged a symposium on the rather broader theme 'Anglo-Scottish Relations 1603–1914'; while James also shared with Elizabeth the Summer 2003 issue of the online *History in Focus*, <http://ihr.sas.ac.uk/ihr/Focus/Elizabeth/index.html>, and a conference at the Université Paul-Valery Montpellier III in France (see J.-C. Mayer (ed.), *The Struggle for Succession in Late Elizabethan England: Politics, Polemics and Cultural Representation*, Montpellier, 2004).

2 For rare anniversary reflections on the expulsion of the Rump, see articles in *Cromwelliana* (2003), pp. 2–26.

3 J. Scott, *England's Troubles: Seventeenth-century English Political Instability in European Context* (Cambridge, 2000), p. 14; S. Adams, 'Spain or the Netherlands? The Dilemmas of Early Stuart Foreign Policy', in H. Tomlinson (ed.), *Before the English Civil War* (London, 1983), pp. 79–101; T. Cogswell, *The Blessed Revolution: English Politics and the Coming of War, 1621–1624* (Cambridge, 1989); A. Thrush, 'The French Marriage and the Origins of the 1614 Parliament', in S. Clucas and R. Davies (eds.), *The Crisis of 1614 and the Addled Parliament: Literary and Historical Perspectives* (Aldershot, 2003), pp. 25–35.

4 The treaty was concluded on 18 August and proclaimed on 19 August 1604.

5 For a recent example, D. Newton, *The Making of the Jacobean Regime: James VI and I and the Government of England, 1603–1605* (Woodbridge, 2005).

6 Adams, 'Spain or Netherlands?', p. 93.

7 For Elizabethan foreign policy as broadly Protestant, see D.J.B. Trim, 'Seeking a Protestant Alliance and Liberty of Conscience on the Continent, 1558–1585', in S. Doran and G. Richardson (eds.), *Tudor England and its neighbours* (Basingstoke, 2004), pp. 139–77.

8 E.g., James VI to the States-General, 10 November 1590 and 26 November 1591, and to Maurice of Nassau 16 May 1592, Het Nationaal Archief, Den Haag [hereafter HNA], 1.01.04: 5882, nos. 92, 199, 201.

9 *The Historie and life of King James the Sext* (Bannatyne Club, XIII; Edinburgh, 1825), p. 335.

10 States-General to James, 26 July 1594, in *ibid.*, 336–37; States-General, extraordinary accounts 1598–1609, HNA, 1.11.01.01: 879, fols. 12v, 24v, 88v, 132, 139.

11 Treatises against peace with Spain and/or urging the importance of the Dutch alliance: All Souls College Oxford, MS 211, fols. 20v–26; Bodleian Library, Oxford, MS Eng. Hist. C.272, pp. 32–35 and MS Rawl. D.719, fols. 272–320; Folger Shakespeare Library, Washington, DC, MS G.a.1, fols. 17–19v and 20–57, and MS V.b.151, fols. 63–73; Henry E. Huntington Library, San Marino, Calif., Ellesmere MSS [hereafter HL, EL] 1594, fols. 18–20, and EL 1600, pt 13; Somerset Record Office, DD/M1/18/78 (I am obliged to Andrew Thrush for this reference); and W. Ralegh, 'A Discourse Touching a War with Spain and of the Protecting of the Netherlands', in T. Birch (ed.), *The Works of Sir Walter Ralegh, Political, Commercial and Philosophical; Together with His Letters and Poems* (2 vols., London, 1751), II, 1–20. Speeches to the House of Commons: Sir Edward Hoby, 12 May 1604, Somerset Record Office, DD/MI, Box 18, FLIV/79 and OB II/90, published by A. Thrush as 'The Parliamentary Opposition to Peace with Spain in 1604: A Speech of Sir Edward Hoby', *Parliamentary History*, 23 (2004), pp. 301–15. Briefer statements of similar sentiments: e.g. William Browne to Robert Cecil, 23 August 1604, Historical Manuscripts Commission [hereafter HMC], *Calendar of the Manuscripts of the Most Hon. the Marquis of Salisbury, preserved at Hatfield House, Hertfordshire* (24 vols., London, 1883–1976), XVI, 270. Also on opposition to the treaty see P.C. Allen, *Philip III and the Pax Hispanica, 1598–1621: The Failure of Grand Strategy* (New Haven, 2000), p. 110.

12 F. Bacon, *Considerations touching a warre with Spain* (1624), in *Certaine miscellany works … Published by William Rawley* (London, 1629), pp. 25–26; J. Spedding, R.L. Ellis and D. Denon Heath (eds.), *The Works of Francis Bacon*, VII, *Literary and Professional Works*, vol. II (London, 1859), pp. 9–36.

13 E.g. S. Alford, *The Early Elizabethan Polity: William Cecil and the British Succession Crisis, 1558–1569* (Cambridge, 1998), p. 216; P. Croft, 'Mildred, Lady Burghley: The Matriarch', in *Patronage, Culture and Power: The Early Cecils*, ed. *idem* (Studies in British Art, VIII; New Haven and London, 2002), pp. 283–84, 291.

14 Salisbury to Thomas Edmondes, 10 October 1605, British Library (hereafter BL), Stowe MS 168, fol. 166. See A.L. Rowse, *The Expansion of Elizabethan England* (London, 1955), p. 321; P. Croft, 'Serving the Archduke: Robert Cecil's Management of the Parliamentary Session of 1606', *Historical Research*, 64 (1991), pp. 289–304, esp. pp. 294, 302; P.E.J. Hammer, 'The Crucible of War: English Foreign Policy, 1589–1603', in Doran and Richardson (eds.), *Tudor England and Its Neighbours*, pp. 256–58; Adams, 'Spain or Netherlands?', pp. 94–95. See also C. Dalton, *Life and Times of General Sir Edward Cecil, Viscount Wimbledon* (2 vols., London, 1885), I, pp. 14–41.

15 D.J.B. Trim, 'Fighting "Jacob's Wars". The Employment of English and Welsh Mercenaries in the European Wars of Religion: France and the Netherlands, 1562–1610' (Ph.D. thesis, University of London, 2002), pp. 177–78; Hammer, 'Crucible of War', p. 258. Thus, *pace* Dr Adams, James did not 'transfer the troops in the Netherlands to the service of the States-General' (Adams, 'Spain or Netherlands?', p. 85).

16 Adams, 'Spain or Netherlands?', pp. 93–94.

17 Trim, 'Seeking alliance and liberty of conscience'; *idem*, 'Jacob's Wars', pp. 194–96 *et passim*.

18 See Trim, 'Jacob's Wars', pp. 102–04, 106–08, 137, 158, 327, 195–96; *idem*, 'Seeking alliance and liberty of conscience', pp. 156–60.

19 See P. Croft, 'England, Spain and Europe 1558–1604', in *Tudor England and Its Neighbours*, ed. Doran and Richardson, p. 199 (and, *pace*, p. 198); M.C. Fissel, *English Warfare 1511–1642* (New York and London, 2001), pp. 177, 254; Hammer, 'Crucible', pp. 259–61, 257–58; Allen, *passim*.

20 A.E.C. Simoni, *The Ostend Story: Early Tales of the Great Siege and the Mediating Role of Henrick van Haestens* (Bibliotheca Bibliographica Neerlandica, XXXVIII; 't Goy-Houten, 2003); Trim, 'Jacob's Wars', pp. 188, 230–31.

21 W. Crosse, *A generall historie of the Netherlands. Newly revewed, corrected, and supplied with observations omitted in the first impression, by Ed. Grimeston. Continued from the yeare 1608 till the yeare 1627 by William Crosse. The second impression* (London, 1627), p. 1198.

22 Ralegh, 'Discourse', p. 11; Salisbury to Edmondes, 11 May 1605, BL, Stowe MS 168, fol. 17.

23 States-General to James I, 8 Apr. 1603, printed in Crosse, p. 1175.

24 Crosse, pp. 1175–76.

25 Example in the National Army Museum: NAM 9612–26.

26 Count d'Arenberg to Archduke Albert, 3 and 13 July 1603, in H. Lonchay and J. Cuvelier (eds.), *Correspondance de la Cour d'Espagne sur les affaires des Pays-Bas au XVIIe siècle*, vol. I (Brussels, 1923), nos. 331, 339, pp. 153, 160.

27 See d'Arenberg to Albert, 8 July 1603 ('ne pourront ny toucher tambor'), *ibid.*, no. 336, p. 157; Salisbury to Edmondes, 11 May 1605, BL, Stowe MS 168, fol. 17; Earl of Southampton to [Salisbury], 29 June [1605], HMC, *Calendar of Salisbury MSS*, XVII, 286; Croft, 'Serving the Archduke', pp. 289–92 (Cecil to Winwood quoted at p. 291); Trim, 'Jacob's Wars', pp. 237–38; R.M. Shurmer, 'Scottish Mercenary Forces in the Revolt of the Netherlands and Anglo-Scottish Relations, 1566–1609' (M.Litt. thesis, University of Aberdeen, 1989), pp. 79–80.

28 Salisbury to Thomas Edmondes, 12 and 27 February 1606, HMC, *Calendar of Salisbury MSS*, XVIII, pp. 50–51, 62.

29 Croft, 'Serving the Archduke'.

30 See Trim, 'Jacob's Wars', app. 2, tables 6–7, pp. 340, 343; app. 10, esp. fig. 18, p. 514.

31 Trim, 'Jacob's Wars', pp. 191, 340; cf. G. Parker, *The Army of Flanders and the Spanish Road* (corr. edn, Cambridge, 1990), app. A, pp. 271–72.

32 Trim, 'Jacob's Wars', pp. 339, 370; S. Murdoch, 'James VI and the Formation of a Scottish-British Military Identity', in *Fighting for Identity: Scottish Military Experience c. 1550–1900*, ed. *idem* and A. Mackillop (Leiden, 2002), pp. 12–14.

33 'That wch Don Diego Sarmiento de Acuna Ambassador of his Catholique Matie … said … about the satisfaction wch the Catholique kinge desireth to be made towchinge the causes of his subjectes', n.d. [but *c.* 1613–4], HL, EL 1639, unfoliated [fol. 1r].

34 Trim, 'Jacob's Wars', pp. 304–06

35 Grants of offices, 15 June 1606, *Calendar of State Papers, Domestic Series, James I* [hereafter CSPDom.] 1603–10, p. 321; A. Ersfeild to Salisbury, [June] 1606, HMC *Calendar of Salisbury MSS*, XVIII, p. 176.

36 Trim, 'Jacob's Wars', p. 193.

37 HoP, *Elizabethan House of Commons*, ed. Paul Hasler (3 vols., London, 1981), I, 570.

38 Chamberlain to Dudley Carleton, 23 January 1609, *The Letters of John Chamberlain*, ed. N.E. McClure, 2 vols. (American Philosophical Society, Memoirs, XII; Philadelphia, 1939), I, p. 282, no. 110. HoP, *Jacobean House of Commons*, ed. A. Thrush (in progress) (hereafter *Jacobean House of Commons*), draft biography of Cary; Winwood to Edmondes, 6 October [1605], and Salisbury to Edmondes, 8 Mar. 1606, BL, Stowe MS 168, fols. 158, 366.

39 Chamberlain to Carleton, 13 July and 5 October 1622 and 25 January 1622/23, *Letters of John Chamberlain*, nos. II, 411, 414, 422, 446–47, 455, 474.

40 See Winwood (by now Secretary of State) to Carleton, 1 April 1617, The National Archives, Kew (hereafter TNA), SP 84/77, fol. 3v.

41 Trim, 'Jacob's Wars', pp. 420, 437; D.J.B. Trim, 'Sir Horace Vere in Holland and the Rhineland, 1610–1612', *Historical Research*, 72 (1999), 345n. 347; T. Wilks, 'The Pike Charged', chapter in this volume.

42 See Trim, 'Jacob's Wars', pp. 384, 506–07; Vere to Adam Newton, 8 April 1610, Koninklijke Bibliotheek, The Hague, MS 134.C.18^A; Trim, 'Sir Horace Vere', pp. 344–46; Murdoch, p. 13n.

43 Chamberlain to Winwood, 2 May 1610, *Letters of John Chamberlain*, I, p. 297, no. 119; E. Herbert, *Life of Edward Herbert Lord Cherbury*, ed. J.M. Shuttleworth (London and Oxford, 1976), pp. 53–57; cf. Wilks in this volume.

44 Vere to Newton, 29 September 1612, Koninklijke Bibliotheek, MS 134.C.18^B. This was for a 'Mr More' – probably the son of Sir George More of Loseley, Prince Henry's Receiver-General: see John Hammond to More, 19 April 1605, Folger Shakespeare Library, MS L.b.620; and n. 50, below.

45 Cf. Dalton, I, pp. 11, 15–16, 65, 72.

46 *Jacobean House of Commons*, draft biography of Wroth; Trim, 'Jacob's Wars', p. 483.

47 *Jacobean House of Commons*, draft biography of Wroth.

48 P. Croft (ed.), 'Introduction', *A Collection of Several Speeches and Treatises of the Late Lord Treasurer Cecil and of Several Observations of the Lords of the Council Given to King James Concerning His Estate and Revenue in the Years 1608, 1609, and 1610*, in *Camden Miscellany XXIX*, Camden Soc., 4th ser., XXXIV (1987) (hereafter *Cecil Collection*), p. 250.

49 HL, EL 6169. See D.J.B. Trim, 'Calvinist internationalism and the English Officer Corps, 1562–1642', *History Compass*, 4 (2000), pp. 1024–48, esp. p. 1031.

50 Panton, at the time of Henry's death, was a Gentleman of the Privy Chamber Extraordinary in the Prince's household, see TNA, LC 2/4 (6). In April, 1612, he wrote from Utrecht to the Prince's Receiver-General, Sir George More, confirming that he was ready to receive More's son, and sending news of 'Vorstius that arch-heretick', HMC *Seventh Report, Appendix*, p. 670. For Sir Edward Cecil's letter of complaint to Henry, written from the siege camp before Jülich on 29 July, 1610, concerning 'the mutinous and unworthy carriage of Sir Thomas Dutton, whom your Highness was pleased to favour beyond his merit', see Thomas Birch, *The Life of Henry Prince of Wales* (London, 1760), p. 199.

51 L.A. Knafla, 'New Model Lawyer: The Career of Sir Thomas Egerton, 1541–1616' (Ph.D. diss., University of California at Los Angeles, 1965), pp. 230–31, 235; Panton to Ellesmere, 8 November 1614, HL, EL 1659; Trim, 'Sir Horace Vere', p. 350 and note; *idem*, 'Jacob's Wars', pp. 396, 423, 507; register of soldiers taking the oath of allegiance before going to serve in the Low Countries, December 1613–December 1614, TNA, E 157/2. But Knafla's suggestion (p. 235n.) that Ellesmere had Dutton appointed surveyor of Gloucestershire probably rests on a misunderstanding of HL, EL 1198; if it was the same Thomas Dutton who held the office, then it was almost certainly much earlier, before Dutton served in the Netherlands.

52 E.g. Devon Quarter Sessions resolutions, 4 October 1603 and 12 January 1604, Devon Record Office, QS 1/2, unfol.; Fissel, *English Warfare*, p. 179; Privy Council to JPs of Wiltshire, 1611, in HMC, *Report on Manuscripts in Various Collections*, I (1901), p. 83; Privy Council, passport for Thomas Hobbes, 16 May 1612, Wiltshire RO, Quarter Sessions Autograph Book, fol. 29. Although my evidence comes from Wiltshire and Devon there are sufficient examples to suggest that these cases were not exceptional, at least in those counties.

53 K. Fincham, 'Prelacy and Politics: Archbishop Abbot's Defence of Protestant Orthodoxy', *Historical Research*, 61 (1988), pp. 36–64 (p. 46).

54 D. Colclough, 'John Hoskyns and the Manuscript Culture of the Seventeenth Century', *Huntington Library Quarterly*, 56 (1999–2000), p. 388; Trim, 'Jacob's Wars', p. 296n.

55 Trim, 'Jacob's Wars', pp. 351, 383, 457–58; Herbert, *Life of Lord Cherbury*, pp. 53–57; R.M. Smuts, 'Rich, Henry, first earl of Holland (*bap.* 1590, *d.* 1649)', *Oxford Dictionary of National Biography*, Oxford University Press, 2004 http://www.oxforddnb.com/view/article/23484, accessed 6 Dec 2006.

56 D. Norbrook, *Poetry and Politics in the English Renaissance* (London, 1984), pp. 184–85, 318.

57 *Epigrammes* (1616), nos. XII, LXXXII, LXXXVII, CVII, in *Poems of Ben Jonson*, ed. G.B. Johnston (London, 1954), pp. 10–11, 38, 40, 54–55.

58 *Ibid.*, no. CVIII, p. 55.

59 *Ibid.*, no. LXVI, p. 32.

60 *Ibid.*, nos. XCIII, cx–cxi, pp. 45, 56–57.

61 *Ibid.*, XCI, p. 43.

62 'Pro Vero Autumni Lachrymae' (1622).

63 R.S. Ide, *Possessed with Greatness: The Heroic Tragedies of Chapman and Shakespeare* (London, 1980), pp. 3–4 (p. 4).

64 See Norbrook, p. 136.

65 I owe this reference to Sears McGee. Lennard is discussed in Timothy Wilks's chapter in this volume.

66 *The Scourge of Folly* (London, 1611), p. 88.

67 J.S.A. Adamson, 'Chivalry and Political Culture in Caroline England', in K. Sharpe and P. Lake (eds.), *Culture and Politics in Early Stuart England* (Basingstoke, 1994), p. 165; Norbrook, p. 107. See D.J.B. Trim and Peter J. Balderstone, 'Introduction', *Cross, Crown and Community: Religion, Government and Culture in Early-Modern England, 1400–1800* (Oxford and Berne, 2004), pp. 12–13.

68 'Considerations upon the likelihoode of the Spaniardes Resoluccon to breake their peace with the state of England on the first advantage or opportunitie meete to be laid hold upon' [1605], HL, EL 1600, pt 13; see Trim, 'Jacob's Wars', ch. 6; D. Maland, *Europe at War 1600–1650* (London, 1980), p. 32.

69 Proclamation in J. Rushworth, *Historical Collections of Private Passages of State, Weighty Matters in Law, Remarkable Proceedings in Five Parliaments, Beginning the Sixteenth Year of King James, Anno 1618, And ending the Fifth Year of King Charles, Anno 1629* (London, 1659), p. 21.

70 Privy Council letter to peers, bishops and Lord Mayor of London, 25 October 1620, *ibid.*, p. 16.

71 C. Bridenbaugh, *Vexed and Troubled Englishmen 1590–1642* (New York and Oxford, 1968), p. 265, citing a contemporary diary.

72 The total was actually £34,617 6s. 8d. A list of donors and donations is in the papers of the Earl of Bridgewater: 'The names of the noblemen and others that gave their benevolences towardes the Defense of the Pallatinate from the first of October 1620', HL, EL 6970.

73 *Ibid.*; Somerset JPs, quoted in Bridenbaugh, p. 265.

74 Privy Council to Earl of Essex (as Lord Lieutenant of Staffordshire and Lichfield), 13 September 1614, Folger Shakespeare Library, MS G.b.14, no. 9; H. Peacham, *A most true relation of the affaires of Cleve and Gulick* (London, 1615).

75 A. Thrush, 'The Personal Rule of James I, 1611–1620', in T. Cogswell, R. Cust and P. Lake (eds.), *Politics, Religion and Popularity in Early Stuart Britain: Essays in Honour of Conrad Russell* (Cambridge, 2002), p. 92.

76 R.C.L. Sgroi, 'Piscatorial Politics Revisited: The Language of Economic Debate and the Evolution of Fishing Policy in Elizabethan England', *Albion*, 35 (2003), pp. 1–24 (p. 23); Crosse, p. 1402; also cf. G. Davies, *The Early Stuarts 1603–1660* (corr. edn, Oxford, 1945), pp. 49–50.

77 See R. Lockyer, *The Early Stuarts: A Political History of England 1603–1642* (2nd edn; London and New York, 1999), pp. 156–57, 161–62; Davies, pp. 51–52; Adams, 'Spain or Netherlands?', p. 84. Salisbury, 'treatise to his Majesty', n.d., in *Cecil Collection*, p. 285, note 92 – Croft indicates that this memorandum is from *c.* 1610: 'Introduction', *Cecil Collection*, pp. 248–49.

78 John Donne to Sir Henry Goodeere, 30 August 1611, in *Letters to severall persons of honour written by John Donne … ; published by John Donne, Dr. of the civill law* (London, 1651), p. 157. Adams, 'Spain or Netherlands?', p. 95; Norbrook, pp. 126–27; J. Rees (ed.), 'Introduction', *Selected Writings of Fulke Greville* (London, 1973), p. 12; Thrush, 'Personal Rule', p. 93.

79 Adams, 'Spain or Netherlands?', pp. 91, 95. C. Giry-Deloison, 'Westphalie 1648: l'Angleterre en marge de l'Europe', in *L'Europe des traités de Westphalie: Esprit de la diplomatie et diplomatie de l'estprit*, ed. L. Bély and I. Richefort (Paris, 2000), p. 405.

80 E.g. see Ellesmere's marginal notes for responses to Acuna's complaints, *c.* 1613, HL, EL 1639; and Thrush, 'French Marriage', p. 29.

81 E.g. Rushworth, *Historical, Collections*, pp. 3, 16.

82 Crosse, pp. 1401–04.

83 Pembroke to Carleton, 9 December 1624, TNA, SP 14/176/34, quoted in Adams, 'Spain or the Netherlands?', p. 87.

84 *Pace* Adams, 'Spain or Netherlands?', pp. 87–88 (p. 88).

85 Cogswell, p. 309; Adams, 'Spain or Netherlands?', p. 101.

86 D.J.B. Trim, 'Sir Thomas Bodley and the International Protestant Cause', *Bodleian Library Record*, 16 (1998), pp. 314–40; W.H. Clennell, 'Bodley before the Bodleian', *ibid.*, 40th Anniversary Commemorative Issue, 17, no. 6 (October 2002), pp. 381–82.

10| 'Grief was as clothes to their backs':[1] Prince Henry's funeral viewed from the Wardrobe

Gregory McNamara

On 7 December, 1612 Prince Henry's funeral cortege processed from St James's Palace to Westminster Abbey as London mourned in black.[2] About a month earlier, on 6 November, the eighteen-year-old Prince died unexpectedly after a persistent fever turned to a much more serious condition for which his physicians could do little of real medical value; above all, these men tried very hard indeed, as one of them put it, to ensure that 'it should never be said in after ages that he had killed the King's eldest Sonne'.[3] This discussion examines Henry's funeral rites in the context of cloth and clothing culture, a subject which may at first seem slight or trivial but which, in fact, tells us a great deal about the mental and material world of the early Stuart court and Early Modern London. In referring to the Prince's funeral rites I mean not only the procession and ceremony of 7 December but also the month-long period of material, social and spiritual preparation undertaken within and around the Prince's residence at St James's. Much of this mourning work found textual expression through the publication of sermons and elegiac works, including *The Funerals of the High and Mighty Prince Henry*, a tract compiled for public consumption by contemporary occasional writers that reveals traces of the archival and heraldic scholarship of William Camden.[4] These are the most commonly referenced literary and historical markers and artifacts of the events; but such documentary and occasional works were elements of a complex social text within which textiles, too, held a prominent place, as is evidenced by records and observations of the manner in which these goods were measured, cut, tailored, distributed, worn, hung, draped, unfurled and flown in courtly and public space during the funeral rites. There is intertextuality – a poetic quality, even – to the garments of majesty and mourning that circulated around St James's Palace in November and early December 1612.

Henry's funeral viewed from the Wardrobe is, in its most basic sense, a study in the outward expression of mourning, exploring well-known norms and customs still regularly enacted, but such a view also directs us toward matters of spatial designation and division within royal and aristocratic contexts and invites consideration of the relationship between privileged and common or public space. Further, the period May 1610 to October 1612 was for Henry and for London a time of grand entries and lavish spectacles which invigorated the capital and the court with exceptional arrays of colours, textures and structures of cloth, clothing and costumes. In both 1610 and 1612, Merchant Taylors were elected to the Lord Mayor's office, and Henry, himself a Merchant Taylor since 1607, was lavishly praised in the proceedings of their guild and of the City.[5] On such occasions, as with the presentation of Anthony Munday's water pageant, *Londons Love to the Royal Prince Henrie,* in June 1610, 'all the worshipfull Companies of the Cittie, were readie … with their Streamers and Ensignes gloriously displayed'.[6] By contrast, November and December 1612 were memorable for the outpouring of grief in response to the unexpected and untimely setting of Great Britain's 'rising sun'.[7] Clothing and livery, formerly symbolic of social status and social bonds, now betokened the imminent disbandment of the Prince's household.[8] In a literal as well as figurative sense, the black draperies and hangings formed the pall over this elaborate period of Stuart pageantry as its principal actor, Henry, made his exit in a lead casket.

Part of why a view from the Wardrobe is an important one to undertake has to do with the profound differences between our own relationship to goods and their modes of production and that of the Early Moderns.[9] Malcolm Smuts has argued in a broader context:

> It is difficult today in an age of machine-made fabrics, to appreciate
> the impression rich clothes made in an age when everything had to be
> spun, woven, stitched, and embroidered by hand, often from costly raw
> material … [W]hen contemporaries described a stately scene, they often
> did so largely in terms of the clothes worn.[10]

In addition to the very pertinent matters material to which Smuts directs us, it should be noted that adjectives such as 'rich' and 'stately' indicate the pronounced social divisions of Early Modern England informing the illusion of power central to the performance and perception of monarchy throughout the early Stuart era.[11] The production and use of fine and rare textiles and ornaments and the production and maintenance of royal space were closely related in the Early Modern imagination.[12] A lavish display of cloth, for example, was essential to the phenomenon of the royal canopy, indoors and out, as in the case of the forty-five yards of yellow tissue cloth composing the symbol of state under which King James rode on the occasion of his first formal entry into the City of London.[13] Descriptions of the most prominent ceremonies of Henry's courtly career, too, frequently emphasize attire and provide a strong foundation for analysis of the symbolic use of cloth and dress and discourse. To consider an entry of a different sort, it is apparent that Henry's role, even from his baptism, was expressed through the textiles surrounding him: William Fowler's account of the 1594 celebration at Stirling reports that, visited by foreign dignitaries, the infant Prince was 'lying in his bed of estate richly decorated, and wrought with embroidered work, containing the story of Hercules and his travels'.[14] Just as the narrative of King James's accession to the English throne seems to conflate cloth and political power, so too with the narratives of Henry's youth, particularly his attaining of majority as expressed in 1610 and the brief period of his court's development until late 1612.

'*The order of his coming was in this fashion …*'[15]

English subjects' lasting memories of the pageantry surrounding the Prince might have centred on the week-long creation festivities of 1610, which included public and private celebrations in addition to the creation ceremony before Parliament on 4 June. The week of celebration began with a magnificent, waterborne entry into London and included the closed performance of the masque *Tethys' Festival* before the court on Tuesday, 5 June. John Finet mentions the next and final day of the June events in a letter to William Trumbull, in which he observes:

> The third and last day did not give place unto any of the former,
> either in stateliness of shew or sumptuousness in performance.
> First we had the runners at the tilt; afterwards in the evening a
> gallant Sea-fight, and lastly, many rare and excellent Fire-works,
> which were seen by almost half a million of people.[16]

These were the first state and civic occasions at which the Prince appeared with a significant measure of autonomy before the citizens and companies of London and the royal court. The Wardrobe expenses were exorbitant. As with most major events, detailed records were kept for purchases of apparel and costuming employed throughout the week, one of the more striking examples of which being for the Prince's furred and perfumed creation robes, which came in at a few pennies under £1292, prompting one auditor of the accounts – possibly the Prince himself – to insert the brisk marginal note 'this is most unresonable and can not be endured'.[17] Reflecting on the week's festivities, Finet, having seen even the Earl of Pembroke's *horses* in 'peach-coloured velvet embroidered all over with fair orient pearls', was effusive, declaring 'in all my life I have not seen once so many riches in bravery, as at this time, embroidered suits were so common, as the richest lace to be gotten seemed but a mean Grace to the wearer'.[18]

By the late Elizabethan and early Stuart periods, public and aristocratic sensitivity to diverse and complex social imagery – particularly in dress – had become, in unprecedented ways, a cultural obsession.[19] Certainly, one place where we might well expect to find dress culture under examination is the contemporary stage; so it seems pertinent to draw a sample of references from plays popular around the time of the Prince's death. By the second line of *The Duchess of Malfi* we find Delio, an attentive and perhaps a little sardonic student of international fashion, noting upon Antonio's return from the French court, 'You have been long in France, and you return / A very formal Frenchman in your habit'.[20] Moll enters Scene III of Dekker and Middleton's play, the *Roaring Girl*, in a frieze jerkin and a black safeguard intending to buy a 'good shag ruff' from Openwork. One stall over, dandy Jack Dapper refuses Mistress Tiltyard's offering of 'the general feather', 'most worn and most in fashion / Amongst the beaver gallants, the stone-riders / The private stage's audience, the twelvepenny-stool gentle-men', demanding instead 'a – spangled feather', which reminds Moll of the bright colours and ornament of 'a nobleman's bedpost'.[21] And, in yet another contemporary play, Gonzalo, es-caping the fury of Prospero's tempest, seems to take greater note of his unspoiled garments than the miracle of his own survival, exclaiming with wonder: 'Our Garments, being, as they were / drench'd in the Sea, hold notwithstanding their / Freshness and Glosses, being rather new Dy'd / than stain'd with Salt-water'.[22] This brief catalogue of characters written and per-formed around 1612, whose thoughts readily gravitate toward the wardrobe, suggests the degree to which cloth, clothing and fashion informed the social landscape through which the Prince's funeral processed that December.

Should the stage, given the theatre's intrinsic relationship to the tiring house, seem a too artificial cultural context, one might look to popular history. In the last decades of Elizabeth's reign, observers such as Phillip Stubbes and William Harrison responded to what seemed to them to be the social preoccupations and international influences associated with contem-porary fashion. In his discourse on national apparel and attire in *The Description of England*, Harrison inveighs:

> Neither was it any merrier with England than when an Englishman was known
> abroad by his own cloth and contented himself at home with his fine kersey
> hosen and a mean slop, his coat, gown, and cloak of brown-blue or [puce],
> with some pretty furniture of velvet or fur, and a doublet of sad tawny or black
> velvet or other comely silk, without such cuts or garish colours as are worn
> these days and never brought in but by the consent of the French, who think
> themselves the gayest men when they have most diversities of jags and change
> of colours about them.[23]

Of colour, Harrison further writes, 'I might here name a sort of hues devised for the nonce wherewith to please fantastical heads, as gooseturd green, pease-porridge tawny, popinjay blue, lusty gallant, the-devil-in-the-head (I should say "the hedge"), and suchlike'.[24] Harrison's frustration with the pace of emergent culture is amusing but also indicative of the rapid deve-lopment and innovation in contemporary vocabulary applied to dress and fashion. Further, Harrison's observations reveal nationalistic tensions inherent to the communication of fash-ion trends from the Continent into the English mainstream.

And what of the psychology of dress from the perspective of the wearer of fine fashions? In a January 1589/90 letter, the 'enthusiastical' William Reynolds – though not quite sane, a nonetheless 'perfectly trustworthy witness' of current events and culture[25] – wrote at length to one Mr Cope,[26] drawing a somewhat melancholy but curiously instructive association be-tween his own apparel, Englishness and Godliness:

Considering the second suit of tawny, I understood it best became my sad and
penitent mind, yet the darkness of my country England, by my cloak of russet
lined with seawater and stockings of seawater, so that I could not step forth of
England but into the sea [with] which I compassed me about, and that the sky,
God's word, was so darkened with the thick clouds of our sins that the sun
Christ could not shine through it.[27]

Reynolds's sentiments about his clothing, fantastical though they are, might remind us of
Malvolio's outlandish imaginings of his potential to preside over Olivia's (no longer mournful)
household in his 'branched velvet gown'[28] and of the frustrated steward's punning on the
humorous implications of his yellow-stockinged, cross-gartered legs.[29] *Hamlet*, another play of
the turn of the century (when Henry was about six years of age), reveals something more of
the psychology of mourning dress and of the limits of dress as a mode of social performance,
as the Danish prince defends his outward display:

'Tis not alone my inky cloak, good-mother,
Nor customary suits of solemn black,
Nor windy suspiration of forced breath,
No, nor the fruitful river in the eye,
Nor the dejected havior of the visage,
Together with all forms, moods, shows of grief
That can denote me truly. These indeed 'seem',
For they are actions that a man might play.[30]

Hamlet's acerbic commentary is as remarkable for his defence of his natural emotions as for his
allusions to dress as a complex and potentially indeterminate performance. Such musings on
dress and behaviour might be heard with some frequency on the popular stage, from the pulpits
and in the streets – or perused in pamphlets bought from the bookstalls of St Paul's Yard.
Although there is nothing to suggest that those who mourned Henry were anything less than
genuine in their inward and outward grieving, Hamlet's words do, when read perhaps a little
against the grain, serve as a reminder of tensions between natural expression and self-conscious
performance experienced by actors in circumstances of collective behaviour. Like the mourning
rites for Old Hamlet, Henry's funeral and the associated transformations of dress and display at
court and within the city – however powerful and sweeping, mournful and dark – were
ephemera surfacing in stark contrast to dominant cultural modes, simultaneously reinforcing
and containing those same modes on material as well as psychological and symbolic levels.

Taking a broad view, increased demand for, and availability of, exotic materials and
fashions informed an enhanced emphasis on the application of descriptive and interpretive

language commonly applied to the elements of fashion in a variety of contexts. The courtly rituals associated with Henry's death provide us with one such context, revealing by contrast something of the normative backdrop temporarily suspended for, and indelibly marked by, the events of November and December 1612. For a court and public accustomed not only to a hopeful and rising prince but also to a prince with whom energetic and colourful display was recently and consistently associated, Henry's unanticipated death was an awesome matter expressed through the hurried replacement of profuse and diverse colour by black.

'Colours should be as good as nothing if there were no eyes to behold them'[31]

Aware that Henry's health had been declining apace since late October, the shipwright Phineas Pett, a Gentleman Servant Extraordinary of the Prince's household, called at the palace on the afternoon of 6 November, no doubt to learn how things stood.[32] Two days earlier, on Wednesday, the King himself was at St James's but 'being advertised … what addition of griefe it would be unto him to see his best-beloved Sonne in that extremity' ceased his regular visits to the Prince, and gave command that 'because his Highnesse was continually molested with a number who out of their love came to visit him, no creature should be admitted to see him, save those who of necessitie must tend on him'.[33] When Pett arrived at about four o'clock in the afternoon, he found 'a house turned to the very map of true sorrow, every man with the character of grief written in his dejected countenance, all places flowing with tears and bitter lamentations'.[34] It had been a rough night: the Prince was out of his senses with his illness and convulsing violently; as he experienced fainting spells, there were raised 'prodigious exclamations of grief in the chamber, court, and adjoining streets'.[35] The narrative of the Prince's illness and death reveals, like his period of lying in state and his funeral, very clear expectations and representations of movement in court space, which was stratified and closely restricted. Descriptions such as that found in the opening of *The Funerals of the High and Mighty Prince Henry* tend to move outward from the bedchamber – the real *locus* of royal decision-making under the early Stuarts – toward public space through a hierarchically defined sequence. Thus it was that:

> Thursday before the Funeralls, his Princely body was brought forth
> of his Bed-chamber into his Privie-chamber.
> Friday, it was brought into his Presence-chamber, and set under his
> cloath of estate.
> Saturday … it was removed into the Guard-chamber, where all his
> chiefe servants and officers being assembled, and the Officers of Arms
> in their coates, the corps was solemnly carried into the Chappell of
> that house, and placed under a canopy in the middest of the quire.[36]

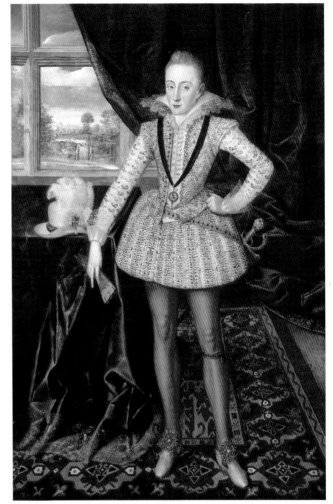

Fig. 1 Robert Peake the Elder, *Prince Henry* c. 1610, National Portrait Gallery, London

This progression illustrates with a morbid difference one of the fundamental observations of Neil Cuddy's influential structural and spatial analysis of the early Stuart bedchamber: that there was a clear relationship between political intimacy and influence and access to privy space. Cuddy's findings are reflective of contemporary descriptions of court space which tend to depict ingress from the outer precincts to more intimate space by chamber and by degree, leading ultimately to the bedchamber, to which access was most strictly controlled; such descriptions tend to depict egress in like style, in this particular case with Sunday chapel as the frontier beyond which one entered into public space.[37]

On more typical days at St James's, Pett's venturing to court would have been a vastly different experience to that of 6 November. Examination of the records of Henry's household indicates a court very much alive with colour and activity, where men of promise gathered in the latest fashions. Two suits provided in 1612 for Archibald Primrose, the Prince's page of honour, offer some insight to the look of the court. Primrose received, and presumably wore, doublet, jerkin, hose and cloak of cloth laid with 'cullered purple silke lace'. These suits cost about £24 each, nearly double the amount paid for a black silk suit presented to no less a courtier than James, Lord Hay, in the same year.[38] Outside the residence, the Prince's carriage men might be seen in 'gownes of Redd cloth lined wth Bayes and trymed wth silke lace'.[39] Of the Prince himself, Robert Peake the Elder's *c.* 1610 portrait (fig. 1),[40] which Roy Strong has called the 'Richmond Portrait', reveals, in ways that lists of clothing purchases cannot, the vibrant colours worn by the Prince and his retinue. In this particular portrait, lush purple draperies embroidered with gold frame a magnificent interior in which the Prince stands upon an intricately woven carpet, wearing a

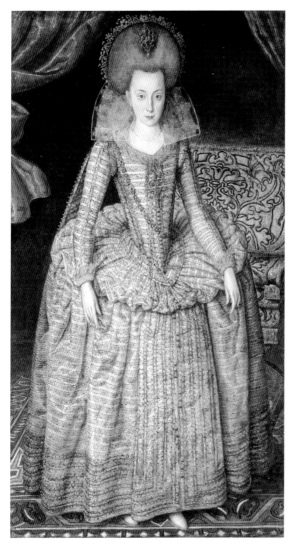

richly embroidered ensemble of doublet and hose, which combines pearl-white and red-orange tones; a jewelled and plumed white hat stands on an elaborately draped table nearby. Peake's portrait of Princess Elizabeth from the same period (fig. 2)[41] reveals a similar focus on interior fineries, particularly draperies and carpets, in addition to the usual emphasis on intricate and majestic apparel one expects from royal portraiture of this era. Household furnishings and decor – not to mention the Prince's art collections – constituted yet another layer of display.[42] Among the accounts of the Prince's revenues for the period from Michaelmas 1611 to the time of his death is listed an entry for 'Rich hangings, Plate, and other Furniture of Howse-houlde which the Kings Ma[tie] gave unto him'.[43] Such, it seems, was the visual splendour of the Prince's household, whether situated at St James's or Richmond, on more typical days.

So it was a pronounced transition when, within three days of the Prince's death, that gloom which was apparent to Pett in the faces of the household 'family' on his 6 November visit was displayed through the palace itself at the Privy Council's command.[44] Interiors were hung with black cloth as a visual and material representation of mourning signifying the relationship between power and the exclusivity of place and space. The palace was newly fashioned in its hierarchically arranged funereal garb, with

> foure chambers hung with blackes, *viz.* the Guard-chamber and the
> Presence, with black cloth; the Privy-chamber with finer cloth, and
> the bed-chamber with black velvet; in the middest whereof was set
> up a canopy of blacke velvet, valanced and fringed; under which, upon

tressels, the coffin, with the body of the Prince, was placed; covered
with a large pall of black velvet, and adorned with scutcheons of arms.[45]

This description provides a clear example of the importance of textiles in defining social space
and social divisions and underscores the correlation between cloth and the construction not
only of scenes of grief but also of scenes of majesty.[46]

Despite the imminent disbanding of the household, the palace was flush with attendant
courtiers, many of whom were undoubtedly stricken not only by the Prince's death but also
by potential loss of place.[47] According to Sir Charles Cornwallis, Henry's treasurer and contemporary biographer, seventy of the Prince's servants were appointed to attend to the
mournful chambers in their blacks 'night and day ... tenne at a time' throughout the month.[48]
Precisely how these attendants were distributed throughout the Guard (or Great), the
Presence, and the Privy chambers is not clear from Cornwallis's account, but some inferences
might be drawn from the normal stationing of men within the major chambers. The Guard
Chamber was the base of the yeomen of the guard, who naturally controlled passage through
it, and for whom the Prince's Book of Household specified additional duties such as attending
at the gates, some with halberds, to 'assist the porters to execute their office and orders to be
observed in time of infection and other occasions'.[49] As the description of black draperies
hung within the chambers indicates, the Guard Chamber and the Presence Chamber were
areas of more ready access furnished and staffed to make an immediate impression on visitors
to the palace at any time, but with a grim difference in the wake of the Prince's death. In addition to the altered visual dynamics, the catastrophe in progress at St James's might have been
most felt on a social level within the busiest chamber in the household, the Presence, the place
for court gossip and general business, which was ordinarily 'well furnished with gentlemen
that strangers and men of quality that shall resort unto his highness court may not find it
emptie'.[50] Pett recalled appearing at the Prince's command to discuss a naval matter on
1 August, 1612, at Richmond Palace, which functioned under the same regulations as St
James's.[51] His account provides a unique and illuminating view of the spatial and social
dynamics of the household:

> The next day being Sunday, I waited on his Highness to chapel and at dinner;
> he had this day a great deal of private conference with me concerning affairs of
> consequence. After his Highness was risen from dinner and had talked with
> me awhile at the bay window of the presence, he was pleased to license me to
> depart to dinner, which was prepared for me and my company by Mr.
> Alexander, the principal gentleman usher, at Mr. Wilson's house, then his
> Highness' tailor.[52]

Even until two days before Henry's demise, his household was a place of vigorous business, with a heavy traffic of suitors and their attendants moving through the sequence of chambers within the palace and in and out of courtiers' houses on the periphery of the court. Certainly, the palaces were still more active given the recent arrival of Frederick, the Elector Palatine, for his imminent wedding to Princess Elizabeth. Henry frequently entertained his brother-in-law to be and his entourage during this time and had his last entertainment playing cards and tennis, and riding with Frederick's uncle, 'Count Henry', Frederik Hendrik of Nassau, while the sixteen-year-old Elector attended the princess and her royal parents.[53] Given the hitherto hopeful atmosphere, it is difficult to imagine the awkwardness at court as Henry, whose increasingly wasted appearance was alarming observers by late October,[54] suddenly declined and disaster struck.

Pett states in his autobiography that he 'had warning to attend at St James upon the preparation of the funeral of our master, and had black cloth delivered to me according to the place I was ranked above stairs, which was as a gentleman of the Privy Chamber extraordinary'.[55] Pett's remembrance of receiving his blacks might be loosely understood as an illustration of his bond to the Prince's household in the context of the elaborate and deeply engrained livery system of the era. Although livery – considered here in the sense of uniforms – was not ordinarily provided for household members of Pett's status but rather for such servants as pages and lesser grooms, clothing given as gifts and provided for special occasions might properly be read as exemplifying deep social bonds. Examining the role of clothing in similar contexts, Peter Stallybrass has reminded us that 'All forms of livery … displayed clothing as a means of incorporation, the marking of the body as to associate it with a specific institution … it bound people in networks of obligation'.[56] Phineas Pett received his allowance of black cloth keenly aware of his 'misfortune and the utter downfall of all my future hopes, to the ruin of all my poor posterity'.[57]

In the same paragraph as Pett's account of receiving cloth for his mourning suit – not coincidentally, I suspect – he recollects Daniel Price's sermon on the eve of the Prince's funeral, with its text from 2 Samuel: 'Rend your clothes, put on sackcloth and mourn before Abner.'[58] 'There were very few present at the sermon', Pett adds, 'that did not bitterly mourn and shed tears in abundance.'[59] Price, one of Henry's chaplains who became somewhat infamous as one of the 'pulpit-hornets',[60] owing in part to some controversial sermonizing over the circumstances of the Prince's death, was, by 10 November, very much engaged in a series of public and private sermons and lamentations. The first of these sermons extant is based on Matthew 26.31 and examines in two parts the theme: 'I will smite the Shepheard, and the Sheepe of the flocke shall be scattered.'[61] Price's dedicatory epistle to the members of the household describes the sermons partly with a sartorial metaphor. Of the two sermons together, Price wrote in his dedication to the 'Princelie familie':[62] 'They are plaine both because sorrow dislikes descant, and plaine stuffes are fittest for mourners.'[63] Meditations on the putting on and taking off of garments and the marking of the body as a performance of identity, community and mourning in Scripture, the classics and in contemporary culture are frequent in Price's sermons throughout November.[64] One of the more interesting features of Price's approach to clothing and apparel is the resonance his references seem to hold with observers like Harrison who celebrated plainness. Indeed, Price's sermons contain much outcry against ostentatious dress, and one might well ponder in what ways the puritan vigilance which drove Price to associate the 'outrage of apparell' with 'new oaths, new exchange of sinnes, and the sluice of vengeance that hell hath opened'[65] informed Henry's own tastes and sensibilities. Although the Prince was sometimes represented in elaborate dress, as in the 'Richmond Portrait', and, given the richness and variety of his wardrobe, undoubtedly had plenty of such finery to call for, the Venetian ambassador reported in 1611 that 'The Prince has abandoned the French dress and has taken to the Italian … as it seems to him more modest'.[66]

The most poignant of Price's sermons considering mourning dress as social discourse was presented on 6 December. The Prince's body, being long since 'bowelled, embalmed, and closed up in lead' was positioned in St James's Chapel, and Price preached before the casket.[67] This is the sermon mentioned by Phineas Pett, which was promptly printed and sold under the title *Teares Shed Over Abner*.[68] Interestingly, Price's dedication is to the courtier considered Henry's closest confidant, Sir David Murray, 'Master of the Great Wardrobe and Robes'.[69] In his dedicatory epistle, Price offers a meditation distinguishing between Murray's earthly office and the great wardrobe of eternity:

> It is my first *service* to you, who were one of the first and
> faithfulest *servants* to him, till the *holy* passage of his *heavenly*
> soule; your *watry* eies having then no other object but *him*,
> and *heaven*, where now he is *cloathed* with the rich *wardrop*
> of his *Redeemer*.[70]

By the time Price presented *Teares Shed Over Abner*, Murray, as keeper of the robes, was, more than any other member of the household, attuned to the chaplain's theme. Murray himself was swamped in a sea of cloth: not the coarse sackcloth called for from the pulpit, but a great variety of fine black cloth to suit many stations of household servants and nobility as well as the requisite assemblage of public poor chosen to march in the funeral. Further, Murray was charged – at least in part[71] – with accounting for the draping of the household and providing for public displays still in the planning stages. And then there was the matter of clothing the body itself and the Prince's effigy. It was not unusual for Murray to account for large volumes of cloth and clothes, but now it was yard upon yard, not of carnation, rose, orange, pink, sage, deereculler, haireculler, blushculler, murreyculler, tawny murrey, or the range of fashionable tones he had often recorded for his master, but predominantly blacks.[72] During the month leading up to the funeral, Murray divided his time among such duties as finalizing the accounts of the Prince's Wardrobe; distributing hundreds upon hundreds of yards of cloth, some in the form of finished suits, for uncertain numbers of the nearly two thousand mourners who would process in the funeral;[73] and ensuring that cloth of many types and grades was provided for the chambers, canopies, horses and wagons, and other royal trappings connected to the daily rituals. The material reality of Daniel Price's sermons on dress and outward show of grief would not have eluded Murray and the members of the Prince's household.

Price preached about dress to a court audience for whom elaborate display was, and always would be, the norm, despite the temporary concession to plainness. Yet Price was undoubtedly conscious of the wider social, not to say commercial, potential of his own performance, immediately releasing for printing and for sale his sermons on the occasion. Perhaps a little defensively, Price contends in *Teares Shed Over Abner*, 'My ende in publishing this Sermon is not popular ostentation; that neither becometh this season, nor this subject …. I desire to confine myself to the sircle of solitarinesse, yet I was put unto this, and the like burdens above my strength, and beyond my will.'[74] Reminding his audience (and readership) that they should exhibit like humility, Price turns to the wardrobe and to fashion itself: 'Not only change your garments, but rent them, tear them to totters, and put on not only sables, semblances of sorrow, but saccloath hairy, dusky, dusty sackcloath …. Put your garments on of lamentation … not as though you did personate sorrow, but as though griefe were as cloathes to your backes.'[75] It is certain that Price's pious, even puritanical, admonitions, themselves wrapped in vivid hyperbole, were by no means a reflection of the realities of dress at court, as is evidenced by the orders for mournful, but still wholly rich and regal, cloth and clothing that Murray recorded for the funeral and through contemporary accounts of the procession itself.

'My text containeth the furniture for a funerall, an Honourable shadow
presented on the stage of mortalitie concluding his last act upon the face of the earth …
Herse, Sepulchre, mourning garments, mourning Elegies be not omitted.'[76]

Among the diverse responses to the Prince's death, occurring as it did in a period enamoured of panegyric, there was a significant body of elegiac poetry produced in the winter of 1612. As the literary historian John Philip Edmond described the phenomenon in 1906, for the month between the Prince's death and burial 'the printing presses literally rained tears of black ink'.[77] Throughout November and the months that followed, more than forty tracts were published in response to the Prince's death, with some exhibiting quite elaborate formatting, as in the case of Joshua Sylvester's contribution, which featured pages ringed with tears and set in xylographic print.[78] The 'Water Poet', John Taylor's collection of elegies, *Great*

Britain All in Black (London, 1612), reflects in its title the spirit of the time, emphasizing the material fact that on 7 December an assembly of thousands in black processed in public mourning for the Prince.[79]

The vivid expressions of grief following the Prince's death were in stark contrast to the public events of 29 October, just a few weeks prior to the funeral, when London observed the annual Lord Mayor's Show, this time honouring Sir John Swinnerton, a Merchant Taylor, and in one tableau assigning Henry to everlasting glory of a very different sort. Thomas Dekker was called upon to compose the inaugural pageant, *Troia-Nova Triumphans*, and it was widely expected that Henry and the Palatine entourage would attend.[80] The highlight of the show was a magnificent representation of the House of Fame, which included a tribute to Henry, who was assigned 'a particular roome' in 'Fames high Temple … this Court of Fame'. Although the Elector Palatine attended the show and was feasted afterwards by the Lord Mayor, Henry himself was languishing at St James's, already in the throes of the fatal illness that ensured his next public appearance would be in effigy (his actual body, autopsied and embalmed, concealed within the casket beneath) at the heart of the massive funeral procession.

In addition to the more predictable reactions to the Prince's death, there were curiosities and singularities as pageantry turned to mourning, palace became mausoleum, and encomia gave way to elegies. As John Taylor and many better poets were composing their dedications, and as Sir David Murray and the servants of the court were ordering affairs, there 'fell out', according to a letter of John Chamberlain's dated 19 November, 'a very ridiculous accident'.[81] It seems blacks were not for all, as, on Friday, 13 November, 'A very handsome young fellow (about the prince's age) and not altogether unlike him, came stark naked to St James's, while they were at supper, saying, he was the Prince's ghost from Heaven with a message to the King'. John Chamberlain, the newsletter-writer continued: 'Some say he is simple, others mad'; nonetheless, 'thousands came to see him', as he was held at St James's in the porter's lodge. This episode illuminates the near-hysteria of the days following Henry's death, heightened by speculation as to the cause – one wonders what message the 'ghost' thought he was bringing. In a similar vein, Cornwallis describes the appearance on 29 October of 'a fatall signe, about two hours or more within the night, bearing the colours and shew of a rainbow, which hung directly crosse and over Saint James House'.[82] Such events and accounts had a prophetic quality about them, which was manifest in the literary response. John Nichols offers a note to Cornwallis's report that 'The Poets on Prince Henry's death, as may be imagined, did not forget to allude to so poetical an assistant as this rainbow', and this is certainly understandable given the contrasting cosmic imagery intrinsic to the sign – witnessed, apparently, by Cornwallis himself and 'divers others' – with its radiant energy appearing in night only to be absorbed back into darkness after a powerful but brief show of colour.

Henry remained as a spectral presence in London, not just in the days and weeks after his death but for years, as his ghost can be found presented as a symbolic character, to note just one example, in John Webster's Lord Mayor's Show for 1624, *Monuments of Honor*. Webster's show for the Merchant Taylor, Sir John Gore, which near its conclusion harkened back to the poet's representation of Henry as a 'perfect diamond set in lead' in his elegy *A Monumental Column*, positioned the lost ascendant within a tableau of 'Artificiall Rocke, set with mother of pearle, and such other precious stones as are found in quarries' shaped into four pyramids as monuments to the dead. Amidst these pyramids, a figure representing Henry stood upon a pedestal of gold 'with his coronet, George and Garter'.[83] More than a decade after his death, the prince – and his garments of majesty – retained significant cultural currency.

George Wither's contribution to the elegiac literature also connects with the theme of mourning dress as social performance while illustrating the spectral power the dead Prince commanded and even giving him new voice. Wither's *Prince Henries Obsequies*, which sold with a magnificent image of the funeral procession on its title page, promised the buyer not only 'mournefull elegies' but also 'A supposed Inter-locution betweene the Ghost of Prince Henrie and Great Brittaine'.[84] While there is much yet to be written on the discourse of otherworldliness and prophecy in response to Henry's death, closer to the emphasis of the present study is Wither's sixteenth elegy from the *Obsequies*, in which he complains,

> Prince Henri's dead! … why mourn I not to open view,
> In sable robes according to the Rites?
> Why is my hat, without a branch of yeugh?
> Alas my mind no complement delights,
> Because my griefe that Ceremonie lothes,
> Had rather be sad in heart than seeme in clothes.[85]

In a court culture obsessed with clothing and fashion, such assertions were commonplace, but the material grounds for the complaint were weighty. Wither was certainly responding to engrained ritual practice but also to a period aesthetic, suggesting resonances of cultural critique from such diverse commentators as William Shakespeare and William Harrison, and incorporating the evocative power of a sermon by Daniel Price or a melancholy portrait by Hilliard or Oliver.

Of those who *were* obliged to mourn in open view much evidence remains. The account of 'The Blackes allowed for the Prince for [the] severall degrees, and their prices, 28 Nov. 1612' records the distribution of no less than eight hundred yards of black cloth of diverse quality to apparel nobility and their followers, guardsmen and poor men alone. Material accounted for in this document is described in fairly broad strokes, noting under the heading 'Prices of severall sortes of cloth' the following cost structure:

Noblemen 30s. a yard

Noblemen's sonnes and Principall 26s. 8d.

Officers, and all Gownsmen

The better sort of clokes 20s.

The meaner sort of cloke s16s.

The poore gownes 12s.

A conservative estimate of the cost for these allotments, based on an average expenditure of 20 shillings per yard, would, therefore, be £800, and this would have been only the official allocation.[86] In the midst of such wide-sweeping distribution and, eventually, display of black cloth, George Wither and so many other commentators produced, not wholly unintentionally, an intertextuality or cultural poetics from which textiles frequently emerge as a dominant trope.[87]

Sir David Murray's itemization of the 'Blackes and other [necessaries] provided after the Princes death' in the accounts of the Prince's Wardrobe offers details specific to the household:

Five blacke sutes for the five groomes of the Princes Bedchamber [£87.5.6]
five Beavers for them and [4] felte for the pages wth silke and woosted
stockinges garters pointe[s] and Rybbon [£51.3.0] And for [69] yards of blacke
cloth for the groomes of the Bedchambe[r] men [20s] the yard [£51.15.0]
In all [£190.3.6]
[4] mourninge sutes for the Pages [£65.9.0]
[3] yardes of blacke clothe to laye over the coffin [60s.]
[16] elle of Holland for a sheete to lay over the coffin wth makeing
the same [£18.2.8]
Scarlett viz [2] yards to wrap the Prince in and [3] [quarters] for the
Chamber at [£4.10] the yarde [£12.7.6]
A Roabe of Crimsin velvett wth Crimsin satin sleeves and two Crownes
for the Princes picture the Robe furred wth powderinge [£39.15]
[Neccesaries] for embalminge the Prince viz [18] elle of Crimsin and
yellow Taffaty at [18s.] the ell [£16.4] [25] elle of stronge Holland at [2s.]
the ell [50s.] [30] elle of fine hollad at [16s.] the ell [£24] and [9] dozen of
Rybbon [£4.10] In all [£47.4.][88]

The majority of the items in this account refer not to the clothing of household servants but to cloth and garments necessary for preparing the Prince's bedchamber, the corpse itself and the effigy fashioned by Abraham van der Doort displayed upon the funeral hearse, which was '(made in so short warning as like him as could be) … as he was appareled at the time of his Creation'.[89] Murray refers to the likeness in painterly terms, calling the work 'the prince's picture',[90] and William Hole's engraving of the hearse provides a static view of the effigy as-sembled under Henry's insignia and composed in state.[91] But a more dynamic image of the hearse in procession might be had from *The Funerals*, which catalogues the successive waves of black-garbed men and horses.

After gentlemen ushers bearing their wands came the funeral chariot, 'covered with black velvet, set with plumes of black feathers, and drawn by six horses, and armed with scuchions, having their chieffrons and plumes'. The canopy itself was borne by six baronets, and ten baronets bore banners alongside the vehicle. Within the lead casket itself, the Prince was firmly ensconced in the crimson and yellow fabrics of embalming. In his funereal representa-tion, the Prince passed through London with no less pomp than that with which he had come for his creation in 1610. The dramatic and emotional force of this spectacle was recorded by Isaac Wake, who observed the procession. Wake's description focuses on the manner in which the Prince's representation was clothed and the effect that the imagery had upon those who stood in prospect of this representation of the death of majesty:

> Under that [canopy] lay the goodly image of that lovely prince
> clothed with the richest garments he had, which did so lively
> represent his person, as that it did not only draw tears from the
> severest beholder, but caused a fearful outcry among the people
> as if they felt at the present their own ruin at that loss. I must
> confess never to have seen such a sight of mortification in my life.[92]

Even in death, Henry remained on the princely stage, as Wake's employment of theatrical metaphor indicates. The people of London stood watching political theatre on a grand scale, yet the representation of the Prince was also a profound illustration of human and dynastic frailty: inside the casket was the corpse that might have been Henry IX, his creation robes on display a potent reminder of his former station.[93] The funeral scene – particularly the pre-sence of the blacks – seems to have particularly affected those who witnessed and participated in the event, as is evident in the desire expressed by John Davies of Hereford to commemorate 6 November as a 'black Death-day'.[94]

Facing uncertain fortune, Sir David Murray fashioned his master for public view one last time. When the chariot rolled through the London crowd, Murray's intimacy with the Prince was evident as ever:

> the corpse of the prince, lying in an open-chariot [was drawn along
> the streets] with the prince's representation thereon, invested with his
> robes of estate of purple velvet, furred with ermines [and] at his feet, within
> the said chariot, sat Sir David Murray, the Master of the Wardrobe.[95]

Such intersections of material and political culture illustrate the connection of cloth, clothing and fashion to Henry's funeral while connecting to the broader social landscape of early Stuart London. The bleak finality of the Prince's death is apparent in the unfinished business that Murray set down last, no doubt trying to be as thorough as the orders of the household indicated he should: itemizing a series of several 'sutes cut out but not made up at the prince's death'.[96]

NOTES

1 My title borrows the image of grief as a garment from Henry's chaplain Daniel Price, whose sermon *Tears Shed Over Abner*, delivered on 6 December 1610, is discussed below. Wardrobe is capitalized when referring here to the Chamber department of that name, strictly the Wardrobe of Robes, as distinct from the Wardrobe of Beds. There appears to have been no office of Great Wardrobe within the Prince's household. Uncapitalized, the term is used here to denote, simply, a person's store of garments.

2 The procession is recorded in detail in *The Funerals of the High and Mighty Prince Henry … Which Noble Prince Deceased at St. James' the Sixt Day of Nov. 1612* (London, 1613), given in John Nichols, *The Progresses, Processions, and Magnificent Festivities of King James I*, 4 vols. (London, 1828), II, pp. 493–512.

3 See Nichols, *Progresses*, II, pp. 480–81; also W.H. [William Haydon?], *The True Picture and Relation of Prince Henry* (Leiden, 1634), pp. 33–46; Charles Cornwallis [assigned to], *The Life and Death of … Henry Prince of Wales* (London, 1641), pp. 22–30; and esp. Thomas Birch, *The Life of Henry Prince of Wales* (London, 1760) pp. 252–72.

4 Nichols cites BL Harl. 5176 and Cotton MSS Vespasian C. XIV. J.P. Edmond's *Elegies and Other Tracts on the Death of Henry Prince of Wales 1612* (Edinburgh, 1906) catalogues forty-four tracts and elegies. This catalogue has since been expanded by other scholars, most recently by Michael Ullyot.

5 See Nichols, *Progresses*, II, pp. 136–43. R.T.D. Sayle, *Lord Mayors' Pageants of the Merchant Taylors' Company in the 15th, 16th & 17th Centuries* (Reading, 1931).

6 Anthony Munday, *Londons Love to the Royal Prince Henrie, Meeting him on the River of Thames* (London, 1610), p. 8. Munday was allotted colours as well as a 'Capp and fether' for his apparel on the day. See Sayle, *Lord Mayors' Pageants*, p. 31.

7 William Basse employs this metaphor in his *Great Brittaines Svnnes-Set, Bewailed With A Shower of Teares* (Oxford, 1613). Earlier, in private correspondence, Richard Sackville, Earl of Dorset, had written to Sir Thomas Edmondes: 'To tell you that our Rising Sun is set ere scarce he had shone', Nichols, *Progresses*, II, p. 490. Roy Strong borrows Dorset's memorable phrase for the Epilogue of *Henry Prince of Wales and England's Lost Renaissance* (London, 1986).

8 The concept of livery is explored further below. Here, I use the word not only in the sense of clothing distributed to lesser servants of the household but also in a more general sense in that clothing given and worn as a clear component of courtly performance reflects, albeit more flexibly and variously, the expectations inherent to the contemporary livery system.

9 On this theme, see most recently Linda Levy Peck, *Consuming Splendor: Society and Culture in Seventeenth-Century England* (New York, 2005).

10 R. Malcolm Smuts, 'Art and the material culture of majesty', in R. Malcolm Smuts (ed.), *The Stuart Court and Europe* (Cambridge, 1996), p. 92.

11 Jane Ashelford has written, 'Like their Tudor forebears, the Stuart monarchs placed great emphasis on the public and flamboyant display of clothing and on the setting in which to 'publish one's clothes'. Throughout

the seventeenth century the monarch, his family and his courtiers formed the circle where new fashions were generated [actively encouraging] public ceremonies and private parties where a lavish display of fine clothes and jewels was expected'. *The Art of Dress* (London and New York, 1996), p. 56. On monarchy as performance, and more particularly the relationship between performance culture, the court masque, and the early Stuarts, see Stephen Orgel, *The Illusion of Power: Political Theater in the English Renaissance* (Berkeley and London, 1975).

12 Henri Lefebvre, in *The Production of Space*, trans. Donald Nicholson-Smith (Oxford, 1991), p. 27, discusses the premise that '(social) space is a (social) product': an argument with profound implications for the construction and reception of the performance of majesty and the creation of 'royal space' through myriad social rituals including dress and ornamentation.

13 Smuts, 'Art and the material culture of majesty', p. 94. Smuts cites NA LC2/4(5), adding that the canopy was 'adorned with gold and silk fringes, ten large plumes and fifty yards of ribbons': the cloth itself cost £10 per yard.

14 William Fowler, *A True Reportarie of the most triumphante baptisme of Frederik Henry: Prince of Scotland* (Edinburgh, 1594), sig. A2r. J.W. Williamson, in *The Myth of the Conqueror* (New York, 1978), has used this image as a point of departure for his argument that Henry was, even from his birth, following a heroic model that he labels 'the myth of the conqueror'.

15 John Finet to William Trumbull, describing Henry's (somewhat delayed) entry at the time of his creation ceremony before Parliament at Westminster Palace on 4 June, 1610, printed in Edmund Sawyer (ed.), *Memorials of Affairs of State … from the original papers of … Sir Ralph Winwood*, 3 vols. (London, 1725) III, p. 179; also Nichols, *Progresses* II, p. 359.

16 This letter is printed in Sawyer, *Memorials* III, pp. 179–81 and in Nichols, *Progresses*, II, pp. 359–61.

17 SP Dom. 14/57 fol. 145. The exact amount is £1291 18s. 9d., with £1080 3s. 4d. to the furrier, Mr Bland, alone. Beside this entry is the marginal note mentioned above; the Prince's autograph can be found below this comment and on the facing page of the account.

18 Sawyer, *Memorials*, III, p. 182.

19 Stephen Greenblatt writes in the 'General Introduction' to *The Norton Shakespeare* (New York, 1997), that a 'virtual clothes cult … prevailed in England in the late sixteenth and early seventeenth centuries, a cult whose major shrine, outside the royal court, was the theater' (p. 5).

20 John Webster, *The Duchess of Malfi*, I, I. First performed in 1614.

21 Thomas Dekker and Thomas Middleton, *The Roaring Girl*, II, I. First published in 1611, and possibly also written and first performed in that year, and no earlier than 1608. See P.A. Mullholland, 'The date of *The Roaring Girl*', *The Review of English Studies*, new series, XXVIII, 109 (February 1977), pp. 18–31.

22 William Shakespeare, *The Tempest*, II, I. First performed at court in the winter of 1611.

23 Harrison, *Description of England*, p. 148.

24 *Ibid.*, p. 148.

25 Katherine Duncan-Jones, '"Much Ado with Red and White": The Earliest Readers of Shakespeare's *Venus and Adonis* (1593)', *The Review of English Studies*, new series, XLIV, no. 176 (November 1993) pp. 479–501 (p. 481).

26 Mr Cope is possibly Sir Anthony Cope (1549–1614) previous to his knighthood; Sir Anthony was later one of the first baronets created by King James and was one of ten baronets who bore a bannerol alongside Henry's funeral hearse. But this Mr Cope may also have been Sir Walter or Sir William Cope prior to receiving their knighthoods. Much grieved at the death of his son, King James came to lodge in Sir Walter's Kensington house on 9 November, where, 'the next morning the young Prince, the Lady Elizabeth, and the Palsgrave went all together in one coach to him; and that afternoon all the Council', Nichols, *Progresses*, II, pp. 488–89.

27 Lansdowne MS 99, fols. 22r–26v. Letter dated 28 January 1589/90. Transcription and modernization by Katherine Duncan-Jones (October 1998) included here with her kind permission. See Duncan-Jones, '"Much Ado with Red and White"', p. 481, for further analysis of this letter and of Reynolds, a prolific writer of 'strange enthusiastical' letters (Lansdowne 99.10).

28 Sir David Murray notes a remainder of above £30 of 'brauncht velvette' in his itemization of cloth left over after the prince's death [NA 351/3085 f. 13r].

29 William Shakespeare, *Twelfth Night*, III, IV, 24–26. Malvolio's caution to bemused Olivia, 'Not black in my mind, though yellow in my legs', reveals an association, presumably popularly understood, between clothing and state of mind and body not dissimilar to Reynolds's observations cited above. Tim Wilks informs me that the fashion for yellow stocking persisted until at least 1620; cf. Nathaniel Bacon's self-portrait, for which see Karen Hearn, *Nathaniel Bacon: Artist, Gentleman and Gardener* (exh. cat., Tate Britain, London, 2005). Nathaniel Bacon may have been the 'Mr Bacon' named among Henry's Gentlemen of the Privy Chamber Extraordinary in LC 2/4(6).

30 William Shakespeare, *Hamlet*, I, II, 77–84.

31 Pamela's discourse on beauty, in Sir Philip Sidney, *The Countess of Pembroke's Arcadia* (1590), III, Ch. 10.

32 Pett, who was among the leading national shipwrights, kept his residence at the Woolwich naval yards, a site visited frequently by the Prince during the construction and launch of his great warship, the *Prince Royal*. He might have been alerted to the grave seriousness of the situation by Thomas Pett, a young Page of the Chamber on wages of £40 and livery of £4 13s. 4d., who was undoubtedly a relative (probably a nephew), and whose place in the household should be interpreted as another mark of favour shown to Phineas. See Birch, *Life*, p. 453.

33 Nichols, *Progresses*, II, p. 480, citing Cornwallis.

34 Phineas Pett, *The Autobiography of Phineas Pett*, ed. W.G. Perrin (London: The Navy Records Society, 1918), p. 100.

35 Cornwallis, in Birch, *Life*, p. 269.

36 *The Funerals*; Nichols, *Progresses*, II, pp. 493–94.

37 Neil Cuddy, 'Reinventing a Monarchy: The Changing Structure and Political Function of the Stuart Court, 1603–88' in Eveline Cruickshanks (ed.), *The Stuart Courts* (Stroud, 2000), pp. 59–85. These spatial divisions were reinforced by cloth and draperies, as in the case of the Presence Chamber, for which household orders specified that at eight in the evening final service was to be brought up and 'the Travers bee drawne' (BL Harl. 642 fol. 263).

38 NA 351/3085 fols. 20 and 24.

39 NA 351/3085 fol. 24.

40 National Portrait Gallery, London, NPG 4515.

41 NPG 6113.

42 On the Prince's collections see Strong, *Henry, Prince of Wales*, especially 'The Prince's Collections', pp. 184–219; also Timothy Wilks, ' "Paying attention to the adorning of a most beautiful gallery": the pictures in St James's Palace, 1609 to 1649', *The Court Historian*, 10, no. 2 (December 2005), pp. 149–72.

43 From William Bray, 'An account of the revenue, the expences, the jewels, etc. of Prince Henry', *Archaeologica*, XV (1806), pp. 13–26.

44 Cornwallis, cited in Nichols, *Progresses*, II, p. 486: 'The Monday after, the Lords of the Privy Councell came to St. James's to give order for all things belonging to so wofull a business'.

45 Nichols, *Progresses*, II, p. 493; and *The Funerals of the High and Mighty Prince Henry*, pp. 4–66.

46 The description of the creation itself emphasizes the form and structure of the textiles arranged in the Court of Requests chamber at Westminster, noting that 'his majesty [King James] entering in his royal robes, his crown upon his head, did first take his place of state'; the chamber itself was: 'very richly hung from the upper end more than half down towards the lower end, where was set up a strong bar of timber thwart the room; in the highest part of the room was placed, for his majesty, a sumptuous cloth of state, and of either side scaffolds for ambassadors of foreign countries' (Nichols, *Progresses*, II, p. 329).

47 The disbanding of the household came soon enough: 'The late princes household brake up the last of December and his servants sent to seeke theyre fortune' (Chamberlain, *Letters*, I, p. 405).

48 Nichols, *Progresses*, II, p. 487.

49 BL Harl. 642 fol. 265.

50 BL Harl. 642 fol. 263.

51 'A declaration of the bouge of court', printed in Birch, *Life*, pp. 463–66, mentions the 'standing Ward-robe at Richmond', where most of Henry's clothes were apparently stored and cared for.

52 Pett, *Autobiography*, p. 97. Pett refers here to Walter Alexander, one of three gentlemen ushers, daily-waiters, and to Alexander Wilson, yeoman of the Wardrobe, whose wages of £100 and livery of £40, placed him among the best–paid of Henry's officers. See Birch, *Life*, pp. 451, 454. Wilson was clearly among 'divers of the Prince's under officers [who] are to be lodged abroad, whose service is such as they must be let in at the gates early in the morning', 'An establishment of orders for the porters', Birch, *Life*, p. 434.

53 Nichols, *Progresses*, II, pp. 467–73.

54 Particularly striking is Cornwallis's relation of the prince playing tennis on 24 October, at which time he 'as though his body had been of brasse did play in his shirt, as if it had been the heat of summer; during which time he looked so wonderful ill and pale, that all the beholders took notice thereof, muttering to one another what they feared' (Nichols, *Progresses*, II, p. 473).

55 Pett, *Autobiography*, p. 101.

56 Peter Stallybrass, 'Worn Worlds: Clothes and identity on the Renaissance stage', in Margreta de Grazia, Maureen Quilligan and Peter Stallybrass (eds.), *Subject and Object in Renaissance Culture* (Cambridge, 1996), p. 290.

57 Pett, *Autobiography*, p. 100.

58 *Ibid.*, p. 101. Pett's language differs somewhat from Price's actual epigraph, for which see Daniel Price, *Spirituall odours to the memory of Prince Henry. In foure sermons* (Oxford, 1613), V. 3: *Teares Shed Over Abner*, sig. M3.

59 Pett, *Autobiography*, p. 101.

60 Another of Henry's chaplains, Lewis Bayly, was called to the Privy Council to explain himself, which he did so effectively that 'Divers other preachers … begin to speake freely'. Chamberlain, *Letters*, I, p. 396.

61 Daniel Price, *Lamentations for the death of Prince Henry. Two Sermons* (London, 1613), sig. B.

62 Sig. A2. Price is of course using the word 'family' in reference to the officers and servants of the household; the leaf previous to that cited above (sig. Av) does, however, offer a dedication to Prince Charles.

63 Price, *Lamentations*, sig. A2.

64 See especially the six sermons contained in STC 20294 and STC 20304 cited above. The depth and systematic complexity with which Price deploys these symbols invites much more complete discussion and consideration.

65 *Lamentations*, 481, sig. Gv. Price's marginal note to these lines, 'Since the year 1603', is openly seditious, like much he wrote and apparently spoke in response to the Prince's death.

66 *CSP Venetian* XII, 1610–13, p. 122. The report goes on to suggest the politics of dress and the role of national influence and allegiance in fashion: 'The Spanish Ambassador, in conversation with his Highness congratulated him on having adopted the Spanish dress, but had for his answer that it was really nearer Italian.'

67 Nichols, *Progresses*, II, p. 493, for text and further references.

68 The title of this sermon might be explored not only in terms of its reference to the rending of garments but more specifically in terms of the circumstances of Abner's death by treachery and of King David's subsequent lament for Abner, 'the Prince of Light' (2 Samuel 3).

69 Murray's title is given in NA E351/3085; elsewhere he is also listed as keeper of the privy purse and as groom of the stool to Henry. Born in Perthshire in 1567, Murray was about twenty-seven years Henry's senior and had served under James VI in 1600 as comptroller of the household. Following the disbanding of the Prince's household, Murray was supported by royal gifts of money under James I and of the estate of Gorthy, Perthshire under Charles I.

70 Price, *Sprituall Odours* [STC 20304 v3], sig. M.

71 There is need for a more detailed examination of payments toward the Prince's funeral from the Wardrobe and from the household of James I and the Office of the Revels than it is possible to offer here.

72 NA E351/3085.

73 Birch, *Life*, p. 274.

74 Price, *Spirituall Odours* [STC 20304 v3], sig. M.

75 Price, *Spirituall Odours*, v.3, sig. M3.

76 Price, *Teares Shed Over Abner*, sig. M2.

77 Edmond, *Elegies*, p. 143.

78 Joshua Sylvester, *The Distillation of Teares Shed for the Untymely Death of the Incomparable Prince* (London, 1612); see also Edmond, *Elegies*, p. 155. I am grateful to Michael Ullyot for his assistance with terminology related to this reference.

79 John Taylor, *Great Britain, All in Black* (London, 1612) [STC 23760.5].

80 In addition to itemizing a chariot drawn by sea horses and other fantastical devices, the Merchant Taylors' records of expense for the event notes such diverse and voluminous purchases of cloth sufficient to warrant a separate study. See Sayle, *Lord Mayors' Pageants*.

81 See Nichols, *Progresses*, II, pp. 488–89.

82 Cornwallis, cited in Nichols, *Progresses*, II, p. 477.

83 John Webster, *Monuments of Honor* (London, 1624).

84 George Wither, *Prince Henries Obsequies* (London, 1612) [STC 25915].

85 Wither, *Obsequies*, sig. B2.

86 This information and the related figures are drawn and extrapolated from BL MS Lansdowne 160, as given in Nichols, *Progresses*, II, p. 496 note 1.

87 The Merchant Taylors of London must have been under considerable strain to meet demands, and materials for this event were probably ordered and imported hurriedly from across the Channel.

88 This for a seemingly erroneously calculated total of £371.20d.; the correct tally should be £376.20d.

89 Cornwallis, *Life*, pp. 84–85.

90 NA E351/3085 fol. 24.

91 *The Herse, and Representacion of our late Highe and Mighty Henry Prince of Wales, &ct.* See A. M. Hind, *Engraving in England in the Sixteenth and Seventeenth Centuries*, 3 vols. (Cambridge: Cambridge University Press, 1952–64), II, p. 323.

92 Isaac Wake to Lady Carleton, 19 December 1612, SP Dom. 14/71 f. 128.

93 Certainly, the implications of Henry's death were variously understood in England and on the Continent. G.P.V. Akrigg, in *Jacobean Pageant, or The Court of King James I* (London, 1962), p. 399, gives a jingle said to be current during Henry's lifetime:
    'Henry the 8. pulld down abbeys and cells,
    But Henry the 9. shall pull down Bishops and bells',
a distinctly puritan prediction. In the event, Henry's hearse and effigy was installed in Westminster Abbey, episcopal Church and divinely appointed monarchy continuing to confirm and honour each other.

94 John Davies [of Hereford], *Muses-Teares for the losse of … Henry* (London, 1613), C1r.

95 Nichols, *Progresses*, II, p. 498.

96 NA E351/3085 f. 14.

11| 'So iust a sorrowe so well expressed': Henry, Prince of Wales and the Art of Commemoration

Elizabeth Goldring

Henry, Prince of Wales, died on 6 November 1612, roughly two weeks after the sudden onset of an illness now thought to have been typhoid fever.[1] He was just a few months shy of his nineteenth birthday. The unexpected death of the young heir to the throne on whom Protestant England – and indeed Protestant Europe – had pinned its hopes unleashed an extraordinary outpouring of grief. Within twenty-four hours of Henry's death, an *Elegiacall lamentinge Poem for the Incomparable losse of losses of Henry our late hopefull Prince* had been registered at Stationers' Hall.[2] This was but one of approximately fifty memorial publications – ranging from elegies to epitaphs, emblems to epicedia – produced in England in the immediate aftermath of the prince's death. Abroad, the reaction from Protestants was one of great dismay. Diplomatic reports from France record that 'The Huguenots are grieved, as they built their hopes on the Prince [of Wales], and had already chosen him as their chief support and head'.[3] Despatches from Cologne, Düsseldorf, Heidelberg, Stuttgart and Zeeland express similar sentiments, demonstrating the extent to which Henry's death was felt not only by English Protestants, but also, as one German mourner put it, by 'the right party in Christendom generally'.[4]

Although the elegies occasioned by Henry's death have received considerable scholarly attention,[5] neither the funeral itself nor the visual artefacts generated by it have been subject to the same analysis – a reflection, perhaps, of the fact that neither the 'rich tomb of marble and porphyry' nor the 'many statues' envisioned in the immediate aftermath of Henry's death were, in the end, built.[6] Yet, as we shall see, both Henry's obsequies and the engraved record of them played a key role in shaping the prince's posthumous reputation, or what J.W. Williamson memorably termed 'the myth of the conqueror'.[7] To that end, this essay begins with a discussion of the funeral, demonstrating how it presented Henry as a Protestant warrior king when in fact he was a young, inexperienced prince who had died in peacetime. It then turns to William Hole's engraving of Henry's effigy lying in state in Westminster Abbey – an image without precedent in England and one which memorialized both Henry and his funeral, so reinforcing the prince's posthumous elevation in status. Finally, this essay examines how, over the course of the seventeenth century, Hole's engraving was reprinted at moments of religious and political instability, itself a weapon in the service of Protantism.

On 7 December 1612, funerals were staged for Henry in Bristol, Cambridge, Oxford and London. This last, which was the primary funeral, was exceptionally lavish, even by royal standards. More than two thousand official mourners accompanied the coffin on its processional route to Westminster Abbey, some 400 more than had marched in the comparable procession staged for Elizabeth I in 1603. Although the total cost of Henry's London funeral is not known, some sense of its splendour can be gauged from the fact that, over a year after the event, more than £16,000 worth of bills were still outstanding.[8] Even in an era marked by the inflation of funeral honours,[9] Henry's stand out for their sumptuousness.[10]

Who orchestrated this elaborate event? Normally, such a task would have fallen to the Earl Marshal, traditionally a member of the Howard family. The office, however, was vacant when James I ascended the throne and was to remain so until 1621, in which year Thomas Howard, 14th Earl of Arundel, was appointed to the post.[11] G.P.V. Akrigg notes: 'During the eighteen-year interim King James gave occasional special appointments to the Earl of Worcester [Master of the Horse] to serve as Earl Marshal when some ceremony required the presence of one. Otherwise he entrusted the duties of the Earl Marshal to a small committee of Lord Commissioners.'[12] On the occasion of Henry's funeral, the basic arrangements were overseen by the Lord Chamberlain, Thomas Howard, 1st Earl of Suffolk, in consultation with the College of Arms, with the procession being managed on the day by the Knight Marshal, Sir Thomas Vavasour, and his bailiffs from the Marshalsea.[13] As for Henry's own household officers, those who might have had some hand in the planning include the chamberlain, Sir Thomas Chaloner; the comptroller, Sir John Holles; and the keeper of the robes and wardrobe, Sir David Murray.

The primary source of information regarding the cortège is a work entitled *The Funerals of the High and Mighty Prince Henry* (London: T[homas] S[nodham] for John Budge, 1613). As is clear from this account, the contents of which are corroborated by other contemporary sources,[14] the funeral procession through the streets of Westminster began, as was traditional in aristocratic and royal funerals in this period, with representatives of the poor – in this particular case, 140 poor men in black gowns. Thereafter – and again in keeping with the conventions of heraldic funerals in Early Modern England – the procession's participants gradually increased in importance, the richness of their mourning garb increasing incrementally to reflect distinctions in rank. The procession reached its climax with the appearance of the coffin, which, as was customary, was preceded by the heralds and followed by the chief mourner, Henry's younger brother, Charles, Duke of York, the new heir apparent, who was to succeed to the throne as Charles I in 1625.

Although the general contours of this cortège followed established models, several aspects of the funeral deviated from convention. Given that Henry had died in bed at St James's

Palace, the inclusion of a fife and drums – signifiers of martial glory and, therefore, normally restricted to military funerals – was unorthodox.[15] Also unusual was the prominent part played in the procession by foreign nobles. Frederick V, Elector Palatine – attended by an entourage of eight counts and three noble pages,[16] together with six of his Privy Councillors – marched in the cortège immediately behind Prince Charles as, in effect, second chief mourner. This role is, so far as is known, unprecedented in English funerals of the period.[17] Also prominent, walking with the Lord Chancellor and the Archbishop of Canterbury immediately ahead of the coffin, was 'Count Henrik': Frederick Hendrick of Nassau, the younger brother of Maurits of Nassau, Stadholder of Holland.[18] Elsewhere in the procession, the Elector's servants marched alongside those of the Archbishop of Canterbury and Prince Charles; Frederick Henry's servants marched alongside those of the Lord Chancellor; and the gentlemen of both the Elector and Frederick Henry marched alongside those of Princes Henry and Charles. According to one English observer: 'There [were] in all eight *Counts* (besides Count *Henry of Nassaw*), some 36 Gentlemen, and the rest do make up about 150'.[19]

The Elector Palatine and Frederick Henry, together with their respective entourages, were in England for the Elector's upcoming marriage to Henry's beloved sister, Elizabeth, an event that had had to be postponed owing to the young prince's unexpected death.[20] A powerful Protestant alliance was in the making, with the Dutch acting as the brokers, and it was thus both unavoidable and desirable that these foreign nobles should play an important role in the proceedings. Just as the Barriers staged in connection with Henry's investiture as Prince of Wales in 1610 have been interpreted as casting 'the Prince into a revival of Elizabethan chivalry that in its wildest fantasies could see England at the head of a pan-Protestant, European, anti-Catholic and anti-Spanish crusade',[21] so the presence in the cortège of a fife and drums and a large number of high-ranking Continental Protestants may be read as an advertisement for the brand of militant, interventionist Protestantism Henry had embraced in life. In particular, these aspects of the funeral procession might be interpreted as gesturing towards Henry's ambitions for a European-wide Protestant league.

Both Henry's installation as Prince of Wales and his funeral were played out against a background of European-wide political and religious upheaval: namely, the aftermath of the Jülich-Cleves succession crisis of 1609–10, which had brought Henri IV of France to the verge of an alliance with the United Provinces of the Netherlands and the recently formed Protestant Union, a coalition of German states including the Palatinate.[22] Although James I appears to have had no intention of joining this military league, Henry, if the Venetian ambassador in Paris is to be believed, had secretly promised, while only sixteen years of age, 'to serve under his Most Christian Majesty [i.e. Henri IV] whenever he marched on Cleves'.[23] In fact, Henri never marched again, for he was assassinated by a Catholic fanatic in May 1610. His funeral, held in Paris the following month, was to be the last occasion on which a French monarch was buried with great pomp and circumstance, as well as the last time that an

effigy was used at a French royal funeral.[24] As Jennifer
Woodward has suggested, some aspects of Prince Henry's
lavish obsequies – including the display of an effigy and the
participation of some 2000 official mourners – may have
been modelled on the French king's funeral,[25] accounts of
which had circulated in England.[26]

Other aspects of the mourning for Henry might have recalled – for those old enough to remember it – the mourning for Sir Philip Sidney, Elizabethan England's model
Protestant soldier and poet-courtier.[27] Fatally wounded in
1586 whilst fighting against the Spanish in the Netherlands,
Sidney had been buried in London the following year with
an almost princely magnificence.[28] As more than one
scholar has noted, the outpouring of elegiac verse elicited by
Sidney's death was similar in size and scope to that pro-
voked by Henry's some twenty-five years later.[29] Moreover,
Sidney's funeral, as Henry's would later do, emphasized the
deceased's military ambitions and Continental ties. Perhaps
most strikingly, both funeral processions offered the militant Protestant elite a public stage on which to champion its
political agenda of the day: in February 1587, this was the
Dutch revolt; in December 1612, it was the Palatine marriage
and, by implication, a Protestant league.[30]

If Henry's funeral deviated from convention in ways that
cast him as a fallen warrior – in spite of the fact that he had
never seen battle – it also did so in ways that elevated him to an
almost regal status. The size and scale of the cortège, as already
suggested, were unusual for a prince. So, too, was the staging
of multiple funerals. But perhaps the most remarkable feature
of Henry's obsequies was the construction and display of a life-
sized effigy, remnants of which are extant in the archives of
Westminster Abbey (fig. 1). The arms, legs and torso are made
of wood; the head and hands, which do not survive, probably
were made of wax.[31] The effigy's visage was probably made
from a death mask taken from the oiled face of the dead Prince.

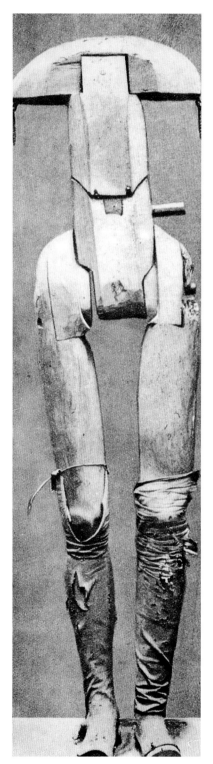

Fig. 1 The effigy of Henry, Prince of Wales, as it appeared in the early
twentieth century

Lifelike effigies had played an integral role in the obsequies of English kings and queens from at least the fourteenth century and in those of French kings and queens from at least the fifteenth, the practice having grown out of an earlier one in which the royal corpse itself was carried on the bier.[32] Henry's funeral, however, marks the first occasion on which an effigy is known to have been made for the son of a reigning English monarch.[33] The extension of this ritual to the Prince of Wales constitutes perhaps the most potent example of the ways in which Henry was buried with the trappings normally reserved for a king or a queen, for the effigy's primary symbolic resonance was as a signifier of the perpetuity of monarchy.[34] As the chronicler Pierre Matthieu observed in the early seventeenth century, 'the effigy was placed upon the coffin … to show that the King never dies.'[35]

According to the records of the Lord Chamberlain's office, the joiner Richard Norris received £9 'for makinge the bodie for the representation';[36] the Dutch wax modeller Abraham van der Doort, who had been a Gentleman Servant Extraordinary to Henry, was paid £10 'for the face and hands of the Princes representacion being verie curiouslie wrought'; and William Peake, the son of Robert Peake, Henry's principal painter, received 30s. 'for one staffe all guilt and burnished with fine gold for the Representacion of the body'.[37] On the eve of the Prince's funeral, the completed effigy was delivered to St James's Palace, where it was dressed and then placed in a recumbent position atop the coffin. According to John Hawkins,

> This Sunday [i.e. 6 December] at night before the Funerall, his representation
> was brought (made in so short warning, as like him as could be) and apparelled
> with cloathes, having his creation robes above the same, his cap and crowne
> upon his head, his Garter, Coller, with a *George* about his neck, his golden staffe
> in his Right hand … it was laid on the back on the Coffin, and fast bound to the
> same, the head thereof being supported by two cushions, just as it was to bee
> drawne along the streets ….[38]

The next morning, Henry's coffin and effigy were borne through the streets of Westminster in an open chariot draped in black velvet. Once inside the Abbey, the coffin and effigy were placed in the outward range for the duration of the service, at the end of which members of Henry's household broke their staves and rods over his coffin. There is also some evidence to suggest that the effigy was used as a prop during the sermon, for Hawkins notes that, during the explication of Psalm 82: 6–7, the congregation's eyes were directed 'for ocular proofe … to the present dolefull spectacle of their late ever renowned *Prince*'.[39] For nearly two weeks after the funeral, the coffin and effigy remained in the Abbey, where they lay in state beneath Henry's hearse, or catafalque.[40] Isaac Wake, another first-hand observer of these rituals, described their effect as follows:

the goodly image of that lovely prince … did so liuely represent his person, as that it did not onely draw teares from the severest beholder, but cawsed a feare-full outcrie among the people as if they felt at the present their owne ruine in that loss. I must confess never to have seen such a sight of mortification in my life, nor neuer so iust a sorrowe so well expressed as in all the spectators whose streaming eyes made knowen howe much inwardly their harts did bleed.[41]

This public display in the Abbey mirrored an earlier, private lying-in-state that had occurred at St James's Palace in the weeks prior to the funeral. Almost immediately after Henry's death, a black canopy had been erected in his bedchamber. There, Henry's coffin – covered with a black pall on top of which were placed his cap and coronet, his state robes, his sword, and his rod of gold – had lain in state for the month or so that elapsed between his death and his funeral.[42] During this time, the Prince's gentlemen-servants had maintained a constant vigil, serving meals to Henry just as they had done when he was alive. A similar lying-in-state had occurred at Richmond Palace during the period between Elizabeth I's death and funeral, and indeed vari-ous versions of this ritual had been an integral part of the obsequies staged for English kings and queens dating back to the death of Edward I in 1307.[43] Henry's death, however, is believed to mark the first occasion on which the lying-in-state ritual was applied to a prince rather than to a monarch.[44] In short, Henry's obsequies, which buried him with the trappings of a Protestant warrior-king, were more reflective of what might have been than of what was.

*

The public display of the effigy and hearse in Westminster Abbey was captured for posterity in an engraving by William Hole, an engraver with close links to George Chapman, Thomas Coryate, Michael Drayton, Angelo Notari and others in the intellectual and artistic circles that had orbited around Prince Henry (fig. 2). As depicted by Hole, the prince's hearse consisted of a base section which supported both the coffin and the recumbent effigy. Resting on this base were six Tuscan columns.[45] This choice of the plainest and stoutest of the classical orders befitted a soldier, and thus might be read as reinforcing the martial overtones of the funeral itself.[46] These columns supported a black canopy, described by the Venetian ambassador as 'raised in the form of a pyramid'.[47] Affixed to this canopy were heraldic devices and emblems, including the badge and motto of the Knights of the Garter and the letters 'HP' surmounted by coronets; ensigns of the principality of Wales, the dukedom of Cornwall and the earldom of Chester; and scrolls bear-ing the prince's motto (*Fax mentis honestæ Gloria*) and that of the hearse (*Iuuat ire per altum*). At the apex – and occupying, in Hole's rendering, a separate, much smaller engraved plate – were the Prince of Wales's feathers and motto. Although it has been plausibly speculated that Inigo Jones, Henry's surveyor of the works and a participant in his funeral procession, might have been

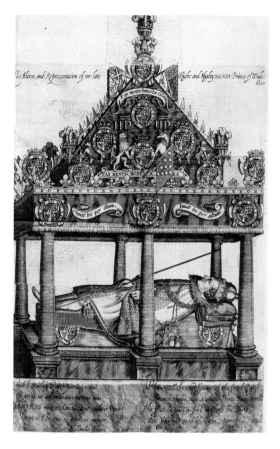

Fig. 2 The effigy of the hearse of Henry, Prince of Wales in Westminster Abbey, engraving by William Hole, printed in George Chapman's *Epicede or Funerall Song* (London: T[homas] S[nodham] for John Budge, 1613)

Fig. 3 The hearse of Sir Philip Sidney in St Paul's Cathedral, engraving (detail) by Theodor de Bry after a preliminary sketch by Thomas Lant, printed in their *Sequitur celebritas et pompa funeris …* (London: n.p., 1588)

responsible for the hearse's design, there is no documentary evidence that this was so.[48]

Hole's engraving, which is now rare, survives in two states, the earlier of which lacks the latter's title (*The Herse, and Representacion of our late Highe and Mighty Henry Prince of Wales, &ct.*), signature (*Guli: Holus sculp.*), and imprint (*Lond: print: for Jo: Budge*).[49] Examples of the second state may be found prefixed to George Chapman's *Epicede* (London: T[homas] S[nodham] for John Budge, 1613), extant copies of which are, more often than not, bound together with the aforementioned *Funerals of the High and Mighty Prince Henry*, a work almost certainly not by Chapman.[50] Some of the surviving copies of the *Epicede* and *Funerals* also contain a solid black leaf on which the Prince of Wales's feathers and motto, together with the letters 'HP', have been imprinted.

The relationship of these texts to Hole's plate is difficult to reconstruct with precision. Although the full title of the composite publication is *Epicede or Funerall Song: On the most disastrous Death, of the High-borne Prince of Men, Henry Prince of Wales … With The Funeralls, and Representation of the Herse of the same*, it is not known whether Hole's plate was always prefixed to the *Epicede* and *Funerals* or whether it was also possible to acquire these texts with-

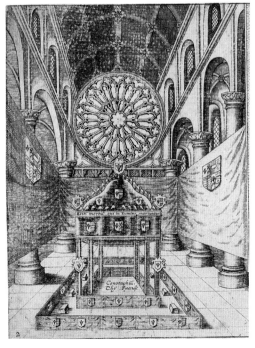

out the illustration advertised on the title page. Several extant copies of the *Epicede* and *Funerals* lack Hole's engraving, though it may be the case, of course, that Hole's print was removed from the copies in question at some point in their history. Also unknown is whether it was possible, at Budge's 'shop at the great south dore of *Paules*',[51] to purchase Hole's engraving on its own. The absence of text on its verso, however, suggests that, in all likelihood, this print was intended for individual sale as well as for inclusion in the *Epicede* and *Funerals*.

In both states of Hole's engraving, two epitaphs – one in Latin, the other in English – are inscribed on the base of the hearse.[52] The latter, by Chapman, who had been sewer-in-ordinary to Henry and had dedicated his translation of the *Iliad* to the Prince,[53] appears in the lower right corner:

> Whome all the vast fframe of the fixed Earth
> Shrunck under; now, a weake Herse stands beneath.
> His ffate be past in fact; in Hope his Birthe:
> His Youth, in good life; & in Spirritt his Death.

The Latin epitaph, by Hugh Holland,[54] appears in the lower left corner:

> *Crudeli crudaque Patri patriæque ruinâ*
> *Raptus, ut æthereis insereretur auis:*
> *Henricvs modicæ (Sanctum Caput!) inditur Vrnæ;*
> *Maximus Ille, suo ni genitore minor.*[55]

These verses by Chapman and Holland also were printed in Scotland – possibly pirated – in *Mavsolevm or, The Choisest Flowres of the Epitaphs, written on the Death of the neuer-too-much lamented Prince Henrie* (Edinburgh: Andro Hart, 1613), a small pamphlet consisting of sixteen epitaphs for Henry.[56] In addition, Chapman's 'Whome all the vast fframe …' appears, along with two other epitaphs, at the end of his *Epicede*, under the heading, 'And this short verse be on his Tomb imprest'.[57] Hole's engraving, in which the lines in question are 'imprest' on Henry's hearse, thus literalizes Chapman's figurative trope – itself an allusion to the early modern practice by which inscriptions were sometimes affixed to the catafalque.[58]

Hole's engraving is not the first image of a hearse to have been printed in England: that distinction belongs to Thomas Lant and Theodor De Bry's engraved depiction of Sir Philip Sidney's hearse in St Paul's Cathedral (fig. 3).[59] Hole's print, however, is believed to be the first engraved image of an English royal effigy.[60] Whether the impetus for the production of this unprecedented image resided with Hole or with the stationer John Budge or with someone else altogether is unclear. But the choice of subject-matter and general format may have been influenced by an engraving associated with the mourning for Henri IV (fig. 4). The image in

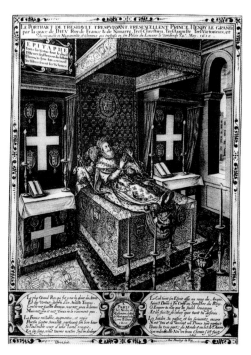

Fig. 4 Henri IV on the bed of state, engraving by Jacques Briot, printed in *Brief Discours des pompes, ceremonies, & obseques funebres d'Henry Le Grand* (Paris: Nicolas de Mathoniere, 1610)

question, by Jacques Briot, depicts Henri IV's effigy lying on the bed of state and was printed in the *Brief Discovrs des pompes, ceremonies, & obseques funebres d'Henry Le Grand* (Paris: Nicolas de Mathoniere, 1610). Although Briot's image places greater emphasis on the depiction of architectural space – whereas Hole's is tightly focused on the hearse and effigy – the general similiarities between the two prints are striking: both were produced to accompany written accounts of a royal funeral and both have commemorative verses on the deceased inscribed beneath the image of the coffin and effigy. Moreover, both engravings would have extended the lying-in-state ritual to an audience beyond those individuals who had been able to experience it in person, whilst also serving as *aide-mémoires* for those who had.

That Hole's engraving should have evoked the mourning for Henri IV is not, perhaps, entirely surprising. There is, as noted, reason to believe that aspects of Henry's funeral were modelled on Henri IV's. Moreover, contemporaries repeatedly likened the loss of the Prince of Wales to that of the French king. The Venetian ambassador in London, for example, reported, 'It has fallen to my lot to be present at the death of Henri of France and now of this other Henry, Prince of Great Britain, his peer in greatness, magnanimity, valour … the only difference was their age'.[61] William Basse's elegy for Henry, *Great Brittaines svnnes-set* (Oxford: Joseph Barnes, 1613), expresses a similar sentiment: 'But *France* whose cheek's still wet, nearest our greife hath / For she from *Henry* Great; wee from Great *Henry* parted'.[62] Such comparisons were not without basis in fact. Henri IV had cultivated his godson and namesake as a political ally, sending him armour and a riding instructor – gifts, in Dennis Kay's words, 'calculated to proclaim the boy's … assumption of the iconographic trappings of empire'.[63] The young Prince, upon learning of the French King's death, is said to have taken to his bed for several days with the lament, 'My second father is dead'.[64]

If the general subject-matter and format of Hole's print echo Briot's, implicitly casting Henry as a second Henri IV, Hole's depiction of the face on Henry's effigy has a source much closer to home – albeit one no less politically charged. The effigy's visage, as depicted by Hole, is so similar to that seen in the artist's 1612 engraving of *Prince Henry practising with the pike* – an image itself closely related to Isaac Oliver's miniature of the prince *à l'antique c.* 1610 (see Wilks's essay in this volume, figs. 2–4, p. 187) – that it seems probable that Hole used his earlier work as a guide. In all three images, Henry is depicted staring straight ahead, his profile characterized by the same distinctively aquiline nose, broad forehead, cleft chin and slightly receding hairline. Whether Hole copied the face for Henry's effigy directly from his own earlier engraving or from the face wrought by Van der Doort is unclear. But, whatever the case, Hole's rendering of the Prince's effigy – and, perhaps, the effigy itself – conformed to and confirmed the politicallycharged tenor of these earlier images, which depicted Henry as the warrior-king-in-waiting of the Barriers.[65]

Who constituted the audience for Hole's effigy engraving? This is a difficult question to answer, for there are enormous gaps in our knowledge of the circulation and reception of prints in early seventeenth-century England – a problem that is directly related to the low survival rate of the prints themselves.[66] Equally elusive is the matter of how Early Modern viewers experienced Hole's image – something which, in any case, must have varied from one individual to the next. That said, engravings of Elizabeth I's tomb are known to have been displayed on the walls of parish churches across England (fig. 5).[67] Moreover, in the case of Hole's engraving of Henry's hearse and effigy, it is possible to comment on the experience of one contemporary viewer, even if he is rather exceptional. The antiquarian Augustine Vincent, who was to be appointed Rouge Rose pursuivant-extraordinary to the College of Arms in 1616, compiled a handwritten description of Henry's obsequies, the text of which is closely related to that of the *Funerals*, and into which he pasted one of Hole's engravings of the Prince's effigy and hearse. This collection of materials, which also includes hand-coloured illustrations of the banners borne in Henry's funeral procession, appears within Vincent's *Precedents*, a manuscript on the correct form for marshalling public ceremonies. Now in the College of Arms, this document also contains, *inter alia*, an account of Elizabeth I's funeral which includes hand-coloured drawings of the banners carried in the procession and of the Queen's hearse; in addition, an engraving of Elizabeth's tomb has been pasted into the manuscript.[68] Whether Vincent's copy of the Hole engraving once had been affixed to the *Epicede* and *Funerals* is unknown, as is the extent to which Vincent had access to the original designs or was able to examine the paraphernalia of the obsequies as described in his *Precedents*. But, given that Vincent was, at the time of Henry's funeral, keeper of state records in the Tower,[69] we may suppose that he was – at the very least – amongst the many thousands of Londoners who witnessed the funeral procession.

*

Hole's engraving of Henry's effigy and hearse in Westminster Abbey had a remarkable afterlife. In 1646, the funeral of Robert Devereux, 3rd Earl of Essex, who had served as Lord-General of the Parliamentary forces, was marked by the publication of a print depicting

Essex's effigy and hearse in Westminster Abbey (fig. 6).[70] As a child, Essex had been one of Henry's closest friends, the two having been educated for a time together; an extant double portrait of Henry and Essex, executed by Robert Peake *c.* 1606–07, speaks eloquently to their childhood intimacy.[71] At Henry's funeral, the young earl had been a prominent participant in the prince's cortège.[72] Just as Essex's obsequies seem to have been closely modelled on Henry's – down to and including the design of his hearse[73] – so the engraving in question self-consciously invites comparison with Hole's. It survives in two virtually identical states,[74] both of which are signed in the lower right corner *W. Hole*, though Hole was long dead by the time of Essex's funeral.[75] This explicit reference, as A.M. Hind first noted, doubtless was intended to reinforce the unknown engraver's debt to Hole's model.[76] Yet it signals more than an artistic debt. As J.S.A. Adamson has argued, the iconographic and ceremonial echoes of Prince Henry's obsequies in those staged for Essex may be read as an attempt 'to order and rationalize the traumatic and dislocated politics of 1646 by an act of relocation in the past; in the romanticized heroic age of Prince Henry and in the values for which that episode was held to stand'.[77] In other words, the militant Protestantism embodied by Prince Henry and epitomized by Hole's effigy print was re-conceived and redeployed at a moment of crisis.

Although this engraving of Essex's effigy and hearse has been much discussed by historians of Caroline political and visual culture,[78] what is less well known is that Hole's image inspired at least three other copies over the course of the seventeenth century. One of these, printed by Abraham de Koninck at Amsterdam, was clearly aimed at an audience in the Low Countries, Hole's title having been replaced with a Dutch one and Chapman's verses on the base of the hearse having been replaced with a vernacular translation of Holland's Latin ones (fig. 7).[79] Otherwise, this copy follows Hole's model very closely, though it has been truncated so that the Prince of Wales's feathers and motto at the apex of the hearse have been omitted. When, precisely, this image was printed is not known. Nor is it clear if this print was issued on its own or as part of a larger publication. But the existence of this engraving speaks to the success with which Hole's engraving of Henry's obsequies – like the obsequies themselves, with their large contingent of Continental Protestant nobles – helped to elevate the Prince's death to an event of international significance.

Hole's engraving of the Prince's effigy and hearse also was copied by Willem or Magdalena de Passe and printed in the *Heroologia Anglica* … (Arnhem: Jan Jansson, 1620), a work devised by the London-based printer and bookseller Henry Holland, but produced in the Netherlands, where it was financed jointly by Crispijn de Passe and the printer Jan Jansson (fig. 8). Although the feathers and motto of the Prince of Wales that appear, in Hole's rendering, at the apex of the hearse once again have been omitted – as have the signature, title and imprint found in the later state of Hole's print – the de Passe engraving is, in all other respects, an extremely faithful copy.

In addition to this image, the *Heroologia* features some sixty engraved portrait busts, beginning with one of Henry VIII and concluding with one of Thomas Holland, Regius Professor of Divinity at Oxford. In between is a roll-call of leading English Protestants, who, roughly speaking, fall into four categories: monarchs, a group that includes Edward VI and Elizabeth I, but pointedly excludes Mary Tudor; courtiers, such as Robert Dudley, Earl of Leicester, Sir Philip Sidney and Robert Devereux, 2nd Earl of Essex; theologians, such as William Perkins, John Whitgift and Edwin Sandys; and explorers, such as Sir Humphrey Gilbert, Sir Martin Frobisher and Sir Francis Drake. Only Elizabeth I and Prince Henry are depicted more than once. Elizabeth's portrait is supplemented by an engraving of her tomb (fig. 5), Henry's by the aforementioned copy of Hole's effigy engraving, as well as by a copy of Hole's pike print. Each image in the *Heroologia* is accompanied by a Latin commentary, written by Holland, who also selected and supplied the models from which the de Passes' engravings were copied. The de Passes's work is believed to have been carried out in the Netherlands, for Magdalena is not known to have travelled to London and Willem did not do so prior to 1621.[80]

The *Heroologia* was produced in an environment of European-wide religious and political upheaval, sparked by the outbreak in 1618 of what would come to be known as the Thirty Years' War. Henry's sister, Elizabeth, and her husband, Frederick, the Elector Palatine, were amongst the first political casualties of this conflict. Having accepted the crown of Bohemia in August 1619 and been crowned king in Prague in November of that year, Frederick reigned for just over a year. In November 1620, his troops were defeated by advancing Catholic armies at the Battle of White Mountain, after which he and Elizabeth were forced into exile in the Netherlands.

The *Heroologia's* appropriation of Hole's images effectively inducted Henry into a pantheon of Protestant heroes. Holland's Preface to the *Heroologia* is explicit about the work's Protestant bias, noting that only avowed enemies of the Papacy have been selected for inclusion. Significantly, it would appear that the images in the *Heroologia* were not intended for individual sale, as nearly every engraving contains text on its verso.[81] In other words, these images derived their meaning and context from being part of a group – in Henry's case, being cast as the successor to the legacies of Elizabeth I and of the Leicester-Sidney-Essex circle at her court. Holland registered the *Heroologia* at Stationers' Hall on 30 September 1619,[82] and – given that all the subjects depicted are British – the London market must have been the principal one. However, as Antony Griffiths rightly notes, the exclusive use of Latin throughout suggests that the *Heroologia* also may have been intended for an international readership, albeit a Protestant one.[83] That Holland chose to include copies of Hole's pike and effigy engravings may be viewed as a testament to the success with which Hole had articulated for posterity a vision of Henry as a Protestant warrior-king.

Another version of Hole's effigy engraving may be found in Francis Sandford's *Genealogical History of the Kings of England and Monarchs of Great Britain …* (London: Thomas Newcomb, 1677; fig. 9). Signed *R. Gaywood fecit'*, it is the work of Richard Gaywood, a prolific etcher whose

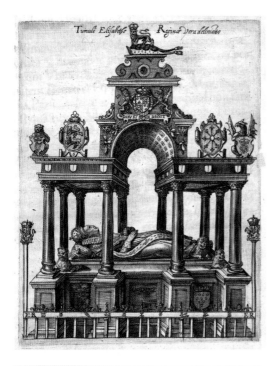

Fig. 5 The tomb of Elizabeth I, engraving by Willem or Magdalena de Passe after an unknown (now lost) source, printed in Henry Holland's *Heroologia Anglica* (Arnhem: Jan Jansson, 1620)

Fig. 6 The effigy and hearse of Robert Devereux, 3rd Earl of Essex, engraving by an unknown artist after William Hole, 1646

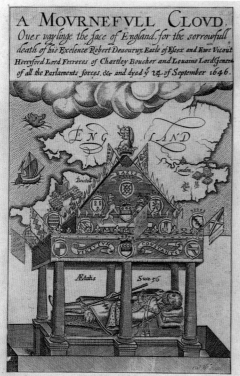

stock in trade was copying printed portraits from other artists. In Gaywood's rendering, all of the inscriptions found in the original have been omitted and the image has been reversed, so that the effigy's head is on the viewer's left. Gaywood may simply have traced from a print on to his plate, but the debt to Hole is unmistakable.

Like the copies of Hole's print already discussed, Gaywood's appeared at a moment of religious and political instability. If the *Heroologia* may be read in the context of the threat to international Protestantism posed by the outbreak of the Thirty Years' War, then the *Genealogical History* may be understood in an English context in which neither Charles II's reign nor the future of Protestantism seemed entirely secure. By 1677, the year in which the *Genealogical History* was published, it was becoming increasingly clear to all that the King was unlikely to produce a legitimate heir. Meanwhile, his younger brother, the Duke of York and future James II, had converted to Catholicism, in 1673 taking the Catholic Mary of Modena as his second wife. Although James's daughter Mary wed the Protestant Prince William of Orange in 1677, the following year was to bring the discovery of the Popish Plot.

A herald and genealogist, Sandford dedicated his *Genealogical History* to Charles II,

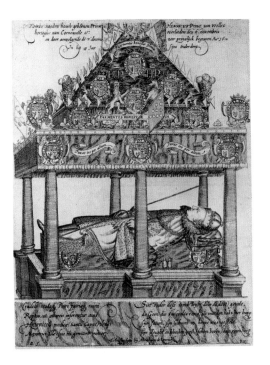

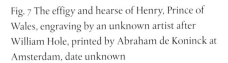

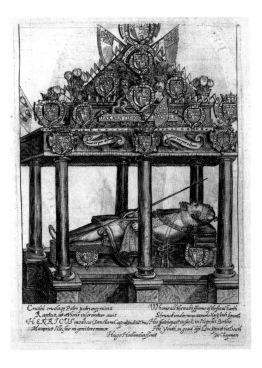

Fig. 7 The effigy and hearse of Henry, Prince of Wales, engraving by an unknown artist after William Hole, printed by Abraham de Koninck at Amsterdam, date unknown

Fig. 8 The effigy and hearse of Henry, Prince of Wales, engraving by Willem or Magdalena de Passe after William Hole, printed in Henry Holland's *Heroologia Anglica* (Arnhem: Jan Jansson, 1620)

Fig. 9 The effigy and hearse of Henry, Prince of Wales, engraving by Richard Gaywood after William Hole, printed in Francis Sandford's *Genealogical History* (London: Thomas Newcomb, 1677)

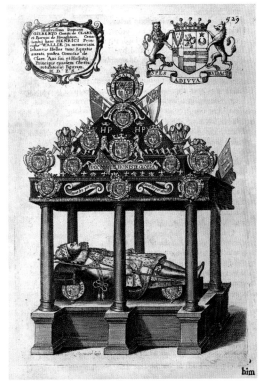

whose reign it seeks both to legitimize and to celebrate.[84] Although it contains no new information, the work consolidated existing knowledge of royal genealogy and provided illustrations of royal tombs and portraits. With its emphasis on setting forth the royal lineage 'From the Conquest, *Anno* 1066. to the Year, 1677',[85] the work explicitly celebrates the Restoration, casting Charles II as the rightful heir to a centuries' old tradition. Henry's inclusion in this roll-call of English kings speaks to the success both of his obsequies and of Hole's depiction of them in fashioning a legacy for him as one, to quote Sandford, 'by his demeanour seeming like a King even whilst he was a Prince onely'.[86]

Conclusions

It is not simply Hole's engraving of Henry's effigy that had an eventful afterlife: so too did the effigy itself. According to Hawkins's account, printed in 1641, when the public lying-in-state came to an end, the Prince's hearse was dismantled and Henry's effigy placed on display alongside those of his forebears:

> the Coffin with the representation … remaining still under the Hearse, to be seene of all, untill the 19. of the said Moneth of *December*, when decked and trimmed with cloathes, as he went when hee was alive, Robes, Coller, Crowne, Golden Rodde in his hand, &c. it was set up in a Chamber of the said Chappell at *Westminster*, amongst the Representations of the Kings and Queenes, his famous Predecessors, where it remaineth for ever to be seene.[87]

Thus, just as both the funeral and Hole's engraved record of it elevated the prince to a regal status, so the ongoing display of his effigy – alongside those of past Kings and Queens – contributed to a posthumous elevation in Henry's status and rank.

The custom of publicly displaying effigies in the Abbey can be dated to at least 1606 and may stretch as far back as 1561, in which year the chief verger was granted 'custodie and oversight of the Tombes and monimentes and of the pictures [i.e. funeral effigies] of kings and quenes within all the saide church remayning'.[88] In 1606, the effigies of seven monarchs had been repaired, rerobed, and placed on display for the benefit of the visiting Christian IV of Denmark. The Abbey's accounts for that year record a payment for 'the making of the presse of wainscott in which the statues do stand',[89] which suggests that the effigies were displayed in an upright, rather than a recumbent, position. It is a point which might account for the fact that the joiner Richard Norris had taken care to ensure that Henry's was equipped 'with severall joynts, in the Armes leggs and bodie to be moved to sonderie attions'.[90]

The subsequent history of the prince's effigy is, however, rather chequered. Within a few years of Henry's death and funeral, his effigy's robes had been stolen.[91] In 1725, when George Vertue visited the Abbey, Henry's effigy was one of twelve on display in a 'great Press' in Abbot Islip's Chapel, though the effigies 'of late years [had been] nailld up & not shown'.[92] This collection – which also included representations of Edward III, Henry V, Henry VII, Elizabeth I and James I – was, according to Vertue, 'commonly calld the Ragged Regiment'. Prince Henry's, in particular, had suffered damage to the head, which had been 'repaird in plaister'. By the late nineteenth century, the head seems to have disappeared altogether.[93] Today, what remains of the prince's effigy is in such poor repair that it is no longer on public display in the Abbey.[94]

Meanwhile, the lavish tomb envisioned in the immediate aftermath of Henry's death was never built. Various interpretations have been offered for the fact that this ambitious project – which the Venetian ambassador predicted would 'take a long time and cost much'[95] – failed to come to fruition. David Howarth, for example, has suggested three possible explanations: that James I was too devastated by the catastrophic loss of his elder son to see through plans for the monument; that, owing to the elaborate funeral, 'justice [already] had been seen to have been done' to Henry's memory; and finally that the funeral itself simply may have bankrupted the Exchequer.[96] By contrast, Nigel Llewellyn sees the absence of a tomb for Henry as reflective of a wider pattern: 'the need for monuments was manifestly greater at the establishment of the dynasty, but once the lineage was safely established, monuments became less important, could be left unfinished or even dispensed with altogether'.[97] Whatever the case, Hole's engraving of Henry's effigy and hearse, together with the many copies it inspired, seems to have come to stand in for the prince's elaborate, unbuilt tomb and for his increasingly decrepit effigy. As Francis Sandford stated of Henry in his *Genealogical History*, 'Memorial he hath none; therefore to supply the place of a Tomb, I have … exhibited the Figure of his Herse set up at his Funeral in the said Abbey'.[98]

NOTES

I would like to thank Christy Anderson, R.J. Knecht, Sarah Knight, Phillip Lindley, Nigel Llewellyn, Mia Mochizuki, Graham Parry, Michael Ullyot and Tim Wilks for their assistance.

1 For the contemporary rumour that Henry had been the victim of foul play, see Horatio F. Brown (ed.), *Calendar of State Papers and Manuscripts, Relating to English Affairs, Existing in the Archives and Collections of Venice, and in Other Libraries of Northern Italy, 1610–1613* (London, 1905), pp. 464, 467, 470, 473; Edmund Sawyer (ed.), *Memorials of Affairs of State … from the original papers of … Sir Ralph Winwood*, 3 vols. (London, 1725), III, pp. 410–11. For the autopsy that was conducted in order to counter such rumours, see *Historical Manuscripts Commission, Downshire*, ed. A.B. Hinds (London, 1938), III ('Papers of William Trumbull the Elder, 1611–1612'), p. 419; and Mary Anne Everett Green (ed.), *Calendar of State Papers, Domestic Series, 1611–1618* (London, 1858), pp. 154, 155.

2 Edward Arber (ed.), *A Transcript of the Registers of the Company of Stationers of London 1554–1640 A.D.*, 5 vols. (London and Birmingham, 1875–1894), III, 228r.

3 *CSPV, 1610–1613*, p. 452.

4 See, for example, *HMC Downshire*, III, 415, 417, 433.

5 See, in addition to Michael Ullyot's essay in this volume, the following: J.P. Edmonds, 'Elegies and other Tracts on the Death of Prince Henry,' *Publications of the Edinburgh Bibliographical Society*, 6 (1906), pp. 141–58; Dennis Kay, *Melodious Tears: The English Funeral Elegy from Spenser to Milton* (Oxford: Clarendon Press, 1990), pp. 124–203; Graham Parry, *The Golden Age Restor'd: The Culture of the Stuart Court, 1603–42* (Manchester, 1981), pp. 88–91; Ruth Wallerstein, *Studies in Seventeenth-Century Poetic* (Madison, WI, 1950), pp. 59–95; Elkin Calhoun Wilson, *Prince Henry and English Literature* (Ithaca, NY, 1946), pp. 128–76.

6 *CSPV, 1610–1613*, p. 469.

7 See J.W. Williamson, *The Myth of the Conqueror, Prince Henry Stuart: A Study of 17th Century Personation* (New York, 1978).

8 Jennifer Woodward, *The Theatre of Death: The Ritual Management of Royal Funerals in Renaissance England, 1570–1625* (Woodbridge, 1997), p. 148.

9 Cf., for example, the case of Sir John Spencer ('Rich Spencer'), whose funeral of 1610 included 1000 mourners (Sawyer, *Memorials of Affairs of State*, III, 136). See also Clare Gittings, *Death, Burial and the Individual in Early Modern England* (London, 1984), p. 226.

10 Estimates as to the cost of Elizabeth I's funeral range from £11,305 1s. (Gittings, *Death, Burial and the Individual*, p. 226) to £20,000 (Woodward, *Theatre of Death*, p. 93).

11 One might expect Arundel to have been given some special responsibility for the funeral: not only was he well known to aspire to his family's hereditary office of Earl Marshal, but he had been close to Henry. However, Arundel was taking a cure at Padua when the prince died and did not return to England until late January or early February 1612/13. See Mary F.S. Hervey, *The Life, Correspondence and Collections of Thomas Howard, Earl of Arundel* (Cambridge, 1921), p. 67.

12 G.P.V. Akrigg, *Jacobean Pageant, or The Court of King James I* (London, 1962), p. 27.

13 See Thomas Birch, *The Life of Henry Prince of Wales* (London, 1760), p. 529.

14 See, e.g., College of Arms, Vincent MSS 87 and 151; Sir Charles Cornwallis [assigned to], *The Life and Death of our Late most Incomparable and Heroique Prince, Henry Prince of Wales* (London: John Dawson for Nathanael Butter, 1641) and *CSPV, 1610–1613*, pp. 467–69.

15 Henry had retained within his household his own drummer (William Pearson) and fife player (Abraham Hardy). Their participation in the funeral, while contributing to Henry's posthumous image as a warrior, also would have evoked memories of his well-known enjoyment of martial music. See Birch, *Life of Henry Prince of Wales*, p. 384.

16 An examination of the *Beschreibung der Reiss …* (Heidelberg: Gotthardt Vögelins, 1613), an account of the

Palatine couple's journey home which includes a German translation of *The Funerals of the High and Mighty Prince Henry*, enables the eight 'Earles strangers' listed in the *Funerals* as 'attendants on Count *Palatine*' (sig. C1v) to be more accurately identified: 'Count *Wigensten*' = 'Graff Bernhard von Wittgenstein' ; 'Count *Lewis de Nassau*' = 'Graff Hans Ludwig von Nassaw'; 'Count *Leuingsten*' = 'Graff Johann Casimir von Lewenstein'; 'Count *Hohenlo*' = 'Graff Philips Heinrich von Hohenloe zu Waldenburg'; 'Count *Ringraue*' = 'Hans Cunrad Rheingraffe'; 'Count *Erback*' = 'Graff Johann Casimir von Erbach'; 'Count *Nassaw Scarburg*' = 'Graff Philip von Nassaw Sarbrucken'; 'Count *Le Hanow*, Iunior' = 'Graf von Hanaw Bußweiler der jünger' (*Funerals*, sig. C1v; *Beschreibung*, p. 22). Likewise, the three pages attendant upon the Elector may be identified thus: 'Count *Isinbersh*' = 'Graff Philip Ernst von Ensenberg'; 'Count *Solmes*' = 'Graff Conrad Ludwig von Solms'; and 'Count *Zerottin*' = 'Johann Dieterich von Zerotin' (*Funerals*, sig. C1v; *Beschreibung*, p. 22). The high status of these nobles generally has gone unrecognized, and, as not all came from the Palatinate, their attendance indicates the breadth of the Elector's Continental following.

17 Woodward, *Theatre of Death*, p. 155.

18 Frederik Hendrik was to succeed his elder brother as Stadholder in 1625.

19 Sawyer, *Memorials of Affairs of State*, III, 404.

20 At the wedding of Princess Elizabeth and the Elector Palatine, Frederick Hendrick represented the house of Orange-Nassau, as Maurits was at the time unable to leave the Netherlands.

21 Roy Strong, *Henry Prince of Wales and England's Lost Renaissance* (London: Thames & Hudson, 1986; repr Pimlico, 2000), p. 113. The Barriers were staged on Twelfth Night 1610 as a prelude to Henry's investiture, which took place in June of that year.

22 The Elector Palatine at the founding of the Protestant Union in 1608 and during the Jülich-Cleves crisis of 1609–10 was Frederick IV, father of Frederick V.

23 Horatio F. Brown (ed.), *Calendar of State Papers and Manuscripts, Relating to English Affairs, Existing in the Archives and Collections of Venice, and in Other Libraries of Northern Italy, 1607–10* (London, 1904), p. 506.

24 See Ralph E. Giesey, *The Royal Funeral Ceremony in Renaissance France* (Geneva, 1960), pp. 180, 122.

25 Woodward, *Theatre of Death*, pp. 149–50.

26 The official French account of the obsequies, *Pompe Funebre du Grand Henry Roy de France et de Navarre. Faites à Paris &. à S. Denys les vingt neuf & trentieme iours de Iuin 1610* (Rouen: Raphaël du Petit, 1610), was translated into English as *The Funerall Pompe and Obsequies of the Most mighty and puissant Henry the fourth, King of France and Navarre, solemnized at Paris, and at S. Dennis, the 29 and 30 daies of Iune last past. 1610* (London: Nicholas Okes, 1610). See also Arber, *Registers of the Company of Stationers*, III, 195r, 204r; and Sawyer, *Memorials of Affairs of State*, III, 188–90.

27 For the 'ideological line of descent' from the Earl of Leicester and Sir Philip Sidney to Prince Henry, via the 2nd Earl of Essex, see Strong, *Henry, Prince of Wales*, pp. 169–70.

28 For first-hand accounts of the funeral, see the following publications: John Phillip's *Life and Death of Sir Philip Sidney* (1587) and Thomas Lant and Theodor De Bry's *Sequitur celebritas et pompa funeris … (1588)*.

29 On this point, see Kay, *Melodious Tears*, p. 125; Parry, *The Golden Age Restor'd*, p. 88; and Wilson, *Prince Henry and English Literature*, pp. 173–74.

30 For the political dimensions of Sidney's obsequies, see Elizabeth Goldring, 'The Funeral of Sir Philip Sidney and the Politics of Elizabethan Festival,' in J.R. Mulryne and Elizabeth Goldring (eds.), *Court Festivals of the European Renaissance: Art, Politics and Performance* (Aldershot, 2002), pp. 199–224.

31 For Henry's effigy, see Anthony Harvey and Richard Mortimer (eds.), *The Funeral Effigies of Westminster Abbey* (Woodbridge, 1994), pp. 59–62; and W.H. St John Hope, 'On the Funeral Effigies of the Kings and Queens of England, with Special Reference to Those in the Abbey Church of Westminster,' *Archaeologia*, 40, part 2 (1907), pp. 517–70 (pp. 32–39). Although it has been suggested that a wooden head presented to the Abbey in 1986 might belong to Henry's effigy, this hypothesis has been convincingly refuted (Harvey and Mortimer, *Funeral Effigies*, p. 62).

32 Harvey and Mortimer, *Funeral Effigies*, pp. 3–4; Woodward, *Theatre of Death*, pp. 62–66.

33 Harvey and Mortimer, *Funeral Effigies*, p. 9. In fifteenth-century England, effigies had been made for bishops as well as for kings, though this practice was considered outmoded (and unusual enough to be worthy of comment) when, in 1556, one was made for Bishop Stephen Gardiner. For Gardiner's funeral, see John Gough Nichols (ed.), *The Diary of Henry Machyn, Citizen and Merchant-Taylor of London, from A.D. 1550 to A.D. 1563* (London, 1848), p. 101. For a negative commentary of *c.* 1560 on the use of the effigy ('the figure is not nowe used'), see London, British Library, MS Egerton 2642, fol. 195r; cited and discussed in Sydney Anglo, *Images of Tudor Kingship* (Guildford, 1992), p. 106.

34 See Ernst Kantorowicz, *The King's Two Bodies: A Study in Medieval Political Theology* (Princeton, NJ, 1957; repr 1997), pp. 419–37.

35 Quoted in Giesey, *The Royal Funeral Ceremony*, pp. 179–80.

36 The records of the Lord Chamberlain's office indicate that Norris also was paid £6 'for making a coffin of strong elme plankes and Setting on the Ironworke to the said coffin and incoffering the bodie of his highness in the same coffin and for his attendaunce about the same business' (Kew, National Archives, LC 2/4 (6), fol. 5r; cited in Harvey and Mortimer, *Funeral Effigies*, p. 59).

37 Kew, National Archives, LC 2/4 (6), fols. 5r–5v; cited and discussed in Harvey and Mortimer, p. 59. Van der Doort and both Peakes marched in Henry's funeral procession. For a list of artificers and officers of the works who attended Henry's funeral, see Timothy V. Wilks, 'The Court Culture of Prince Henry and his Circle, 1603–1613' (unpublished doctoral thesis, University of Oxford, 1987), Appendix III.

38 Cornwallis, *The Life and Death*, p. 85.

39 *Ibid.*, p. 88.

40 In early modern usage, the term 'hearse' refers not, as today, to the vehicle for conveying the coffin, but rather to the ephemeral structure erected around the coffin in the church.

41 Kew, National Archives, SP 14/71, fol. 128r; cited in Strong, *Henry Prince of Wales*, p. 1.

42 On 3 December, the coffin had been moved from the bedchamber to the privy chamber and the following day from the privy chamber to the presence chamber. On 5 December, it was carried into the Great Chamber, and Henry's crown and cap moved to a cushion at the head of the coffin. Finally, the coffin was transported – via the court – to the chapel choir, where it was to remain until the morning of 7 December.

43 Woodward, *The Theatre of Death* , pp. 115–17. According to Woodward (p. 116), the formalization of the lying-in-state ritual may be dated to the death of Henry VII in 1509.

44 *Ibid.*, p. 149.

45 Although Hawkins recalled that there were eight columns (Cornwallis, *The Life and Death*, p. 87), this seems an unlikely arrangement for what appears to have been a double-cube design.

46 For the contemporary association of the Tuscan order with military architecture, see Robert Peake's translation of Serlio (Book 4, chapter 5, especially fols. 6r and 9r), published in 1611 and dedicated to Prince Henry.

47 *CSPV*, 1610–1613, p. 468.

48 See John Peacock, 'Inigo Jones's Catafalque for James I,' *Architectural History*, 25 (1982), pp. 1–5. The profusion of heraldic decoration does not obscure the clarity of the design, which is essentially architectural and, as Peacock notes (p. 2), 'adapted in the direction of Florentine models – which may mean it is by Constantino de' Servi and not Jones'.

49 Arthur M. Hind, *Engraving in England in the Sixteenth and Seventeenth Centuries*, 3 vols (Cambridge, 1952–1964), II, p. 323.

50 W.A. Jackson has suggested that the *Funerals* is probably 'by some hack, possibly John Taylor, whom Budge hired for that purpose' (*The Carl H. Pforzheimer Library: English Literature, 1475–1700*, 3 vols (New York, 1940), I, 151). For a discussion of various extant copies of the *Epicede* and *Funerals*, see also Phyllis Brooks Bartlett (ed.), *The Poems of George Chapman* (New York and London, 1941), pp. 451–55.

51 Chapman, *Epicede*, sig. A1r.

52 Given that the verses are slightly oversized for the base, it seems probable that they were copied out by a

professional penman and that Hole then cut the letters onto the already finished engraving of the hearse.

53 Chapman's *Twelve Bookes of the Iliad* was printed in 1609, his complete *Iliads* in 1611. Both were dedicated to Henry.

54 Holland also belonged to the literary fraternity closely linked to Prince Henry's court. He contributed verses to Thomas Coryate's *Crudities* (London: W[illiam] S[tansby], 1611) and also to his *Crambe* (London: William Stansby, 1611), and was 'Hugo Inferior-Germanus' at the gathering of wits known as the 'Mitre Convivium'. See Michael Strachan, *The Life and Adventures of Thomas Coryate* (Oxford, 1962), pp. 279–80; and Colin Burrow's entry on Holland in the *Oxford Dictionary of National Biography*.

55 'He was snatched away, to the cruel, savage detriment of his father and homeland, / So that he might be united with his ancestors in heaven: / Henry (sacred life!) is placed on the modest urn; / He is the greatest, lesser only than his own father.' Translation by Sarah Knight.

56 Holland's verses are item no. 10 in the *Mavsolevm*, Chapman's no. 14.

57 Chapman, *Epicede*, sig E2v.

58 Although it is not inconceivable that Chapman's verses also appeared on the actual hearse, there is no evidence that this was the case. For the custom of affixing inscriptions to catafalques, see Nigel Llewellyn, *The Art of Death: Visual Culture in the English Death Ritual, c. 1500–c. 1800* (London, 1991), p. 64. For the practice by which epitaphs and prints were sometimes buried with the coffin, see Roger Chartier, *The Cultural Uses of Print in Early Modern France* (Princeton, 1987), p. 161.

59 This image is the second of thirty plates in Lant and De Bry's *Sequitur celebritas et pompa funeris …* (London: n.p., 1588), a sequence of engravings depicting Sidney's funeral procession. For these images, see Jayne Archer, Elizabeth Clarke and Elizabeth Goldring (eds.), *Sequitur celebritas* in *John Nichols's The Progresses and Public Processions of Queen Elizabeth I: A New Edition of Early Modern Sources*, 4 vols. (Oxford, forthcoming). See also Elizabeth Goldring, '"So lively a portraiture of his miseries": Melancholy, Mourning, and the Elizabethan Malady,' *The British Art Journal*, 6.2 (2005): pp. 12–22 (pp. 16–17); and Elizabeth Goldring, '"In the cause of his god and true religion": Sir Philip Sidney, the *Sequitur celebritas* and the Cult of the Protestant Martyr,' in *Art Re-formed? Reassessing the Impact of the Reformation on the Visual Arts*, ed. Tara Hamling and Richard Williams (Cambridge, forthcoming).

60 Harvey and Mortimer, *Funeral Effigies*, p. 61. There are, of course, drawings of royal effigies that pre-date Hole's engraving. See, e.g., London, British Library, Add MS 35324, fols. 16r and 37v.

61 *CSPV, 1610–1613*, p. 448. See also *HMC Downshire*, III, 415; and *CSPV, 1610–1613*, p. 452.

62 Basse, sig. C2v.

63 Kay, p. 133. Henry appears in a portrait wearing the armour given to him by Henri IV; the painting is now at Dunster Castle.

64 Strong, *Henry Prince of Wales*, p. 54.

65 For the connection of these images to the Barriers, see Roy Strong, *Tudor and Jacobean Portraits*, 2 vols. (London, 1969), I, p. 164.

66 See, e.g., Antony Griffiths, *The Print in Stuart Britain, 1603–1689* (London, 1998), pp. 20–21; and Tessa Watt, *Cheap Print and Popular Piety, 1550–1640* (Cambridge, 1991; repr 1996), pp. 141–43.

67 Nigel Llewellyn, 'The Royal Body: Monuments to the Dead, For the Living,' in Lucy Gent and Nigel Llewellyn (eds.), *Renaissance Bodies: The Human Figure in English Culture, c. 1540–1660* (London, 1990; repr 1995), pp. 218–40 (pp. 229–30).

68 See London, College of Arms, Vincent MS 151, pp. 464–73 (for Henry's funeral); p. 475 (for Hole's engraving of Henry's effigy and hearse); pp. 522–33 (for Elizabeth's funeral); pp. 534–35 (for the drawing of Elizabeth's hearse); and p. 537 (for the engraving of Elizabeth's tomb). For another colour drawing of Elizabeth's hearse, see London, British Library, Add MS 35324, fol. 39r.

69 Vincent, though not a Londoner by birth, had taken up this post at the Tower in about 1599. For his life and career, see A.E. Brown's entry in the *Oxford Dictionary of National Biography*.

70 Essex's funeral was the first of a handful of mid-seventeenth-century non-royal funerals for which effigies

were constructed and displayed. Others include those of Oliver Cromwell (d. 1658) and of George Monk (d. 1670), Duke of Albemarle. (The 1735 obsequies of Edmund, Duke of Buckingham, constitute the last occasion on which a recumbent effigy was borne above a coffin at an English state funeral.) Beginning with the funeral of Charles II, in 1685, the obsequies of English monarchs have substituted an imperial crown for an effigy. See Woodward, *The Theatre of Death*, pp. 199–201.

71 For this image, see *The Tudor, Stuart and Early Georgian Pictures in the Collection of Her Majesty the Queen*, ed. Oliver Millar, 2 vols. (London, 1963), I, 79 (no. 100).

72 Essex was one of twelve assistant mourners to the chief mourners.

73 In addition to John Morrill's entry on the 3rd Earl of Essex in the *Oxford Dictionary of National Biography*, see J.S.A. Adamson, 'Chivalry and Political Culture in Caroline England,' in Kevin Sharpe and Peter Lake (eds.), *Culture and Politics in Early Stuart England* (London, 1994), pp. 161–98 (pp. 191–93).

74 In the later state, reproduced here as fig. 6, the words *Aetatis suae 56* appear under the pall and the hearse's columns are more heavily shaded. See Hind, II, pp. 319–20.

75 Hole died in 1624.

76 Hind, *Engraving in England*, II, p. 320.

77 Adamson, 'Chivalry and Political Culture in Caroline England', pp. 191–93.

78 See also David Howarth, *Images of Rule: Art and Politics in the English Renaissance, 1485–1649* (Basingstoke, 1997), pp. 171–73.

79 The Dutch title reads: '*Tombe van den hoochgebornen Prinse Henricus Prince van Walles hertoghe van Cornewaile &c overleeden den 6 novembris & en daer aenvolgende de 7 decemb. zeer princelijck begraven Anno 1612 In het 18 Jaer suis ouderdons*' ['Tomb of the high-born Prince Henry, Prince of Wales, Duke of Cornwall, etc. died 6 November and the following 7 December was given a very princely burial in the year 1612 in his 18th year.']. Translation by Mia Mochizuki.

80 Griffiths, *The Print in Stuart Britain*, p. 52.

81 *Ibid.*, p. 52.

82 Arber, *Registers of the Company of Stationers*, III, p. 303v.

83 Griffiths, *The Print in Stuart Britain*, p. 53.

84 Cf. also Sandford's *The order and ceremonies used for and at the solemn interment of … George, duke of Albemarle* (London, 1671), produced on the orders of Charles II (for which see Griffiths, *The Print in Stuart Britain*, pp. 203–04).

85 Sandford, *Genealogical History*, title-page.

86 *Ibid.*, p. 529.

87 Cornwallis, *The Life and Death*, pp. 92–93. According to Carola Oman, Princess Elizabeth and Frederick, the Elector Palatine, were amongst the first to pay a visit to Westminster Abbey in order to see Henry's effigy displayed alongside those of his predecessors (*Elizabeth of Bohemia* (London, 1938; repr 1964), p. 73). Unfortunately, Oman does not give her source for this anecdote.

88 London, Westminster Abbey, Lease Book IV, fol. 33r; cited in Hope, p. 52.

89 London, Westminster Abbey, MS 33659, fol. 6v; cited in Woodward, *The Theatre of Death*, p. 130.

90 Kew, National Archives, LC 2/4 (6), fol. 5; cited and discussed in Harvey and Mortimer, p. 59.

91 *CSPD, 1611–1618*, p. 361.

92 'Vertue Note Books Volume 1,' *Walpole Society*, XVIII (1930), p. 158.

93 Harvey and Mortimer, *Funeral* Effigies, p. 61.

94 The effigy has deteriorated significantly since being photographed in the early twentieth century (fig. 1).

95 *CSPV, 1610–1613*, p. 469.

96 Howarth, *Images of Rule*, pp. 172, 177.

97 Llewellyn, 'The Royal Body,' p. 225.

98 Sandford, *Genealogical History*, p. 530.

Photograpic Credits

INDEX